Prison Labour: Salvation or Slavery?

Oñati International Series
in Law and Society

GENERAL EDITORS

William L.F. Felstiner
Eve Darian-Smith

BOARD OF GENERAL EDITORS

Johannes Feest
Peter Fitzpatrick
Hazel Genn
Eliane Junqueira
Hubert Rottleuthner
Ronen Shamir

TITLES

*Totalitarian and Post-Totalitarian Law*
Edited by Adam Podgorecki and Vittorio Olgiati

*Foreign Courts: Civil Litigation in Foreign Legal Cultures*
Edited by Volkmar Gessner

*Family Law and Family Policy in the New Europe*
Edited by Jacek Kurczewski and Mavis Maclean

*Procedural Justice*
Edited by Klaus F. Röhl and Stefan Machura

*Emerging Legal Certainty: Empirical Studies on the Globalization of Law*
Edited by Volkmar Gessner and Ali Cem Budak

Oñati International Series
in Law and Society

# Prison Labour: Salvation or Slavery?

## International Perspectives

Edited by Dirk van Zyl Smit
and Frieder Dünkel

A Series published for
THE OÑATI INTERNATIONAL INSTITUTE
FOR THE SOCIOLOGY OF LAW

Taylor & Francis Group
LONDON AND NEW YORK

First published 1999 by Dartmouth and Ashgate Publishing

Reissued 2018 by Routledge
2 Park Square, Milton Park, Abingdon, Oxon, OX14 4RN
52 Vanderbilt Avenue, New York, NY 10017

*Routledge is an imprint of the Taylor & Francis Group, an informa business*

Copyright © Oñati I.I.S.L. 1999

All rights reserved. No part of this book may be reprinted or reproduced or utilised in any form or by any electronic, mechanical, or other means, now known or hereafter invented, including photocopying and recording, or in any information storage or retrieval system, without permission in writing from the publishers.

Notice:
Product or corporate names may be trademarks or registered trademarks, and are used only for identification and explanation without intent to infringe.

Publisher's Note
The publisher has gone to great lengths to ensure the quality of this reprint but points out that some imperfections in the original copies may be apparent.

Disclaimer
The publisher has made every effort to trace copyright holders and welcomes correspondence from those they have been unable to contact.

A Library of Congress record exists under LC control number: 99011976

Typeset by Manton Typesetters, Louth, Lincolnshire, UK.

ISBN 13: 978-1-138-38628-0 (hbk)
ISBN 13: 978-1-138-38630-3 (pbk)
ISBN 13: 978-0-429-42687-2 (ebk)

# Contents

| | | |
|---|---|---|
| Preface | | vii |
| 1 | Austria<br>ARNO PILGRAM | 1 |
| 2 | Botswana and Ghana<br>KWAME FRIMPONG | 25 |
| 3 | England and Wales<br>JON VAGG AND URSULA SMARTT | 37 |
| 4 | Germany<br>FRIEDER DÜNKEL | 77 |
| 5 | Hungary<br>FERENC NAGY | 105 |
| 6 | Israel<br>LESLIE SEBBA | 115 |
| 7 | Japan<br>YUICHI KAIDO AND KATSUSHIKO IGUCHI | 145 |
| 8 | Namibia<br>GAIL SUPER | 153 |
| 9 | The Netherlands:<br>    Work in the Dutch Prison<br>CONSTANTIJN KELK | 169 |
| 10 | The Netherlands:<br>    Labour Imposed as a Criminal Punishment<br>    outside the Dutch Prison<br>MIRANDA BOONE | 185 |
| 11 | Poland<br>ZBIGNIEW HOLDA | 197 |
| 12 | South Africa<br>DIRK VAN ZYL SMIT | 211 |
| 13 | Spain<br>ESTHER GIMÉNEZ-SALINAS | 241 |

| | | |
|---|---|---|
| 14 | Switzerland<br>ANDREA BAECHTOLD | 259 |
| 15 | United States of America:<br>  Prison Labour: A Tale of Two Penologies<br>JAMES B. JACOBS | 269 |
| 16 | United States of America:<br>  Inmate Work and Consensual Management in<br>  the Federal Bureau of Prisons<br>MARK S. FLEISHER AND RICHARD H. RISON | 281 |
| 17 | International Perspectives<br>HELENA HENRIKSSON AND RALPH KRECH | 297 |
| 18 | Still 'Slaves of the State': Prison Labour and<br>International Law<br>GERARD DE JONGE | 313 |
| 19 | Conclusion: Prison Labour – Salvation or<br>Slavery?<br>DIRK VAN ZYL SMIT AND FRIEDER DÜNKEL | 335 |
| Index | | 349 |

# Preface

Prison labour is a controversial issue. It is not difficult to understand why. Over the years penal activists of all kinds have made large and sometimes diametrically opposed claims about penal labour. Some have asserted in the religious language of redemption and salvation that an appropriate system of prison labour can reform prisoners and ensure that they do not reoffend. More have declared that prison labour, properly managed, will be profitable: so profitable that the prison system may cease being a drain on the fiscus. Indeed, bright-eyed prophets have proclaimed that the two goals can be met simultaneously.

For other equally passionate reformers prison labour has epitomized the exploitation of prisoners. The image not only of forced labour but also of prison labour as slavery has been prominent. Critics have pointed to the exploitative nature of such labour and hinted that large profits may be squeezed from those who are unable to resist the might of the state that backs the prison authorities.

Nor have social theorists been shy in attaching significance to changes in approaches to penal labour. The long historical view has been prominent. The study by Rusche and Kirchheimer (1939) that found a direct link between changing modes of production and the evolution of penal practices has continued to inspire inquiries into the direct connection between prison labour and economic developments. Also enormously influential has been the work of Foucault (1977) and of Melossi and Pavarini (1981) who, in very different ways, focused not so much on the direct economic significance of prison labour but on the way in which prison labour was used and continues to be used to shape and 'discipline' not only prisoners but workers in general for the evolving world of work.

Without eschewing either the humanist ideals of the reformers or the theoretical endeavours of the social theorists, the aim of this volume is somewhat different. It is in the first instance a stock-taking exercise designed to elicit basic information as a foundation for reconsidering fixed assumptions about prison labour. In planning this exercise we started from the assumption that prison labour is embedded in national prison law and national practices. These laws and practices need to be researched closely. They cannot simply be deduced from major economic changes or shifts in attitudes to work. From this basis fresh analyses can be attempted.

At one level, prison labour presents a classic field of study for the sociology of law. This is the challenge of understanding what is happening in an area in which the aspirations of law, in general, to uphold human dignity seem to be compromised not only by specific legal enactments (allowing prison labour of various kinds) but also by institutionally embedded practices that undermine both the 'higher law' and, on occasion, the specific legal safeguards (designed in theory to prevent the exploitation of prison labour).

The Oñati International Institute for the Sociology of Law provided the ideal setting for a meeting to consider law and practice of prison labour in a comparative and international context. It enabled us to bring together a group of scholars who could describe developments in their own countries and at an international level in a way that would remain sensitive to the large questions raised by reformers and social theorists, but at the same time could provide the detailed information that would allow a better informed re-evaluation of these questions.

In drawing up guidelines for participants at the seminar we, as the organizers, were conscious of the need to have sufficient information on law and practice in different countries in order to have a basis for a discussion about trends and developments. On the other hand, our intention was to explore the significance of prison labour in the late twentieth century and not merely to collect material for an encyclopaedia. For this reason, participants who were invited to submit papers on specific countries were given suggestions they could follow, but were not to be bound by them. In each instance they were invited to begin with a brief overview of the history of prison labour. They were then asked to deal with the current position and to indicate in quantitative terms, if possible, how important prison labour was in the context of the respective national prison systems. They were also asked for a short exposition on the official justification for prison labour.

In the invitation to participate, specific questions were posed for participants to consider as a basis for the discussion. These questions referred to six different areas within the wider field of prison studies.

- Firstly questions were asked about imprisonment and involuntary servitude. Whether prisoners have to work and, if so, what limits there were on this duty, were the key questions in this first group.
- The second set of questions concerned prisoners' right to work.

- The third was a single question about whether there was any connection between work and release.
- The fourth set of questions was more detailed and asked about the links between work in prison and national labour law.
- The fifth set of questions dealt with compensation of prison labour.
- The sixth and final set of questions asked participants writing on prison labour in the national context to consider also whether international human rights law had any significant influence on prison labour.

The incorporation of international human rights law into the discussion was designed to ensure that the focus was not exclusively on national concerns. In addition, two participants were invited to consider the question of prison labour specifically from an international perspective. Helena Henriksson and Ralph Krech approached this question primarily from the perspective of the United Nations, whilst Gerard de Jonge ranged widely but focused particularly on the role of the International Labour Organization in this regard.

This mix of semi-structured national accounts and international overviews provided the basis for an extremely lively discussion at a seminar at Oñati, which was held on 9 and 10 May 1996. After the meeting the participants used the opportunity to revise and update their contributions to reflect the insights that they had gained. The results are reflected in this collection. In addition we were able to commission further chapters on Switzerland and Hungary, which were not presented in Oñati. We have also added a final chapter in which we have included some of the ideas that emerged from the discussion at Oñati, to which we have added some synoptic conclusions about tendencies in the use and control of prison labour and the significance of these tendencies.

We would like to thank all the contributors, particularly for their assistance in the difficult task of clarifying terminology and ideas developed in different traditions of legal scholarship and administration. These differences have made the editorial task more difficult but also more challenging. In developing the early papers for publication the detailed critique provided by the editors of the Dartmouth series, Professors Felstiner and Darian-Smith, has been invaluable. Special thanks is also due to Ricky Röntsch for her editorial assistance.

The seminar would not have been possible without the financial support of the Oñati International Institute for the Sociology of Law and the Thyssen Foundation of Cologne in Germany. In Oñati,

Johannes Feest, as Director of the Institute, combined to perfection the role of genial host and that of academic godfather.

DIRK VAN ZYL SMIT AND FRIEDER DÜNKEL
*Cape Town and Greifswald*
*October 1998*

## References

Foucault, Michel. 1977. *Discipline and Punish: The Birth of the Prison*. Translated by A. Sheridan. Harmondsworth: Penguin.

Melossi, Dario and Massimo Pavarini. 1981. *The Prison and the Factory: Origins of the Penitentiary System*. London: Macmillan.

Rusche, Georg and Otto Kirchheimer. 1939. *Punishment and Social Structure*. New York: Columbia University Press.

# 1 Austria

ARNO PILGRAM

## 1 History and Current Situation

### 1.1 Introduction: Methods of Research and Available Information

Imprisonment and prison labour have only occasionally been the object of historical or sociological research in Austria. Hitherto, all the available reports and surveys have been based on sources taken from the administration of justice and legislation: on law, decisions, decrees and, in some few cases, on reports and comments in the media. This has meant that there has been a judicially and hierarchically dominated discourse with its own specific criteria for what is relevant. The available material nevertheless suffices for us to estimate the significance of prison labour as part of the government's representation of its activities towards the relevant sectors of the public. The political and administrative designs concerning prisons and prisoners are, in each era, an expression of the 'rationality' of governmental policy on matters of order and the exercise of authority, or they reflect the historical dispute about this 'rationality'.

The practical aspect of prison labour and its real effect on the prisons and the prisoners' daily life is quite a different matter. Reports or written testimonies are scarce and have not been granted sufficient attention; nor has their historiographic significance been evaluated. There are many questions about the conformity between the logic of the central administration and the logic of the decentralized executive institutions; about the applicability of concepts of prison labour in everyday prison life; about perceptions and construction of reality by the custodians and the prisoners themselves; and about the underlife in prisons and prison workshops.

There is good reason to assume that prison labour has always acted as a major trigger for establishing subcultures and contracultures among the prisoners, an effect which has been completely ignored by the official policy on prison labour. We can safely assume that the daily interaction between staff and prisoners on labour matters produces a number of 'secret' arrangements that do not correspond to norms and regulations. As to the prisoners' and the junior staff's opinions on the issue of prison labour and on how prison labour is and has been handled, there are far more open questions than there are answers. Complaints and directives occasionally offer insight into the real state of affairs: for example, when so-called 'corruptive agreements' between staff and prisoners have come to light or when means have been sought to prevent staff members from dealing privately with commodities produced by the inmates (Stekl, 1978: 232). Most scientific surveys and reports, however, have completely neglected the subject of prison reality.

## 1.2 The History and Tradition of Prison Labour in Austria

Prison labour in Austria can be traced back to at least two roots, one of which has since died out. One is the policy of physical punishment, the other the policy of work provision and discipline of the period of absolutism. Hard labour was introduced as a demonstration of public physical punishment. This was considered a more reasonable form of punishment than that of pure chastisement.

Labour penalties that deliberately took into account a possibly destructive effect on the delinquents' health were introduced as a substitute for the abolished death penalty in the penal code of 1787 under Joseph II and were sharply criticized by enlightened citizens (Wangermann, 1995: 648). By introducing sentences of forced labour in fortification construction work, mining, and even the manual towing of vessels against the current of the Danube, a 'semi-enlightened' absolutism endeavoured temporarily to combine a set of conflicting principles of governance. Law (codification), mercy (abstention from torture and the death penalty, retention of the extra-curial granting of mercy) and terror each had a role to play. (The most cruel public labour penalties were abolished under the reign of Leopold II (1790–92) but labour penalties were not fully repealed until 1852.)

This penal policy had little or nothing to do with economic considerations. The lack of any mercantile approach only reflects the underdeveloped state of mercantilism in general during the time of Austrian absolutism. The early chastisement institutions and workhouses in Austria were also a manifestation of this reality. Their introduction in the seventeenth century was based on illusory conservative ideals. There was a strong desire to reinstate an order for the '*Ganze Haus*'.[1] This was a reaction to the rapid decline of the old social order. Economic development was leading to the emancipation of large parts of the population from their respective traditional social groups. In order to find remedies for the ever-growing problem of poverty, both the traditional channels of distribution and the moral attitude towards those who had lost the social basis formerly provided by the old social structure required revision. The solution was the institutionalization of marginalized persons (orphans, children who had run away from their homes, servants, vagrants, pedlars, beggars and the like).

It was argued that labour could and had to be expected from the able-bodied poor in exchange for public board, protection and schooling, and as a contribution to cost reduction. (Nevertheless, the bulk of the income used for prisons for hard labour and workhouses was not drawn from labour profits. Specifically earmarked taxes on gambling, entertainment or tobacco provided the required means.) The utilization of manpower in innovative governmental or municipal manufacturing projects, a specifically mercantilist form of rationalization, was not mentioned in any of the documents concerned with the establishment of the workhouses. Such endeavours were first pursued at the beginning of the eighteenth century, when new forms of labour houses were introduced. Consequently, the efficiency of operational and labour processes was widely ignored. In addition, means to invest in more sophisticated lines of production were scarce. As a result, simple textile manufacture prevailed (Stekl, 1978: 300).

From the very beginning, all hard labour institutions and workhouses also served as prisons for those subjected to detention or serving sentences; these groups were naturally also part of the poverty-stricken population (Stekl, 1978: 304). Until the late nineteenth century, such institutions, together with prisons and jails for delinquents, remained under the control of the police authorities.

The original distinction between 'voluntary' labour houses offering work, schooling and wages for the innocent poor, on the one hand, and the forced labour institutions for the 'dishonest' poor and the convicts, on the other hand, gradually dissolved. The aspect of productive unemployment welfare eventually lost ground to the notion of exemplary punishment. As early as the end of the eighteenth century, the city of Vienna was strongly opposed to any

[1] Literally: 'Whole House', an absolutist claim of government involvement in all levels of society.

extension of the 'voluntary' workhouse system. The opposition was fully in accordance with the ideas of the liberal economists who opposed government intervention and guaranteed employment. They were in favour of labour and provision of services in the home and the emergence of a job market on a pure supply and demand basis (Stekl, 1978), that is, a kind of 'repressive de-institutionalization' of services.

The remaining voluntary workhouses were eventually transformed into correctional and disciplinary institutions that were frequently administered very strictly. (Most of today's prisons originated as such institutions.) In spite of this trend, the forced labour institutions were not placed under the control of the Department of Justice or coordinated until 1873: that is, not until the end of the period of neo-absolutism. The reasons for custody in such institutions were now clearly defined as statutory offences (vagrancy and prostitution) and the procedure for incarceration subjected to legal rules.

The idea of improvement and rehabilitation by means of labour nevertheless originated in the tradition of the workhouses. This idea also implied schooling, wages as motivation, honourable release and financial relief, as well as cooperation with and recruiting for private business enterprises. Not only certain organizational structures, but many of these ideas, including the general duty of all able-bodied prisoners to work, were applied in the new system of penal institutions.

In the middle of the nineteenth century, both hard labour institutions and a large penitentiary were run by Catholic orders in the area of present-day Austria. These monasteries were granted government funds and the permission to utilize prison manpower as they saw fit. The connection ('*Wahlverwandtschaf*'[2]) between monastery, factory and prison (Treiber and Steinert, 1980), all of them being laboratories of discipline and work, and the concept of know-how transfer between them are expressed in this system. Factory premises and prison manpower were leased to private companies as well. There was constant debate about whether this system was most profitable to the community (cost reduction), to those exploiting prison manpower directly (market advantage) or to the prisoners themselves (opportunities to earn an income, albeit varying and often inadequate). Did the system produce better vocational training, education and discipline among the prisoners, or did it not in

---

2   Literally: 'Elective Affinity', the title of a novel by Goethe.

fact jeopardize such aims? This uncertainty led to the specification of general norms, increasing attention to uniformity and, finally, to the state taking over the administration of penal institutions as well as any connected labour-intensive operations (Saurer, 1995).

The normative determination of the nature of prison labour and its limitation to correctional institutions and to unskilled work, and the disconnection from both modern production and sociopolitical claims, all reflected the era of liberal economy in Austria towards the end of the nineteenth century. The effects of this period are strongly felt even in our day. In 1873, the Ministry of Justice issued an order decreeing that prisoners were not entitled to payment for their work and that any profits from such work would accrue to the government's account. Furthermore, the business communities' right to veto any competition from prison workshops was acknowledged (Hautmann, 1995: 667). The short and generally rather uninfluential period of liberalism in Austria had a long-term impact on penal policy.

## 1.3 Turning to the Present: the Penal Amendment of 1993

There is a large administrative literature (Wahlberg, 1882; Marcovich, 1899; Grossmann, 1905; Hoegel, 1916) and several secondary survey reports on the situation in the latter days of the Austrian monarchy, but the history of penal practice in twentieth-century Austria has yet to be written. In view of the repeated periods of national emergency and exceptional circumstances (World War I, Austro-fascism and Nazi rule), scholars have tended to focus on ruptures and turbulence rather than on continuity. The administration, for its part, has also lost any interest in tradition or wide-ranging cultural comparisons. There are indications that the Austrian policy on penal and correctional matters remained untouched by the developments in the rest of Europe (such as early decriminalization and deinstitutionalization processes) and that Austria was increasingly incarcerating a higher proportion of its population than other European countries. This trend continued until the 1970s, when Austria had the highest rates of imprisonment in Europe (Kaiser, 1983; Stangl, 1988). However, there are no studies of the social and political processes that caused this lack of progress in Austria.

The current law on the implementation of prison sentences came into effect in 1969. For the first time, prison orders were cast in legislative form, although in practice little was changed.

The first substantial amendment of the Prison Act, concerning prison labour among other issues, did not follow until 1993. The amendment did not revise the existing duty of sentenced prisoners to work, nor did it change the obligation of the institutions to provide all inmates with useful activities, to have all suitable work in the institutions done by prisoners themselves and otherwise to provide prison labour for public administration, for public benefit or for private companies and principals. Other guidelines for the distribution of tasks that were not reviewed in the amendment were those relating to the length of the sentence period, the prisoner's behaviour and his special skills, abilities and interests, as well as the opportunities for making a living when no longer in custody. If the inmate has no skills or qualifications at all or none that can be put to use, he is entitled to vocational training – that is, if the institution in question is in the position to offer the facilities required for training.

A new feature is that prisoners are to be paid in accordance with wage rates determined in national collective bargaining arrangements for workers generally. This was a precondition for giving them access to unemployment insurance, higher wages than before and allowing them to use their income for a wider range of purposes. Prisoners' rights to spend their income on goods and services and dispose of the accumulated balances ('reserve' savings for the time after release) have been extended to allow for the support of family members, compensation for damage done, or for paying off debts. On the other hand, the amendment introduces a wage deduction as a means to recover the costs of custody. Another novelty is the more liberal rules on contracts between institutions and private companies regarding the use of prison labour. (Such contracts no longer require the approval of official district labour bureaux.) Additionally, labour activities on a day-leave basis and attendance of vocational or educational programmes outside prison grounds can be granted more readily.

These reforms were mainly brought about by lobbies striving to improve prisoners' legal status as far as their contacts with society were concerned: visits, correspondence, telephone conversations and open custody (so-called 'derestrictive measures'). Professional associations (prison pastors and psychologists), political groups (the Green Party in particular) and the organized legal profession all lobbied for improvements. Since it was well known that penal practices in Austria lagged behind European standards, the lobbies succeeded in stressing the urgency of reforms.

A very special concept stated in the Prison Act was that of *Stufenvollzug*. This system distinguished between several 'levels of penalty measures', ranging from the quite severe kind to penalty relief by means of different sets of 'benefits' granted to prisoners as rewards.[3] As a consequence, the prisoners' basic rights were made subject to their individual progress within the institutional system of these penal 'levels'. This was not in conformity with European standards, and therefore the reforms abolished the system of *Stufenvollzug* and transformed some of the former privileges into prisoners' rights. This led to a general discussion of prisoners' exceptional status in society and its legitimacy, also with regard to labour and social rights. Even though the structural reform of prison labour was not originally given priority, questions concerning equal labour rights now became urgent. The fact that labour in prison was not compensated by 'fair' wages, or by any access to social security for the future,[4] now became a pressing problem, as did the exclusion of working prisoners from the general unemployment and pension insurance schemes. Eventually, full pay according to national wage agreements was introduced, a deal that implied more than just an increase in wages. However, less than full equality was achieved as far as social security was concerned. Only unemployment insurance (ALV) for prisoners was recognized. Although not in principle opposed to ALV for prisoners, the ÖVP[5] succeeded in limiting even this form of protection to below the social norm. The result is that prisoners are given insurance credit for only 75 per cent of the hours spent on work in prison and that there are no restrictions on the nature of the work that released prisoners must be prepared to do if they are to qualify for unemployment benefits. In the report (Justizausschuss, 1993: 12) on the penal code negotiations, the Parliamentary Board of Justice stated that working prisoners could be granted access to pension financing at a later date (Holzbauer and Brugger, 1996: 929). The cost of the measures that were to be introduced was estimated at 90 million

---

3   For example, in terms of the *Stufenvollzug* approach, prisoners on a 'low' level were very rarely permitted to receive visitors and the number of granted visits increased with each 'higher' level.

4   In Austria it is mandatory that all employees are charged social insurance fees. They are therefore entitled to a number of insurance benefits.

5   *Österreichische Volkspartei*, the Austrian Peoples Party: traditionally conservative.

Austrian Schillings (ATS), to be covered by the Ministry of Justice, and an additional 52 million ATS provided by the ALV premiums. These amounts were budgeted accordingly and the amendments were approved unanimously by Parliament in 1993.

To understand the nature of the reforms, one should ask what they did not seek to achieve. The objective was not a general reform of the prison economy. Increased productivity and incentive wage structures for the efficient part of the prison system were not on the agenda, or if they were, only implicitly. The new system is not applied according to productivity standards. On the contrary, conditions have become less competitive than they were before the reform, or are on the free market. These include longer approved breaks from work for a variety of reasons, more money, and ALV insurance credits for time served, as well as for those prisoners who are involuntarily unemployed. The reforms do not stipulate investments in vocational training programmes or rehabilitation measures aimed at reintegration in the free job market, although, in view of the new status of released prisoners as persons entitled to payments from the ALV insurance funds, the official unemployment agency is likely to prove more eager to help them to find jobs. There is also a total absence of practical measures to create an environment that would encourage vocational rehabilitation or at least to counteract unfavourable trends.

The 1993 amendment must be understood as the result of a general public effort to ensure that each individual citizen, for better or for worse, acts independently, without assistance or influence from the state. According to this policy, government-run institutions should not jeopardize individual self-help initiatives on the part of prisoners.

The 'extraordinary authority relationship'[6] and discrimination to which prisoners had been subjected were now identified as counterproductive when it came to encouraging them to preserve social networks, social competence and the ability to resume responsibility for their own future welfare. These old relationships had to be revised.

The amendment sought to contradict any allegations that the state necessarily disadvantaged the prisoners where labour matters are concerned and thus 'desocialized' them. Simultaneously, the

6   The legal doctrine which holds that the constitutional rights of prisoners are automatically restricted by their status as sentenced prisoners. (*Editors*)

amendment introduced the released inmates to the brave new world of self-sufficiency. The amendment can be defined as a kind of material compensation – a quite inadequate one, of course – for the insufficiency of the measures that should have guaranteed resocialization during custody. Paradoxical as it may seem, the amendment reflects a defensive social and rehabilitation policy. It links ideas from different periods: labour and social rights for prisoners and the disengagement of the government from attempts to guarantee jobs and develop the labour market while cutting social services.

### 1.4 Consequences of the Amendment

A survey which began as soon as the amendment came into force has yielded insights into the legal reforms as well as into their practical impact (Pilgram, 1995). The survey covers the development of the labour situation in correctional institutions between 1980 and 1994, the extent to which the increased cost of prison labour has influenced the system; and how the reforms are perceived by the prisoners and warders.

The first results of this survey record the daily practice of prison labour and tell us something about how the reforms are interpreted and incorporated into daily institutional life by the prisoners and the staff. The data give credit to the argument that the amendment went into effect in the prisons under circumstances that would have caused any private business to close plants and branches, discontinue lines of production, dismiss employees and cut back on welfare and other fringe benefits. In spite of these clear signs of the time, the productive performance of prison workshops and production units was not on the reform agenda at all throughout the preliminary discussions (Pilgram, 1995).

At the same time, the prison population has fluctuated dramatically in the course of the last two decades, featuring the highest and lowest figures since World War II within a period of only a few years. The major reforms of the Prison Act and of court procedures, on the one hand, and the substantial geopolitical transformations that resulted in petty crime by eastern European citizens, on the other hand, caused these extremes. The number of available jobs in custody could not be matched to the fluctuating number of prisoners. The number of persons held in custody began declining in 1982 and the lowest point was reached between 1985 and 1989. Consequently, the employment rates in prison actually went up, despite both the general recession in the early 1980s and the poor demand for prison manpower. Later, when the Austrian economy expanded in the second half of the decade, the prisons did not have the capacity to take advantage of the market situation and to establish a network of business relationships. Lulled by the relatively high employment rates in the institutions, which, as it turned out, were only temporary, no one seemed to think that steady market activity was called for.

Towards the beginning of the 1990s the number of persons held in custody increased quite considerably and, at the same time, the Austrian economy as a whole, and the job market in particular, began to feel the competition from the eastern European countries where labour costs were much lower. More and more work assignments were cancelled and many contractors moved production units to eastern Europe or discontinued production altogether. The employment rates in prison dropped and would have collapsed entirely if it had not been for the increased distribution of in-house tasks.

The incompatibility between the number of persons in custody and the fluctuating markets caused the loss of numerous jobs in prisons (Renk, 1993). As a result, an ever-increasing proportion of the jobs available is of an inferior nature, and many serve only to maintain the system itself. In 1981, 30 per cent of the work was done for private principals, in 1993 (the year before the reforms were introduced) this figure had dropped to 15 per cent, whereas 9 per cent was carried out for public institutions and a total of 76 per cent was done directly for the prisons. In 1981, an annual total of 100 days of prison work were required for prison maintenance for one prisoner. By 1993, the requirement had increased to 130 days. As conditions for the prisoners have not improved in any way, there is reason to assume that the administration tends to inflate the work done in order to report satisfactory employment rates (see Tables 1.1 and 1.2, and Figure 1.1).

The data on labour and the economy in prison have hardly changed as a result of the amendment. Thanks to a reform of criminal court procedures, the number of pre-trial detainees in prison was considerably reduced in 1994 and so the employment rates in prison have remained constant in spite of the loss of available jobs. The structure of employment also remains the same, although the long-term tendency of an ever-increasing proportion of in-house work, higher credits for time spent at work and almost full automatic payment of rewards has been reversed, at least temporarily.

The reform of the system of remuneration does, however, allow the possibility of adopting an economically more sound approach to

## Table 1.1: Number of Prisoners Incarcerated and Employed, 1981–94

| Year | Total Prisoners | Pre-trial Detainees | Sentenced Prisoners | Psychiatric Detainees |
|---|---|---|---|---|
| | | Average Daily Population | | |
| 1981 | 8,650 | 2,522 | 5,843 | 244 |
| 1982 | 8,636 | 2,246 | 6,087 | 266 |
| 1983 | 8,538 | 2,066 | 6,178 | 255 |
| 1984 | 8,471 | 1,957 | 6,079 | 371 |
| 1985 | 8,463 | 1,945 | 6,075 | 380 |
| 1986 | 8,050 | 1,785 | 5,853 | 371 |
| 1987 | 7,560 | 1,666 | 5,493 | 353 |
| 1988 | 6,318 | 1,440 | 4,505 | 316 |
| 1989 | 5,946 | 1,602 | 3,992 | 286 |
| 1990 | 6,390 | 1,954 | 4,053 | 291 |
| 1991 | 6,750 | 2,168 | 4,189 | 315 |
| 1992 | 7,029 | 2,307 | 4,293 | 342 |
| 1993 | 7,184 | 2,211 | 4,522 | 357 |
| 1994 | 6,909 | 1,692 | 4,676 | 371 |

| | Average Daily Population: Employed/Rate of Employment in % | | | | | | | |
|---|---|---|---|---|---|---|---|---|
| 1981 | 4,987 | 58 | 478 | 19 | 4,313 | 74 | 185 | 76 |
| 1982 | 4,998 | 58 | 439 | 20 | 4,362 | 72 | 190 | 71 |
| 1983 | 5,059 | 59 | 428 | 21 | 4,418 | 72 | 204 | 80 |
| 1984 | 4,972 | 59 | 377 | 19 | 4,400 | 72 | 186 | 50 |
| 1985 | 5,073 | 60 | 337 | 17 | 4,506 | 74 | 214 | 56 |
| 1986 | 4,976 | 62 | 333 | 19 | 4,390 | 75 | 242 | 65 |
| 1987 | 4,928 | 65 | 389 | 23 | 4,282 | 78 | 243 | 69 |
| 1988 | 4,357 | 69 | 418 | 29 | 3,705 | 82 | 220 | 70 |
| 1989 | 3,981 | 67 | 505 | 32 | 3,245 | 81 | 204 | 71 |
| 1990 | 4,056 | 63 | 601 | 31 | 3,230 | 80 | 188 | 65 |
| 1991 | 4,187 | 62 | 665 | 31 | 3,296 | 79 | 201 | 64 |
| 1992 | 4,152 | 59 | 670 | 29 | 3,236 | 75 | 213 | 62 |
| 1993 | 4,265 | 59 | 656 | 30 | 3,318 | 73 | 245 | 69 |
| 1994 | 4,181 | 61 | 491 | 29 | 3,386 | 72 | 248 | 67 |

Source: Pilgram (1995, Tables 1 and 2).

Table 1.2: Users of Prison Labour in Days Worked, 1981–94

| Year | Prisons | Prison Staff, Prisoners | Public Service | Private Customers |
|---|---|---|---|---|
| 1981 | 912,928 | 123,846 | 118,055 | 307,903 |
| 1982 | 962,858 | 119,752 | 113,398 | 282,912 |
| 1983 | 975,739 | 125,767 | 130,850 | 231,846 |
| 1984 | 1,003,984 | 114,348 | 117,984 | 225,088 |
| 1985 | 991,598 | 124,732 | 121,321 | 227,320 |
| 1986 | 994,121 | 121,440 | 119,233 | 200,538 |
| 1987 | 925,718 | 110,997 | 126,700 | 205,046 |
| 1988 | 855,727 | 100,531 | 108,328 | 178,615 |
| 1989 | 815,462 | 84,066 | 83,390 | 150,237 |
| 1990 | 846,955 | 63,924 | 84,119 | 148,463 |
| 1991 | 901,260 | 56,161 | 70,452 | 145,663 |
| 1992 | 925,883 | 52,221 | 64,850 | 128,077 |
| 1993 | 945,025 | 50,500 | 68,427 | 129,342 |
| 1994 | 837,625 | 48,430 | 68,260 | 107,168 |

Index: 1981 = 100

| Year | Prisons | Prison Staff, Prisoners | Public Service | Private Customers |
|---|---|---|---|---|
| 1981 | 100 | 100 | 100 | 100 |
| 1982 | 105 | 97 | 96 | 92 |
| 1983 | 107 | 102 | 111 | 75 |
| 1984 | 110 | 92 | 100 | 73 |
| 1985 | 109 | 101 | 103 | 74 |
| 1986 | 109 | 98 | 101 | 65 |
| 1987 | 101 | 90 | 107 | 67 |
| 1988 | 94 | 81 | 92 | 58 |
| 1989 | 89 | 68 | 71 | 49 |
| 1990 | 93 | 52 | 71 | 48 |
| 1991 | 99 | 45 | 60 | 47 |
| 1992 | 101 | 42 | 55 | 42 |
| 1993 | 104 | 41 | 58 | 42 |
| 1994 | 92 | 39 | 58 | 35 |

Source: Pilgram (1995, Tables 8, 9 and A20).

prison labour (Pilgram, 1995). Since the total cost of compensation for the labour of prisoners before the reform was nearly as high as the entire income gained by work for private principals (according to

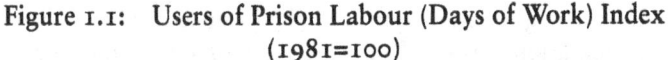

Figure 1.1: Users of Prison Labour (Days of Work) Index (1981=100)

♦ Number of prisoners    ■ Labour inside prison
▲ Labour for public service    ● Labour for private contractors

the Ministry of Justice), approximately 50 million ATS, even the 100 per cent rise in the net payments to the prisoners (a somewhat higher rise had been expected) resulted in a negative balance.[7]

A poll taken among prison staff (Hammerschick and Pilgram 1994, 1996) shows that the majority appreciated the results of the reform as far as the labour- and social rights are concerned. The staff felt that both the increased net wages and the eligibility to draw from unemployment funds after release meant that they were less likely to be held responsible for failures (the inevitable repeated offence). The reform also meant that they did not have to apply 'discriminatory' labour policies. Forced labour seems to be nearer extinction and the prisoners have become more self-disciplined. Since work in prison is no longer merely a means of dealing with stress but has become a means to satisfy personal needs through access to consumer goods, increasing pressure on the prison staff to provide work now also comes from the inmates.

The staff did not see the amendment only as a first step towards full equality of conditions of labour in and outside prison. To them the amendment remained a purely political construction. Most of the

7    Detailed information on the production value of prison labour according to the nature of the production units is not available in Austria.

staff hardly recognized the symbolic significance of the tariff wages and the integration in the ALV and were opposed to doing away with any remaining anomalies in the prisoners' rights to payment and insurance. The predominant opinion was that, by its very nature, labour in prison could not be subject to general norms and that it could not be made profitable, or even bring sufficient returns to finance the institution itself. The deterioration of the economic base was met with resignation: remedies such as the systematic differentiation of correctional institutions, prison enterprises, and prisoners according to productivity, were rejected as not conforming to the system, as well as being unjust. For the majority of prison staff, payment and other forms of compensation for prison labour remain merely a necessary, and therefore acceptable, concession for the maintenance of order and discipline in the institutions. These novelties are not understood as part of a rational economic plan and as a normal interaction of financial and labour processes. The emphasis that the staff places on the abnormal reality and the rules of the institutions neutralizes and deflects the purpose of the reforms.

As far as the inmates were concerned, the poll disclosed some satisfaction, as well as a severe lack of information (Hammerschick and Pilgram, 1994, 1995). Many inmates, however, described an acute gap between material improvement, on the one hand, and the treatment they are exposed to and the manner in which other personal rights are dealt with by the administration, on the other hand. Well educated prisoners in particular complained about inexplicable decisions, mismanagement of production units and other operations, artificially bloated activities, deliberate waste and idleness (this point is bound to remind many of the situation of conscripts to the armed forces), lack of prisoner involvement in decision making and absence of individual responsibility. All these circumstances were described as typical, and the reform had not changed anything in this regard.

Hardly any of the poll participants could detect any changes in the reality of prison labour or in relevant factors such as rationality and efficiency. Because of the increased payment for work, the significance of prison experience and knowledge of the informal rules and networks increased and thus undermined the effect of the new law, thus confirming, to the disappointment of some, the extent to which the intention of paper laws can be undermined during their implementation in the prison context.

Integration into society and integration into work life in prison vary greatly. Some groups have greater or lesser opportunities of being integrated or employed in prison than outside. The required 'qualifications' are different. On this point the prisoners' and the staff's views of the isolated reality in the institutions are in agreement. Most prisoners also share the pragmatic viewpoint and do not reflect on the intentions or the character of the law. They try instead to take advantage of the real new material possibilities. This usually means compensating for the ordeal of imprisonment by indulging in consumer goods. Most prisoners have insufficient means or support to make long term financial and social arrangements. The prisoners do not acknowledge that the reform was also intended to improve their relationship with their social environment outside prison and to transform their financial dependency into a system of mutual trade of services.

A critical résumé of the institutional handling of the amendment would report that the prisoners' new financial situation and social rights position is a consequence of developments in society and social policy as well as a new set of functions to be fulfilled by the prisons. However, the reality of prison economy, work and life tells a different story. Seen against this background, the latest benefits have their own very special logic. As long as prisons are not business organizations that encourage self-sufficiency and efficiency of their own accord and call for laws and circumstances that enable normal business activities, the adjustment of the wages for prison labour and the access to the ALV appear to be superficial, albeit welcome, changes. These 'rewards' are aimed at keeping the prisoners from demanding further rights and promoting the prisoners' obedience of the rules and principles of peace and order. As far as daily reality in prison is concerned, the reforms of the Prison Act and of prison labour in particular are less radically influential than many thought or desired them to be. The next step will have to be to bring about concrete changes to the economy and organization of the prison rather than reforms of the law.

## 2  Information for International Comparison

### 2.1  *Prisoners and Forced Labour*

If prisoners are validly sentenced and fit to work, labour is an obligation (art. 44(1) StVG).[8] Unsentenced prisoners, the ill and

8   For ease of use, when referring to a specific clause in the Prison Act, the Act will be referred to as the StVG, being the Austrian abbreviated form of the *Strafvollzugsgetsetz* (Prison Act).

the disabled are exempt from the obligation to work. Prisoners must execute the work they are assigned. The work must be of a nature that is not hazardous to life or health (art. 44(1) StVG). In order to ensure that the assigned work is not degrading or punitive, there are regulations on the supply and distribution of work. Prisoners should be provided with 'useful' work (art. 45(1) StVG) and the prisoner's 'age, health, *skills* and *abilities* as well as the sentence period, the prisoner's behaviour, *chances of making a living* after release, and finally the prisoner's *interests* should all be taken into account' (art. 47(1) StVG; emphasis added). Whether the prisoners' work actually meets these standards depends solely on the prison administration. Prisoners do have the right to submit complaints concerning labour assignments, but in fact the likelihood of their being changed is poor.

Any work that is required for the administration and maintenance of the institutions and the execution of penal measures and that can be given to prisoners to do must be done by them (art. 47(2) StVG). It is not the case that every inmate is obliged to contribute directly to his own keep, but a large number of prisoners are involved in in-house maintenance and services (food production, preparing meals, laundry, cleaning, renovation and so on).

Work may not be imposed as a form of punishment. The so-called 'workhouse' was abolished by the penal reform of 1975. It used to be an establishment for repeat offenders (mostly drifting delinquents guilty of petty crimes), who could be detained there for a certain period after the sentence itself had been served. This extra detention was – as the name suggests – seen as a period of time spent under the strictest labour discipline. Labour can no longer, in this sense or in any other, be assigned as part of a sentence.

Prisoners who disregard the norms of prison order cannot officially be assigned work as a sanction and only in exceptional cases can they be denied the right to work. Temporary exclusion from work can be a consequence of the harshest sanction imposed for disciplinary offences (confinement). Informally, however, the reaction to disobedience can be to assign unattractive jobs, to withdraw a prisoner from attractive tasks or to assign less work altogether.

Working hours and conditions in prison usually observe the norms of labour on the free market. 'General regulations on protection of life, health and physical security of the employees are accordingly valid' also for jobs and units in prison (art. 49(3) StVG). The general maximum working hours also apply. Exceptions from the general regulations are only granted for such cases as are otherwise exempt, such as forestry and agriculture (art. 50(1) StVG). Work may not be done on Sundays and national holidays, except for activities that are required to run the institution, such as in the kitchen or sick wards (art. 50(3) StVG). Although the general norms for working hours basically apply to prisons as well, two significant anomalies must be pointed out: prisoners in Austria are not entitled to annual holidays[9] and they remain subject to the obligation to work beyond retirement age (art. 50(3) StVG).

### 2.2 Prisoners and the Right to Work

Strictly speaking, there is no legal commitment on the part of the administration to provide prisoners with jobs, let alone acceptable jobs that suit the demands of the prisoners. The prisoners' duty to work thus does not correspond to the administration's obligation to provide work. Article 45(1) StVG, which stipulates that 'provisions are to be made that enable each prisoner to work' is a very loosely defined guideline: nothing but a recommendation to the institutions to make every effort to employ the prisoners in a reasonable manner. An explicit right to work cannot be derived from this. Since the Austrian Constitution does not otherwise guarantee work for anyone, this regulation must nevertheless be regarded positively. At least it declares that full employment is a goal in prison.

When prison administrative bodies in fact do take pains to provide work for as many of the (willing) inmates as possible, they are not responding primarily to the normative guidelines but are concerned about maintaining peace and order and avoiding public criticism should able and healthy young people kept in costly public institutions be idle. Providing work is not the only way to avoid inactivity, keeping the peace and ensuring the legitimacy of the system. Article 48 StVG grants the prisoner the right to vocational training according to his individual skills, abilities and interests. It applies where the inmate does not have a profession or if the profession he has cannot be exercised in prison. In reality, however, only a very limited number of prisoners are in the position to take advantage of this claim as any vocational training must take place in the vicinity of the institution and must be completed within the sentence period. These criteria can hardly ever be met. There are very few prisons with educational facilities and so prisoners often

---

9   In Austria it is mandatory to grant all employees an annual five weeks' paid holiday.

have to be transferred to distant institutions in order to attend training, or they must finance external courses privately: they cannot of course be forced to spend their earnings on education.

Forced passivity is actually not the simple counterpart of forced labour. Both states are closely interwoven in prison. Because the number of prisoners that should work, and are willing to, exceeds the number of available jobs, prisoners are obliged to take on work that is characterized by inferior productivity, that presents a minimal challenge and that undermines their self-esteem. In view of the fact that, on average, only 21 per cent of Austrian prisoners were without jobs in 1994 (only 54 per cent of these were inactive owing to a lack of available work), involuntary passivity does not appear to be such a great problem at first glance. It must, however, be pointed out that the majority of the active (79 per cent) are dissatisfied; they feel that they are not challenged and that they are redundant (Hammerschick and Pilgram, 1995).

It is quite obvious that pre-trial detention encourages prisoners to remain passive since there is no legal duty to work during this form of detention: 29 per cent of the prisoners detained before trial were active on a voluntary basis in 1994, and 71 per cent were 'unemployed'. According to penal statistics, as many as 57 per cent of these were 'unemployed' because of a lack of available jobs; that is, their failure to work was not voluntary.

The fact that many sentenced prisoners are involuntarily without work does not infringe the legal right to rehabilitation, simply because there is no positive right to rehabilitation. Reintegration into society is in fact a professed aim in Austrian penal policy, but the means by which this goal should be achieved are not adequately specified. Prisoners are guaranteed access to a minimum of information about the outside social environment. Contacts with society and future prospects of integration do exist, but this does not include professional activities, vocational training or professional reintegration. The recent amendment of the Prison Act has, however, removed some of the former obstacles and to some extent has enabled the prisoners to seek information independently, to attend educational programmes and to maintain social relations. It can be conceded that the penal system no longer fully destroys opportunities for rehabilitation, but it is far from providing any real relief of the kind that employment would offer.

### 2.3 Interaction between Work in Prison and Release

Austria still has a very low rate of prisoners released on parole. Only approximately a fifth of the prisoners are granted early conditional release. The most prominent criterion considered when deciding on such release is the previous criminal record of the prisoner. Work achievements are not given priority. The court that makes this decision is supposed to take the prisoner's behaviour in custody into account when determining conditions of release. However, a correlation between the ability to assimilate to prison conditions and the ability to become a law-abiding citizen is not generally assumed. None of the court decisions on early release that are known to me have made an issue of the prisoners' achievements or employment in prison, except in those very rare cases in which disciplinary procedures were involved. Work does not entitle prisoners in Austria to any reduction of their original sentences.

### 2.4 Prisoners and Labour Rights

There is no law that forbids trade in goods produced in prison. The law, however, does require that consideration be given to the social economy (art. 46 StVG); that is, the prices of prison products and the costs of hiring prison labour should not be lower than the market standard. Prison staff alone are allowed to purchase such goods at nominal prices. Prison labour hired by private principals must be paid according to general wage rates, but without the social security dues that are otherwise mandatory.[10]

The administration is obliged to take socioeconomic factors (the job market) into consideration when establishing new production units. This means that they must apply for permission to do so from the official district employment office. However, the institutions no longer require the approval of the employment offices to conclude contracts regarding the lease of manpower from prison. This has greatly reduced bureaucratic barriers to the hiring out of prison labour.

Labour rights generally do not apply to prisoners, except for the restrictions on the employment of minors, for employee protection (regarding job security on the job, see Article 49(3)) and for working hours (as stated above). Prisoners are not protected against transfer to other units or dismissal and can therefore be 'fired', even

---

10   In Austria the total dues charged to the employer amount to approx. 50 per cent of the gross.

if the prison legislation recommends continuous labour activity and demands statements on the reasons for withdrawal of work (art. 47(1) StVG). Prisoners do not have the right to be represented by collective, officially recognized lobbies, or by an elected trade union official. In wage negotiations, the interests of prisoners have recently been represented by the Metal Workers' Union. The level of the prisoners' wages has been determined by the outcome of this union's collective negotiations.

Prisoners are not explicitly exempt from minimum wage provisions. On the contrary, the minimum wages for prisoners are related to the wages in the metal industry for unskilled workers over 18 years of age. To be precise, the current rate is between 60 and 90 per cent of the unskilled metal workers' wage. (In 1994, it was between 42.20 and 67.80 ATS per hour: art. 52(1) StVG.) According to the legislator's intention this wage may be raised to between 75 and 112.5 per cent of the metal workers' rate. Prison wages are in fact below the minimum wage in the metal industry, but are comparable to low wage industries such as textiles or foods. The rates of the metal workers were chosen for the Prison Act simply to have one single standard. Many other decisions in wage tariff policy are also based on the metal workers' standards.

All accumulated credits for disability pensions or official retirement pensions are suspended during the sentence period. If an accident or a long-term illness caused by labour in custody results in a decreased ability to work, the prisoner explicitly has the same legal right to compensation, health care or a pension as any other employee (art. 76 StVG). Accident insurance also covers voluntary work for the government or work for charitable purposes. Family members of prisoners are entitled to pensions in cases of fatal accidents in prison.

Since 1994, the government has covered the equivalent of the contributions of the 'employers' and the prisoners themselves pay the contributions of the 'employees' to the unemployment insurance scheme so that the released prisoners are insured against unemployment. The ability to claim insurance payments does not depend on whether the prisoners were in active work in custody or not, as long as any 'unemployment' in custody was involuntary (art. 66a(5) of the Unemployment Insurance Act (ALVG)). A prisoner who has not been given work by the institution administration is not released from custody without access to unemployment insurance payments. In providing this insurance access, the penal policy takes the assignment of full employment seriously. In this instance, the legal rules in fact favour prisoners above normal employees. An adult prisoner who has not accumulated any insurance credits has to have worked or have been willing to work during a sentence of at least 16 months in order to be eligible for ALV funds. This is four months more than a normal employee must accumulate. (Any work done during pre-trial detention is not calculated.) In this case the prisoners are disadvantaged. Prisoners who are juveniles become eligible in a shorter period of time. If the prisoner has accumulated the required credits for the insurance, is able and willing, and reports to the local employment office after release, he is entitled to receive long-term payments from the ALV funds until an (acceptable) position can be found. (Because of the low wages in prison, the relative payments from the insurance funds are modest: between 4,100 and 5,800 ATS.)

Medical care for prisoners is not covered by the official health insurance scheme. It is covered in full by the penal budget (art. 68 StVG) – also when treatment is not carried out by the prison physician or in the prison hospital.

Labour in prison does not currently provide access to insurance credits in the official pension scheme. When the amendment of 1993 was passed, Parliament expressed the intention of integrating the prisoners into the pension insurance scheme in the future. This statement of intention has no binding force (Justizausschuss, 1993).

## 2.5  Compensation for Prison Work

Work of all kinds done by the prisoners is compensated by payment, except for the cleaning of prison cells. Work required for the 'maintenance of the system' provides an ever-increasing percentage of the inmates with work that is not really productive but which the government is prepared to pay prisoners to do. As the employment rates in prison are considered significant, the administration is led to define work as including 'maintenance of the system'. The fact that this work is compensated by full pay supports this definition.

Of a prisoner's wage, 75 per cent is deducted to cover the costs of custody. According to the reasons given in the preliminary government statement to the amendment of 1993, the 75 per cent corresponds to the expenses for board and lodging; staff salaries and building maintenance are not included. The premiums for the ALV (2.65 per cent) of the assessment are deducted from the remaining 25 per cent. Pre-trial detainees may dispose freely of the balance and sentenced prisoners may dispose of half of it. The second half is held back until release; this 'reserve' can only be drawn upon under exceptional circumstances during the sentence period.

Prisoners who work on a day-leave basis for public or private principals are not bound by these rules. If such prisoners are highly qualified, the employer must pay high gross salaries to the government. These prisoners do not receive any higher payments than other prisoners working in custody. In such cases the contributions to the costs of custody are based on real costs and at times can amount to more than 75 per cent of the tariff wage.

### 2.6 International Human Rights and Prison Labour

Trade in products made in prison should only be forbidden if the conditions of work, the wages and the social security of prisoners in custody do not meet certain minimum standards.

International human rights have a role to play in setting standards for prison labour. Prisoners should not be forced to work. If the supply of jobs in prison and the work itself meet certain minimum standards, which are yet to be discussed, more prisoners will show interest in working than there are jobs available. In Austria today, for example, the prison administration can pick and choose from a number of prisoners that are willing to work and does not really have any problems at all getting the necessary work done. If the compulsion to work were abolished under these circumstances, the economic system of the institutions would not be jeopardized, but the administration would be deprived of the means of applying task assignments as sanctions.

## References

Grossmann, Stefan. 1905. *Österreichische Strafanstalten*. Vienna and Leipzig: Wiener Verlag.

Hammerschick, Walter and Arno Pilgram. 1994. *Wirtschaftliche Vollzugsziele und der Umgang mit der Arbeitskraft von Gefangenen (Einsatz, Qualifizierung, Entlohnung. Ergebnisse einer Befragung von Vollzugspraktikern und Gefangenengruppen nach Inkrafttreten der StVG-Novelle. Teilbericht 1 zum Forschungsprojekt 'Zur Position Gefangener/Entlassener auf dem österreichischen Arbeitsmarkt. Veränderungen durch die Strafvollzugsnovelle 1993'*. Vienna: Institut für Rechts- und Kriminalsoziologie.

Hammerschick, Walter and Arno Pilgram. 1995. *Zur Position Gefangener/ Entlassener auf dem österreichischen Arbeitsmarkt. Veränderungen durch die Strafvollzugsnovelle 1993. Teilbericht 3A: Zweite Befragung Gefangener – ein Jahr nach der Strafvollzugsreform*. Vienna: Institut für Rechts- und Kriminalsoziologie.

Hammerschick, Walter and Arno Pilgram. 1996. *Zur Position Gefangener/ Entlassener auf dem österreichischen Arbeitsmarkt. Veränderungen durch die Strafvollzugsnovelle 1993. Teilbericht 4: Zweite Befragung von Experten – ein Jahr nach der Strafvollzugsreform*. Vienna: Institut für Rechts- und Kriminalsoziologie.

Hammerschick, Walter and Arno Pilgram, eds. 1997. *Arbeitsmarkt, Strafvollzug und Gefangegenenarbeit. Jahrbuch für Rechts- und Kriminalsoziologie 1997*. Baden-Baden: Nomos-Verlag.

Hautmann, Hans. 1995. Fragen des Strafvollzugs in der Endphase des Habsburgerreiches (1872–1918). In *Justiz und Zeitgeschichte. Symposiumsbeiträge 1976–1993*. Volume 1, edited by Erika Weinzierl, Oliver Rathkolb, Rudolf G. Ardelt and Siegfried Mattl. 1995. Vienna: Jugend and Volk.

Hoegel, Hugo. 1916. *Freiheitsstrafe und Gefängniswesen in Österreich von der Theresiana bis zur Gegenwart*. Graz and Vienna: Ulrich Mosers Buchhandlung.

Holzbauer, Albert and Sepp Brugger, eds. 1996. *Strafvollzugsgesetz (StVG)*. Vienna: Österr. Staatsdruckerei.

Justizausschuss. 1993. *Bericht des Justizausschuss über die Regierungsvorlage zur Strafvollzugsnovelle 1993*. Vienna. 1253 der Beilagen zu den Stenographischen Protokollen des Nationalrates XVIII. GP. 30 September.

Kaiser, Günther. 1983. *Strafvollzug im europäischen Vergleich*. Darmstadt: Wissenschaftliche Buchgesellschaft.

Marcovich, Anton. 1899. *Das Gefängniswesen in Österreich unter Berücksichtigung der Gesetze, Verordnungen und Vorschriften*. Vienna: Manz'sche Buchhandlung.

Pilgram, Arno. 1995. *Zur Position Gefangener/Entlassener auf dem österreichischen Arbeitsmarkt. Veränderungen durch die Strafvollzugsnovelle 1993. Teilbericht 2A: Statistische Übersicht über Arbeits- und Ausbildungswesen des österreichischen Strafvollzugs (1981–1994)*. Vienna: Institut für Rechts- und Kriminalsoziologie.

Renk, Christian. 1993. Kommende Auswirkungen im Beschäftigungsbereich der Insassen. In *Management in Justizanstalten. 28. Arbeitstagung der Arbeitsgemeinschaft der Leitenden Strafvollzugsbeamten Österreichs*. Vienna: Bundesministerium für Justiz.

Saurer, Edith. 1995. Strafvollzug im 19. Jahrhundert. In *Justiz und Zeitgeschichte. Symposiumsbeiträge 1976–1993*. Volume 1, edited by Erika Weinzierl, Oliver Rathkolb, Rudolf G. Ardelt and Siegfried Mattl. Vienna: Jugend und Volk.

Stangl, Wolfgang. 1988. *Kriminalpolitik in der Ersten Republik*. Vienna: Institut für Rechts- und Kriminalsoziologie.

*Statistische Übersicht über den Strafvollzug* (an annual administrative report). Vienna: Bundesministerium für Justiz.

Stekl, Hannes. 1978. *Österreichs Zucht- und Arbeitshäuser 1671–1920. Institutionen zwischen Fürsorge und Strafvollzug*. Vienna: Verlag für Geschichte und Politik.

Treiber, Hubert and Heinz Steinert. 1980. *Die Fabrikation des zuverlässigen Menschen. Über die 'Wahlverwandtschaft' von Kloster- und Fabriksdisziplin*. Munich: Heinz Moos.

Wahlberg, Wilhelm Emil. 1882. Die Gebrechen und die Verbesserung des Gefängniswesens in Österreich. In *Gesammelte Schriften* (collected works). Volume 3. Vienna: Hölder Verlag.

Wangermann, Ernst. 1995. Kriminalverbrechen und Bestrafung im Josephinischen Österreich. In *Justiz und Zeitgeschichte. Symposiumsbeiträge 1976–1993*. Volume 1, edited by Erika Weinzierl, Oliver Rathkolb, Rudolf G. Ardelt and Siegfried Mattl. Vienna: Jugend und Volk.

## The Author

**Arno Pilgram** is research fellow at the Institute of Sociology of Law and of Criminology in Vienna, Austria.

# 2 Botswana and Ghana

KWAME FRIMPONG

## 1 Introduction

The notion that imprisonment should not be an end in itself has gained a wider acceptance in practice within the international community. Consequently, various methods are being used, either on an experimental basis or as established practice, to minimize the apparently harsh conditions in prisons. It is in this light that prison labour must be seen. An important consideration to examine is how best prison labour can be used.

In this chapter, the practice of prison labour in two selected African countries (Ghana and Botswana) is discussed with a view to highlighting the beneficial aspects and also identifying the inherent weaknesses which require closer scrutiny for possible changes. A very broad definition of prison labour is adopted. This involves any type of work undertaken by an inmate in connection with his[1] incarceration. Accordingly, the limitation of prison labour to work that is beneficial to the inmate is not followed. It is worth noting that the prison labour under discussion refers to work undertaken by convicted prisoners and does not address any work done by unconvicted prisoners.

## 2 Prison History

As has been argued by Frimpong (1983, 1986) and Ramokhua (1985), imprisonment as a method of punishment of criminals was unknown under the indigenous systems of the two countries. The formal introduction of this form of punishment came with the advent of colonial rule, in the eighteenth century in the case of the Gold Coast (now Ghana)[2] and in the nineteenth

---

[1] The use of 'he', 'him' or 'his' has no gender connotation and refers to both male and female and is also consistent with section 44 of the Interpretation Act of Botswana (Act 20 of 1984).

[2] The colonial name given to the area now known as Ghana had much to do with the abundance of gold which had been discovered in the area during that time.

century in the case of Bechuanaland (now Botswana).³ Prison labour was a necessary part of the new form of punishment for the 'Natives', as the indigenous people were generally classified by the colonial masters.

Prison labour has had a relatively long history in Ghana (Report on Ghana Prisons, 1980). Initially, imprisonment in Ghana rested on what was popularly known as 'the three pillars'. By this method, following the English Prison Act of 1865, three goals of imprisonment were maintained: a separate system of confinement, penal labour and a restricted diet. The penal labour envisaged here was a very strong punitive measure as the aim was to ensure that the inmate suffered the most severe form of pain. However, by 1926, the situation had changed completely, as there had been tremendous influence from reforms in Britain, the mother country, especially after the publication of the Gladstone Report of 1895 which put more emphasis on reformation than on punishment. The result was that the then governor, Guggisberg, announced that:

> The chief object of the Gold Coast Prisons today is reform rather than punishment.... The chief way in which it is hoped to secure the reform of the prisoners is through trade training. (Government Report, 1926, para. 310)

In the case of Botswana, prison labour was not formally introduced until 1959 (Ramokhua, 1985). Prison labour was initially limited in its application. Only a limited number of inmates were employed in areas such as tailoring, carpentry, upholstery and canvas work (ibid.). It is to be noted that prison labour also served as a form of punishment for the inmates. For instance, it was not uncommon for inmates to be involved in stone breaking or road works, or to be used to bury the dead. But, as shall be noted later, prison labour for punitive purposes is no longer permissible.

Apart from the use of prison labour in the punitive sense, it was not uncommon for the two countries to use the inmates in another form of prison labour. This had the inmates undertaking various kinds of activities for their own benefit. Among other things, they were required to clean their surroundings, fetch water and firewood, learn some kind of trade and carry out some specific duties, as permitted by the institution. It was this type of prison labour that

---

3   The apparent mispronunciation of Botswana by the colonialist had resulted in the country being called Bechuanaland.

Governor Guggisberg was pleased to have found operating in the Gold Coast in 1926.

## 3   Prison Labour in Modern Botswana

Prison labour as understood in post-independence Botswana is elaborately provided for under the Prisons Act (Cap.21: 03) and its Regulations. The primary goal of prison labour is to 'prepare prisoners for the conditions of normal occupational employment' (s.91(6), Prisons Act). Accordingly, the 'organisation and methods of work shall resemble, as nearly as is reasonable, those of similar work outside prison' (ibid.). The use of prison labour as a form of punishment is rejected by s.91(1) of the Act: 'Prison labour shall not be afflictive.' The Act looks beyond the immediate period of the incarceration of the inmate and focuses on his future life. The prison labour for the inmate must thus take into account its usefulness to the inmate after his release. Section 91(3) of the Prisons Act provides: 'So far as reasonably practicable, the work provided shall be such as will maintain or increase the ability of the prisoner to earn an honest living after his release from prison.'

The Act envisages two types of prison labour. The first deals with the labour required in the prisons and the second is associated with work that is done outside the prisons. This finds support in s.91(8) of the Act: 'Every convicted prisoner shall be given, within or without the precincts of the prison, such employment as the Commissioner may direct.'

The work in the prison itself is of three kinds. First, the inmate may be required to undertake any type of work for his own immediate need. For example, he may be required to wash himself or his clothes, or clean his own surroundings. The second is the type of work that he does for the benefit of the institution itself, although in the final analysis it directly or indirectly benefits the inmate as well. An example of this is when an inmate is charged with the responsibility of painting the prison walls or cleaning the offices of the staff. Finally, there is the employment that is vocational or training in nature and is part of the programme for the inmate's rehabilitation. In some cases the end product of such vocational work or training may be of commercial value (this is discussed below). It is this type of work that is commonly associated with the term 'prison labour'.[4] While a broader definition of prison labour is

---

4   Extramural labour is not discussed in connection with prison labour.

adopted, much of the discussion is focused on its commonly accepted understanding.

The Act provides for two types of work outside the prison walls. It is work undertaken either for the benefit of a public authority or for a private person. In the case of the former, it is mainly for the government that prison labour has been utilized. The prison authorities have so far not been able to make prison labour available to private persons. This invariably has a major limitation on the discussion of prison labour in general, as some important issues which fall within this area cannot be considered from a Botswanan perspective. Among other things, one would be required to address issues such as the remuneration for the inmate who works for a private person. This and other relevant issues are considered in the next section in the context of practices in Ghana.

### 3.1  *Botswanan Prison Labour in Practice*

In theory, the Botswana Prisons Act has elaborate provisions for prison labour. However, not all the provisions have been put into practice. As was noted earlier, for the work outside the prison walls, the main beneficiary has been the government. This is a major limitation on the practical use of prison labour, as the types of work that the government can offer are limited. Furthermore, the issue of the inmate's entitlement to some form of remuneration is overlooked. Where a prisoner is employed by the government, the position is taken that an inmate is deemed to be undertaking such work as part of his incarceration and therefore is not entitled to any financial reward. The same position is adopted in connection with any work that the inmate does within the institution, whether directly for himself or for the prisons. In all these cases the prisoner is deemed to be only contributing, even if in a limited way, to the

---

Under ss.96 and 97 of the Act, a convicted person may be employed by a public authority instead of being in gaol. To qualify for extramural labour, a person must have been sentenced to a term of imprisonment not exceeding six months or committed by a court for non-payment of a fine not exceeding P400.00 (about $120.00). The convicted person may not have to enter the prison gates if this is determined by a court; but if he is already in jail then his release for extramural labour will have to come from either the Commissioner of Prisons or an official visitor. For a detailed discussion of the subject, see Frimpong (1992).

cost of his maintenance. But, as will be argued later, there is an element of unfairness in this system.

On the other hand, if an inmate were to be employed by a private person outside the prisons he would be entitled to be paid (s.94(2)). Although the payment in terms of this section is not made directly to the inmate, he is nevertheless entitled to a limited portion of the pay. But since the section has not been put into operation, the opportunity for the inmates to benefit from an earning scheme has not been realized.

To some extent all prisoners participate in some form of earning scheme. Under this scheme, the prisoners are grouped into three categories, Grades 'A', 'B' and 'C', on the basis of their conduct and skill in their trade. A Grade 'A' prisoner is classified as being of exemplary conduct and also skilled in his trade. He is entitled to 75 thebe a month (about 20 American cents). The Grade 'B' prisoner is of good conduct and semi-skilled in his trade and earns 60 thebe (about 15 American cents) per month. All other prisoners engaged in the scheme are Grade 'C' and earn 45 thebe (about 10 American cents) per month. From the earnings the inmate may opt to purchase luxuries such as cigarettes and tobacco.

It is worth noting that these earnings are not payment, since they do not conform to any standard of appropriate remuneration for the work inmates actually do in the prisons. The position adopted by the prison authorities is that the inmates, because they have fallen foul of the law and are in gaol, cannot claim to be entitled to any payment for the work they perform, either in the prisons or outside the prison walls. The work that the inmates perform is seen as their contribution to the cost of maintaining themselves for their commission of offences. The very limited earnings are available to all the inmates, with some slight differentiation based solely on their skills and behaviour in prison. As was noted earlier, the payments to them merely serve as some form of savings for the purchase of luxuries. As regards essentials, the authorities are expected to cater for the prisoners.

A different approach is adopted when the inmate works on Sundays, during public holidays and after working hours. Under normal circumstances, no prisoner is expected to work during these days and after hours without the permission of the Commissioner (Regulation 62). When an inmate works on a Sunday, a public holiday or after hours, he is entitled to be paid, provided that the labour is in connection with an item of a commercial nature. For his payment, the prisoner gets one-eighth of the profit that is derived from the sale of the item in question. The profit is determined by calculating 45 per cent of the total cost of creating the item. This is deemed to represent the labour cost. Therefore, if only one inmate was responsible for manufacturing the item in question, he alone gets the one-eighth of the profit. If, on the other hand, more than one inmate produced the item, they will share the one-eighth. The payment is not of any substantial value and is termed 'hobbies and handicrafts incentives'. The rationale for this type of payment is that the inmate is required to work during a period of rest. Thus, in lieu of rest, he is compensated.

## 4 Prison Labour in Ghana

Ghana, like Botswana, also has two types of prison labour: activities outside prisons and activities within the prisons. It is important to note that an activity may take place outside the prisons but nevertheless be for the benefit of the inmates or the Prisons Service as a whole. For example, if prisoners go into the bush to fetch firewood this activity, which has taken place outside the prison, is for the benefit of the prison.

In Ghana, prison labour is heavily utilized for the benefit of both the Prisons Service and the general public. The Prisons Service Decree (N.R.C.D. 46), the legislation which regulates the affairs of the Prisons Service, makes provision for the two types of prison labour. The service itself relies heavily on prison labour for a number of activities for the benefit of the service. Among other things prison labour provides an easy source for some projects within the service itself. For instance, through prison labour the service engages in agricultural activities, and the produce from such farms is used to feed the inmates. In 1988, the Agricultural Unit started experimenting with Settlement Farms. The rationale for these Settlements was outlined in the 1989 *Annual Report*:

(1) To ease congestion in the existing prisons,
(2) To produce more foodstuffs and to cut down the feeding cost of the inmates and also to sell the surplus to the public,
(3) To reduce fuel and transportation costs by settling the farm gangs at one location instead of travelling long distances to the farms,
(4) To train the inmates in modern methods of farming and to inject into them an active interest in rural life so that, when they are discharged, they will stay in the rural areas and farm rather than stay in the urban areas and get involved in criminal activities again. (*Annual Report*, 1989: 18)

The experiment became so successful that by 1992 more than 10 farms had been established. The only labour permitted on the farms is related to agricultural activities. No other industrial training is permissible.

It is gratifying to note that the Ghana Prisons Service has finally come to realize the value of using the inmates for farming activities. The Report of a Committee[5] that the writer chaired in 1980 had recommended that the service should embark upon large-scale farming in order to reduce the cost of feeding the inmates (Ghana Prisons Service, 1980: paras 441–6).

There are other activities such as brickmaking, carpentry, soapmaking and shoemaking, which are very beneficial to the service. These activities take place within the precincts of the prisons. In this regard, the emphasis is on vocational training.

Over the years, the Industrial Wing of the service has undertaken some private work outside the prisons. For instance, in the late 1980s and early 1990s, the Wing completed a privately owned house in Accra. It also carried out painting work for the Ghana Industrial Holding Corporation and did renovation work on the Cape Coast Prison Officers' Living Quarters. In all these cases the Industrial Wing relied substantially on the prison labour available. The officers merely provided the technical advice and supervision.

One area that evokes much controversy is prison labour for private use. Unlike Botswana, this is heavily utilized and patronized and, to some extent, even abused. For instance, when an investigation was conducted into the prisons in Ghana in the late 1970s and early 1980s, it was discovered that only a small group of people, mainly foreigners, were utilizing the labour and at a very cheap fee (Ghana Prisons Service, 1980: para. 446). Prison labour for private use is mainly used in agriculture, especially on large plantations. There are, however, cases where the labour has been tapped for other purposes. For instance, it is not uncommon for inmates to do work outside, clearing bush for people or cutting hedges, or even assisting at a construction site.

It is interesting to note how the remuneration aspect and other implications, which arise as a result of the outside prison labour, are handled. The applicable fee is not paid directly to the inmate, but rather to the government through the Prison Service. However,

5   This was a Committee of Inquiry set up by the Government of Ghana to conduct an investigation into the alleged malpractices in Ghanaian prisons.

a small percentage of the payment is kept for the inmate pending his release.

Most inmates prefer labour rendered to a private person. There are three reasons for this. First, this is an opportunity for the prisoner to be exposed to the outside world. It affords him a limited release from gaol. Secondly, the remuneration aspect is very important to him, even if it is small. Finally, prisoners find the contact with the outside world highly advantageous as often they receive gifts from the employers. But the receipt of gifts is a highly contentious issue. The inmates maintain that the prison officers allow them to receive the gifts, only to seize them from the inmates inside the prison compound – a ploy on the part of the officers to obtain the gifts for themselves.[6] The officers, on the other hand, argue that the items seized are usually prohibited items that the inmates want to smuggle into the prison compound at the end of their labour outside the prison walls. This unfortunate state of affairs compelled the Committee to recommend that there should be a complete ban on the bestowing of gifts on the inmates by private persons, especially when the gifts were prohibited items (Ghana Prisons Service, 1980: 165, para. 412). It was the view of the Committee that, even if the gifts were prohibited items, it was not right that prison officers should allow inmates to bring the gifts into the prisons and then, once inside the prison walls, seize the gifts.[7]

### 4.1 Vocational and Industrial Training in Ghana

Prison labour for the purpose of vocational and industrial training in Ghana is not very well organized. It suffers from both logistical and personnel problems. While the facilities are there for the proper trade training of the inmates for their eventual return into society, the appropriate machinery is not put into force to ensure the successful implementation of the objective of reforming and rehabilitating the inmates.

As discussed below, this state of affairs is not only detrimental to the inmates, but it also has a demoralizing effect on the staff,

---

6   This complaint was forcibly brought to the attention of the Committee of Inquiry (Ghana Prisons Service, 1980).

7   The following recommendation was made: 'Their [the prison officers'] conduct of allowing the prisoners to carry gifts only to be seized either by themselves or by the gate-keeper is not only reprehensible but fraudulent' (Ghana Prisons Service, 1980: para. 412).

especially when inmates have very little to do for most of the period of their incarceration.

## 5   Rights and Obligations in Respect of Prison Labour

Much controversy has arisen, particularly in the industrialized countries, over the question of whether or not a prisoner has a right to work. The debate is no longer confined to the industrialized world, but has spilled over into the two countries under discussion. The controversy is, however, not of the same intensity as in the western part of the globe.

In Botswana, on the basis of the statutory provisions, it can be argued that a prisoner has a right to work. This conclusion is based on the combination of a number of provisions in the Prisons Act. Section 91(2) of the Act reads: 'Sufficient work of a useful nature shall be provided to keep every prisoner who is required to work actively employed for a normal working day.' The question that arises is, who is required to work? This finds an answer in s.91(8) which states: 'Every convicted prisoner shall be given, within or without the precincts of the prison, such employment as the Commissioner may direct.'

However, when this is read alone it does not help. It must be read in conjunction with the proviso contained in subsection (8): 'Provided that the medical officer may, after the examination of a prisoner, order on medical grounds that the prisoner shall be exempt from such employment for such period of time as the medical officer shall specify.' It thus follows that every convicted prisoner is obliged to work and that the Commissioner is expected to find suitable employment for him, unless he is exempt on medical grounds.

The same argument can be made about the prisoners in Ghana, but not as forcefully as in Botswana. Both the Prisons Decree and its Regulations are emphatic on the need to provide work and training for the inmates. For instance, s.41(1) of the Decree reads:

> With the view to encouraging prisoners to lead useful and responsible lives after their release, the Director of Prisons shall, after consultation with such Government, welfare and other bodies as he may think fit, establish in every prison courses of training and instruction designed to teach simple trades, skill and crafts to prisoners who may benefit from such training.

The question that arises is whether we can argue that the inmates in both Ghana and Botswana do have a right to work and, if so, what are the consequences if the right is denied. In other words, if there is such a right, is it enforceable and also justiciable?

In Botswana, the statutory provisions state clearly that the inmate has a right to work. They are more likely to be justiciable because of the strength of constitutional rule in the country. Regulation 57(1) reinforces this position by providing that 'every convicted prisoner shall be required to engage in useful work'. Nevertheless, in spite of the fact that there is provision for a right to work in Botswana and to a lesser extent in Ghana, it can be argued that the right exists only in theory and not in practice. There are some compelling reasons why this right cannot be put into practice. Some of them are discussed below in the section on the societal implications of prison labour policy.

### 5.1 *Overcrowding*

The prison population in both countries is high, although Botswana's is much higher than that of Ghana.[8] With a very large prison population, any meaningful rehabilitation programme does not work. Furthermore, it is impracticable to find work for all the inmates. This has serious psychological problems for the inmates. The Committee of Inquiry (Ghana Prisons Service, 1980) found that the worst part of the incarceration was not so much the denial of freedom but the fact that the inmates were idle most of the time. The phrase, 'Eating, Idleness and Sleeping' was coined to describe the conditions in which most of the inmates were found.

### 5.2 *Limited Resources*

Even where the prison population is manageable, the non-availability of resources makes it difficult to enforce a right. The situation is not too critical in Botswana, where the economy has been performing very well, but in Ghana, because of neglect over the years as a result of national economic decline, the Prisons Service suffers from severe shortages that make the implementation of most plans difficult.

---

8   Ghana's prison population per 100 000 inhabitants ranges between 60 and 70. The corresponding figure for Botswana is between 200 and 300 (Frimpong, 1992).

### 5.3 Societal Implications

There are some wider implications for the entire society when the issue of an inmate's right to work is pursued vigorously. In Africa, this could have serious consequences for most countries, especially when one takes into consideration the high rate of unemployment in many countries on the continent. In both Botswana and Ghana, the unemployment rate is very high, but relatively higher in Ghana. For the average citizen of these two countries, imprisonment does not evoke any sense of concern. An inmate is seen as one who has breached the law of the nation and must pay for the transgression. It is therefore not uncommon for the average citizen to complain about the comfortable treatment meted out to the inmates, when the ordinary person in the street cannot afford even a decent meal a day. It will therefore be not only politically unwise, but also economically suicidal, to allow the inmates to compete with the unemployed and law-abiding citizens for the limited employment opportunities available.

In view of the peculiar circumstances of Botswana and Ghana, and the limited opportunities for employment in most African countries, the issue of the right to work for inmates has to be handled with great caution. It is not only impracticable, for logistic reasons, but also inappropriate to grant such a right, let alone to enforce it when many law-abiding citizens do not have the opportunity to work. Ideally, we should talk about 'creating opportunities for every prisoner who wants to work to be able to work' within the constraints of the economic realities of a country.

## 6 Conclusion

This has been a brief attempt to examine prison labour in two countries on the African continent. While there is no doubt that prison labour is an important element in the prison system as a whole, its practical application continues to prove difficult. Botswana seems to be in better control of the situation than Ghana.

Although the empirical information in this chapter has been limited to Botswana and Ghana, it is not too presumptuous to regard most of the views expressed as applicable to other countries on the African continent. A few general comments are therefore apposite.

In many ways, answering questions about prison labour, and particularly its implementation, is another means of addressing symptoms rather than causes. This writer has argued elsewhere

(Frimpong, 1992) that the use of imprisonment should be restricted as much as possible and that more emphasis should be placed on alternative sentences. There can be no doubt that prison labour would be manageable if the prison population were reduced to the barest minimum, thus permitting very limited resources to be utilized for the upkeep of the inmates. It is therefore imperative for the world as a whole to reassess the whole purpose of imprisonment and its overall implementation with a view to putting more emphasis on alternative sanctions. This is even more compelling in the case of many African countries who are unable to cope with the social and economic needs of their citizens, and that find themselves diverting limited scarce resources for the upkeep of able-bodied persons who are merely languishing in gaols.

## References

Frimpong, Kwame. 1983. Some Reflections on Ghana's Penitentiary System. *Yearbook of African Law* 3: 85–103.

Frimpong, Kwame. 1986. Some Observations on Botswana's Prison System. *Zimbabwe Law Review* 4: 136–48.

Frimpong, Kwame. 1992. Searching for Alternatives to Imprisonment: An African Experiment. *South African Journal of Criminal Justice* 5: 233–55.

Ghana Prisons Service. 1980. *The Report of the Committee of Inquiry into Prisons in Ghana.* Accra: Government Printer.

Ghana Prisons Service. 1989. *Annual Report,* Accra: Government Printer.

Government Report. 1926. *The Gold Coast: A Review of the Events of 1920–1926 and the Prospects of 1927–1928.* Accra: Government Printer.

Ramokhua, Lucas. 1985. A History of the Prisons Service in Botswana. In *The Law, the Convict and the Prisons,* edited by K. Frimpong. Gaborone: University of Botswana.

## The Author

**Kwame Frimpong** is associate professor in the Department of Law at the University of Botswana in Gaborone.

# 3 England and Wales

## JON VAGG AND URSULA SMARTT

Over the last quarter-century the prison system in England and Wales has experienced so many dramatic events that prison labour may well seem a mundane topic.[1] Yet many of the developments and crises in the prison system have had important repercussions for prison labour, while recent developments in prison labour may have important implications for prison regimes in the future.

The first section of the paper looks at the development of prison labour in penal ideology and practice. Later sections deal with the current situation, recent developments, and the issues and problems they raise. These should be viewed against the chronology of changes in the prison service as a whole (Table 3.1), and the answers to some specific questions may be found in summary form in Table 3.2.

## 1 The Development of Prison Labour

### 1.1 *Until the 1840s*

Prior to the 1840s, penal institutions were under the control of local magistrates and sheriffs. Gaols typically held persons awaiting trial, while houses of correction held sentenced prisoners. Until the 1770s, punishments such as transportation meant that relatively few sentenced prisoners were held and their sentences were often short, though by the 1840s transportation had largely ceased, leading to a corresponding increase in the number of long-term prisoners.

There was no national legal provision requiring prisoners in gaols or houses of correction to work, and a mix of local arrangements existed. For example, Wakefield House of Correction employed prisoners in wood sawing and vegetable growing; other establishments used prisoners to maintain the prison buildings; and

[1] This study will concentrate on prisons in England and Wales. Scotland and Northern Ireland are separate jurisdictions with different legislation, prison rules and, to some extent, different circumstances in prisons. They are thus not included here.

Table 3.1: Chronology of Events in the England and Wales Prison Service, 1986–97

| Year | Event |
|---|---|
| 1986 | Riots and disturbances in about 40 establishments following POA (Prison Officers' Association) industrial action banning overtime. Northeye category C prison burned out, one wing of Bristol (local prison) destroyed. |
| 1987 | HMCIP (HM Chief Inspector of Prisons) reports on the 1986 disturbances. Although it criticizes staff for refusing to carry out orders, it blames the disturbances on generally poor prison conditions.<br><br>Changes to rules governing remission. Sentences of 12 months or less to attract half (previously one-third) remission. Remission unchanged for longer sentences.<br><br>Introduction of 'Fresh Start' working arrangements, designed to make prison staff more efficient through group working procedures etc. |
| 1988 | *Leech* and *Prevot* decisions determine that governor's disciplinary hearings may be challenged by way of judicial review.<br><br>Additional home leave privileges for category C prisoners, reduction in censorship, installation of payphones in prisons. |
| 1990 | Major riot at Strangeways prison, Manchester, in which the prison is out of staff control for some 25 days. Disturbances occur simultaneously in several other prisons. |
| 1991 | The Woolf Report on the Strangeways riot criticizes many aspects of prison management and prison conditions, and argues for an approach to prisoners based on the concept of justice.<br><br>The 1991 Criminal Justice Act contains provisions allowing private prisons.<br><br>The 'Lygo Report' argues that the prison service should cease to be a government department, instead having 'agency' status.<br><br>The ECPT (European Committee for the Prevention of Torture and Inhuman or Degrading Treatment or Punishment) publishes a report on three English prisons (Wandsworth, Brixton, Leeds) and considers that conditions there amount to inhuman and degrading treatment of prisoners. |
| 1992 | Boards of Visitors (independent local inspectors of prisons) cease to have powers to discipline prisoners. |

The first private prison, The Wolds, is opened (for remand prisoners).

1994 A Prisons Ombudsman is appointed to deal with prisoner complaints (one of the Woolf Report recommendations).

An 'earned privileges' scheme is announced. This is a bastardized form of the Woolf recommendations that prisoners should have a core of rights that cannot be removed, coupled with a range of privileges dependent on behaviour. In future, prisoners will have to earn through good behaviour privileges such as extra visits, access to private cash, wearing their own clothes and recreation in association.

In view of various highly publicized incidents, more rigorous risk assessment is to be employed in making decisions on home leave.

The Chief Inspector (Judge Tumim) calls for experiments with outside contracts paying prisoners realistic wages in return for a full working day, and suggests that low wages may contribute to predatory behaviour and drug dealing by some prisoners.

Following the attempted escape of several prisoners from Whitemoor high-security prison, the 'Woodcock Report' recommends a comprehensive review of prison security (and also that staff should follow existing instructions on security procedures).

1995 Three high-security prisoners escape from Parkhurst prison, Isle of Wight. They are recaptured after several weeks. The 'Learmont Report' on the escape recommends much tighter security in prisons. The head of the prison service, Derek Lewis, is fired by the Home Secretary but claims that he was wrongfully dismissed; a compensation payment is later agreed by the Home Secretary.

A comprehensive programme of random drug testing for prisoners is announced, with a rolling start date. It is expected to be in place in all prisons by mid-1996.

1996 Ann Widdecombe, junior minister with prisons responsibility, announces a plan to pay prisoners wages comparable to those outside prisons.

1997 Mandatory Drug Testing (MDT) is introduced into all English prisons, testing a weekly 10 per cent of the total prison population in each of the 135 prisons (this includes schedule A and B drugs).

Table 3.2: Main Characteristics of Prison Labour in England and Wales, 1997

| | |
|---|---|
| What rights and protections do prisoners have not to work? | Convicted prisoners are obliged to work, but may be exempted on medical grounds by a doctor, or assigned to specific kinds of work (e.g. non-strenuous work, or work that can be carried out while sitting down) on a doctor's recommendation. Remand prisoners may work, but are not required to do so. This assumes that work is available. In reality, few workplaces are available for remand prisoners, though those registered as willing to work receive 'unemployment' payments. |
| Is all work compensated? | Yes, though at rates that vary widely. In general, prisoners are paid about £7 per week. A relatively small number of prisoners who participate in 'enhanced work' schemes earn in the region of £23–35 a week, and a small handful earn substantially more (£70–135 a week). Methods for calculating pay vary; some workshops have piece rates. In general, in the event of workshops being closed for reasons of security, staffing, etc., payments are made as normal. Unemployed prisoners are paid a minimal 'unemployed' rate. |
| Can work be imposed as a punishment for certain special crimes or prison rule violations? | No. Nor are there special categories of work such as 'hard labour'. Certain punishments, e.g. confinement to cell, preclude participation either in work as such or in work in association with others.<br>Refusal to work, or idleness at work, constitute disciplinary offences. |
| What restrictions are there on the type of work, hours of work, etc.? | Prison rules state that prisoners should work a maximum 10–hour day. It is not clear that this necessarily means 10 continuous hours, since some prisoners, working e.g. in kitchens or staff canteens, are probably present in the workplace for longer; however, such jobs are normally regarded as 'high status' by prisoners because of the freedom and informal privileges that often attach to them. |

# ENGLAND AND WALES

Prisoners must also be allowed at least one day of rest per week on the day of their religious observance, though they may waive this right.

Workplaces are subject to normal heath and safety legislation and in principle are maintained to the same standards as ordinary industrial premises. Some jobs (e.g. tending intensively grown vegetables in polythene tunnels) may take place in relatively uncomfortable circumstances and appropriate safety procedures should be followed. There is no question of prisoners being required to do certain kinds of work because they are too dangerous for free workers.

| | |
|---|---|
| Can parole or remission depend upon volunteering for work? | Remission is currently automatic, and lost only for disciplinary offences (technically, loss of remission is now described as 'extra days' to the sentence).<br><br>Work record is one factor that may be considered in a parole decision, but only to the extent of a prisoner refusing to work, being disruptive at work or having an exemplary record. |
| Does the state make deductions from prisoners' wages for maintenance, taxes, social insurance etc.? | Not currently, though it has been argued for many years that the prison system should contribute to prisoners' national insurance (i.e. state pension), since a gap in payment records is a possible sign to future employers that an applicant has had a spell in prison.<br><br>Current legislation allows the prison service to pay prisoners in some workshops wages much higher than normal. Currently this applies to only a small proportion of prisoners. Deductions are made for 'bed and board', compulsory savings etc. although specific authority to do so is not yet in place |

some used devices such as the crank and the treadmill to occupy prisoners.²

Prison labour in this period was justified in three ways. First, penal reformers saw work as an alternative to the corrosive influence of other prisoners. Secondly, reformers, especially those associated with religious organizations, argued that work was morally improving. John Howard, perhaps the best-remembered prison reformer, referred to the reformatory aspect of prison labour in his *The State of Prisons* (1777) and similar claims by other reformers are detailed in Forsythe (1987). Finally, where work was profitable, it could defray the costs of imprisonment and provide prisoners with cash or savings. Indeed, an Act of 1782 entitled prisoners – such as those in Wakefield House of Correction mentioned above – to receive half the profits of their labour.³

2   Neild (1812: 568) describes Wakefield House of Correction as using prisoner labour to grow vegetables, saw wood, and so on for use within the institution; surpluses were sold to defray the costs of imprisonment, and inmates who worked received one-half of the income in addition to the allowance of six pence per day provided by the local magistrates. Fox (1952) provides extracts from the reports of the prison inspectors in 1836. Newgate Prison, in London, provided no work for prisoners. In Cambridge, the House of Correction employed men on treadwheels and women in laundry though the Spinning House (operated by the University) provided no work. In Huntingdon, the County Gaol used a treadmill and crank, while no form of employment was mentioned for the Borough Gaol. In Ipswich, the County Gaol and House of Correction used the treadwheel, while no work was mentioned for the Borough Gaol. Gloucester County Gaol and Penitentiary possessed a treadwheel, and some prisoners worked in cooking, cleaning and so on; the debtors were permitted to work at other trades provided the prison was not crowded. In Winchester County Gaol, by contrast, no hard labour was practised and although domestic work and building repairs were carried out by prisoners, no other regular form of employment existed.

3   It is not clear how far this entitlement was honoured in practice. The *Law Magazine,* in 1861-2, detailed a dispute as to whether the Keeper of a particular gaol had the right to keep income produced from prisoners' labour (issue nos. XXI, pp.125-124; XXII, pp.247-91; XXIII, pp.99-126).

That said, it is clear that, for at least some prisoners, labour was intended to be punitive whatever formal justification might have been provided for it. This may be inferred from the existence of a sentence of 'imprisonment with hard labour'; the fact that some institutions used devices such as cranks and treadmills; and the use in, for example, Leicester prison of the work of 'powdering bathbrick' – rubbing bricks together until they were reduced to powder. Moreover, working conditions could be very poor.

Not all commentators, however, were in favour of prison labour. For example, a visiting judge in Bedford, Higgins (Home Office, 1835), objected to any form of labour that could be perceived as vocational training, primarily on the grounds of less eligibility (that is, prisoners should be less eligible than free labourers to receive training).

### 1.2 The Second Half of the Nineteenth Century

The refusal of many of Britain's colonies to accept convicts, and the subsequent commutation of many sentences of transportation to long prison terms, led to the accumulation of a large number of long-term prisoners throughout the first half of the 1800s. In 1840, a network of nationally administered 'convict prisons' was established to hold these prisoners.

Convicts in these prisons were expected to work under a regime of hard labour. They began their sentence under a 'separate' system, graduated to work in associated conditions within the institution, and might ultimately work on large public works projects such as the building of Broadmoor mental institution, and Navy dockyards at Chatham and Portsmouth. Arrangements existed for early release on licence, with the proviso that anyone attempting to escape from a labour gang while outside the prison would forfeit this privilege (Forsythe, 1987).

Once the convict prisons had been established, central control was gradually extended to the gaols and houses of correction. The Prison Act, 1865, consolidated gaols and houses of correction into a single type of institution, the 'local prison'; it required that prisoners should be confined in separate cells and laid down specifications for the previously ill-defined sentence of 'imprisonment with hard labour'. This was divided into first- and second-class hard labour, with the former including the use of the treadwheel, crank and so on, and the latter any form of labour determined by local Justices (Fox, 1952). The Prison Act, 1877, then transferred control of the local prisons to central government. This was primarily intended to produce economies of scale (some smaller institutions were closed) but also meant that prison policies, including those on labour, were henceforth determined centrally.

In short, the justifications for prison labour mentioned above had become, by the 1880s, the declared aims of the system. In 1885, Sir Edmund du Cane wrote:[4]

> The punishment of hard, dull, useless, uninteresting, monotonous labour is necessary for its penal effect ... There are three objects to be attained by the employment of prisoners at labour: first, to create a deterrent effect on the prisoner himself and on the criminal class, second, to produce a reformatory effect on the prisoner himself, and thirdly, to recoup as far as possible the cost of maintaining the prison. (du Cane, 1885: 175ff)

The harshness of the work regime was slightly mitigated by the Prison Act, 1898. The Act abolished first-class hard labour (cranks and treadwheels); all prisoners were to be employed from the beginning of their sentence on 'useful industrial labour'. Meanwhile, the Prison Rules, introduced for the first time in the 1898 Act, provided that, for the first 28 days of any sentence of hard labour, the prisoner should be held in segregation while carrying out work harder than that given to him subsequently. It is likely that the hard, but individual, task originally envisaged was oakum picking (picking apart strands of ship's rope), but, when this work was discontinued as uneconomical, these provisions on hard labour seem to have been dropped (Fox, 1952).

Finding labour for prisoners was a perennial problem. As the Controller of Accounts and Stores on Prison Industries reported in 1907:

> During the year 1906–7, great difficulties have been experienced in finding suitable and sufficient employment for all the prisoners of our prisons owing to a serious scarcity of Government work adapted to the capacity of our workers, who are mostly unskilled. (Home Office, 1907: 53ff)

Government work undertaken by the prisoners ranged from making hammocks for the Admiralty, seamen's bags, cotton picking and

---

4   Du Cane was the first Chairman of the Prison Commissioners after the nationalization of the prison system in 1877.

mailbag sewing. The Controller continued to report that employment was found for 84 per cent of the total prison population, the remaining 16 per cent being invalids and prisoners on remand, awaiting trial, or under punishment. Trial prisoners were encouraged to perform voluntary tasks for which they were remunerated, though few of them were keen to work (Home Office, 1907).

### 1.3 Borstal Training

The 1898 Prison Act also created a new type of penal establishment, Borstals, designed to offer indeterminate sentences with training for young offenders aged between 16 and 21.[5] Until 1948, it was envisaged that only young offenders whose character, health and mental condition suggested that instruction and discipline would be beneficial would be sent to Borstal.[6] In essence, the aim was to provide individualized treatment using a progressive system, and with differences between the institutions in order to widen the range of regimes available. That said, Fox (1952: 373) described work as the 'back-bone' of all Borstal institutions, since 'these boys must learn how to work hard, and above all they must learn how to stick to a job'. We shall see shortly how the reality of Borstals matched this aspiration.

### 1.4 A 1922 Snapshot

In 1919, the Labour Party established a Prison System Enquiry Committee, whose purpose was to create 'a description ... of the English Prison System as it is actually working to-day, accompanied by a study ... of its physical, mental, and moral effects upon those who are subjected to it'. The enquiry was conducted in the face of opposition from the Prison Commissioners, but succeeded nonetheless in taking a great deal of evidence. Its report (Hobhouse and Fenner Brockway, 1922) painted a less rosy picture of prison labour than the Commissioners might have liked.

Hobhouse and Fenner Brockway concluded that prison labour had a low priority within prisons. Some ambitious projects had been completed (for example, the construction of a chapel in

5   The name 'Borstal' derived from the village in Kent where the first such institution had been opened on an experimental basis. In 1908, the upper age limit was raised to 23, but this was later repealed. There were a few Borstals for girls as well as boys.

6   After 1948, the legal specifications changed, so that most young offenders were sent there.

Wormwood Scrubs prison), but there was a lack of trained instructors, many work processes were labour-intensive because better-equipped workshops would provide less employment, and some non-productive or counterproductive tasks (such as unpicking finished mailbags) were used to absorb prisoner time. Hobhouse and Fenner Brockway commented that 'work is regarded as a means to an end, emphatically not as a craft, but as a prescribed task to be fulfilled as part of the punishment of imprisonment' (1922: 113). They continued: 'In criticising the character of manual labour enforced in prisons, we do not forget that much modern factory work is both monotonous and degrading too' (ibid.: 114); however, many of the tasks given to prisoners could have been made more purposeful and instructive, rather than compelling prisoners 'to do mechanical work by hand, in a word, *to become inefficient machines*' (ibid.: original emphasis). Similar conclusions were reached with regard to work in women's prisons (ibid.: 341–4).

Hobhouse and Fenner Brockway were equally critical of the situation in the Borstals. Little trade training was done and instructors were overstretched and lacked proper machinery, so that after release the prisoners were unfitted for work in normal factory conditions.

Finally, it is worth noting that Hobhouse and Fenner Brockway argued strongly for a system of payment for prison work, a view that led them to consider whether prison labour did or should compete with free labour. On this point they concluded that: 'all useful work done in prison is necessarily competitive with free labour. It is no use restricting prison labour. The right course is to demand that it should be done under Trade Union conditions' (ibid.: 118–19).

## 1.5 The Late 1950s: Poor Conditions but High Aspirations

As we have seen, in the 1800s and early 1900s, prison labour was justified as morally improving, a means of preventing idle prisoners from corrupting others, and a way of defraying costs. In practice, however, there was also strong adherence to the idea that prison labour should have some punitive elements. By the 1960s, much of this had changed, largely through a process of neglect.

One of the most influential prison studies ever conducted in England is a detailed sociological account of Pentonville prison, London (Morris and Morris, 1963). Prison labour was not a major topic of this study, and indeed a wide-ranging review of labour policies was going on as the research was under way. However, Morris and Morris's comments probably represent the situation in many large local prisons in the late 1950s and the first years of the 1960s.

The kinds of work available included mailbag sewing, rag-stripping, mat-making, and tailoring, which occupied just under half the prisoners (Morris and Morris, 1963: 24). The remainder were mainly employed in the maintenance of the institution (cleaning, painting and glazing, gardening, and so on). The 7 per cent who were unemployed comprised those who had just entered or were about to be released, or who were in hospital or under punishment.

Rule 56 of the prison rules at that time provided that 'Every prisoner shall be required to engage in useful work for not more than ten hours per day, of which so far as is practicable, at least eight hours shall be spent in associated or other work outside the cells.' Refusal to work constituted a disciplinary offence. However, Morris and Morris assert that much of the work performed was 'purely symbolic'. The timetable of the prison and problems of finding enough work combined to make the average workshop day, including security checks and the issue of tools and so on, about three hours. The prisoner population included a large number of drunks and others physically incapable of sustained work. As far as the workshop instructors were concerned, therefore, the fulfilment of outside contracts rested mainly upon the work of a small number of prisoners, who tended to become an elite able to earn a variety of unofficial privileges.

## 2   Prison Labour since 1960

### 2.1   *Legislative and Administrative Frameworks*

#### 2.1.1   *The Prison Act and the prison rules*

The Prison Act 1952, as amended by later legislation such as the Criminal Justice Act 1991,[7] remains the key legal provision governing prisons. It makes only one tangential reference to prison labour. Section 47(1) enables the Home Secretary, the minister of state responsible for prisons, to 'make rules for the regulation and management of prisons, remand centres, detention centres and youth

---

7   The Criminal Justice Act 1991 included in ss.84–92 provisions for certain prisons to be 'contracted out', that is, privatized.

custody centres respectively, and for the classification, treatment, employment, discipline and control of persons required to be detained therein'. More detailed provisions are thus contained in the prison rules.

The Prison Rules 1964 (as amended) make specific reference to work in Rule 28, and other sections contain additional and consequential arrangements. Rule 28 reads:

(1) A convicted prisoner shall be required to do useful work for not more than 10 hours a day, and arrangements shall be made to allow prisoners to work, where possible, outside the cells and in association with one another.
(2) The medical officer may excuse a prisoner from work on medical grounds, and no prisoner shall be set to do work which is not of a class for which he has been passed by the medical officer as being fit.
(3) No prisoner shall be set to do work of a kind not authorized by the Secretary of State.
(4) No prisoner shall work in the service of another prisoner or an officer, or for the private benefit of any person, without the authority of the Secretary of State.
(5) An unconvicted prisoner shall be permitted, if he wishes, to work as if he were a convicted prisoner.
(6) Prisoners may be paid for their work at rates approved by the Secretary of State, either generally or in relation to particular cases.

The main additional provisions are the following:

- Rule 15 states that prisoners shall not be required to 'do any unnecessary work' on days of religious observance. Thus prisoners doing 'necessary' work, for example in the kitchens, may be required to work on such days, though presumably they may elect not to take employment that requires it.
- Rule 27(1) permits prisons not to provide prisoners with outdoor exercise if they are engaged in outdoor work. So far as we know, this provision is applied only to prisoners working on prison farms, and so on, who may not have periods specifically identified as 'outdoor exercise'.
- Rule 47 deals with offences against discipline and one subsection, Rule 47(18), creates the offence of one who 'intentionally fails to work properly or, being required to work, refuses to do so'. Other

subsections, dealing with assaults, intentionally endangering the health or safety of others, possessing or selling unauthorized articles, issuing threats, being absent from part of the prison where the prisoner is supposed to be, disobeying lawful orders and so on, apply in the context of prison labour as they would in any other situation. Further rules then set out the procedure for disciplinary hearings and the maximum punishments – in most cases, forfeiture of privileges, stoppage of earnings, an award of 'extra days' (that is, cancellation of automatically granted remission) all for periods of up to 28 days; exclusion from associated work for up to 14 days; and cellular confinement for up to three days.[8]

Young Offender Institutions (YOIs) hold persons aged 15–21 undergoing a specific sentence, a Youth Custody Order.[9] Provisions under the Young Offender Institution Rules of 1988 differ from the equivalent adult rules, and reflect the historically different attitude to prison labour for young offenders. Hence the YOI Rules simply state, in Rule 37:

(1) Work shall, so far as practicable, be such as will foster personal responsibility and a prisoner's interests and skills and help him to prepare for his return to the community.
(2) No prisoner shall be set to do work of a kind not authorized by the Secretary of State.

Paralleling the prison rules, YOI Rule 32 prevents prisoners being required to work on days of religious observance, while YOI Rule 50(18) creates the offence of failing to work properly or

[8] Certain other punishments are also available, including a caution, forfeiture of certain minor items (such as newspapers bought at the prisoner's expense) for indefinite periods and the prospective addition of 'extra days' for prisoners not yet sentenced. A governor may punish an offence with only one, or a mixture, of the measures discussed here. Special provisions also govern punishments where more than one charge arises out of an incident. Multiple punishments may operate consecutively, except in the case of 'extra days', which remain subject to a maximum of 28 days per incident.

[9] The Youth Custody Order is the standard custodial provision for young offenders, and is a determinate sentence. In certain circumstances young offenders may be given other types of custodial sentence, including imprisonment.

refusing to work. Rule 36(2) makes a provision, not mirrored in the rules for adult prisons, requiring YOIs to operate training courses 'such as will foster personal responsibility and a prisoner's interests and skills and improve his prospects of finding suitable employment after release'. Finally, the provision for education is more extensive than the equivalent adult rule, requiring prisoners of school age to receive education or training classes for at least 15 hours a week within the normal working week (Rule 35(2)).[10]

### 2.1.2 *The framework document for the Prison Service*

This document is a managerial mission statement that outlines the main functions of the prison service and links each one to a Key Performance Indicator (KPI).[11] One of the functions is to 'deliver positive regimes which help prisoners address their offending behaviour and allow them as full and responsible a life as possible'. One of the corresponding measures of performance is KPI5, 'the number of hours a week which, on average, prisoners spend engaged in purposeful activity'. From this perspective, labour is only one of several 'purposeful activities' provided to prisoners, and there is no KPI relating specifically to the number of prisoners employed or the number of hours worked. For 1993/4, for example, the goal was to provide an increase of 3 per cent in the average number of hours of purposeful activity per prisoner, to 24.9 hours per week. In fact, this was slightly exceeded, with an average increase of 4 per cent.

### 2.1.3 *Heath and safety legislation and so on*

While convicted prisoners are required to work, they are not employees of the prison (*Pullen v. The Prison Commissioners* (1957)), nor is there a master–servant relationship (*Davis v. The Prison*

---

[10] In addition to the Prison and YOI Rules, Prison Service Orders and Instructions (previously known as Standing Orders and Circular Instructions) provide administrative guidance to staff.

[11] The functions, or 'relevant goals', are as follows: to keep prisoners in custody; to maintain order, control, discipline and a safe environment; to provide decent conditions for prisoners and meet their needs, including health care; to provide positive regimes which help prisoners address their offending behaviour and allow them as full and responsible a life as possible; to help prisoners prepare for their return to the community; and to deliver prison services using the resources provided by Parliament with maximum efficiency.

*Commissioners* (1963)). Consequently, various employee rights and employer obligations, such as invalidity benefits, access to industrial tribunals and insurance requirements, contained in legislation such as the Health and Safety at Work Act 1974 do not apply to them. Nor are any contributions made to the state pension scheme. Prisoners can litigate for injuries sustained at work, but only on the basis that the prison owes them a general duty of care and that they are able to demonstrate that the prison was negligent. In practice, prisoners injured while at work would be more likely to receive an *ex gratia* payment at rates equivalent to disablement benefits provided by the Department of Social Services.[12]

Conditions of work may be inspected by the Health and Safety Executive, which inspects prisons exactly as it does any other workplace. It is service policy to observe all relevant legal, health and safety provisions. However, since prisons are owned by the Crown they benefit from 'Crown immunity'; that is, they cannot be prosecuted for breaches of these provisions. The Crown does not prosecute itself. The only exception to this relates to prison kitchens, where Crown immunity was specifically lifted in the mid-1980s. It remains possible, nonetheless, for individual governors or other staff to be prosecuted for wilful or reckless disregard of health and safety requirements, or to face internal disciplinary action (though this would not occur for honest mistakes or breaches occurring as the result of management deficiencies).

HM Chief Inspector of Prisons has a wide remit to review the propriety and humanity of conditions in all establishments. There is a rolling programme of inspections; inspection teams normally spend about a week in any one establishment, and their findings are published. Prison labour is only one among many areas dealt with in inspections, and is specifically mentioned in only about one-quarter of the recent reports. Where comments have been recorded,

12   This continues to be the case in privatized prison industries. HMP Coldingley turned over the operation of its workshops to Wackenhut UK (a subsidiary of Wackenhut Correctional Corporation of America) on 1 November 1997, for an initial five-year contract. While Wackenhut operates the workshops, comprising a laundry, sign-making shop and light engineering plant, the liability for prisoner injury, damage caused by prisoners and the payment of wages still lies with the Crown. The general principle that the prison authorities owe a duty of care to prisoners was established in *Ellis v. Home Office* (1953).

about half praised prison labour practices and/or facilities (while often criticizing other aspects of the prisons) and half made adverse observations on the poor use of workshops and/or the number of prisoners left idle. Brief details appear in Table 3.3.

## 2.2 Prison Labour, 1960–68; the Advisory Council on Prison Labour

At the time Morris and Morris were conducting the study discussed earlier, plans were afoot for major changes in prison labour. In 1960, the prison service established an Advisory Council on the Employment of Prisoners. Its three reports set out two principles for prison labour, namely that (1) 'offenders in custody shall be given training (including vocational training where appropriate) and experience that will assist them to get and keep jobs on discharge' and (2) 'the best possible economic use [should] be made of prison labour' (cited in Home Office, 1977: 55).

These two aims were set against several additional considerations. First, the type of work provided had to take account of personal aptitudes, but it was expected that most would need to be semi-skilled manufacturing jobs. Secondly, it was recognized that some prisoners would not wish to work, or would find any but the most simple job too taxing. Special provisions were necessary for such groups. Thirdly, it was thought unlikely that most offenders would find the same work after release that they had done in prison. The aim was thus not to equip prisoners with particular skills but to 'encourage the habit of regular and purposeful work at a tempo and in conditions as close as possible to those of outside industry' (Home Office, 1977: 56). Finally, given the prison setting, the work provided had to take account of security considerations and a range of practical matters, including levels of overcrowding and population turnover, the available workshop space within the prison estate (including issues such as power supplies to workshops) and other claims on staff time, such as – until recently – escorting remand prisoners to and from courts. The net effect of these caveats was to rob the two primary aims of much of their practical force, since they amounted to a recognition that they could only be achieved with part of the prison population and where other circumstances – population levels and turnover, security considerations, and so on – were favourable.

The Advisory Council had, in the end, little impact on the prison labour situation, yet the year after its final report was published, though for reasons unconnected with it, the first thoroughgoing industrial prison was opened in England.

## 2.3 The Industrial Prison

### 2.3.1 Coldingley

In the 1960s, industrial sociologists such as Blauner (1964) and Halmos (1965) advocated the introduction of contemporary industrial processes in prisons, partly because of their profitability and partly because they would also require prisoners to be more psychologically involved in their own rehabilitation. Two developments flowed from this perspective. In 1972 prison industries were given a corporate identity ('Prindus'), and reorganized to concentrate on a small number of industries (clothing and textiles, weaving and knitting, engineering, woodwork, laundering, light engineering and assembly, electrical and mechanical production, and plastic injection mouldings). And slightly earlier, in 1969, the first and only 'industrial prison', Coldingley, had been opened with modern manufacturing workshops in paint-dipping, engineering, laundry services and sign-making, supported by vocational training.[13]

The original intention was to operate the prison like a business, and its staff included a management consultant. Prison officers supervising the workshops at Coldingley never wore uniforms, so as to imitate the world of work outside. Works managers were recruited from the civilian sector to make the prison industries work, regarding the governor as their chief executive. And the prison employed marketing staff and sales representatives who succeeded in getting a variety of prestigious orders; for example, the whole of the German Army of the Rhine had their shields and royal arms made at the prison, intricate silk screen printing work produced to a high standard. However, the business aims were compromised by the special demands of the prison environment. It was not possible to operate workshops efficiently because other activities, such as exercise and education, had to be incorporated into the working day; staff unions resisted proposals for shift arrangements that would have solved such problems; and, since Coldingley was a category B prison with a high security element, security considerations sometimes supervened. Moreover, unemployment

13  A second was planned for Featherstone, in the Midlands. Featherstone was opened in the 1970s, but has never run on such uncompromisingly industrial lines as Coldingley.

Table 3.3: Samples of Comments on Prison Labour in Reports on Individual Establishments by HM Chief Inspector of Prisons

| Establishment | Type | Comment |
| --- | --- | --- |
| Kingston | Training (the only prison with an all-lifer population) | Prisoners should be more involved in workshops or full-time education. |
| Exeter | Local | Workshops and time out of cell at recreation were commended, though problems were noted with education. |
| Northallerton | Remand centre, with some sentenced males aged 18–21 | Thought to have an ineffective management structure, and education, PE and workshop facilities were all underused. |
| Coldingley | Training (the only 'industrial' prison) | Equipment was considered obsolete and wages too low. |
| Stoke Heath | Prison and YOI | Had impressive, but underused, workshop facilities. |
| The Mount | Training (category C) | Too many idle prisoners. The 20-hour working week was improved from the last visit, but still unsatisfactory. |
| Channings Wood | Training (category C) | Workshops praised, though almost every other aspect of the prison regime was severely criticized. |

Table 3.3: Concluded

| Establishment | Type | Comment |
|---|---|---|
| Holme House | Training (category B) opened 1992 | Found to have design faults resulting in insufficient workshop and education places. On a spot check, 45 per cent of prisoners were found locked in their cells during the working day. It was later announced that two new workshops would be built at the prison. |
| Hindley | Remand and sentenced male prisoners aged under 21 | Praised for having increased the numbers of work places since the last inspection, despite abandoning one workshop. |
| Elmley | Local and training (category B) | Praised for the variety of work available, although there were some difficulties caused by having category C prisoners in a category B establishment; the security restrictions on the latter effectively acted as a block on the introduction of more opportunities for the former. |
| Lancaster Farms | YOI and remand centre opened two years previously | Praised as a model institution on a number of counts including its work opportunities, though it was noted that prison service intentions to increase the prison's population would threaten the regime. |

Source: Reports of 48 inspections published July 1994–September 1995.

remained a problem for the prison's management, just as it was on the outside. Coldingley had 310 prisoners on four wings in 1970, but only gave full industrial employment to two-thirds of them. At the same time, prisoners were not initially receptive to the idea of an industrial work culture. Some motivation was provided by the de facto abolition of selected prison rules, such as restrictions on the number of letters they could write each week. Prisoners' pay rates were enhanced: the normal weekly wage in 1969 was 70 pence a week, while Coldingley paid £1.40. And the normal procedure of charging inmates with a disciplinary offence if they refused to work was dropped in favour of a simple withdrawal of privileges. Those who refused work were denied access to the canteen (prison shop), cigarettes or home leave.

Despite its problems, Coldingley was a qualified success. It was the 'flagship' for a new approach to prison labour, received scores of visitors from home and abroad, and in time became a popular allocation option among prisoners, not least because it had a reputation for being a prison from which a high proportion of inmates were released on parole.

In more recent times, Coldingley has been criticized by the Chief Inspector of Prisons, Sir David Ramsbotham (who succeeded Judge Tumim in 1995). Following an unannounced short inspection, a report was published in March 1996 listing several faults, including discarded food left to rot, poor maintenance of electrical installations, and fire risks including designated fire control staff who were not trained in fire-fighting. Ramsbotham concluded that management had spent too much time seeking to develop prison industry and had not paid attention to basic regime elements. Finally, and strangely for an industrial prison with a design capacity of 288, he noted that there were only 136 prisoner work places (HM Chief Inspector of Prisons, 1996).

In November 1997, the Coldingley workshops (though not the prison as such) were privatized. This is described in more detail below.

### 2.3.2 Developments elsewhere in the system

Throughout the 1970s and 1980s, there were periodic aspirational statements about the importance of labour in prison regimes. The May Committee (Home Office, 1979), an inquiry into the prison service that took place following a major riot, recognized that work provision was important, if for no other reason than that 'Industrial work is ... valuable in providing some outlet for prisoners' physical and mental energies and so aids the maintenance of good order and morale' (para. 3). While accepting that strenuous efforts to provide good-quality work had been made in the past, the May Committee referred to what it saw as the 'fatalistic and defeatist attitude' of the Prison Department and its staff towards prison industries and called for a greater sense of purpose, though without suggesting alternatives or solutions (paras 4.27–38).

In 1984/5, the Prisons Board issued a mission statement, the *Statement of the Functions of Prison Department Establishments*.[14] Item 17 stated that the service aimed 'to provide, with a view to occupying prisoners as fully as possible throughout the whole week, a balanced and integrated regime, which may include work, education, physical education, access to libraries and individual and collective leisure facilities'. Work thus became one item among several that were to be 'balanced and integrated'. However, a continuing series of pressures, including the problems posed by an increasing prison population, ensured that work remained consistently low in operational priorities (Stern, 1987). Throughout most of the 1980s, workshops in local prisons experienced frequent and often unscheduled closures due to the redeployment of staff to escort prisoners to court. Indeed, given the degree of difficulty in running workshops in local prisons, some locals closed their shops, usually to expand the space available for other kinds of activities.

There was also some managerial inefficiency. Stern (1987) cites reports of HM Chief Inspector of Prisons that detail, for example, an admitted 'error of judgement' in the installation of an industrial woodworking machine at Frankland prison in 1980, which was used only for a trial period and then left idle; and the installation of 18 plastic moulding machines in Shepton Mallet prison that had to be run a minimum of 12 hours a day to be commercially viable, when the moulding workshop could normally operate for only 25 to 30 hours a week. It is fair to say that the Shepton Mallet machines could be described as successful, in that prisoners were able to work on state-of-the-art equipment, yet the inability of the workshop to operate at commercially viable levels of production meant that this experience was provided to them at a substantial cost to the prison service.

Indeed, Prison Service Industries and Farms made substantial losses in the early 1980s.[15] Stern (1987) cites accounts for 1982/3

14  Reprinted in Maguire *et al.* (1985).
15  The headquarters organization has been renamed and reorganized

detailing a loss of £11.6 million, and in 1984/5 a loss of £29 million. The losses were so serious that, in January 1986, the administrative head of the Home Office was called to appear before the House of Commons Public Accounts Committee to explain them.

Although on that occasion the issue was one of mismanagement, it may be that some part of the losses is a function of the way that costs are attributed in the bookkeeping, rather than 'real' trading losses. In England and Wales, the full cost of supervision by discipline staff in the workshops is included as a workshop cost, even though it is possible to argue that the officers would have to be employed anyway. In other countries, different practices exist and this probably led to some confusion when English officials began, as described below, to make comparisons with Germany.

### 2.4 The Current Situation

As the previous sections have indicated, by the mid-to-late 1980s, labour had again dropped down the list of priorities. Only one fully industrial prison, Coldingley, was in operation and labour had become only one item in a corporate goal that related to prisoner activities as a whole.

In 1987, a new programme of prison staffing was introduced. The 'Fresh Start' programme was largely intended to buy out staff overtime and eliminate what the prison service saw as restrictive staff practices. A promise to recruit additional staff to cover the workload previously borne through overtime was never kept, so that there was a net decrease in the number of officer hours available within the system as a whole. However, new working practices, coupled with developments outside the Fresh Start framework, such as the use of private companies to carry out prisoner escorts to court, did result in some improvements in regimes.

King and McDermott (1995), in a wide-ranging study of changes in imprisonment, compared average weekly hours in purposeful activities for 1987 and 1992 in five prisons. With one exception, the prisons achieved longer hours in activities in 1992 than in 1987. However, this was achieved primarily through increases in the availability of physical education and study. So far as work was concerned,

> several times. In 1992, it changed from 'Prison Service Industries and Farms' (PSIF) to 'Prison Enterprise Services' (PES), and in May 1997 it was further renamed and integrated into a larger 'Regime Services' division.

the results were more mixed. Local prisons achieved increased hours at work: in the case of Birmingham, from 2 to 2.5 hours a week and in Nottingham, from 1.5 to 3.3 hours a week. In the three training prisons, however, hours had fallen, in one case (Gartree) by over 40 per cent (see Table 3.4).

Table 3.4: Average Prisoner Hours in Work and Other Activities in Five Prisons, 1987 and 1992

| Prison | Work Hours | | Work and Training Hours | | Hours in All 'Purposeful Activities' | |
|---|---|---|---|---|---|---|
| | 1987 | 1992 | 1987 | 1992 | 1987 | 1992 |
| Birmingham | 2.03 | 2.52 | 2.03 | 2.75 | 3.90 | 5.44 |
| Gartree | 9.42 | 5.53 | 9.42 | 6.84 | 15.37 | 15.65 |
| Nottingham | 1.52 | 3.28 | 4.80 | 7.50 | 11.26 | 13.95 |
| Featherstone | 15.13 | 10.81 | 17.74 | 12.93 | 23.67 | 18.11 |
| Ashwell | 8.06 | 7.56 | 12.16 | 10.72 | 18.54 | 19.18 |

Source: Adapted from King and McDermott (1995: 240).

Other information is patchy. Fairly substantial data are available in relation to the activities of Prison Enterprise Services (PES), albeit that this accounts for only a small proportion of prisoners. Less good data are available for locally based employment because the regime monitoring data collection system that provides information on KPI5 (prisoner activities) is being overhauled.[16] Meanwhile, much of the responsibility for budgeting has been devolved to prison governors, who can now decide (in consultation with PES and area managers) how best to spend their budget for prisoner labour, and in consequence how many domestic,

[16] These data were collated at institutional level on a weekly basis, using a form that recorded, inter alia, the numbers of prisoners in each workshop, the hours worked and a number of other activities such as education and hours of association. In more recent years the information has been downloaded to a central database, using a now-archaic computer system. Moreover, some prisons were never connected to the system and their data were not included.

maintenance, orderly and other jobs will be available for prisoners.[17]

In terms of the system as a whole, the current (June 1998) population is slightly more than 64,000 prisoners, of whom 53,000 are sentenced. Of these sentenced prisoners, 8,000 work in PES workshops, 2,000 on PES farms and gardens, and a further 8,000 in locally created jobs as cleaners, orderlies, building maintenance labourers, and so on.[18] The implication is that only about one-third of sentenced prisoners (or about 28 per cent of all prisoners) are at work, though a large number of the rest may have other activities, such as education. The proportions of prisoners working have fallen over the last few years owing to the increase in the prison population. In May 1996, for example, the numbers working were approximately the same, but they comprised about 55 per cent of sentenced prisoners or one-third of all prisoners.

A limited amount of more structured information is also available in relation to PES, through the prison service's annual reports. The data provided are, however, typically one to two years out of date. Thus in mid-1995, for example, figures for 1993/4 were reported. In that year, prisoners employed within PES worked on average 21 hours a week in the workshops and 29 hours a week in the farms and gardens (cf. the system-wide average of 24.9 hours of *all* purposeful activity per prisoner cited earlier). The majority of the work done (92 per cent by value of goods of services produced) related to the 'internal market', that is items for use within the prison system or other government agencies or departments.[19] The remaining 8 per cent was produced for the 'external' market, that is on contract for outside companies (the amount of external work is likely to increase in the future, for reasons indicated below). Several positive developments were taking place, such as the accreditation of workshops for British Standard 5750, dealing with quality control; 32 workshops had been accredited and 28 were being prepared for accreditation in March 1994. Most prison farms with livestock

17   There are 13 areas in the prison service. Each has an area manager, whose role it is to monitor and advise on developments in his or her area. The area system (which replaced four regions in the 1980s) is itself under review.
18   Estimates provided to Ursula Smartt by prison officials.
19   Prison farms produce all the bacon, pork and preserves used in prison kitchens, and about 80 per cent of the vegetables and 70 per cent of the milk.

had established units for rare breeds. However, taken globally, industries and farms were running at a loss, costing the prison system some £69.4 million (approximately 5.6 per cent of the total prisons budget) while producing £58 million of goods and services.

Another view of the situation 'on the ground', and of the impact of the recent rise in the prison population, comes from looking at the experience of individual prisons.[20] Hull, for example, is a 'community' prison: a local prison holding remand and short-term prisoners (adult males and young offenders on Youth Custody Orders) from the Hull area. In October 1994, the prison had a design capacity of 295, held 403, and planned to provide daytime activities for 335 (83 per cent of the population). By June 1998, its design capacity had been increased to 432, but it held 520 prisoners (including remand and convicted adults, and young offenders aged 15–21) and had 432 planned places for daytime activities. It was therefore providing activities for 83 per cent of its new, higher, population figure.

The increased numbers of activity places came mainly from the workshops. Indeed, other types of places had been reduced. In 1998, the prison offered the following (corresponding 1994 figures in brackets):

- 200 workshop places, of which 50 were contractual work centrally provided by PES (112 in 1994);
- 36 prison works: labourers, kitchen, industrial training, gardening (62);
- 66 orderlies (84);
- 90 education (78);
- 20 pre-release group and community work (20);
- 20 induction: just arrived, not yet available for employment (20).

In addition, in 1998, 25 prisoners were in either the prison hospital or the segregation unit. It follows from these figures that industrial work was provided for about 38 per cent of the population; a further 20 per cent were involved in domestic functions of the establishment and 25 per cent were enrolled in other daytime activities. Against system-wide figures for activities, this is a comparatively positive picture.

If we look at the time-sheets for individual workshops, we can get a clearer picture of the difficulties besetting the prison. For example, in 1996, the mid-point of the two dates used above, one

20   The information on Hull was collected by Ursula Smartt.

manufacturing workshop had places for 28 prisoners and, in a given week, 30 prisoners actually worked in it, divided as follows:

- 11 worked for the whole week, missing at most one morning or afternoon, for example for visits;
- 4 worked on three or four days, the others being taken up with, for example, court appearances;
- 1 worked on three days and was returned to cells as 'not required' on the others, owing to a lack of supervisory staff;
- 2 worked on one or two days and were not required on the others for the same reason;
- 4 were transferred to the workshop in mid-week and worked only on two days;
- 8 were returned to cells as 'not required' *every* day because the workshop was short of supervisory staff (though in the course of the week some of these were transferred elsewhere anyway).

We can therefore say that the total amount of activity in the workshop amounted to 163 person-sessions (mornings or afternoons) or 66 per cent of the maximum of 246 that were possible, allowing for prisoners being transferred in or out of the prison, and so on. The largest single cause of this shortfall was prisoners being returned to cells as 'not required' because there were not sufficient supervisory staff.[21]

The range of weekly earnings in this workshop, for prisoners who could have worked the full week, ran from £2.50 for those not required at work at any time to £10.00 for those who worked both mornings and afternoons on every working day in the most responsible jobs. Most prisoners received between £9.00 and £9.50 for a full week, though the average amount across the workshop as a whole, including those who were only at work part of the time, was £7.19. This was above the average for the institution as a whole, which amounted to £5.77 per week. On an average week, in Hull, and again without adjusting the figures to account for court appearances and prisoners 'not required', and so on, kitchen workers received £9.46, orderlies £6.11, workers in the textile shop £5.98, those on vocational training £5.86, cleaners £5.84 and those in education £4.93.

21   In the tabulated information, the statement that a prisoner 'worked on one day' may mean that in fact he only worked for half of that day.

The situation in Hull may not fairly represent that of training prisons where there are many fewer absences from work for court appearances and so on (though the lack of supervisory staff may still be an issue). However, the global figures are also difficult to work with since they mask a great deal of variation between prisons and types of prisoner. Taking all the data discussed above as a whole, however, we may reasonably reach two conclusions. Firstly, a large proportion of prisoners who do work are working substantially less than a full working week. Secondly, while many of those who do not work are on education courses and so on, probably more than 10 per cent and possibly as many as 20 per cent of prisoners have no daytime activity other than exercise and association.

### 2.4.1 The Workshop Expansion Scheme and 'enhanced work'

While the prison service largely neglected prison labour issues in the 1980s and early 1990s, there have been recent signs that attention is again being focused on it. Two points are worth mentioning in this connection: the 'Workshop Expansion Scheme' and arrangements that increase the pay of a few selected prisoners very substantially.

The Workshop Expansion Scheme is a programme that has mutated rapidly in its short life. It began life as the 'Prison Enterprise Partnerships' scheme. The partnerships amounted to a concerted attempt to obtain outside contracts. The official brochure suggested that inquiries made to headquarters will be referred to the prison that has the productive capacity most suited to the contract, though in practice it seems that most contracts were generated locally. The advantages to businesses were claimed to be flexibility, short production runs and short supply chains; the advantages to the prison were the opportunities for prisoners to learn new skills and apply them in more flexible ways, enhanced job opportunities after release and additional revenue to the prisons. The scheme most often mentioned as an illustration of a successful contract was a designer label tailoring operation (a contract with the Red or Dead company) at Full Sutton maximum security (dispersal) prison near York.[22]

22   In mid-1996 the Red or Dead company went into receivership for bankruptcy. Although the workshop survived, this illustrates one of the problems of using prison labour to fulfil commercial contracts: namely, that the prison is exposed to commercial risks and faces the same economic uncertainties as any other company.

The partnerships were subsequently renamed the 'Pathfinder' scheme and some also became involved in offering 'enhanced work'; that is, higher than normal wages in return for productivity approaching that of normal commercial operations. For example, in 1996, 'enhanced' pay in four of the prisons involved averaged £8.20 a week as opposed to £7.20 in most establishments. As indicated the current name for the programme as a whole is the 'Workshop Expansion Scheme'.[23]

Prisons in the scheme commit themselves to targets of an increase in overall workshop productivity to 60 per cent (measured against industry norms for outside factories), an increase of the working week to 35 hours and an emphasis on full prisoner employment. The effect of this has been that prison governors and their industrial managers are seeking more lucrative contracts on the outside rather than taking in contracts from PES to produce goods for the internal (Prison Service) market.

Meanwhile, some other more or less experimental enterprises have been developed, though not all depend on outside contracts. They include furniture production at Albany training prison (Isle of Wight) and a vegetable preparation plant at Leyhill open prison, near Bristol. In general, these experiments are self-funding, with increased prisoner pay generated from increased production. Thus, at East Sutton Park in Kent, four prisoners earn 'real' wages: £134.61 a week (£3.45 per hour) working a 39-hour week to produce Italian cheeses under a private contract. And at Latchmere House, a category C low-security prison near Kingston, Surrey, 120 out of 190 prisoners work on a day-release basis in jobs such as driving delivery vans and working in local factories. These prisoners are directly employed by outside firms and are paid normal wages; they pay normal tax and national insurance contributions, but are also required to make contributions to a compulsory savings scheme and to the prison for board and lodging. Those working inside earn about £60 a week producing plastic flowerpots and buckets. Coldingley, the industrial prison, was paying 30 prisoners £80 for a

23  The original 'Pathfinder' scheme, in April 1996–7, included 10 prisons: Acklington, Ashwell, Featherstone, Kirkham, New Hall, Ranby, Stocken, Stoke Heath, Wakefield and Wymott. In 1998, when the scheme became the Workshop Expansion Scheme, nine futher prisons were added. The scheme now includes 19 prisons: the original 10, plus Albany, Camp Hill, Channings Wood, Ford, Gartree, Littlehey, The Mount, The Verne and Wandsworth.

40-hour working week (including overtime) by June 1997, but made a 50 per cent deduction from wages for compulsory savings and financial support.

Paying enhanced wages has demonstrated a clear link between additional pay and productivity and increasing workshop numbers. At Styal women's prison, for instance, 38 additional workshop places were created in the tailoring workshop in 1996 and at Wakefield (dispersal) prison all workshops increased their productivity by over 15 per cent, to the point that it frequently outstripped the supply of raw materials in the engineering shop. Establishments have found that enhanced wages acted as an incentive for prisoners to go to work, resulting in an increased awareness of the benefits of employment and leading to improved levels of behaviour within the establishment.

### 2.4.2 Private prisons

The 1991 Criminal Justice Act allowed the Home Secretary to contract out prisons to private companies. Existing prisons have been offered out to tender following refurbishment (Strangeways, Blakenhurst, Buckley Hall) and tenders have also been invited for the operation of new establishments built by the prison service. By 1995, four private prisons had been opened (The Wolds, Blakenhurst, Doncaster and Buckley Hall). An internal prison service team bid against outside competition and won the contract for Strangeways in Manchester. Since 1995, several additional prisons have been offered for tender and the contract period has been extended; the first contracts were for periods of five years, while the latest ones are for 25 years. This programme has survived the change from a Conservative to a Labour government following the general election of May 1997.

The first private prisons were originally intended to be remand establishments, and had this remained the case they would have had no obligation to offer prisoners work. The first newly built private prison, The Wolds, originally had no workshops for this reason. In the event, all the private prisons have operated with a mix of remand and sentenced prisoners and have needed to provide at least some of their population with work opportunities. In the main this has been done through the establishment of workshops. The Wolds developed workshops after the then Chief Inspector of Prisons, Judge Tumim, criticized its lack of work and educational facilities for prisoners. Workshop staff, like all staff in private prisons, are hired by the contractor. Prisoners' pay and the flow of workshop contracts follow the same arrangements outlined in respect of the prison service's own establishments.

In November 1997, a further experiment in privatization took place when Wackenhut was awarded a contract to operate the workshops, though not the rest of the prison, at Coldingley. The financial arrangements are confidential, though it is believed that Wackenhut rent the facilities, contract with the prison to provide labour, and seek production contracts in the normal way. Their profit would thus come from whatever surplus they generated, after costs, from their commercial contracts. As with most prison projects, the devil is likely to be in the detail. In principle, the establishment is now insulated from commercial risk (this becomes Wackenhut's concern) but covers its costs and provides work to prisoners. In practice, the prison is now dependent on Wackenhut for its supply of prisoner activities.

### 2.4.3 Latest developments

In February 1996, the then Conservative Prisons Minister, Ann Widdecombe, speaking at the Prison Service Conference in Brighton, stated:

> It would certainly not be right for prisoners to accumulate large amounts of money as disposable income ... I would like to see deductions being made as contributions towards the prisoners' board and lodging; the support of his or her dependants; for savings to be paid on release, and – perhaps most important – to go towards helping victim support and crime prevention measures.'[24]

The idea that prisoners should be paid a near normal salary for their work, out of which they could then pay for their keep, is not new (see, for example, Hobhouse and Fenner Brockway (1922), discussed above). Moreover, by the time of Ann Widdecombe's speech, experimental programmes paying enhanced (and in a handful of cases 'near-normal') wages had been in place for some time, although no formal arrangements had been made for deductions from salary. The significance of the speech was that, for the first time, government support was being given to a thoroughgoing industrial approach to prison labour. It is worth outlining how this came about.

24   'Prisoners to pay victims of crime from their wages', *Daily Telegraph*, 13 February 1996.

In 1988, Judge Stephen Tumim, then Chief Inspector of Prisons, argued that prison work should be meaningful industrial work in prison workshops, farming, gardening, specialized skilled work or work in the community. He repeated the argument in September 1993, drawing particular attention to the experience of Straubing prison in Bavaria where, he had been told, prison industries had made an operating profit of some DM3.9 million in 1992.[25]

In April 1995, a pressure group, the Penal Affairs Consortium, argued in favour of a substantial increase in prisoners' wages to bring their earnings more in line with outside pay rates. And in July of the same year, Judge Tumim once again suggested that Britain should follow the German and other European penal systems in which outside firms employed prisoners to produce goods in return for wages.[26] A few months later, a similar view was expressed in the Learmont Report (Home Office, 1995b). While this was primarily a report on security arrangements, Learmont endorsed the idea that prisons

> should also offer meaningful work with realistic wages. This would enable prisoners to pay their way in prison, save a little in preparation for release and avoid a financial burden on their families. It would also assist security and control by giving prison staff the opportunity of employing financial sanctions against those who do not conform. (1995a: para. 5.72)

The Trades Union Congress had already, by 1989, dropped objections to increased industrial work in prisons and been persuaded that an 'enhanced wages' policy for prisoners should be adopted. In consequence, there were few criticisms of the scheme, even though it could mean that prison wages might exceed those on offer in the local job centres.[27]

25   *Daily Telegraph*, 3 September 1993. See also quotes attributed to Tumim in a report on a meeting at Westminster Abbey, London (*The Guardian*, 25 July 1995). It is, however, likely that he was misinformed as to the way in which prison labour in Straubing was costed; see Fulton and Smartt (1995).
26   'Tumim calls for "industrial prisons"', *The Guardian*, 25 July 1995.
27   Following the abolition of Wages Councils (which suggested minimum wage rates for different industries), it emerged that school leavers in some parts of the country could earn as little as £60 per week (January 1996) as a shop assistant, £50 in an office or £40 as

The Prisoners Earnings Bill 1996 had an easy passage through Parliament and received Royal Assent in July 1996. However, its implementation will require amendment of the prison rules and prison service administrative instructions. These will need to detail procedures for paying enhanced wages and making deductions from prisoners' earnings for compulsory savings, family and/or victim support, board and lodging, and so on. In early 1999 civil servants were still working on these amendments. Prisons in the Workshop Expansion Scheme already paying enhanced wages, and the few already making deductions from earnings, have been doing so in advance of any official guidelines.

Prison Enterprise and Regime Services believe the Workshop Expansion Scheme will only create about 8,000 to 10,000 additional jobs for the current prison population of about 64,000. Nevertheless, it could generate nearly £10 million in income tax and £5 million in other revenue if the prisoners were obliged to pay for their keep. A further £5million could be channelled into crime prevention and victim support funds. Prisoners would be left with about £60 a week (as opposed to an average of £7 a week now), a third of which they would be compelled to save. Arguably, this scheme would, for some prisoners at least, meet objectives that penal reformers have advocated since the days of John Howard. They would be released with substantial savings, working skills and the habit of work; and would have few immediate reasons to return to crime.

Allegations of 'forced labour' in relation to contracting out have been rejected by the government, which has noted that art. 4(3) of the European Convention on Human Rights excludes from the term, 'forced or compulsory labour', 'any work required to be done in the ordinary course of detention imposed according to the provisions of art. 5 of this Convention or during conditional release from such detention'. Meanwhile, prisoners are unlikely to have the right to enhanced wages. The European Commission has regularly rejected applications by prisoners claiming higher payment for their

> tailoring assistants. Such rates are far below the £7,000 a year now envisaged for prisoners. See the comments of Gabrielle Cox, Director of the Low Pay Unit in Manchester, quoted in *The Sunday Times*, 28 January 1996. Indeed, the rates envisaged for prisoners may be slightly higher than the figure now under consideration in parliamentary debates of proposals to introduce a national minimum wage.

# ENGLAND AND WALES

work, or claiming the right to be covered by social security systems.[28]

Many of the problems that remain to be faced are detailed ones of accounting practices. For one thing, current accounting procedures, geared to internal sales and revenue, produce 'shadow' figures that give little indication of commercial profit. For another, there was a period in which it was unclear whether profits on external contracts would be clawed back by the Treasury. These points came together in the report of the Chief Inspector of Prisons, in May 1998, on HMP Featherstone:

> Firstly I commend the Prison Service 'Pathfinder' initiative, which will, I hope, encourage the work ethic that is missing in so many prisoners, and without which they will remain excluded from the job market that is so important for a crime-free future. But the issue of the internal market, and how much prisons are entitled to claim from work done for the Prison Service, is raised with us in a number of prisons, in the same way that it was at Featherstone. In a prison which is facing cuts of a possible £600,000 next year, lack of revenue from successful workshops, no matter for whom they are working, is galling to say the least. The workshops at Featherstone, and the work done in them, is excellent. Gaining advantage from both, in financial terms, would be even better. (HM Chief Inspector of Prisons, 1998: 3)

One of these issues is likely to be resolved with an agreement, not yet formally announced, that prisons will be able to bid to retain up to 50 per cent of the operating surplus from external contracts. Meanwhile, and remembering that the Workshop Expansion Scheme covers only 19 prisons, by 1998 most prison governors appeared to believe that there was no service-wide industrial strategy. The majority were looking to local contracts with firms to provide the main work. There is no requirement on prisons to obtain work from PES, which has become little more than a resource to which prisons may turn for advice and help in obtaining contracts – and which has no central capital to develop and equip workshops.

28  Apps. 3134/67, 3172/67 and 3188–206/67, 'Twenty-one Detained Persons v. Federal Republic of Germany' (1968) *Yearbook of the European Commission*, 11: 528. See also 'The Norwegian Dentist Case on Compulsory Labour' (1964) *Yearbook of the European Commission*, 6:26.

In short, because the Prison Service operates a diverse range of prisons, there is an increasing danger of having 'winners' and 'losers' in the industrial and prison workshop sector. Prisons with appropriate, well-resourced workshops, in favourable locations and with medium-to-long-term prisoners are likely to be better able to attract work, provide a fuller working day, and pay enhanced or 'real' wages. Others, which are likely to include local prisons and remand centres, will be disadvantaged. In some cases, partnership approaches have been developed in which work is taken on by a combination of prisons (for example, with one cutting cloth for shirts and another stitching the garments). Yet there do not seem to be systematic attempts to ensure that available work is spread equitably across the prison estate.

### 2.4.4 A changed ideology of prison labour?

Although the ex-Chief Inspector, Judge Stephen Tumim, the former Prisons Minister, a security advisor, businesspeople and trades unions are now all agreed that more contracting out and enhanced wages are good ideas, they appear to subscribe to these views for different reasons. It is therefore worth asking whether this new consensus has occurred by chance, is the outcome of some compromise, or contains the seeds of a new ideology of prison labour.

The key factor in the new attitude is the idea that prisoners, like workers outside prison, can, *and should*, be motivated by money. Although official pronouncements suggest that inculcating a habit of work is desirable, and there is some suggestion that an emphasis on work will act to 'normalize' prisons (that is, make them more like non-prison environments), it is assumed that what will get prisoners into the workshops will be wages comparable to those outside.

At this point several other factors come into play. It is also assumed that prisoners do not have the same expenses (rent, food and so on) as other workers, and that for prisoners to amass large sums of money would be socially unacceptable since they would appear to be profiting from their offence. As a result, some charge must be made for 'bed and board', which defrays the cost of imprisonment at a time when, coincidentally, cost reductions are critically important to the Prison Service. In addition, the suggestion that some deductions from prisoners' earnings must be made – almost along the lines of a compensation order or fine – to repay the offender's 'debt to society', is now becoming a reality. Further, just as an offender who is working and paying a fine must also support himself and his family, so a proportion of the wages may be paid directly to the prisoner's dependants.

This amounts to a 'deal' offered to the prisoner. If it is accepted, the prisoner will be in a position comparable to that of a worker paying a financial penalty, albeit that he is doing so while in custody. If it is not accepted, the prisoner will simply 'do his time', but it will nonetheless be clear to him that this is financially disadvantageous to him in the long term and perhaps to his family in the short term.

However, the precise nature of the 'deal' will depend on its details. It is as yet unclear, for example, what level of deductions may be made for bed and board; whether victims would be able to seek compensation orders payable from the prisoner's wages instead of or in addition to more general payments to a victims' fund; and whether payments to prisoners' dependants would result in their losing state welfare benefits. The success or failure of the policy will thus depend on policy decisions by the tax authorities, the Department of Social Security and the Treasury.

If the scheme is successful, the prisoner will be transformed from a person 'serving time' to a person quite literally 'paying a debt to society' in much the same way as any offender paying off a fine, save that he will be doing it while in custody. Yet, as we know from the broader literature on imprisonment and from other recent policy developments in relation to parole, remission and so on, the fact of custody is likely to remain supremely important to the prisoner himself. In consequence, while the psychological gap between imprisonment and non-custodial penalties may, in official rhetoric, be closed in quite significant ways, unless the arithmetic is right, prisoners may begin to see themselves as little more than an army of sweatshop labourers.

### 2.4.5 A continuing problem? Race issues and racial discrimination

Racial discrimination has for many years been regarded as a problem area within prisons. It is therefore no surprise that evidence of racial discrimination has emerged in relation to work. Genders and Player (1989) concluded that some discrimination existed in terms of the kinds of work given to racial minorities. In order to reach this conclusion, Genders and Player ranked jobs on the basis of prisoners' assessments, which in practice were largely based on the 'perks' attached to them. The 'best' jobs included work as orderlies in the reception area, office work, kitchen work, cleaning, laundry work and outdoor tasks. All these jobs allowed prisoners opportunities to ease the experience of imprisonment, whether by providing access to information, opportunities for stealing, smuggling or trading goods, or simply by giving them some degree of control of the work flow, so that they were able to relax with a cigarette and a coffee from time to time. Industrial workshops were universally regarded as the 'worst' jobs, where prisoners had little control over the workrate and were more closely supervised.

In one of the prisons which Genders and Player studied, a significantly higher proportion of black prisoners than white were left unemployed or worked in the industrial workshops. In another, comparisons of work records, controlled for the length of time each prisoner had spent in the establishment, indicated that 14 per cent of blacks, but 45 per cent of whites, worked in jobs assessed by prisoners as among the best. One hypothesis for this situation, raised by an earlier study conducted by prison psychologists, was that there may be a difference in the ability levels of blacks and whites that led to differences in prison work allocation. However, Genders and Player analysed the work records of 1,255 medium- and long-term prisoners and concluded that there was no indication of a difference in ability levels. These findings led Genders and Player to state that 'credence must be given to the suggestion that racial bias lies at the root of the racial imbalance evidenced in labour allocation' (1989: 127).

In 1988, a prisoner of West Indian origin, Alexander, successfully sued for damages after he was refused a higher-paying job in a prison kitchen on the basis of two assessment reports which contained racially discriminatory remarks. Alexander challenged his treatment, invoking s.20(1) of the Race Relations Act 1976, which prohibits discrimination in the provision of goods and services to the public or a section of the public, rather than s.4, which relates to discrimination in employment. The Home Office originally defended the action on the grounds that prisoners were not a 'section of the public', but abandoned this point at trial (Livingstone and Owen, 1993).[29]

The issue of race discrimination in employment in prisons may, on this reading, become more pointed over time. What could be at stake is a substantial financial benefit, made available to only a small proportion of prisoners. Any discriminatory practice in employment could therefore have serious consequences and it appears

---

29   *Alexander v. Home Office* (1988).

that monitoring of employment in prisons is already taking this into account.

## 3  Summary and Discussion

Historically, England and Wales have had a confused series of prison labour policies. This has included the use of labour as an element of punishment specified in addition to custody (this ended in the last years of the 1800s), as a means of training (especially in relation to young offenders, but this is also part of the reason why prisons for medium- and long-term prisoners are described as 'training prisons') and as a justifiable way of occupying prisoners' time, given that the regime would otherwise be impoverished. In practice, however, for many years labour took place in a fashion that could best be described as 'symbolic' or 'tokenistic', and for many prisoners – in particular remand prisoners, who were under no obligation to work – work places were not available.

Roughly once every dozen years there has been an attempt to give labour a higher priority within prisons. In practice, these efforts have amounted to very little, usually because other issues – riots, organizational reform, and so on – have pushed labour policies aside within a short space of time. Indeed, at the moment it appears that there is no industrial work for over two-thirds of the prison population. Even if some of these prisoners are taking training courses or full-time education, this suggests that there is a high level of unemployment among prisoners.

Steps have recently been taken, not only to obtain more work from outside contractors, but to enable selected prisoners to work full working weeks and to be paid substantial wages. In some cases they are paid more than some lower-paid workers outside prison. It is unlikely that these arrangements will cover more than about 10 per cent of the prison population for the foreseeable future; nonetheless, they appear to introduce a new conception of prison labour. Firstly, the idea of labour as a 'treatment', through the inculcation of regular habits of work, is weakened and to some extent replaced by the idea that wage labour, the opportunity to earn a realistic level of wages, may concentrate prisoners' minds and exert a reforming effect, since they will be able to save comparatively large amounts and may also be able to contribute to family finances from prison. Secondly, the meaning of imprisonment itself may be shifted, because those who experience the new system will be required to make payments to schemes for victim compensation and so on.

'Imprisonment', for these prisoners, will be 'normalized' in the sense that it will become closer to the everyday experience of ordinary workers. It could even become analogous to the payment of a compensation order while in custody.

It is too early to make moral judgments about the probity of this scheme, since much will depend on the details. The attractiveness of the scheme to prisoners may well also depend on details such as the level of compulsory deductions from wages and the alternatives (for example, the gap between the new scheme and employment in regular workshops). Meanwhile, the extent to which it can be implemented will depend on the willingness of companies to contract with the prison service. The only sure prediction we can make about the scheme is that, even if it reaches its immediate target of 5,000 additional jobs in prisons, it will lead to a much greater diversity of prison experiences for prisoners in terms of the gap between those involved in the scheme and those who are not.

## Postscript

As this chapter was going to press, new information emerged concerning the Wackenhut UK contract to run private sector ('contracted-out') workshops at Coldingley prison, discussed on page 66. The contract started in November 1997, but in December 1998 a Home Office audit team recommended that the five-year contract be terminated. On the one hand, Wackenhut UK had experienced severe difficulties in obtaining work for the workshops and was making a substantial loss. On the other, there were allegations of financial irregularity concerning a loan made by the prison administration to Wackenhut UK. The contract is now terminated – an embarrassing end to what might have been an interesting experiment.

## References

Blauner, Robert. 1964. *Alienation and Freedom*. Chicago: University of Chicago Press.

Council of Europe. 1964. The Norwegian Dentist Case on Compulsory Labour. *Yearbook of the European Commission* 6:26. Brussels: Editions Delta.

Council of Europe. 1968. Twenty-one Detained Persons v. Federal Republic of Germany. *Yearbook of the European Commission* 11: 528. Brussels: Editions Delta.

du Cane, E. 1885. *The Punishment and Prevention of Crime.* London: Macmillan.

Forsythe, William J. 1987. *The Reform of Prisoners 1830–1900.* London: Croom Helm.

Fox, Lionel W. 1952. *The English Prison and Borstal Systems.* London: Routledge & Kegan Paul.

Fulton, Robert and Ursula Smartt. 1995. *German Prison Industries, a working paper and report to the HM Prisons Board.* London: HM Prison Service.

Genders, Elaine and Elaine Player. 1989. *Race Relations in Prison.* Oxford: Clarendon.

Halmos, Paul, ed. 1965. *Sociological Review Monograph No. 9.* University of Keele.

HM Chief Inspector of Prisons. 1996. *HM Prison Coldingley: Report of an Unannounced Short Inspection by HM Chief Inspector of Prisons.* London: Home Office.

HM Chief Inspector of Prisons. 1998. *HM Prison Featherstone. Report of an Unannounced Full Inspection, 26–30 January 1998.* London: HMSO.

Hobhouse, Stephen and A. Fenner Brockway. 1922. *English Prisons Today. Being the Report of the Prison System Enquiry Committee.* London: The Labour Party.

Home Office. 1835. *First Report from the Select Committee of the House of Lords: 'Gaols and Houses of Correction in England and Wales'.* HL 42. London: HMSO.

Home Office. 1907. *Report of the Commissioners of Prisons and the Directors of Convict Prisons.* Cd 3738. London: HMSO.

Home Office. 1977. *Prisons and the Prisoner. The Work of the Prison Service.* London: HMSO.

Home Office. 1979. *Report of the Committee of Enquiry into the United Kingdom Prison Service* (the 'May Report'). Cmnd 7673. London: HMSO.

Home Office. 1995a. *Prison Service Annual Report and Accounts April 1993–March 1994.* HC 185. London: HMSO.

Home Office. 1995b. *Review of Prison Service Security in England and Wales and the Escape from Parkhurst Prison on Tuesday 3rd January, 1995* (the 'Learmont Report'). Cmnd 3020. London: HMSO.

Howard, John. 1777. *The State of Prisons in England and Wales with preliminary observations, and an account of some foreign prisons and hospitals.* 4th edn. London, printed for J. Johnson, C. Dilly and T. Cadell.

King, Roy D. and Kathleen McDermott. 1995. *The State of Our Prisons.* Oxford: Clarendon.

Livingstone, Stephen and Tim Owen. 1993. *Prison Law: Text and Materials*. Oxford: Clarendon.

Maguire, Mike, Jon Vagg and Rod Morgan, eds. 1985. *Accountability and Prisons: Opening up a Closed World*. London: Tavistock.

Morris, Terence and Pauline Morris. 1963. *Pentonville: A Sociological Study of an English Prison*. London: Routledge & Kegan Paul.

Neild, John. 1812. *State of the Prisons in England, Scotland, and Wales. Extending to Various Places Therein Assigned, Not for the Debtor Only, but for Felons Also, and Other Less Criminal Offenders. Together with some useful documents, observations, and remarks, adapted to explain and improve the condition of prisoners in general*. London: John Nichols and Son.

Stern, Vivien. 1987. *Bricks of Shame: Britain's Prisons*. Harmondsworth: Penguin.

## Cases

Alexander v. Home Office [1988] 2 All ER 118.
Davis v. The Prison Commissioners, The Times, 21 November 1963.
Ellis v. Home Office [1953] 2 QB 135.
Pullen v. The Prison Commissioners [1957] 3 All ER 470.

## The Authors

**Jon Vagg** is a senior lecturer in criminology at Loughborough University in Loughborough, England.

**Ursula Smartt** is senior lecturer in law at Thames Valley University in London, England.

# 4 Germany

FRIEDER DÜNKEL

## 1 Introduction

The organization and remuneration of prison labour has become a major issue in the German prison reform debate. On the one hand, the costs of prisons burden the budgets of the federal states ('Länder'), which are responsible for the execution and implementation of the Federal Prison Act of 1976. At the beginning of the 1990s, the prison system in the old federal states cost about 2.2 billion Germans Marks (DM) a year, of which only 0.324 billion (14.7 per cent) was covered by income generated mainly by the prison industries. The net cost of a prisoner per day in 1995 amounted to more than DM150[1] (see Figure 4.1). On the other hand, one of the major reform proposals of the early 1970s, that prisoners should be remunerated adequately, has still not been realized. In fact it has been blocked repeatedly by the finance ministers of the federal states. For nearly 20 years now they have refused to agree even to a small increase in prisoners' wages. They have persisted although s.200(2) of the Prison Act of 1976 provides that, by the end of 1980 (!), an amendment should have been introduced in order to increase the remuneration of prisoners. From 1991 onwards, several cases were referred to the Federal Constitutional Court (*Bundesverfassungsgericht*) in which prisoners claimed that the only marginal remuneration for prison labour violated the Constitution (*Grundgesetz*). The matter was decided on 1 July 1998 and the Federal Constitutional Court ruled that the existing remuneration would have to be reviewed as it was unconstitutional since it violated the principle of resocialization. This decision will force the federal states to increase prisoners' remuneration considerably (see sections 3 and 7 below).

---

[1] See Neu (1995b: 151).

**Figure 4.1:** A Comparison of the Average Daily Cost per Prisoner per Day in the Federal States in 1995

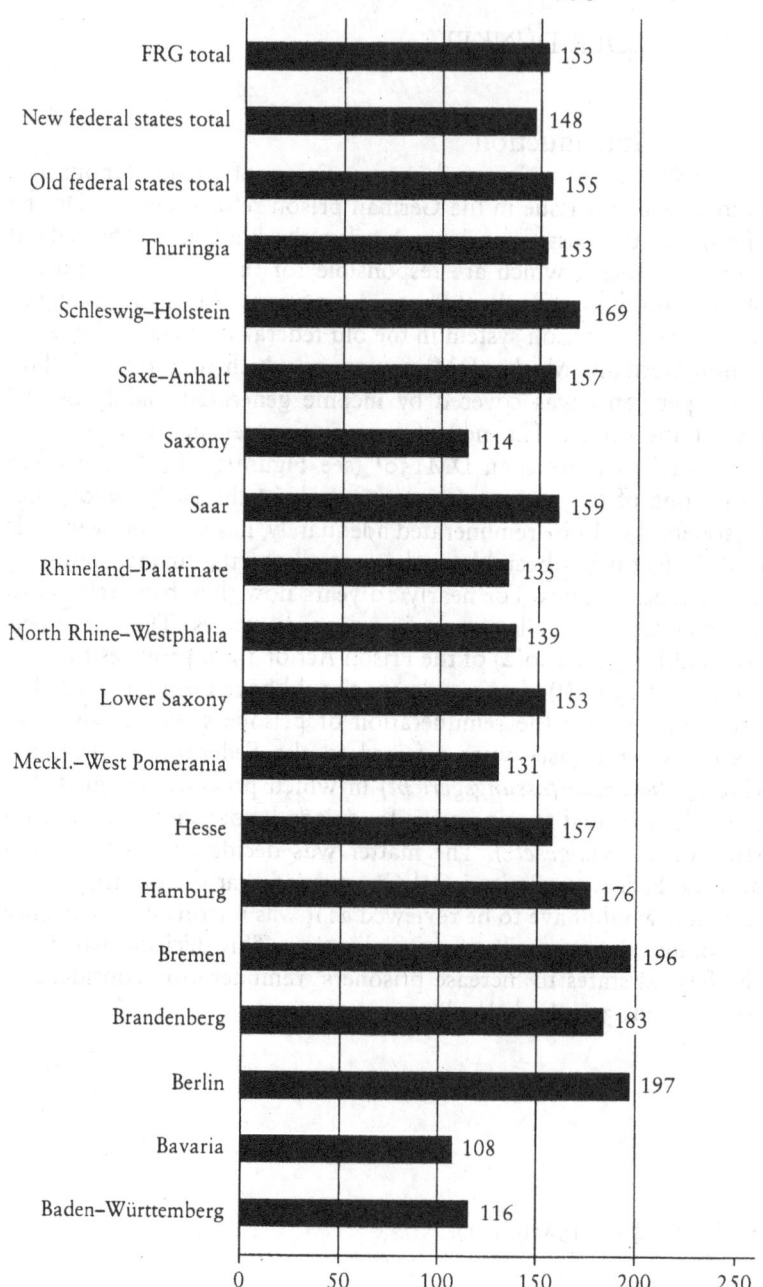

## 2 Prison Labour According to the Prison Act of 1976

Before 1976, prison labour was given a clear priority as a means of rehabilitation and of keeping order in prisons. Rule 80 of the Federal Administrative Rules of 1961 (*DVollzO*) stated that prison labour 'is the basis of an orderly and effective prison system'. Furthermore, it was claimed that prison industries had to ensure that they did not compete unfairly with the free market outside the prison system. This principle was abolished by the Prison Act of 1976, which obliges the prison authorities to provide economically productive prison labour that suits the prisoner's abilities, skills and inclinations and which should develop these abilities in order to assist prisoners when they are released (ss.37(1) and (2) of the Prison Act). Therefore the prison authorities are obliged to create enterprises (run by themselves or by private entrepreneurs), facilities for vocational training and therapeutic working institutions (s.149(1) of the Prison Act).

As a rule, these lofty goals have not been achieved (see section 4 below). The same applies to the related goal of having prisoners admitted to medical and pension insurance schemes; for financial reasons, this goal has been postponed by the legislator.[2] The consequences is that long-term prisoners are considerably disadvantaged and in a sense punished for a second time when they reach retirement age (normally age 65). As a result, they often only receive the minimum social welfare pension, although they may have worked for many years while in prison. Some critics regard this as an unacceptable double punishment, as it is not an inherent element of the original sentence.[3]

Although the Prison Act has retained the prisoners' obligation to work (see s.41(1) of the Prison Act),[4] prison labour may not be of a

2   Only in exceptional circumstances are prisoners in the same position as free workers: when prisoners work outside the prison in a work-release scheme, they have normal contracts of employment, which include premiums to the pension system, see section 6, below.

3   See Rosenthal (1998: 14) who emphasizes the fact that the family and, possibly, after the offenders' death, their widows may be disadvantaged in a way that cannot be justified by the original sentence. However, the Federal Constitutional Court, in its decision of 1998, ruled that this was not a violation of constitutional rights. See section 3, below.

4   This kind of forced labour is allowed by the Constitution; see art.12(3) *Grundgesetz*.

punitive nature. Again, reality often does not meet this goal.⁵ Instead, prison labour is seen as one of several means of rehabilitation. Therefore the legal rules concerning prison labour are included in the same chapter as the regulations on education and vocational training. The participation in such educational or training programmes is put on a par with prison labour (see s.37 of the Prison Act). Such programmes take place during the normal working day and prisoners participating in such educational and training programmes get the same remuneration as those prisoners who work (see s.38(2) of the Prison Act).

Prison labour, however, cannot be seen as an opportunity to earn sufficient money and as an opportunity to really advance in terms of rehabilitation. The 'true dilemma of prison labour' is that wages are still not adequate (Dünkel and Rössner, 1991: 221; see also Preusker, 1988). The prisoners' wage amounts to a mere 5 per cent of the average wage of all persons who contributed to the national pension scheme during the previous calendar year (see s.43, in combination with s.200(1) of the Prison Act). The daily rate per prisoner was about DM10 in 1991 (Neu, 1995b: 152, 159).⁶ The actual average wage per prisoner per day may not exceed DM12; that is, about DM250 a month. One-third of this money is kept by the prison authorities in an account in the prisoner's name in order to provide the so-called bridging finance ('*Überbrückungsgeld*'; see s.51(1) of the Prison Act), the money which is handed out to the prisoner on the day of his release from prison and which enables him to 'survive' the first few weeks after release. The reality, however, is not very encouraging. According to an empirical study in the state of Schleswig-Holstein, male adult prisoners received 'release money' of, on average, DM615 and female prisoners DM503.⁷ This amount sometimes does not even cover rent for a small flat for the first month.

5   One has to consider the ambiguity of prison labour. A culpable violation of the duty to work can result in disciplinary measures. Suspension from work, on the other hand, can be used as a disciplinary measure. Its function is similar to a fine since a prisoner who culpably does not work gets no money, not even pocket money (see s.46 of the Prison Act).
6   The average daily rate was DM10.29 with considerable variations within the Federal States: the lowest rate of DM8.38 in Bremen was about half of that in Berlin (DM16.46 per day).
7   See Dünkel (1992: 113,284); (for young offenders released from a young offenders institution in 1989, the average was DM542).

Working prisoners on average are paid about DM150 to DM180 a month, with which they can make purchases and buy tobacco, sweets, fruit and so on. The low wages do not enable them to make reparation for the damages caused by their offence to the victim (restitution) or to contribute to the maintenance of their families.

Another aspect of the prisoners' duty to work is the obligation of the prison system to provide work for all prisoners. Here, too, the prison system does not meet this goal fully (see section 4 below). The Prison Act recognizes this obligation of prison authorities by at least granting 'appropriate pocket money' to prisoners who, through no fault of their own, have no work (see s.46 of the Prison Act). In practice, however, the pocket money amounts to only about a quarter of the remuneration that working prisoners receive.

Prison-owned or public industrial enterprises inside prisons have to conform, as far as possible, to the labour conditions outside (see s.149(2) of the Prison Act). In prisons the same safety and labour protection regulations have to be observed as outside prisons (s.149(2) of the Prison Act). Prisons are regularly inspected by the trade supervisory board.

## 3 Constitutional Principles Relating to Prison Work: Decision of the Federal Constitutional Court on Work Remuneration

The decision of the Federal Constitutional Court on prison labour, (decision of 1 July 1998), represents a belated success in one of the areas in which the reforms introduced by the 1976 Prison Act were incomplete. Because of budgetary constraints, the federal states had repeatedly postponed raising the wage of prisoners beyond 5 per cent of the average wage of all persons contributing to the national pension scheme (s.43, read with s.200(1) of the Prison Act). In so doing, the federal states ignored the unanimous criticism of experts on imprisonment (Calliess and Müller-Dietz, 1998: para 200, and the sources cited there). The decision of the Court not only strongly criticizes the inaction of the legislature but confirms that the principle of resocialization as derived from the Constitution, particularly from the concept of the *Sozialstaat*, must be regarded as a key principle in the implementation of prison sentences. At a time in which the ideal of reintegration of prisoners does not reflect the *Zeitgeist* axiomatically and conditions of imprisonment are increasingly repressive or oriented only to the containment of prisoners (not least because of prison overcrowding), this return to principle must be seen as a sign that a humane penal policy, oriented to human rights, could be in for a revival.

A noteworthy feature of the decision is also that, when the Court held public hearings on 11 March 1998, questions were put first to criminologists about the relationship between prison labour and resocialization. The importance of the empirical data as background to the normative arguments of the judgment should not be underestimated. The applicants might not have succeeded to the extent that they did had it not been made clear that prison labour and the manner in which it is rewarded play a significant role in the eventual reintegration of prisoners (see section 6 below). Indeed, the judgment as a whole is based on empirical findings (or at least assumptions) of prison researchers about the contribution of appropriate remuneration to resocialization.[8]

In the view of the Federal Constitutional Court, the *Grundgesetz* compels 'the legislator to develop an effective concept of resocialization and to build the implementation of the sentence of imprisonment on it' (Guiding Principle 1, p. 242); 'Work that a prisoner is compelled to do in prison is an effective method of resocialization only if the work that is done is recognized appropriately. This recognition does not necessarily have to be financial. It must, however, be capable of demonstrating to the prisoner, by the tangible advantage it offers, the value of regular work for a responsible and crime-free life in the future' (Guiding Principle 2a, p. 242).

Although the Federal Constitutional Court left open the question of the remuneration required by the principle of resocialization, it did lay down that, by 31 December 2000, the legislator had to increase the remuneration for prison labour to an extent that 'the prisoner can be made aware that gainful employment makes sense in order to restore the basis of his life' (Guiding Principle 2b, p. 249). In practice this should mean, as the various experts have proposed,[9] that prisoners receive at least 20 per cent to 25 per cent of the average wage (Wrage, 1997; Sigel, 1995).

It is conceivable that an arrangement will be introduced whereby prisoners are paid wages that are (largely) comparable to those earned in free society, with deductions for the costs of imprisonment. At the hearing, the Austrian model played a prominent role.

8    See in this regard the international comparisons made by Dünkel and van Zyl Smit (1998) and in the concluding chapter of the present volume.
9    See, for example Wrage (1997: 436).

In this model, prisoners are paid the wages set after collective bargaining agreements applicable to society as a whole, but with 75 per cent deducted for the cost of imprisonment.[10] In this context the Federal Constitutional Court emphasized that costs of imprisonment should be calculated in such a way 'that the prisoner was left with a significant amount of the remuneration' (p. 246). 'The protection of social insurance and pension systems' was expressly mentioned as something into which prisoners could be incorporated, although the *Grundgesetz* did not mandate it. In this respect, the constitutional objections were rejected and the legislator was allowed an area of discretion in deciding how best to meet the requirements of art. 3(1) of the *Grundgesetz* as regards equality of treatment.

Of considerable interest, from the perspective of penal policy, was the indication by the Federal Constitutional Court that it would be acceptable to recognize work by a system according to which 'a prisoner by working could have his term of imprisonment reduced, that is be granted "good time", or could be granted other privileges' (p. 246). Although such 'good time' arrangements are increasingly the exception rather than the rule internationally, they could make an interesting contribution as a counterweight to the long average prison sentences in Germany and to reducing the pressure on overcrowded prisons. Such an arrangement presupposes, however, that all prisoners who are willing to work can be offered work; that is, have a 'right to work', something that will not be easy to implement. At the moment the information gathered by the Federal Constitutional Court itself shows that at least 20 per cent of prisoners are unemployed (see section 4, below).

There is also some dynamite in the determination by the Court that the exception, contained in art.12(3) of the *Grundgesetz*, to the constitutional prohibition of forced labour is limited to institutions 'at which the prison authorities retain the responsibilities granted to them by public law for the prisoners in their care' (General Principle 3, pp. 246–7). Reducing prisoners to objects (*Verdingung*) under the control of private persons is therefore not acceptable. This means that the privatization of prisons, which is becoming more and more significant in the USA, Canada, Australia, New Zealand and England, would be narrowly restricted, if it were to be introduced in Germany.

Firmly condemned in the judgment, as had already become apparent at the hearing, was the so-called 'false work release' (*unechter*

---

10   See Chapter 1 in the present volume.

*Freigang*), a 'legal' concept not uncommon in Bavaria. This concept refers to the practice whereby a prisoner who qualifies for work release is allowed to work outside prison but is paid only the minimal remuneration that prisoners who work inside prison earn instead of the full wage for that kind of work in the open market. The Court gave the authorities until 31 December 1998 to end this practice.

Because the Court allowed the existing practices to continue for interim periods, none of the five applicants who brought the original applications on which the constitutional process was based, formally succeeded with their constitutional claims. Nevertheless, from a wider perspective, the outcome was an unexpected triumph, the consequences of which as yet can hardly be estimated. This decision is surely the most important judgment of the Federal Constitutional Court on the implementation of the sentence of imprisonment since the *Lebach* judgment in 1973.[11]

## 4 The Practice of Prison Labour: Organization, Remuneration, Profits of Prison Industries and so on

Prisoners carry out everyday chores as 'domestic workers' (see s.41(1) of the Prison Act)[12] or work in prison-owned or public industrial enterprises. Work in industrial enterprises is mostly simple and dull. Cleaning and sorting chores are frequently imposed as interim measures until other work becomes available. The prison service makes space and the prisoners' labour power available to entrepreneurs who, in turn, have the authority to manage the enterprise and who bear the financial risk. The prison-owned enterprises are mainly trades or crafts which are conducted in workshops maintained by the prison institutions; training facilities are quite often attached to them.

In line with the objective of resocialization, the prisoner should at least be freely employed outside the prison towards the end of his

11 The *Lebach* judgment was the first decision of the Federal Constitutional Court to recognize resocialization as a constitutional principle deduced from the concept of the *Sozialstaat*; see BVerfGE 35: 202ff. See Dünkel (1996b) for the development of the Federal Constitutional Court judgments.

12 The obligation to carry out 'domestic work' is fixed to a maximum of three months per year. With the consent of the prisoner, it can be longer.

term of imprisonment ('work release', in terms of s.39 of the Prison Act; see section 6 below).

Comprehensive research concerning the economic situation of the prisons in the old federal states (former West Germany) at the beginning of the 1990s revealed that, on average, in the years 1989 to 1991, 35 per cent of the prisoners had no work. About 10 per cent of those prisoners who did work were pre-trial detainees who had asked for work. Pre-trial detainees have no obligation to work and about half of them did not want to work. On the other hand, the prison authorities were not able to offer any profitable work in about 50 per cent of the cases where a pre-trial detainee asked for work. The unemployment rate of the sentenced prisoners (who are obliged to work) was rather low (7 per cent) (Neu, 1995b: 150, 157). About 12 per cent of the working prisoners, which is equal to 8 per cent of the total prisoners' figures, had employment outside prison (work release).

Of those prisoners who were employed, 29 per cent worked in prison service enterprises such as the kitchen and laundry. Another 5 per cent participated in school and 9 per cent in vocational training programmes.[13]

An inquiry via the Ministries of Justice of the 'Länder' showed an increased unemployment rate for 1996 in most of the federal states, ranging from 16 per cent in North Rhine–Westphalia and 24 per cent in Baden-Württemberg to 64 per cent in Lower Saxony and 81 per cent in Saxony–Anhalt (see Table 4.1 below). The average of 37 per cent unemployed sentenced prisoners, however, does not reflect those prisoners who attend school programmes or are working outside in so-called 'work release programmes' (see section 5, below). Thus an unemployment rate of about 25 per cent would be more realistic.

It has already been mentioned that the total costs for the prison system are considerable and that in the early 1990s only 14.7 per cent of the costs are covered by the income of the prison enterprises. The labour administration in prisons needs about 30 per cent of the income, 18 per cent is paid into the unemployment schemes for prisoners and 25 per cent is spent on the remuneration

13 Another 2 per cent were exempted from the obligation to work because they had worked for at least one year in prison. According to s.42 of the Prison Act, such a prisoner has the right to be free of work (a kind of prison furlough without leaving the prison) for 18 days.

Table 4.1: The Proportion of Working Prisoners in the Various Federal States in 1996

| Federal State | Average Number of Prisoners Serving Sentences[1] and in Preventive Detention | | Employed (Average) | |
|---|---|---|---|---|
| | | | Number | Percentage |
| Baden–Württemberg | 5,074 | | 3,875 | 76.4 |
| Bavaria | 6,893 | | 4,750 | 68.9 |
| Berlin | 3,154 | | 2,286 | 72.5 |
| Brandenburg | 969 | | 941 | (including preventive detention) |
| Bremen | 717 | (excluding preventive detention[2]) | 452 | 63.0[3] |
| Hamburg | 1,859 | | 977 | 52.5 |
| Hesse | 3,754 | | 1,900 | 50.6 |
| Mecklenburg–Western Pomerania | 793 | | 561 | 70.7 |
| Lower Saxony | 5,825 | | 2,094 | 36.0 |
| North Rhine–Westphalia | 11,243 | | 9,454 | 84.1 |
| Rhineland–Palatinate | 2,290 | (excluding preventive detention[2]) | 1,678 | (including preventive detention) |
| Saarland | 538 | (excluding preventive detention[2]) | 250 | 46.5 |
| Saxony | 2,214 | | 1,093[4] | 49.4 |
| Saxony–Anhalt | 1,668 | | 317 | 19.0 |
| Schleswig–Holstein | 1,053 | | 737 | 70.0 |
| Thuringia | 657 | | 327 | 49.8 |
| Total without Brandenburg and Rhineland–Palatinate)[5] | 45,507 | | 29,073 | 64.0 |
| Total | 48,666 | | 308,197 | 63.3 |

Notes
1. Including juveniles.
2. In terms of agreements between the federal states, prisoners may serve preventive detention in states other than their own.
3. Estimated number.
4. The figure is based on information for the second half of 1996.
5. For Brandenburg and Rhineland–Palatinate, the proportion of unsentenced prisoners who were included in the original figure was estimated at 1/3 of the figures in the table.

Source: Ministry of Justice (1996).

of prisoners. Therefore about 28 per cent of the income (DM 78 million) is left as net profit of the prison industries. This makes up about 4 per cent of the total costs of the prison system (Neu, 1995b: 152, 158).[14]

The analysis of the net profit of prison labour revealed that a prisoner in prison-owned enterprises contributed about DM9,000 a year.[15] The net profit of free enterprises within prisons was higher and every prisoner contributed to about DM13,000 in 1991.[16] This means that the productivity of prisoners in comparison to the free enterprises outside prisons is only about 15 per cent to 20 per cent.

What are the reasons for this low productivity? The main reasons are low skills and the absence of professional training of prisoners. Another reason is the high turnover of prisoners, which means that new prisoners have to be trained constantly. The prisoners are not very motivated or interested in increasing the productivity of prison enterprises because they are paid so little,[17] thereby perpetuating a vicious circle). A prisoner joke goes: 'If you pretend to pay us, we pretend to work.'

Free enterprises operating within the prisons are keen to use prison labour because of the low wages they pay to the prison administration. The wages are about 20 per cent lower than average and there are no additional costs. The prison authorities provide the space where work takes place and supervise the prisoners. So the free enterprises' risk is rather limited in comparison to the free market.

In spite of the rather limited productivity of prison industries, it is clear that prisoners currently receive remuneration which is only about half (prison-owned enterprises) or one-third (free enterprises) of the amount that the prison administration makes as profit from their work. This leads to the current debate about the possibility of increasing prisoners' wages. If the productivity of prison labour were taken into account, there would be grounds for a considerable increase, indeed the doubling or tripling of the current wages (see section 7, below).

14  In former years, this proportion had been much higher; see Dünkel and Rosner (1982), Dünkel (1987).
15  There are considerable regional differences: approximately DM3,800 in Schleswig–Holstein and about DM15,300 in Berlin.
16  Here again there were considerable regional differences, with about DM6,700 in Hamburg and DM17,600 in Hesse.
17  See Jehle (1994: 263).

## 5 Work Release Programmes: Legal Prerequisites and Developments of the Practice since 1977

Permission to work outside prison without supervision (*Freigang*) is regulated in ss.39 and 11 of the Prison Act. The opportunity to work outside prison under conditions applicable to free workers (that is, regularly, with a formal employment contract granting full remuneration) will be given to a prisoner when this seems to be appropriate 'to impart, maintain or promote professional abilities or skills which will be useful after release from prison'. The prison authorities must, however, consider that there is no risk of the prisoner absconding or committing further crimes (see s.11(2) of the Prison Act).

Work-release programmes in most federal states regularly comprise the last term of the execution of prison sentences, often the last three to six months, after the prisoner has served the greater part of the sentence in a closed institution. In some federal states, however, administrative regulations provide for an immediate transfer to an open prison in order to avoid the detrimental effects of closed institutions (prison subculture, losing the job outside prison, and so on). So, for example, in Baden–Württemberg, prisoners with sentences of up to two years who have a job outside prison can keep that job by being admitted to work release immediately.[18] This programme seems to be successful in terms of the small number of failures during the programme as well as in terms of recidivism after release. In other federal states, too, there is provision for immediate transfer to open prisons and work release is provided, such as in Bremen and Hesse (sentences up to 18 months or even up to five years).

In the last 20 years, work-release programmes have been developed in all federal states, but on very different levels. In general, about 20,000 prisoners were granted work release each year, which in 1990 corresponded to 54 admissions per 100 sentenced prisoners on a particular census day. In comparison to 1977, this implies an increase of 69 per cent. However, this figure had decreased by 15 per cent to 46 admissions per 100 prisoners in 1995. This is due partly to the increasing problems on the general labour market, with high unemployment rates, but partly also to the changing composition of the inmate population, with high proportions of drug offenders and/or foreigners. According to the administrative

---

18   See Dolde and Jehle (1986), Dolde and Rössner (1987), Dolde (1992).

rules applicable to s.11(2) of the Prison Act, only in exceptional cases may such persons be admitted to work-release programmes.

A comparison of the practice of leave of absence (*Hafturlaub*, prison furlough for several days), *Ausgang* (day leave for several hours) and work release, in the federal states, reveals considerable regional differences. These have less to do with the type of inmate (number of prisoners who were likely to abscond, for example) than with the manner in which the prisons are managed.

Figures for the various kinds of relaxations of the prison regime for the *new federal states* in the former East Germany have been available only since 1992. In contrast to the figures of the states of the former West Germany, the practice in the East was significantly more restrictive in 1995. In the case of permissions for short-term day leave (*Ausgang*), in the East German states there were 251 instances of it being granted compared to 1,013 instances of permission being granted per 100 prisoners in the West German states. There were also interesting differences amongst the various new federal states. In Brandenburg (531) and Thuringia (331), permission to leave prison for a few hours per day was granted about two to four times more often than in Saxony (137), Mecklenburg-Western Pomerania (236) and Saxony–Anhalt (145). Also, as far as relaxations to the prison regime and leave of absence (prison furloughs) were concerned, the first empirical findings give reasons to fear that the Prison Act is being interpreted very differently in the different eastern states, a practice strongly influenced by the partnership agreements which states in the East have with states in the West.[19]

As far as permission to work outside prison without supervision (*Freigang*) is concerned, there are also significant variations between states. In Saarland, 48 and in Rhineland–Palatinate, 50 instances of permission per 100 prisoners on a particular census day were recorded in 1995, and in North Rhine–Westphalia as many as 68, while in Hamburg there were only 23 and in Baden-Württemberg 25 (see Figure 4.2). The practice of allowing prisoners to work unsupervised outside prison is relatively recent in the new federal states. The average in these states is 13 per 100 in 1995, as compared to an average of 46 in the old federal states. In this respect, too, the state of Brandenburg is the most advanced (22) whilst in Mecklenburg–Western Pomerania, Saxony and Saxony–Anhalt the practice hardly existed in 1995 (seven cases each per

---

19   For an overview, see Dünkel (1995).

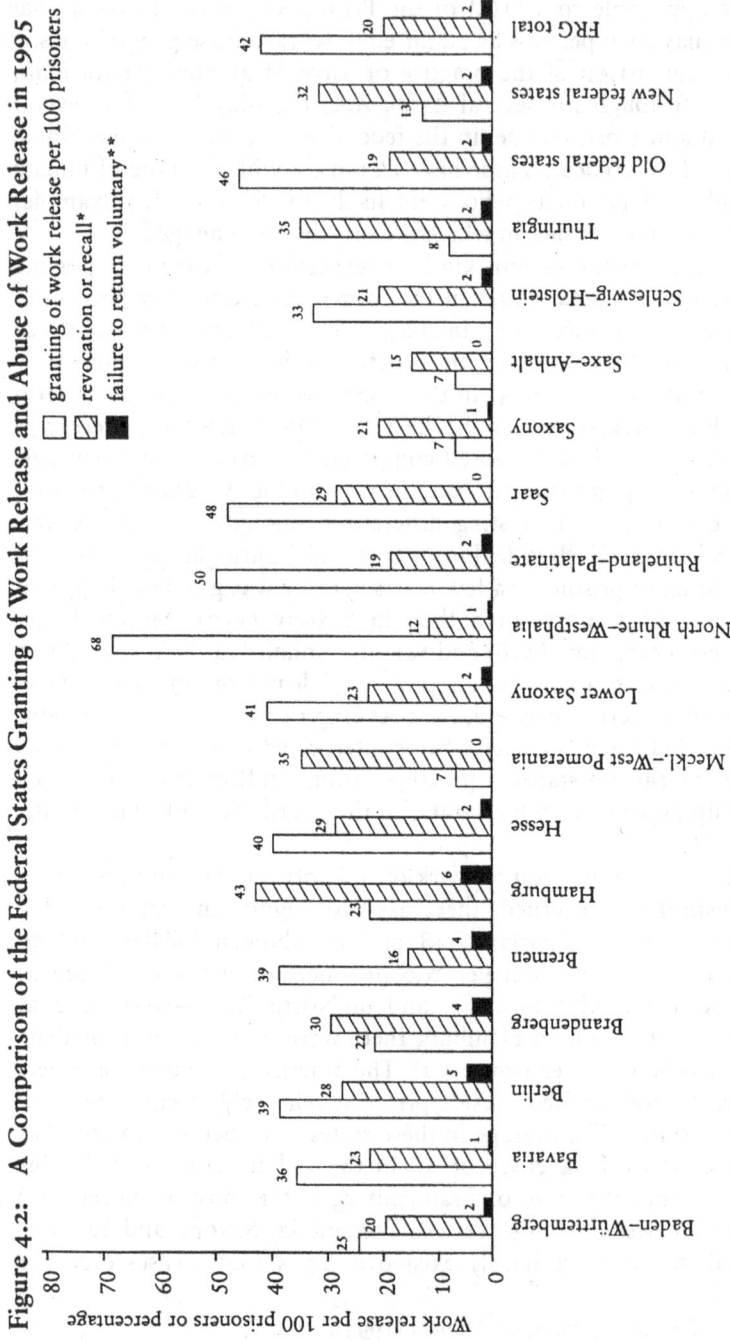

Figure 4.2: A Comparison of the Federal States Granting of Work Release and Abuse of Work Release in 1995

Note: * related to all completed cases of work release (%); ** related to the annual grants of work release (%).

100 prisoners on a particular census day were reported). Naturally, structural difficulties in the sense of the absence of jobs are the most obvious causes of these differences. This is also the explanation why the rate of withdrawing permission to work outside was so much higher. Permission to work outside had to be withdrawn in Brandenburg in 30 per cent of the cases (1992, two-thirds!), in Saxony in 21 per cent (1994, 48 per cent!) and in Saxony–Anhalt in 15 per cent (1994: 28 per cent), presumably mainly because of the lack of employment. In Saxony–Anhalt and Mecklenburg–Western Pomerania, in 1994, there has not been a single case of abuse of this privilege (failure to return in time after being allowed to work outside) registered. In Brandenburg, in spite of a significant increase in the number of cases in which permission was granted in 1993 as compared to 1992 (an increase of 21 to 38 per 100 prisoners), only three instances of abuse of the privilege were recorded (2.2 per cent when calculated in terms of the annual numbers of cases in which permission was granted). The failure rate in general is very low (1.9 per cent in the old, 1.7 per cent in the new federal states. In 1995, no federal state had a failure rate of more than 6 per cent, which can be seen as an indication that neither a more liberal nor a more restrictive practice of work release influences the risk to the public of victimization by work-release detainees.

The statistical patterns observed in the old federal states can be explained in some cases in terms of wider sociopolitical changes. After the change of government in Saarland and in Schleswig–Holstein, the number of leaves of absence, instances of permission to work outside and day leave was markedly increased.[20] What is noteworthy in this context is that the significantly increased use made of relaxation measures did not increase the number of cases in which abuse of privileges was reported. This also explains the fact, mentioned above, that there is no significant statistical relationship between a restrictive or a generous practice of granting relaxations, on the one hand, and higher failure rates, on the other. In other words, the Bavarian practice does not guarantee greater protection against offences committed by prisoners allowed leave of absence. It follows that the argument that a restrictive implementation practice is justified by the need to protect the public is not sustainable. Naturally, careful examination is required of the risk that a prisoner will abscond or abuse his leave. However, in instances where serious offences against the person have been committed, such abuses happen so rarely that

20   For an overview, see Dünkel (1992: 23 ff; 1996a).

none of the prognostic methods currently available to the prison authorities can predict them with certainty. The restrictive granting of relaxations can therefore only be recommended where there is a concrete risk of absconding or abuse.

The overall finding is that the prison authorities in federal states with a more liberal practice have in no way been irresponsible in the granting of relaxations of the regime. In the final analysis, one has to deal with the general risks, which are far higher immediately after release from imprisonment. In other areas of social life we have followed another road to modernity, towards the so-called 'risk-taking society' in which risks that can hardly be calculated are taken on behalf of society as a whole (Beck, 1986). The way in which the mass media singles out some risks as a scandal (and this is particularly true of matters relating to imprisonment) should rather be seen as a diversionary tactic in the light of the overall risks which our society runs.

## 6 Empirical Research on Prison Labour, Vocational Qualifications in Prison, the (Material) Situation of Released Prisoners and Resocialization

Research on recidivism in Germany in the 1960s and the 1970s focused intensively on the relationship between employment prior to incarceration and qualifications, on the one hand, and subsequent reintegration, on the other. An evaluation conducted by Blath, in 1984, of 20 empirical studies came to the conclusion that there was a significant correlation between professional training prior to incarceration and a lower recidivism rate. The difference amounted to between 15 per cent and 30 per cent (Blath, 1984: 353). There was an even clearer distinction in respect of continuity of the employment relationship. Those who worked irregularly or who changed their jobs often prior to incarceration did significantly worse afterwards: a difference of 24 per cent to 44 per cent. Long-term unemployment also proved to be an indicator of a negative prognosis (Blath, 1984: 356 ff).

Similar findings were made in the early 1980s by the criminological research group at the Max Planck Institute in Freiburg in a study of prisoners who were released on probation directly from pre-trial detention. In respect of the recall of probation, seven factors (recorded three months after release) were shown to be of great prognostic significance. Of these there were four factors that relate directly to the material situation as influenced by incarceration: (1) available case of less than DM500, (2) debts of more than DM5,000, (3) no plan to deal with debt, and (4) unemployment. As the number of these negative factors increased there was a linear increase in the likelihood of the probationer being recalled: from a likelihood of 29 per cent with none or one of the factors present to a likelihood of 91 per cent if there were between five and seven of the factors (Spiess, 1982: 590 ff). These factors were more significant variables than the biography of the prisoner prior to detention.[21] These findings confirm the importance for subsequent resocialization of dealing with prisoners' debts (preferably while they are in prison) and of the material situation of prisoners at their release, a situation that is determined to a significant extent by low prison wages. Because prisoners earn so little, the prison social services can (contrary to s.74 of the Prison Act) only make arrangements in a few cases for prisoners to pay their debts.

A study of the ability of inmates in a juvenile institution, in comparison to juveniles who were not detained, to deal with interpersonal conflicts in the workplace, something that is vital for subsequent social integration, showed that the inmates were prepared only to a very limited extent to solve problems in the workplace constructively (Blath *et al.*, 1980: 38 ff; Blath, 1984). This meant that they were more likely either to react in a provocative or aggressive way, or to withdraw by leaving the place of work, than in the comparable group. It appears that the emotionally unsatisfactory atmosphere at work, more than the low wages and the limited stimulation offered by the work ('boring work'), led to work being discontinued (Blath, 1984: 323, 343). Attributing 'work shyness' to prisoners was therefore premature. Furthermore, it must be borne in mind that 'for this group society has not created the conditions that make it appear worthwhile to develop a binding relationship to work or a profession' (Blath, 1984: 343).[22] These findings refer to the 1970s. Since then, and particularly since the beginning of the 1990s, social conditions have worsened.

Of particular significance for the development of penal policy are studies that focus on the impact of professional or educational

---

21  This conclusion is supported by the most recent prognosis research; for an overview, see Spiess (1993, 1996).

22  See also Jehle (1994: 259) who comments that 'in prisons there is an over-representation of people, who for various reasons, cannot integrate fully into the world of work'.

training measures in prison on the subsequent reintegration of offenders into society. There are, of course, well known methodological problems with evaluating research of this kind that cannot be examined in depth here.[23] In particular, the question of the adequate control group plays an important role, as those prisoners who complete programmes successfully can differ a priori from the other prisoners and the effects of selection can limit or exclude conclusions about causality (Geissler, 1991; see also Wirth, 1988, 1996a). Moreover, changing social conditions may also influence the effectiveness of measures adopted in prison.[24]

For these reasons there is continuing controversy about the extent to which educational or professional training programmes lead to a reduction in recidivism. To the extent to which it has been possible to do systematic research with an appropriate control group, however, there are indications that training programmes have positive effects (Berckhauer and Hasenpusch, 1982; Baumann et al., 1983: Baumann, 1984; Wirth, 1988, 1996a; Geissler, 1991). Only in very few instances has it been possible to evaluate integration into the labour market or applicability of the training, received in prison, in the post-release situation. The study conducted by Wirth in North Rhine–Westphalia is an exception. He shows that success depends less on the qualification gained in prison and much more on the opportunity of using what was learnt after release. In other words, what matters is whether the released prisoner can find a job (Wirth, 1996a: 80ff). For example, 80 per cent of the professionally trained prisoners (as against 90 per cent of those who were not trained) became recidivists if they could not find work after release. The percentage of 'returnees' was only 33 per cent amongst those who found employment of a kind that was appropriate for their training. In this way reintegration into the community is best complemented by training in prison.

A further study of considerable relevance is that conducted in Austria by Hammerschick et al. (1997). They come to the conclusion that there is a significant correlation between integration in the labour market before and after imprisonment. It emerges that,

23   In Germany, this question has been discussed intensively in the context of sociotherapeutic institutions: see, for example, Kury (1986), Lösel et al. (1987), Lösel (1993, 1994).
24   See the accessible overview of the methodological problems with such research conducted in institutions for juveniles in Wirth (1996b: 467 ff, 496).

to a large extent, the inmates of prisons are people who for long periods of their lives have been disconnected from both social and working life. The authors also make clear the links between working and obeying the law. Those who succeed in finding a permanent job after release are only sentenced to imprisonment again in 20 per cent of cases; for those who are employed for less than 50 per cent of the time subsequent to their release, the reconviction rate is 40 per cent: in other words, twice as high (ibid.: 186). Long-term 'careers' in unemployment and criminal careers overlap to a large extent. This underlines the necessity for increased efforts by prison authorities and social workers involved with offenders, to break the vicious circle of unemployment, crime and incarceration by focusing on labour in programmes for the reintegration of prisoners.[25]

An overview of all the current empirical research provides a basis for arguing that a well-structured overall training programme in prison, in which the prison regime allows for communal living and is relaxed by allowing work release coupled with post-release support from the probation services, provides a significantly improved opportunity for successful reintegration into the community. This is particularly true if it is combined with a permanent integration into the world of work, with its concomitant improvement of the material conditions of the ex-prisoner. The research also demonstrates that longer prison sentences for comparable groups of offenders cannot be regarded as well, considered from the point of view of special prevention, even when the longer period of detention in a closed institution is connected with the objective of treatment.

Recent analysis of international research on treatment in prison by Lösel (1993, 1994) has shown that well-structured programmes that focus on the specific problems and the conditions of life of offenders have the potential to succeed (see also Dünkel and Geng, 1993; Egg, 1993). This is particularly true of programmes that use methods of social training that are designed to improve the ability to solve problems and interact in society. From the 1970s onwards, American studies have shown that the lack of success of treatment in prison can also be attributed to unsuitable social conditions such as unemployment, homelessness and racial discrimination that

25  Wirth (1996a: 83ff) also emphasizes the importance of work projects in the context of social work assistance for prisoners and probationers.

neutralize therapeutic interventions (Palmer, 1992; Gendreau and Andrews, 1990; Gendreau and Ross, 1995; Sherman et al., 1998; Goldblatt and Lewis, 1998; Lipton, 1998). It follows that treatment programmes are more likely to be effective if the focus is on increasing the opportunities and improving the living conditions of ex-prisoners (Dünkel, 1996a: 24ff; Lipton, 1998).

There is no reason for resignation if one expects realistically only to make a modest contribution to reducing recidivism. The objective of reintegrating the offender (see also s.3(3) of the Prison Act) can only be achieved to a limited extent by the withdrawal of liberty. Imprisonment, as longitudinal studies of juvenile incarceration have shown, does not necessarily reinforce 'criminal careers', for, when observed over a long period of time, these careers tend to stabilize even in the case of groups who are deeply involved in illegal activities (see Kerner and Janssen, 1983; Dolde and Grübl, 1988; Hermann and Kerner, 1988; Hermann, 1990). Nevertheless, the process of reintegration is, if anything, delayed by the negative effects of incarceration, which can neutralize well-intended resocialization programmes. This does not mean, however, that one should cease to offer opportunities for resocialization and not improve the situation in prison. On the contrary, the shortcomings in socialization and education of prisoners strongly confirm the need for increased (compensatory) efforts. The point of departure derived from comparative empirical research on penal sanctions must remain, as before, that non-custodial alternatives such as probation and other community-based sanctions or conditional early release are as effective, and in many instances are more effective, from the perspective of special prevention (Kerner, 1996: 14ff). The empirical evidence supports the penal policy of the past 20 years, which has sought to reduce the use of imprisonment by using it only as the punishment of last resort. This approach has been confirmed by the reform of juvenile justice law in Germany and in Austria, in 1988 and 1990, respectively (Dünkel et al., 1997).

In general, there can be no doubt that the inadequate material provision made for the average prisoner on release is at least partially responsible for the high rate of recidivism. Just how difficult the position of German prisoners is on release can be illustrated with a few examples. An investigation in Schleswig-Holstein at the end of the 1980s revealed that both men and women prisoners had an average debt burden of DM10,000, but on release received an average of DM472 for men and DM396 for women. Even juveniles owed on average DM3,386 at release, yet they received an average pay-out of only DM451 (Dünkel, 1992: 122 ff, 284 ff). With such payments, the desperate situation of these prisoners merely continued after their release. Of those released, 62 per cent to 73 per cent were unemployed before they were imprisoned. Of the men, 29 per cent lived off social security payments and a further 33 per cent survived on unemployment benefits. Amongst women, no fewer that 42 per cent had been dependent on social security.[26] In the light of the low level of educational and professional training of the prisoners (59 5 of the men had completed no professional training; amongst women, the figure was a staggering 79 per cent) it is not difficult to conclude that they had virtually no chance of finding employment in the formal sector.[27] The extent to which not only prisoners are affected by the side-effects of imprisonment is demonstrated impressively by a study by Busch et al. (1987), who found that, in the mid-1980s, 59 per cent of female members of prisoners' families were living below the poverty line (as opposed to 17 per cent of the total population) (Busch et al. 1987: 240; Bundesarbeitsgemeinschaft für Straffälligenhilfe, 1993: 175).

## 7 Criminal Political Questions and Perspectives of Prison Labour in Germany

For a long time after 1945, the organization of prison labour did not play a very important role in prison reform. In the last few years, however, it seems that questions of prison management concerning prison industries as well as the allocation of prison staff have become more important. The aim of reducing budgetary deficits has brought with it cost–benefit analyses and has led to a rethinking in terms of management and so on.[28] An economic analysis of the prison system showing that only a marginal part of the costs is covered by profits of prison enterprises has encouraged considerations of increasing the productivity of prison labour and thereby joining the principle of normalization as required by s.3(1) Prison Act. However, this principle is of limited value as other aims, not directly related to profit making, also have to be considered. Prisoners should be trained in professional skills and this is not always

26   Amongst woman prisoners in Berlin, the percentage was a high as 47 per cent (Dünkel, 1992: 374ff).
27   This has been confirmed by the Austrian study of Hammerschick et al. (1997).
28   See Dünkel and Kunkat (1997: 33).

possible in the same way as in enterprises working under the conditions of the free market. Prison enterprises cannot get rid of unmotivated, lazy or difficult workers. They have to try somehow to improve the sometimes very poor professional skills of the prisoners.

The issue of privatization in Germany is not yet as far developed as in other countries, such as England, Australia or France, but in spite of some reservations about the constitutionality of privatizing traditionally state-run services,[29] the reform of prison industries is seen as possible and as useful in this context. An interesting attempt to improve prison enterprises and their productivity has been made by the Hamburg prison industries, where prisoners are employed inside prisons under normal working contracts (that is, a kind of 'intramural work release'). The productivity has increased considerably. Therefore Hagemann concludes from the Hamburg model that an alternative organization of prison labour which increases productivity is realistic (Hagemann, 1995: 24; 1995b; 1997).

This leads one back to the question of remuneration, which dominates the current debate about prison labour in Germany. An increase in remuneration is justified since the productivity of prisoners is much higher than the 5 per cent actually allowed. The recent decision of the Federal Constitutional Court posits a constitutional obligation to increase prisoners' wages so that they represent compensation for the work performed and demonstrate to the prisoner that it is worth engaging in legal occupations in order to be reintegrated into society. Furthermore, the inclusion of prisoners in the pension system is seen as an urgently required penal reform. Prison labour could be the catalyst for prison reform and the modernization of prison systems. However, not only is an improvement in the quality of the work offered and the conditions under which it is performed required, but prisoners' rights in general should not be forgotten.

## References

Baumann, Karl. H. 1984. Der Einfluß von Bildungsmaßnahmen im Strafvollzug auf das Rückfallverhalten. *Zeitschrift für Strafvollzug und Straffälligenhilfe* 33: 31–6.

Baumann, Karl H., Wolfgan Maetze and Hans G. Mey. 1983. Zur Rückfälligkeit nach Strafvollzug. *Monatsschrift für Kriminologie und Strafrechtsreform* 66; 133–48.

29 See Jung (1988).

Beck, Urich. 1986. *Risikogesellschaft. Auf dem Weg in eine andere Moderne.* Frankfurt/M.: Suhrkamp.

Berckhauer, Friedhelm and Burkhardt Hasenpusch. 1982. Legalbewährungen und Strafvollzug. Zur Rückfälligkeit der 1974 aus dem niedersächsischen Strafvollzug Entlassenen. In *Modelle zur Kriminalitätsvorbeugung und Resozialisierung*, edited by H.D. Schwindt and G. Steinhilper. Heidelberg: Kriminalistik-Verlag.

Blath, Richard. 1984. *Die Neigung zum Verlassen des Arbeitsplatzes.* Jur. Diss. Erlangen. Unpublished PhD thesis.

Blath, Richard, Peter Dillig and Hans P. Frey. 1980. *Arbeit und Resozialisierung.* Weinheim and Basle: Beltz.

Bundesarbeitsgemeinschaft für Straffälligenhilfe. 1993. Tarifgerecht Entlohnung für Inhaftierte. *Zeitschrift für Strafvollzug und Straffälligenhilfe* 42, S. 174–80.

Busch, Max, Peter Fülbier and Friedrich W. Meyer. 1987. *Zur Situation von Frauen der Inhaftierten.* Bonn: Bundesministerium für Jugend, Frauen und Gesundheit.

Calliess, Rolf-Peter and Heinz Müller-Dietz. 1998. *Strafvollsugsgesetz. Kommentar.* 7th edn. Munich: C.H. Beck.

Decision of 1 July 1998 of the Federal Constitutional Court on Prison Labour. 1998. *Zeitschrift für Strafvollzug und Straffälligenhilfe* 47: 242.

Dolde, Gabriel. 1992. Zehn Jahre Ergahrung mit dem Vollzug der Freiheitsstrafe ohne soziale Desintegration. *Zeitschrift für Strafvollzug und Straffälligenholfe* 41: 24–30.

Dolde, Gabriel and George Grübl. 1988. Verfestigte 'kriminelle Karriere' nach Jugendstrafvollzug? Rückfalluntersuchungen an ehemaligen Jugendstrafgefangenen in Baden-Württemberg. *Zeitschrift für Strafvollzug und Straffälligenhilfe* 37: 29–34.

Dolde, Gabriel and Jörg-Martin Jehle. 1986. Wirklichkeit und Möglichkeiten des Kurzstrafenvollzugs. *Zeitschrift für Strafvollzug und Straffälligenhilfe* 35: 195–202.

Dolde, Gabriel and Dieter Rössner. 1987. Auf dem Wege zu einer neuen Sanktion: Vollzug der Freiheitsstrafe als Freizeitstrafe. *Zeitschrift für die gesamten Strafrechtswissenschaften* 99: 424–51.

Dünkel, Frieder. 1987. *Die Herausforderung der geburtenschwachen Jahrgänge – Aspekte der Kosten-Nutzen-Analyse in der Kriminalpolitik.* Freiburg I. Br.: Max-Planck-Institut für ausländisches und internationales Strafrecht.

Dünkel, Frieder. 1992. *Empirische Beiträge und Materialien zum Strafvollzug. Bestandsaufnahmen des Strafvollzugs in Schleswig-Holstein und des Frauenvollzugs in Berlin.* Freiburg I. Br.: Max-Planck-Institut für ausländisches und internationales Strafrecht.

Dünkel, Frieder. 1995. Imprisonment in transition. The Situation in the New States of the Federal Republic of Germany. *British Journal of Criminology* 35: 95–113.

Dünkel, Frieder. 1996a. *Empirische Forschung im Strafvollzug*. Bonn: Forum-Verlag.

Dünkel, Frieder. 1996b. Die Rechtsstellung von Strafgefangenen und Möglichkeiten der rechtlichen Kontrolle von Vollzugsentscheidungen in Deutschland. *Goltdammer's Archiv für Strafrecht* 143: 518–38.

Dünkel, Frieder and Bernd Geng. 1993. Zur Rückfälligkeit von Karrieretätern nach unterschiedlichen Entlassungsformen. In *Kriminologische Forschung in den 90er Jahren*, edited by G. Kaiser and H. Kury. Freiburg i. Br.: Max-Planck-Institut für ausländisches und internationales Strafrecht.

Dünkel, Frieder and Angela Kunkat. 1997. Zwischen Innovation und Restauration. 20 Jahre Strafvollzugsgesetz – eine Bestandsaufnahme. *Neue Kriminalpolitik* 9, no. 2: 24–33.

Dünkel, Frieder and Anton Rosner. 1982. *Die Entwicklung des Strafvollzugs in der Bundesrepublik Deutschland seit 1970 – Materialien und Analysen*. 2nd edn. Freiburg I. Br.: Max-Planck-Institut für ausländisches und internationales Strafrecht.

Dünkel, Frieder and Dieter Rössner. 1991. Germany. In *Imprisonment Today and Tomorrow. International Perspectives on Prisoners' Rights and Prison Conditions*, edited by D. Van Zyl Smit and F. Dünkel. Deventer, Boston: Kluwer.

Dünkel, Frieder and Dirk van Zyl Smit. 1998. Arbeit im Strafvollzug – ein internationaler Vergleich. In *Internationale Perspektiven in Kriminologie und Strafrecht. Festschrift für Günther Kaiser zum 70. Geburtstag*, edited by Hans-Jörg Albrecht, Frieder Dünkel, Hans-Jürgen Kerner, Joseph Kürzinger, Heinz Schoech, Klaus Sessar and Bernhard Villmow. Heymann: Cologne.

Dünkel, Frieder, Anton van Kalmthout and Horst Schüler-Springorum, eds. 1997. *Entweicklungstendenzen und Reformstrategien im Jugendstrafrecht im europäischen Vergleich*. Mönchengladbach: Forum-Verlag.

Egg, Rudolf, ed. 1993. *Sozialtherapie in den 90er Jähren. Gegenwärtiger Stand und aktuelle Entwicklungen im Justizvollzug*. Wiesbaden: Kriminologische Zentralstelle.

Geissler, Isolde. 1991. *Ausbildung und Arbeit im Jugendstrafvollzug. Haftverlaufs- und Rückfallanalyse*. Freiburg: Max-Planck-Institut für ausländisches und internationales Strafrecht.

Gendreau, Paul and Don A. Andrews. 1990. Tertiary Prevention: What the Meta-analysis of the Offender Treatment Literature Tells us About 'What Works'. *Canadian Journal of Criminology* 32: 173–84.

Gendreau, Paul and Robert R. Ross. 1995. Correctional Treatment: Some Recommendations for Effective Intervention. In *The Dilemmas of Corrections*, edited by K.C. Haas and G.P. Alpert. Prospect Heights/Ill.: Waveland Press.

Goldblatt, Peter and Chris Lewis eds. 1998. *Reducing offending: an assessment of research evidence on ways of dealing with offending behavior.* Home Office Research Study 187. London: Home Office.

Hagemann, Otmar. 1995a. Gleiche Arbeit, gleicher Lohn. *Neue Kriminalpolitik* 7, no. 4: 21–4.

Hagemann, Otmar. 1995b. Leistungsgerechte Entlohnung im Strafvollzug: das Hamburger Modell. *Monatsschrift für Kriminologie und Strafrechtsreform* 77: 341–51.

Hagemann, Otmar. 1997. 'Leiharbeit' als Stufe der Reintegration von Strafgefangenen in den Arbeitsmarkt. In *Jahrbuch für Rechts- und Kriminalsoziologie '97. Arbeitsmarkt, Strafvollzug und Gefangenenarbeit.* Edited by Walter Hammerschick and Arno Pilgram. Baden-Baden: Nomos.

Hammerschick, Walter. 1997. Arbeit im Strafvollzug – Rechtslage und Realität im europäischen Vergleich. In *Jahrburch für Rechts- und Kriminalsoziologie '97. Arbeitsmarkt, Strafvollzug und Gefangenenarbeit.* Edited by Walter Hammerschick and Arno Pilgram. Baden-Baden: Nomos.

Hammerschick, Walter, Arno Pilgram and Andreas Riesenfelder. 1997. Zu den Erwerbsbiographien und Verurteilungskarrieren Strafgefangener und Strafentlassener, rekonstruiert anhand von Sozialversicherungs- und Strafregisterdaten. In *Jahrbuch für Rechts- und Kriminalsoziologie '97. Arbeitsmarkt, Strafvollzug und Gefangenenarbeit.* Edited by Walter Hammerschick and Arno Pilgram. Baden-Baden: Nomos.

Hermann, Dieter. 1990. Inhaftierung und Rückfall. *Zeitschrift für Strafvollzug und Straffälligenhilfe* 39: 76–82.

Hermann, Dieter and Hans-Jürgen Kerner. 1988. Die Eigendynamik der Rückfallkriminalität. *Kölner Zeitschrift für Soziologie und Sozialpsychologie* 40: 485–504.

Jehle, Jörg-Martin. 1994. Arbeit und Entlohnung von Strafgefangenen. *Zeitschrift für Strafvollzug und Straffälligenhilfe* 43: 259–267.

Jung, Heike. 1988. Paradigmawechsel im Strafvollzug? Eine Problemskizze zur Privatisierung der Gefängnisse. In *Kriminologische Forschung in den 80er Jahren*, edited by G. Kaiser, H. Kury and H.-J. Albrecht. Freiburg i. Br.: Max-Planck-Institut für ausländisches und internationales Strafrecht.

Kerner, Hans-Jürgen. 1996. Erfolgsbeurteilung nach Jugendstrafvollzug. Ein Teil eines umfassenderen Problems vergleichender kriminologischer

Sanktionsforschung. In *Jugendstrafvollzug und Bewährung*, edited by H.-J. Kerner, G. Dolde and H.-G. Mey. Bonn: Forum-Verlag.

Kerner, Hans-Jürgen and Helmut Janssen. 1983. Rückfall nach Jugendstrafvollzug – Betrachtungen unter dem Gesichtspunkt von Lebenslauf und krimineller Karriere. In *Festschrift für H. Leferenz*, edited by H.-J. Kerner, H. Güppinger and F. Streng. Heidelberg: C.F. Müller.

Kury, Helmut. 1986. *Die Behandlung Straffälliger*. Vols. 1 and 2. Berlin: Duncker & Humblot.

Lipton, Douglas S. 1988. *The Effectiveness of Correctional Treatment Revisited Thirty Years Later: Preliminary Meta-Analytical Findings from the CDATE study*. Paper presented at the 12th International Congress on Criminology. Seoul, Korea. 23–8 August.

Lösel, Friederich. 1993. Sprechen Evaluationsergebnisse von Meta-Analysen für einen frischen Wind in der Straftäterbehandlung? In *Sozialtherapie in den 90er Jahren. Gegenwärtiger Stand und aktuelle Entwicklung im Justizvollzug*, edited by R. Egg. Wiesbaden: Kriminologische Zentralstelle.

Lösel, Friederich. 1994. Meta-analytische Beiträge zur wiederbelebten Diskussion des Behandlungsgedankens. In *Straftäterbehandlung für eine Revitalisierung in Forschung und Praxis*, edited by D. Steller, K.-P. Dahle and M. Basqué. Pfaffenweiler: Centaurus.

Lösel Friederich, Peter Köferl and Florian Weber. 1987. *Meta-Evaluation der Sozialtherapie: Qualitative Analysen zur Behandlungsforschung in sozialtherapeutischen Anstalten des Justizvollzugs*. Stuttgart: Müller.

Neu, Axel D. 1995a. *Betriebswirtschaftliche und volkswirtschaftliche Aspekte einer tariforientierten Gefangenenentlohnung*. Berlin: de Gruyther.

Neu, Axel D. 1995b. Betriebswirtschaftliche und volkswirtschaftliche Aspekte einer tariforientierten Gefangenenentlohnung. *Zeitschrift für Strafvollzug und Straffälligenhilfe* 44: 149–61.

Palmer, Ted. 1992. *The Re-emergence of correctional interventions*. Newbury Park, London and New Delhi: Sage.

Preusker, Harald. 1988. Zur Situation der Gefängnisarbeit. *Zeitschrift für Strafvollzug und Straffälligenhilfe* 37: 92–5.

Quittmann, Joachim. 1982. *Haftentlassung und Reintegration*. Weinheim and Basle: Beltz.

Rosenthal, Michael. 1998. Arbeitslohn im Strafvollzug. *Neue Kriminalpolitik* 10, no. 2: 12–16.

Sherman, Lawrence W., Denise Gottfredson, Doris MacKenzie, John Eck, Peter Reuter and Shawn Bushway. 1998. Preventing Crime: What Works, what doesn't, what's promising. *National Institute of Justice, Research*

*in Brief*. July. (Extended version: http://www.ojp.usdoj.gov/nij or: http: //www.preventingcrime.org).
Sigel, Walter. 1995. Alternative Überlegungen zur Verbesserung der Gefangenenentlohnung. *Zeitschrift für Strafvollzug und Straffälligenhilfe* 44: 81–3.
Spiess, Gerhard. 1982. Probleme praxisbezogener Forschung und ihrer Umsetzung am Beispiel der Bewährungsprognose. In *Prävention abweichenden Verhalterns – Maßnahmen der Vorbeugung und Nachbetreuung*, edited by H. Kury. Cologne, Berlin, Bonn and Munich: Heymanns.
Spiess, Gerhard. 1993: Kriminalprognose. In *Kleines kriminologisches Wörterbuch*. 3rd edn, edited by Gunther Kaiser, Hans-Jürgen Kerner and Fitz Sack. Heidelberg: C.F. Müller.
Spiess, Gerhard. 1996. Prophetie oder Prognose? *Neue Kriminalpolitik* 8, no. 1: 31–6.
van Zyl Smit, Dirk and Frieder Dünkel eds. 1991. *Imprisonment Today and Tomorrow. International Perspectives on Prisoners' Rights and Prison Conditions*. Deventer and Boston: Kluwer.
Walter, Michael. 1991. *Strafvollzug*. Stuttgart, Munich and Hanover: Boorberg.
Wirth, Wolfgang. 1988. Widereingliederung durch Ausbildung? Zur Wirkungsweise berufsfördernder Maßnahmen im Jugendstrafvollzug. In *Kriminologische Forschung in den 80er Jahren*, edited by G. Kaiser, H. Kury and H.-J. Albrecht. Freiburg i. Br.: Max-Planck-Institut für ausländisches und internationales Strafrecht.
Wirth, Wolfgang. 1996a. Notwendigkeit und Schwerpunkte von Arbeitsprojekten in der Straffälligenhilfe. In *Verarmung – Abweichung – Kriminalität. Straffälligenhilfe vor dem Hintergrund gesellschaftlicher Polarisierung*, edited by R. Hompesch, G. Kawamura and W. Reindl. Bonn: Forum-Verlag.
Wirth, Wolfgang. 1996b. Legalbewährung nach Jugendstrafvollzug: Probleme und Chancen von Aktenanalyse, Wirkungsanalyse und Bedingungsanalyse. In *Jugendstrafvollzug und Bewährung*, edited by H.-J. Kerner, G. Dolde and H.-G. Mey. Bonn: Forum-Verlag.
Wrage, Nikolaus. 1997. Die ökonomische Situation der Strafgefangenen oder: Die Achillesferse des Resozialisierungsvollzugs. *Zeitschrfit für Rechtspolitik* 30, 435–7.

# The Author

**Frieder Dünkel** is professor of criminology, penology and juvenile justice at the Ernst-Moritz-Arndt-University of Greifswald in Germany.

# 5 Hungary

FERENC NAGY

## 1 Prisoners and Involuntary Servitude

The obligation of prisoners to work is prescribed in art. 33(1)(d)(e) of the current Hungarian Prison Act. In law, this obligation cannot be regarded as forced labour. This is guaranteed in the regulations by specifying that the prisoner must be remunerated according to the amount and quality of work completed, and that the assigned labour must not be meaningless but socially useful. Moreover, the most important conditions of prison labour are regulated, in accordance with the provisions of Hungarian labour law, by the Prison Act, which governs matters such as working hours, protection of women and youth, times for rest, paid holidays and safety at work.

The general rule is that prisoners must be paid for their labour. Exemptions, created by art. 33(1)(e) of the Prison Act, apply when prisoners work in the cleaning and maintenance of the institution. The time that may be spent on unpaid work of this kind is restricted by a decree of the Minister of Justice. Such restrictions are contained in art. 102(2) IM Decree No. 6/1996 (VII. 12). In terms of this decree, the time spent on unpaid work should not exceed four hours a day and 24 hours a month.

Article 104(2) IM Decree No. 6/1996 (VII. 12) specifies that prisoners must be granted relief from the duty to work in the following cases:

(a) for time spent fulfilling civil duties, prescribed by law, such as attendance before a civil or criminal court;
(b) in the case of serious illness or death of a close relative, when the prisoner may be granted two days' leave;
(c) if the prisoner is incapable of working because of illness;
(d) for compulsory medical examination;
(e) if the absence is caused by an emergency (such as a security measure);
(f) if the employer otherwise permits it.

Perhaps 'reformative and educational labour' and 'restrictive reformative and educational labour' should be mentioned here, as types of sentences that have been abolished. Work can no longer be imposed as punishment for violation of prison regulations. Penal labour as a disciplinary measure has not been available since 1954.

The varied backgrounds of the prison workers, their low level of education, lack of skills, poor performance, low work morale and high rate of turnover impose extra burdens on enterprises that depend upon the labour of prisoners. As can be seen from Tables 5.1 and 5.2, reproduced below, the percentage of prisoners who actually work has declined in recent years. From 1948 onwards, prison work in Hungary took two forms: prison maintenance subsidized by the state budget and work at the state-owned production units. Although the economic system changed drastically in the 1990s (Fekete, 1993), prison labour continued to be divided between maintenance and production work. The only significant development was that the former state-owned production units

Table 5.1: Proportion of Prisoners in Work, and Levels of Wages in Hungarian Forints (HUF) per Prisoner between 1987 and 1996 (31 December each year)

| Year | Numbers and Percentages of All Prisoners in Work | | | Monthly Gross Average Earnings (HUF) | |
|---|---|---|---|---|---|
| | Prison Maintenance* | State-owned Enterprises | Employment percentage (%)** | Prison Maintenance | State-owned Enterprises |
| 1987 | 4,370 | 14,260 | 82.64 | 2,357 | 2,309 |
| 1988 | 4,124 | 13,469 | 84.09 | 2,496 | 2,449 |
| 1989 | 3,095 | 11,037 | 94.37 | 2,703 | 3,082 |
| 1990 | 3,206 | 6,817 | 81.36 | 2,859 | 3,330 |
| 1991 | 3,081 | 4,907 | 53.94 | 3,487 | 4,020 |
| 1992 | 3,113 | 4,609 | 48.55 | 3,985 | 4,475 |
| 1993 | 3,084 | 4,411 | 56.80 | 4,365 | 4,630 |
| 1994 | 3,348 | 4,291 | 58.00 | 4,100 | 5,076 |
| 1995 | 3,420 | 4,244 | 59.17 | 4,185 | 5,399 |
| 1996 | 3,280 | 3,963 | 56.20 | 4,820 | 5,890*** |

Notes:
 * These wages come from the state budget.
 ** In terms of all prisoners.
 *** The minimum wage for employees on the open market in 1996 was HUF14,500 per month.

Source: Prison Administration Statistics, Hungarian Ministry of Justice (1997).

were changed into state-owned enterprises constituted as companies with limited liability. There was also a slight decline in the prison population between 1992 and 1997 (see Table 5.3).

Table 5.2: Prisoners' Employment (1997)

|  | Average Number of Prisoners | Average Income (HUF/Prisoner/Month) |
|---|---|---|
| Industrial sector | 2,622 | 6,044 |
| Agricultural sector | 1,424 | 6,206 |
| Total (all limited companies) | 4,046 | 6,101 |
| State budget | 3,020 | 5,301 |
| Total | 7,066 | 5,478* |
| Total number of prisoners | 9,408 | |
| Employment rate (%) | 75 | |

*Note:* * The minimum wage was HUF17,000 in 1997.
*Source:* Prison Administration Statistics, Hungarian Ministry of Justice (1997).

Table 5.3: Total Number of Prisoners

| | Number of Prisoners Year end | | | | | |
|---|---|---|---|---|---|---|
| | 1992 | 1993 | 1994 | 1995 | 1996 | 1997 |
| Pre-trial detention | 4,272 | 3,557 | 3,433 | 3,183 | 3,455 | 3,660 |
| Sentenced to imprisonment | 11,424 | 9,390 | 9,390 | 8,928 | 8,986 | 9,408 |
| Compulsory medical treatment | 143 | 130 | 121 | 128 | 147 | 165 |
| Confinements | 74 | 119 | 196 | 215 | 174 | 172 |
| Preventive detention | 0 | 0 | 0 | 1 | 1 | 0 |
| Total | 15,913 | 13,196 | 13,140 | 12,455 | 12,763 | 13,405 |

*Source:* Prison Administration Statistics, Hungarian Ministry of Justice (1997).

## 2  Prisoners' Right to Work

Hungarian professional literature and practical experience with the execution of sentences of imprisonment both emphasize the absolute necessity for the application of prisoners' abilities, since work helps improve their chances of reintegration into society while decreasing the harmful effects of incarceration. Our empirical research indicates beyond doubt that idleness gives rise to restlessness, depression and aggression in prisoners (Lõrincz and Kabódi, 1996; Lõrincz and Nagy, 1997). At the legal level, art. 36(1)(*d*) of the current Prison Act also confirms prisoners' right to work.

Condemning prisoners to idleness is generally held to be counterproductive and damaging to their personality and, as such, contradictory to the legally recognized aims of the execution of prison sentences, namely the special and general prevention of reoffending (art. 19 of the Prison Act; Fejes, 1994). Given this legal objective, a close relationship can be identified between prison work and vocational training. The importance of the latter is further emphasized by the fact that the overwhelming majority of prisoners have no vocational qualifications, which further reduces their chance of finding employment after release. A basic objective of vocational training should be to take the real demands of the labour market into consideration, and to enhance the reintegration of released prisoners into society. Amongst the numerous practical obstacles to this are the fast-changing demands of the labour market, prisoners' lack of basic education, the short duration of many prison sentences and the expense of vocational training. Notwithstanding these obstacles, almost 1,000 prisoners participated in some kind of vocational training in 1995: 245 of them attended courses financed from special state funds, the limited companies organized courses for 300, and another 400 took part in short-term or therapeutic training. In 1996, the total number of prisoners receiving vocational training increased to 1,153 (Prison Administration Yearbook, 1997).

## 3  The Interconnection between Work and Release

It has become extremely difficult for released prisoners to find employment in Hungary in the last 10 years. This is due, not only to prejudice, but also to the increasing rate of unemployment. The high unemployment rate has been factored into the Prison Act since the Act does not make conditional release dependent upon securing employment. Article 96(b) of the Prison Act states that released prisoners, who are greatly in need of instruction and supervision by a probation officer, should 'as far as possible' be employed.

## 4 Prisoners and the Labour Law

The products manufactured by state-owned companies, until 1993, and since then by limited companies in Hungarian prisons are ready-to-wear clothes, furniture, shoes and agricultural products, which are released into commercial circulation without any legal limitations. The free market demand for prison labour has decreased in the last few years. This has been accompanied by a growth in the Prison Administration's own utilization of it. Similarly, in order to promote the sale of prison-made goods, art. 9(4) of Act CVII of 1995 has required the army and the security forces to give preference to these goods when purchasing for themselves.

The legal regulation of prison work is a matter partly of general labour law and partly of the Prison Act. The basic restrictions on employment, such as working hours, work schedule and workers' protection, are regulated by labour law. However, because of the special features of prison work, the designation of work, salary and working conditions fall under the Prison Act. What is different about working in prison during the enforcement of a prison sentence is that such work is not based on a contract between employer and employee. It is the law that prescribes compulsory work for the prisoner and the compulsory provision of work by the Prison Administration.

In this special situation, the powers of the employer over the working prisoner are not without limits; these limitations can be found within the basic rules of labour law, and include the above-mentioned regulations on working hours, work schedules, safety regulations and IM Decree No. 6/1996 (VII. 12) of the Minister of Justice. However, owing to the special position of prison labour, the Prison Administration exercises greater power in areas like work assignment, fee settlement and working conditions. On the other hand, its responsibility is also greater: such as the obligation to provide work, and to maintain prisoners when they do not work (clothing, food and so on).

The minimum wage of working prisoners is set by the IM Decree No. 6/1996 (VII. 12), according to which 'the minimum wage should be one-third of the minimum wage of those in regular employment' (art. 124(2)).

The appropriate regulations of the labour law and the abovementioned IM Decree are used to draw up rules regarding the regular working and rest hours of prisoners, irregular work (overtime, work on Sundays and national holidays), trainees' and students' paid holidays, and working hour allowances.

Prisons are generally liable under civil law for any injury or damage suffered by a prisoner. If such an event arises in connection with prison work, the prison is bound by rules derived from the labour law. The prisoner may make his or her claims against the prison where the damage occurred. The prison makes a formal decision about the claim which, if unfavourable, can be taken to court by the prisoner within 30 days (Prison Act, as amended by Act CVII of 1995).

Since there is no contractual relationship between the prisoner and the prison, the time spent at work there does not count towards years of service for superannuation. Nor is the prisoner entitled to sick leave during the term of imprisonment. However, prisoners are entitled to 20 days' annual paid leave, during which they do not have to work, although of course they must remain in prison during this time. If the prisoner is entitled to a retirement pension, or to a specific benefit paid to those who suffered long-term accidental injury before he or she started to serve the prison sentence, he or she will continue to receive it without interruption. If the prisoner suffers an accident at work, or is taken ill in connection with work, he or she is entitled to emergency treatment and health care to help recovery (art. 36(1)(f) of the Prison Act).

## 5 Compensation for Work by Prisoners

In theory, any kind of work carried out during imprisonment has to be remunerated, with the exception of cleaning and maintenance duties (see section 1 above). The prisoners' average income is shown in Tables 5.1 and 5.2.

Prisoners are required by law to contribute to the costs of their maintenance, except when they are unable to work through no fault of their own or do not receive retirement pension or accidental injuries benefit (art. 33(1)(g) of the Prison Act). This contribution amounted to HUF57 per day per prisoner in 1998, which covered about 2 per cent of the real cost of a prisoner's daily maintenance. There are no further deductions from a prisoner's wage for tax or social insurance. Nevertheless, questions may be raised about the acceptability of the contributions that prisoners are compelled to make, for, in theory, the Hungarian state has a duty to provide for all costs of imprisonment.

## 6  International Human Rights Law and Prison Labour

From the list of internationally recognized human rights, art. 70/B(I) of the much-amended Hungarian Constitution recognizes the citizen's right to work and the Prison Act formally extends this to prisoners. Paragraph 5 of Recommendation No. R/89 of the Ministerial Committee of the Council of Europe insists that the education of prisoners should not be held in lower esteem than work, including its remuneration. The financial restraints of the Hungarian Prison Administration do not yet allow this latter recommendation to be implemented in practice. The Hungarian legislature, when enacting amendments to the Prison Act in 1995, intended to encourage prisoners to further their education by declaring that 'if the prisoner pursues studies instead of work, he or she is entitled to monetary subsidy, its amount to be determined by law' (art. 45(4) of the Prison Act). However, for the moment this provision has no practical force.

## 7  The Main Features of the Prison Work in Hungary

In conclusion, it is useful to note a number of general features of prison work in Hungary. The profile of production and the products manufactured need to be adjusted to the (changing) type of workforce that prisons provide. Consequently, market demands can be met only within certain limits. The reality is that modern technology, dependent on highly skilled workers, cannot easily be introduced. Because of the turnover of skilled prisoners, the mode of work at prison enterprises has to be constantly modified. Because these enterprises have to compete in a market environment, work is only available unevenly and a fluctuating level of employment is inevitable. Moreover, the safety regulations that apply in prison and the educational requirements of prisoners place constraints on the capacity of prison enterprises to deploy their labour force that do not apply to outside industries.

Another important feature of the management of prison labour is the trend that the level of professional skills of prisoners entering prison with them seems to be decreasing continuously. At the same time, the proportion of socially and mentally retarded prisoners is increasing. The retarded prisoners' work performance is weaker and their productivity is much lower than that of similarly handicapped workers in the civil (outside) enterprises (Borka Katonáné, 1994)

The majority of prison enterprises engage in light industry. This causes several problems. For one, the majority of the prisoners are male, but in light industry on the outside most employees are women. Therefore it is unproductive to train the prisoners for these kinds of jobs, as it is expensive, takes a long time and their general productivity is low. A related problem is that this type of prison work does not promote the later social resettlement of the prisoner. It means that the employment problem is more or less solved only during the sentence period. After release, many former prisoners cannot gainfully use the skills they have learnt, or in the case of male prisoners simply cannot find the kind of job, such as sewing or weaving, for which they have been trained. Secondly, the demand for the products of light industry is decreasing, thus further exacerbating the difficulty of finding work in this sector.

The statistical data, which show that 70 per cent to 75 per cent of prisoners have work, appear very positive (see Tables 5.1 and 5.2). In reality, the situation is worse. According to the law, state subsidy of the industrial and agricultural enterprises depends on the number of employed prisoners. In order for these enterprises to get a higher subsidy, it is in their interest to report higher numbers of prisoners in work than are actually employed. Consequently, only half of the number of prisoners reported to be in work are actually employed.

An amendment to the Prison Act in 1993 made provision for milder enforcement rules. According to this amendment, the prison judge may order a milder application of the Prison Act than is usually the case for prisoners who are in medium and minimum security prisons. Such prisoners may work without supervision for private employers outside the prison. In such cases, the employment contract is signed by the prison and by the private employer. This kind of employment does not appear separately in the statistics.

There is one more general and fundamental problem. The Prison Administration has not received the state subsidy that has been promised for many years.

## References

Borka Katonáné, K. 1994. Az elítéltek munkáltatásának problematikája. In A büntetés-végrehajtási intézetekben folyó munkáltatás problémái (The problem of employment for prisoners; in The problems of employment in prisons), *Kriminológiai Közlemények*, edited by K. Kerezsi. Budapest: Magyar Kriminológiai Társaság.

*Büntetés-végrehajtási Évkönyv 1997* (The Prison Administration's Yearbook 1997). 1998. Edited by Gy. Csorba and Gy. Hegedûs. Budapest: a Büntetés-végrehajtás Országos Parancsnokság kiadványa (Paper of the Hungarian National Prison Service).

Fejes, Imre. 1994. Reszocializáció vagy(és) gazdaságosság (Social resettlement or/and Profitability). *Börtönügyi Szemle* 4: 30–39.

Fekete, Mihály. 1993. Átalakulás (Proposals for the changes in the field of prison work). *Börtönügyi Szemle* 3: 1–10.

Lammich, S. and F. Nagy. 1989. Die Freiheitsstrafe und deren Vollzug in Ungarn. *Zeitschrift für Strafvollzug und Straffälligenhilfe* 38: 210–15.

Lörincz, J. and C. Kabódi. 1996. A szabadságvesztés-büntetés végrehajtásának hatásrendszere (The effect mechanism of the imprisonment). In *Knowledge of Criminology – Criminality – Criminality Control*, edited by K Gönezöl, L. Korinek and M. Lévai. Budapest: Corvina.

Lörincz J. and F. Nagy. 1997. *Börtönügy Magyarországon* (Prison matters in Hungary). Budapest: Büntetés-végrehajtás Országos Parancsnokság (Hungarian National Prison Administration).

Nagy, Ferenc. 1990. Sanktions- und Strafvollzugspraxis in der Bundesrepublik Deutschland und in Ungarn im Vergleich. In *Deutsch-ungarisches Kolloquium über Strafrecht und Kriminologie*, edited by A. Eser and G. Kaiser. Baden-Baden: Nomos.

Nagy, Ferenc. 1991. Hungary. In *Imprisonment Today and Tomorrow*, edited by D. van Zyl Smit and F. Dünkel. Deventer and Boston: Kluwer.

Nagy, Ferenc. 1993. Arten und Reform punitiver und nicht-punitiver Sabktionen in Ungarn. In *Von totalitärem zu rechtsstaatlichem Strafrecht*, edited by A. Eser, G. Kaiser and E. Weigend. Freiburg: Eigenverlag Max-Planck-Institut.

Nagy, Ferenc. 1995. Die äußere Kontrolle der Gesetzlichkeit des Strafvollzugs. In *Zweites deutsch–ungarisches Kolloquium über Strafrecht und Kriminologie*, edited by A. Eser and G. Kaiser. Baden-Baden: Nomos.

Walmsley, Roy. 1996. *Prison Systems in Central and Eastern Europe*. Heuni Papers 29. Helsinki: Heuni.

## The Author

Ferenc Nagy is professor of criminal law and criminology at the University of Szeged in Hungary.

# 6 Israel

LESLIE SEBBA*

At the time of the establishment of the Houses of Correction in the sixteenth century, or the 'Pennsylvania system' in the nineteenth century, the nature of the work with which prisoners would be occupied was one of the focal issues in prison policy (Sellin, 1976). In modern times this issue has generally been secondary to issues such as overcrowding, security and, to a lesser extent, rehabilitation; within the parameters of this last topic, however, prison labour may also sometimes be considered.

The situation in Israel follows this general pattern. While the prison authorities have in fact expended considerable energies on the planning of prison labour and its structural reform,[1] the wider debates in which parliamentarians, the press and the public have been involved have tended to focus on the other issues referred to in the preceding paragraph. However, since prison labour issues are closely affected by, and interrelated with, the wider issues (particularly rehabilitation, but also security, overcrowding and other questions), an analysis of prison labour is best presented against the background of a general description of the main characteristics and orientation of the Israeli penal system and particularly Israeli prison policy.

---

\*     This chapter is based on a paper presented at a workshop on Contemporary Prison Law and Practice: Special Focus on Prison Labour, held at the Oñati Institute for the Sociology of Law in May 1996. Thanks are due to Profs Frieder Dünkel and Dirk van Zyl Smit, convenors of the Workshop, and to Prof. Johannes Feest, Scientific Director of the Institute, for its sponsorship. I also wish to thank Hava Cohen, of the Ministry for Internal Security, Dr Gavriel Shavitt of Bar-Ilan University, and Adv. Ayana Unger-Latin for the sources they brought to my attention. This chapter was revised in 1998, while the author was a Visiting Fellow at the Centre for Socio-Legal Studies at Wolfson College, Oxford.

1     Implementation of the reforms, in terms of their day-to-day administration, has been less energetic: see section 2.6 below, on 'Administration of the System: Structure and Information Flow'.

## 1 Characteristics and Orientation of Israeli Prison Policy

In *physical* terms, the Israeli prison system is characterized by overcrowding and poor conditions. Such conditions do not facilitate enlightened employment policies. At the time of the establishment of the independent state in 1948 it was believed that crime (particularly among Jews) would not be a problem, and a single prison held over from the period of the British Mandate, with a maximum capacity of 120 inmates, was thought to be sufficient to meet the penal needs of the new state (Eaton, 1964). The figure in fact reached a peak of nearly 10,000 in 1993, although it subsequently declined[2] to below 8,000 (Israel Prison Service, 1996: 45, 48 (H)[3]). Even if security prisoners and pre-trial detainees are discounted from this, the number of convicted 'criminal' inmates exceeds 5,000 (State Comptroller, 1996; Israel Prison Service, 1996: 49).[4] For a country with a population approximating 5 million, the number of prisoners is high. Inmates have been housed mainly in Tegart forts built by the Mandatory authorities (Shavitt, 1998: 278). The first purpose-built prison has only recently been constructed.

In *ideological* terms, the history of prison development and indeed of Israel's criminal justice system in general has been characterized by a perpetual tension between an orientation towards *rehabilitation* and concerns for *security*. In the 1950s, when Israel's penal and social policies were strongly welfarist in orientation (Sebba, 1996a), a penologist with rabbinical qualifications (Dr

2  The reduction was achieved, inter alia, by means of a law providing for administrative release when the maximum capacity of the prisons was reached. Further, more than 2,000 prison places were lost in 1995 when a number of installations in the occupied territories were vacated on withdrawal from these areas; and while many of these prisoners had to be absorbed in the prisons within the 'Green Line', some 800 were transferred to the control of the army (Israel Prison Service, 1996: 37–8E). By 1997, however, the overall figure had again increased somewhat.

3  The report of the Israel Prison Service is published with an English and a Hebrew side, each with its own pagination. Addition of an 'E' indicates that the reference is to the English side, 'H' to the Hebrew.

4  This figure, however, includes a number of Israeli resident security offenders.

Z. Hermon), was appointed to the post of Prison Commissioner. However, a break-out of security offenders in 1958 led to his demotion to the role of scientific adviser, thereby reversing the priorities.

Nevertheless, rehabilitationist reforms have continued over the years, albeit generally low-budget reforms. In 1954, a discretionary release system, on the 'medical model', was established for prisoners who had served two-thirds of their sentence (Sebba, 1996a). After the 1958 break-out, and after much deliberation, it was decided not to adopt a comprehensive parole system. However, prison rehabilitation officers are provided for under the Prison Regulations (s.51 of the Prison Regulations, 1978) and a Prison Rehabilitation Authority (focusing on prisoners on release) was established under a 1983 law (Prison Rehabilitation Authority Law, 1983). Further, legislation of 1963 provided that prisoners with drug addiction could be committed to psychiatric institutions and, while this legislation has since been repealed, a special rehabilitation unit for addicts has recently been constructed in the Sharon prison (formerly a youth prison). Martinsonian-type 'nothing works' scepticism, it seems, has not yet penetrated into prison policy.

As indicated, however, rehabilitationist policies have consistently been tempered by security considerations. Occupation of the West Bank and the Gaza Strip in 1967 did little to reduce this problem. Moreover, the development of organized crime in general and drug commerce in particular, as well as public concern with sex offenders, have created a demand for law and order oriented policies. These policies appear to be affecting the duration of prison terms but not prison conditions.

By way of addition to the rehabilitationist and security orientations, a new dimension has been developing lately in Israel's criminal justice system, namely a human rights orientation. This was given an impetus by the adoption in 1992 of two Basic Laws, which will be referred to below, as well as by Israel's ratification in 1991 of the main international human rights treaties (Cohen, 1992). Moreover, a system facilitating petitions by prisoners to the courts was already developed by this time.[5]

5  In 1980, the right of a prisoner to challenge the administration in the High Court of Justice was replaced by a system of petitions to the district courts: see s.62A of the Prisons Ordinance (New Version) 1971 (as amended). This transfer of jurisdiction was arguably a limitation on previously existing remedies, but appears to have

Human rights organizations have also been active, resulting, inter alia, in the dissemination among prisoners of information on prisoners' rights.

Finally, all the concerns of rehabilitation, security and human rights have combined in support of policies designed to develop *alternatives* to imprisonment. Such policies have been in the forefront of criminal justice legislation since the 1950s and, as will be evident, have had implications for the topic upon which this volume focuses.

### 1.1 *Legislative Framework*

The formal statutory basis for the functioning of the prisons, including the provision for prison labour, derives from legislation introduced by the British Mandatory authorities. The Prisons Ordinance, enacted in 1940, but issued in a New (Hebrew) Version in 1971, states that prison labour will be in accordance with the Penal Code, inside or outside the prison, 'anywhere in the country and in whatever work as shall be determined' (s.25 Prisons Ordinance [New Version] 1971).[6]

The Penal Code to which the above Ordinance refers, originally the Criminal Code Ordinance of 1936, but now s.48 of the Penal Law of 1977,[7] lays down the principle that prisoners are obliged to work 'in accordance with the Prisons Ordinance ... and the Regulations issued under it', and that such regulations will include 'provisions relating to wages and to the conditions applicable to prisoners working outside the area of the prisons' (s.48(*a*) of the Penal Law 1977). Section 48 authorizes the Release Board to exempt a prisoner from the duty to work (or to limit this duty) in certain circumstances, related primarily to health and rehabilitation. It also provides that a prisoner shall not be employed outside

---

made access easier – and probably more successful. Several hundred such petitions are filed each year.

6   The Ordinance also provides that 'Prison labour will be under the supervision of the prison governor' (s.27). Section 26 applies only to female prisoners and will be referred to below.

7   While this is in principle a reissue of the 1936 Code, there have been substantial revisions over the years of many of its chapters. This applies in particular to the provisions relating to the penal system, which were reformulated in 1954, and have been frequently amended since then.

state institutions except with his[8] consent and 'in accordance with usual conditions of work' (s.48(c)).[9]

Regulations under the Prisons Ordinance were issued in 1978 by the Minister of Police (recently renamed Minister for Internal Security) who is responsible for the prisons. These regulations incorporate a chapter (C) elaborating upon the duty and conditions of work. A separate and more detailed chapter (H), entitled 'Rehabilitative Treatment', in fact focuses on prisoners' work, again emphasizing the symbiotic relationship between work and rehabilitation in the lawmaker's perception. The chapter provides for prisoners who have served a substantial proportion of their term to work outside the prisons (day release) – one of the topics referred to in the Penal Law.

The base of this normative pyramid[10] is completed by the standing orders of the Prisons Commission (somewhat confusingly also termed an 'Ordinance'), a compendium of administrative instructions issued by the Prison Commissioner. Standing Order 12.14.01 issued in 1983 is entitled Rules for the Employment of Prisoners in Prisons in Israel; Standing Order 12.14.02 relates to the National Employment Committee; while Standing Order 12.14.04 is entitled The Rehabilitation Framework for Criminal Prisoners in Israeli Prisons. Each of these standing orders is several pages long (in the last case more than 20). Both the Regulations and the Standing Order (or 'Ordinance') will be referred to where relevant to the ensuing discussion.

At the other end of the normative hierarchy, additional tiers (or at least one such tier) have recently been added. While the Knesset, Israel's Parliament, was traditionally perceived as being sovereign on the British model, two recently enacted 'Basic Laws' appear to have constitutional (or quasi-constitutional) status, in that they purport to restrict the possibility of future legislation inconsistent with their content.[11] These Basic Laws may be relevant to the topic

---

[8] Since the legislative provisions are all in the masculine form, and the focus here is on male prisoners, the masculine form will be used throughout. (A brief reference to female prisoners will be found in section 3 below.)

[9] On the question of pay, however, see section 2.4 below.

[10] The metaphor assumes that the 'basic norm' is in fact at the apex: (cf. Freeman, 1994: 284, esp. n.69).

[11] In the case of the Basic Law: Freedom of Occupation (see below) the invalidation of inconsistent legislation is also to operate retrospectively.

at hand, since one is concerned with dignity and liberty of the person, and the other with freedom of occupation.[12]

The other additional tier refers to the international human rights conventions that Israel ratified in 1991. In principle, these do not form part of Israel's domestic law unless specifically enacted, although they may be expected to provide guidance to the courts. While these conventions (unlike the UN Standard Minimum Rules) do not deal with the specifics of the prison regime, certain provisions, particularly of the International Covenant on Civil and Political Rights, may be of some relevance.[13] Article 10 of this Covenant requires that persons deprived of their liberty 'shall be treated with humanity and with respect for the inherent dignity of the human person'.[14]

The content of the legislative provisions in general, and of the constitutional developments in particular, may be of practical significance, since prisoners are able to petition the courts, and do use this power extensively.[15] Observance of the law may also be monitored by the State Comptroller, both in his national audit and in his Ombudsman capacity (Basic Law: State Comptroller and State Comptroller Law [Consolidated Version] 1958).

It should be observed, however, that this relatively simple legal structure is complicated by certain variables that impinge upon the legal status of persons held in custody. In particular, the status of *security* offenders will vary (a) according to whether they have been convicted or are held in custody as administrative detainees, (b) if

12  Basic Law: Human Dignity and Liberty, and Basic Law: Freedom of Occupation. Both laws were adopted in 1992 and amended in 1994. An enormous literature has been concerned with analysing their constitutional significance and proper interpretation. (For a brief overview in English, see Kretzmer, 1992.) Case law is also emerging, including one decision relating to prisoners' rights, on the topic of freedom of expression and the right to publish newspaper articles: see *Golan v. Prison Service* (1996) 704.
13  On the possible effects of the human rights conventions on the Israeli penal system, see Sebba (1996b). A separate issue is the applicability of the Geneva Conventions to the treatment of prisoners in the occupied territories: see, generally, Rodley (1987).
14  Article 8 of this Covenant prohibits compulsory labour, but exempts 'work or service ... normally required of a person who is under detention in consequence of a lawful order of a court'.
15  See n.5.

# ISRAEL

convicted, whether trial was in a criminal court or a military court, (c) if tried by a military court, whether it was convened in the occupied territories or within the 'Green Line', (d) whether the sentence is being served in a military camp or within a prison installation, and (e) whether the place of custody is located in the territories or within the 'Green Line'. The status of a pre-trial (or pre-conviction) detainee is of course also different from that of a convicted person.[16] This differentiation is further complicated according to where the detainee or convicted person is held; for not only are pre-trial detainees often held in prisons,[17] but convicted prisoners sometimes remain in police lock-ups for lack of space. (In the latter case, the provisions of the Prison Ordinance will not be applicable.)

In this section we will focus mainly on convicted, non-security, prisoners serving their sentences in the regular prisons.

## 1.2 Main Categories of Prisoner in Terms of Employment

Information on the different categories of occupation in which prisoners are engaged and in particular on the relevant *statistics* is derived from the recent report published by the State Comptroller (1996), based on an investigation conducted in that office, and from the annual report of the Israel Prison Service (1996). The former source incorporates data based on two separate samples, and it is not always easy to reconcile the data emerging from the three sources.

The State Comptroller's first sample (hereinafter: sample 'A') was based upon data from nine prisons collected in respect of three months in 1994. It was found that 1,809 prisoners were employed, and this was described as 44 per cent of all the prisoners. The second sample (hereinafter: sample 'B' – which in fact appeared earlier in the report) was based on data collected between December 1994 and January 1995 in 'ten prisons within the Green Line and the Nitzan detention centre, in which most of the criminal prisoners are held' (State Comptroller, 1996: 111). The number of criminal prisoners found was 5,061, of which some two-thirds –

---

16 Conditions applicable to pre-trial detainees have been specified (for the first time) in a recent amendment to the code of criminal procedure: see ss.7–11 of the Criminal Procedure Law (Powers of Enforcement – Arrests), 1996.

17 See n.50.

3,411 prisoners – were found to have been placed in work, training or study positions. The Israel Prison Report (hereinafter: sample 'C') provides the identical figure (3,411), although it claimed that 'the number of prisoners employed *rose* during 1995' (Israel Prison Service, 1996: 51(E); emphasis added). Only some of these discrepancies may be accounted for from the context of the sources.[18]

The general picture emerging from these and the other available sources suggests that, in the context of prison labour, prisoners may be divided into six main categories.

1. Prisoners working for the Prison Service in service and maintenance work. This category accounts for approximately one-third of the prisoners who are described as 'employed', a classification which, in the Prison Service reports, includes prisoners who are attending training courses or studying. (See samples A and C.[19]) It seems that, at the time of the State Comptroller's survey, most of these prisoners were earning only three New Israel Shekels (NIS) per day (approximately US$1).
2. Prisoners working in building or manufacturing, either for the Prison Service itself (again, approximately one-third of all working prisoners[20]) or for manufacturers with whom the Prison Service has contracted to supply certain goods (a further 12 per cent[21]). It seems that the

18    In particular, the lower figure for the first sample of the State Comptroller may be partly explained by the somewhat earlier date to which the period relates; the fact that it relates to prisoners actually found to be working, rather than *placements* – and the report specifically noted that a discrepancy between the two was found; and, while prisoners undergoing *training* appear to have been included in all the accounts, the first of the State Comptroller's samples does not appear to have included persons *studying*. See on these categories the following text.

19    The English translation in this latter source, which has a figure of 36.6 per cent for this category, has (in error) 'Outside Prison': see Israel Prison Service (1996: 54(H)).

20    See sample A – but this purports to include prisoners undergoing training, here dealt with in category (5) below. These categories (together with those engaged in services and maintenance) are paid for out of the state budget.

21    Sample C has 17.5 per cent 'Sub-contract Work for Prison'. It seems that manufacturing tasks for the Prison Service itself may be included in the 36.6 per cent figure referred to in n.19.

average pay here would vary between NIS 4.20 to NIS 26.40, depending on the nature of the activity, but in the case of contracted work the earnings reached several hundred shekels per month.

3. Prisoners employed by outside entrepreneurs who have established plants within the prisons. Some 8 per cent of working prisoners fall within this category.[22] They are generally paid the equivalent of the national minimum wage. At the time of the survey, the average pay was around NIS 1,300, indicating that they were not working full-time.

4. Another 15 per cent of employed prisoners are day-release prisoners who work for various employers outside the prisons.[23] The earnings here are similar to those of the previous category. This system is described by the prison regulations as 'Rehabilitation Work'. In spite of the relatively small numbers involved, more of the prison regulations and standing orders are devoted to this topic than to the topic of prison labour in general. This may be an indication of the importance attributed to this arrangement, as well as the complexities involved from the point of view of entitlement, responsibility and so on.

The regulations deal with the minimum qualifications for such work, the conditions attached and implementation aspects. The main requirement is that the offender must have been sentenced to a term of at least one year's imprisonment, that he has served one-third of this term, and that there is less than 18 months left before the completion of two-thirds of his sentence (when he would be eligible for discretionary release) (s.52(a) of the Prison Regulations, 1978). One of the main features of work release is that the prisoners involved are held separately from other inmates (s.56).[24]

The standing orders, however, have added another category here. They differentiate between 'individual rehabilitation work', in accordance with the aforementioned prison regulations, and 'group rehabilitation work', also to be implemented outside the prison grounds, but only under the supervision of a senior prison officer. Both of these categories may be held in rehabilitation wings in the prison, but only those selected for individual rehabilitation work may live in a hostel.[25]

22   See sample C.
23   See sample C. The identities of outside employers, entrepreneurs and contractors appear in the Prison Service report.
24   Such prisoners are held in hostels known as Rehabilitation Houses, from which they have direct access to the outside world.
25   See sections A, C and I of the Standing Orders.

5. More than a fifth of the 'employed' prisoners are either undergoing professional training (4 per cent), studying in a religious learning group (6 per cent) or engaged in conventional school education (13 per cent). These forms of training are classified by the Prison Service as forms of employment and prisoners who are undergoing such training are paid for it.[26]
6. The remaining prisoners, approximately one-third of the total number of non-security prisoners, have no employment or other regular activity.

For the sake of completeness, mention may also be made here of a novel form of sentence introduced in recent years, known as *service work*.[27] This mode of punishment resembles a community sanction since the convicted person remains at home, and works at some form of public service in the community. However, such offenders must initially have been sentenced to imprisonment, and formally remain *prisoners*.[28] Supervision of their work is the responsibility of the Prison Service. According to the Prison Service (1996: 39E)), 1,700 prisoners received service work in 1995. The implications of this will be considered later.

## 2 Focal Issues

There are a number of topics related to prison labour in Israel and in general that raise interesting issues.

26  Sample C describes 450 prisoners as being 'employed' in education. However, a total of 1,185 are described elsewhere in the Prison Report as receiving either primary or secondary schooling – presumably on a part-time basis. (See Israel Prison Service, 1996: 41(E), 54 (H).) Sample C also has 201 prisoners in religious academies, and 129 in training, totalling 780 for the three categories paid to learn. (The same figure appears for sample B.)

27  This was introduced in 1987 by way of amendment to the Penal Law of 1977 (see s.51A ff). It is distinct from community service (governed by s.71A ff of the same law), which is for only a few hours a week, and is supervised by the probation service.

28  Since such offenders are not, however, physically 'under detention', the work imposed on them might raise problems under art. 8 of the International Covenant on Civil and Political Rights (see above, n.14), which predated sanctions of this type. See Sebba (1996b: 205–6).

## 2.1 Objectives of Prison Labour

This topic has both ideological and practical aspects, with implications for the other topics (for example, whether there is an obligation to work). It also has implications for deciding on appropriate measures for determining the 'success' of prison work programmes.

The primary legislation on prisons in Israel, the Prisons Ordinance and the Penal Law, does not address the objectives of prison labour, except insofar as these may be implicit in legislative policy regarding the granting of *exemptions* from work, as reflected in the provision cited above. The prison *regulations*, however, state unequivocally that 'prisoner's work should be directed as far as possible to his rehabilitation' (s.15 of the Prison Regulations, 1978).[29]

The standing orders related to prison labour are considerably more elaborate, and indicate that a variety of objectives are involved. Six aims are referred to in Standing Order 12.14.01:

(1) the prisoner's acquisition of work and occupation habits ...;
(2) the prevention of idleness and atrophy in prison with all its negative repercussions;
(3) the reduction of pressures and tensions among the prisoners and between the prisoners and the staff;
(4) the chance to give expression to talents, to a sense of creativity, personal ability and improvement of self-image;
(5) economic gain for the prisoner with the object of assisting him in supporting his family and his rehabilitation following his release from prison;
(6) covering in part the cost of the maintenance of prisoners in prison.

Most of these considerations, too, reflect, or are at least consistent with, the rehabilitation ethos, although the last one is more in keeping with a neo-classical, neo-retributive or market economy approach. However, this list of aims is followed by another list of 14 'basic principles', including the principle that 'the work of a prisoner will be directed as far as possible to his rehabilitation. Considerations of profit and income for the Prisons Service will not take priority, but the prisoner as an individual – his best interests and welfare...' (Standing Order 12.14.01).

29    Cf. also s.51 of the Regulations which authorizes the Prison Commissioner to make rules designed to help prisoners find suitable work *after* their release; this section falls under chapter H of the Regulations, entitled 'Rehabilitative Treatment'.

The Annual Report of the Israel Prison Service (1996: 51(E)), on the other hand, places the main emphasis on *managerial* concerns (cf. Feeley and Simon, 1992), designating as the primary objective 'to assist the efficient administration of prisons by reducing tension and providing useful activity'. The prison master plan of 1989 (prepared by private consultants) identified three main considerations: security, economic and rehabilitation (State Comptroller, 1990: 445). Explicitly punitive objectives are no longer mentioned in the official documents.[30]

### 2.2 *Work as an Obligation*

As reflected in the title of this volume as well, prison labour has historically been represented in a negative light as a form of slavery (Sellin, 1976), but since the advent of the modern prison in the nineteenth century as the salvation and subsequently the rehabilitation of the prisoner. Paradoxically, both approaches would tend to *require* prisoners to work.

In this respect, Israel is no exception, and under Israeli law all convicted prisoners (as distinct from civil prisoners, pre-trial detainees and administrative detainees) are, in principle, obliged to work. As noted earlier, the principle is laid down in the Penal Law of 1977. The Release Board (so called because of its role in granting early release to prisoners who have served two-thirds of their terms) may exempt a prisoner from this obligation (or restrict its ambit), where it finds one of the following:

(1) the state of his health necessitates doing this;
(2) the exemption or the restriction will be effective, in its opinion, to rehabilitate him;
(3) another reasonable cause. (Section 48(b) of the Penal Law, 1977)

As a matter of principle, it may be questioned whether the obligation to work is still appropriate in an age in which prisons are widely seen as a form neither of slavery nor of salvation; the need

---

30  Cf. the three main objectives of prison labour identified in an early Supreme Court judgment: 'The state makes prisoners work by virtue of the law – partly *as a part of the punishment*, partly to teach them an occupation to be followed on their release, and partly because idleness may lead to the breach of prison order' (Judge Silberg, *Ketib* v. *Governor of the Central Prison Ramle* 1963; emphasis added). See also Shavitt (1976).

to contribute to the prisoner's upkeep (that is, to finance his own punishment) is, in the light of prevailing market-economy theories, more likely to be cited in justification. In the context of the Israeli provision, one might speculate as to what might be considered a 'reasonable cause' for being exempted from work, in addition to factors related to health and rehabilitation. It seems that training and study, including religious study, are regarded by the authorities as forms of work (as indicated above, prisoners are paid for these activities), thus obviating the need for recourse to the Release Board in these cases.

These provisions and practices might give rise to petitions by prisoners invoking the principle of equality, whether by virtue of the Basic Law: Human Dignity and Liberty, or on the basis of rights traditionally recognized by the courts (Raday 1996). This could apply to a prisoner wishing to undertake a learning activity not currently recognized either as education or as religious study.[31]

### 2.3 Work as a Right

More frequently, the problem is the reverse of the above. As in most countries, there are problems finding a sufficient number of work places for prisoners, and a substantial proportion remains idle. The lack of available employment may be a cause of frustration for a prisoner who wishes to earn money.

This may equally apply where a prisoner is in a category whose work is remunerated at approximately $1.00 per day for prison maintenance, and who wishes to be employed by an 'entrepreneur', or to work outside the prison, for the statutory minimum wage. (Hence prisoners' grievances are often related to their classification, since this is the key to many other rights and privileges, including access to employment.) Moreover, many of those employed are only able to work for a limited number of hours. Indeed, the State Comptroller (1996) found that although the number of prisoners employed in the better-paid placements of contract and 'outside' labour had been increasing, between 1991/2 and 1993 the average earnings *declined*.

The possibility of legal claims by prisoners based on inequality of treatment was referred to in the context of *exemption* from

---

[31] It is unclear whether this should be classified here as a request for an exemption from work or a request to engage in an alternative form of work since, as we have seen, education and religious learning are regarded by the authorities as 'work', and earn remuneration.

work. A prisoner might alternatively claim a *right* to employment similar to that of another prisoner of a similar profile. A claim might also be put forward on the basis of the Basic Law: Freedom of Occupation, for example, if a prisoner wished to follow his own profession, or some other occupation of his choice, in particular if no other work was available in prison.

Some support for this type of argument may be gleaned from the case of *Golan v. Prison Service* (1996). The appellant was a prisoner who wished to contribute articles to a local newspaper. The authorities refused him permission on various grounds, including the formal argument that prisoners could only undertake 'outside' work if they were in the category qualifying for 'Rehabilitation Work'. Their refusal was upheld by the District Court, but was overturned by the Supreme Court on appeal by a two to one majority.

The lengthy judgment in this case revolved mainly around the right to freedom of expression and the interpretation of the Basic Law: Human Dignity and Liberty. However, the appellant also cited the Basic Law: Freedom of Occupation. Judge Matza, giving the main judgment for the majority, stated that, since he had found for the appellant on the basis of the Basic Law: Human Dignity and Liberty and the freedom of expression, it was not necessary to consider in depth how far the decision of the authorities was also in contravention of the Basic Law: Freedom of Occupation. He nevertheless expressed the view that 'as a rule, and within the limitations necessarily [following] from the imprisonment, *the basic right to freedom of occupation was also granted to the prisoner*' (*Golan v. Prison Service* 1996, para. 25, emphasis added).[32] He also specifically rejected the relevance of the argument that the appellant was not in the category of prisoners who worked 'outside' the prison, stating that 'this type of activity resembles a hobby that a prisoner may follow in his free time... It was not part of the usual activities of prisoners for the administration of which the respondent is responsible, and the rules applicable to the activities of prisoners do not apply to it' (*Golan v. Prison Service* 1996, para. 25). It is not

---

[32] It followed that any restriction on this right had to comply with the conditions laid down in the Basic Law for such restriction. The conditions were that the restriction was provided 'in a law appropriate to the values of the State of Israel, intended for a suitable objective, and to an extent not in excess of what is necessary...' (*Golan v Prison Service* 1996 para.25). These provisions have been subject to extensive analysis.

clear from this analysis whether the activity was nevertheless seen to be covered by the Basic Law: Freedom of Occupation;[33] but support for the applicability in principle of this law to the prison situation was expressed unequivocally.

## 2.4 Remuneration

The question of remuneration for prison labour raises many complicated issues. Remuneration is not only important for the practical uses to which it may be put and for the sake of enhancing motivation, but it also has symbolic significance in formally differentiating penal labour from slave labour. The issues to be faced include the following:

(a) the level of remuneration, and in particular whether statutory minimum wage levels should be respected;
(b) whether other legal provisions applicable to the payment of wages, such as taxation and pension deductions, should apply;
(c) on what grounds wage levels may vary between prisoners, and in particular whether these should be related to the status of the prisoner, the identity of the beneficiary of the labour (private employer, contractor, or the prison service itself), or the skills required by the work, as well as (presumably) productivity and hours on the job; and
(d) how the moneys received should be allocated. Possibilities here, apart from free availability for present or future spending, include contribution to the prison service for upkeep; payment to the prisoner's dependants, if any; compulsory saving until release from prison; and payment of compensation to victims.

Relatively little attention appears to have been devoted to these issues in Israel, at least insofar as they are reflected in the formal norms. The drafters of the Penal Law indicated their awareness of

33  If the journalistic activity were merely a hobby, its protection may have been unconnected to the freedom of occupation. On the other hand, the Basic Law refers to the freedom of 'activity', and the judgment of Judge Matza used the same expression when applying to the appellant's hobby. It should also be noted that, when the appellant had written newspaper articles on an earlier occasion, when held in another prison, he had been paid for this, so that, in any case, the decision would seem to have relevance to a prisoner's right to earnings.

the problems by specifying that 'regulations [issued by virtue of the Prisons Ordinance] will include provisions relating to remuneration' (s.48(a) of the Penal Law 1977).[34]

The Minister of Police,[35] however, implemented this mandate in a somewhat laconic regulation. Only one prison regulation deals with remuneration. Section 16 of the Prison Regulations, 1978 states: 'Every prisoner will receive remuneration for his work. The rate of remuneration and its form will be determined by the [Prison] Commissioner.'[36]

The general remuneration policy, presented above, requires outside employers to pay prisoners the statutory minimum wage. Such an obligation seems also to be implicit in the provision, cited earlier, which specified that employment outside state institutions should comply with the 'usual conditions of work'.[37] However, in a series of recent cases, Judge Baizer of the Tel-Aviv District Court held that the statutory minimum wage was not binding either in the case of prisoners employed on the premises by private employers or in the case of prisoners working outside as part of their rehabilitation programme.[38] The judge specified four grounds for his decision: (1) there was no express reference in the legislative provisions to this requirement, unlike that of compliance with the law applying to hours of work;[39] (2) the main objective of prison labour was rehabilitation rather than earning a wage; (3) there was a statutory provision which specified that the rate of remuneration will be

34  The other area specified in this provision for which regulations were mandated related to the working conditions of prisoners employed outside the prisons.
35  At the time the regulations were issued, the minister responsible in fact bore the title of Minister of the Interior.
36  Perhaps the rather unusual full stop appearing here, splitting the regulation into two sentences, serves to comply with the requirement of including 'provisions' on this matter!
37  See n.9 and accompanying text.
38  See petitions 198/97 (*Hazan*), 2143/97 (*Gutman*) and 2258/97 (*Turgeman*). These cases focused upon the practice whereby lower wages were paid during the initial months of employment, which was supposedly a training period. While approving this system, the judge condemned its alleged abuse, whereby prisoners were sometimes dismissed at the end of this training period, and subsequently re-employed, so as to maintain the low levels of pay.
39  See section 2.5, below.

determined by the Prison Commissioner – and this applied also to private plants; (4) incentives were required to encourage private contractors to employ prisoners.[40]

The payment of a paltry wage might arguably be challenged not only on the basis of the 'usual conditions' provision, but also on the basis of Israel's quasi-constitution. Such payment, or indeed the inability to provide any work or payment, is arguably an infringement of human dignity, and thus in breach of the Basic Law: Human Dignity and Liberty. However, Professor Aharon Barak, the President of Israel's Supreme Court and the most articulate exponent of the significance of the Basic Law, has expressed the view that social rights are not included in the concept of human dignity (Barak, 1994).

### 2.5 Legal Status

Apart from the matter of remuneration, other legal questions arise in the context of prison labour. The prison regulations specify that the Hours of Work and Rest Law of 1951 applies to prison labour.[41] However, a decision of the Israel Supreme Court in the 1960s held that no employer–employee relationship was created between the state and the prisoner, and that the prisoner was not therefore entitled to a vacation under the provisions of the Annual Vacation Law of 1951.[42]

This issue was raised again more recently in the Tel-Aviv District Court in the context of a prisoner employed by a private

40 See also the discussion in section 2.5 of vacation-redemption payments.
41 Section 14 of the Prison Regulations of 1978 states: 'The [Prison] Commissioner will determine the hours of work and rest of prisoners subject to the provisions of the Hours of Work and Rest Law, 1951.'
42 See *Ketib* v. *Governor of the Central Prison Ramle* (1963). The prisoner's request was to be relieved of his working obligations for the duration of the vacation – not to be absent from the prison. Judge Silberg, in denying the petition, held that the prison's working status derived from the law, and could not be construed as being contractual – even as a 'coerced contract' (ibid.: 2413; cf. an apparent misinterpretation of this point in the judgment in the *Ashkenazi* case discussed below (see n.43), where the *Ketib* case was said to have held that the relationship between prisoner and authorities *was* that of a coerced contract).

entrepreneur.[43] The prisoner claimed that, after being employed for 17 months in a privately owned plant, he was entitled to a 'vacation-redemption payment', such as he had received in the course of earlier prison employment. It appeared, however, that the Prison Service, which had difficulty in finding employment for prisoners in the private sector, had, in their agreements with employers, exempted them from making such payments. (The court assumed that the authorities had taken into account the earlier Supreme Court ruling regarding the absence of an employer–employee relationship.) The petitioner argued that he was legally entitled to such payment on the basis of s.48(c) of the Penal Law, which states that persons employed 'outside the state institutions' will be subject to 'accepted working conditions'.[44]

In her judgment, Judge Serota noted that the 1960s precedent was not relevant, since the present case related to a private employer. She also observed that the paying for vacations would create a positive relationship with the prisoners and that the expression 'accepted working conditions' was wide enough to incorporate the 'social idea' of an annual holiday. She nevertheless dismissed the petition, mainly on the grounds that the exemption granted to the entrepreneurs had been necessary as an incentive for their participation, while the alternative of placing the financial burden on the prison authorities would amount to discrimination against prisoners working in prison-related jobs, who would not be entitled to such remuneration.[45] This argument seems problematical, since (a)

43   *Ashkenazi v. Prison Service* (1992) 187. The petition was also directed at the employer plant, but the latter was not called upon to respond, since the procedure was by way of petition under s.62A of the Prisons Ordinance (see n.5), which only makes provision for petitions to be brought against official bodies.

44   The sub-section reads as follows: 'A prisoner shall not be employed outside the state institutions except with his consent and in accordance with accepted working conditions.' 'Outside the state institutions' presumably relates to the identity of the employer rather the physical location, and is thus applicable also to work for entrepreneurs *within* the prison walls.

45   Two additional and more formal arguments appear in Judge Serota's judgment (although it is unclear whether they, too, form part of the *ratio decidendi* of the case): (a) not all working persons are entitled to vacations: take contractors and independent persons, for instance; and (b) the true aim of the Annual Vacation Law is to grant

prisoners working for the entrepreneurs in any case receive higher wages, so that the issue of vacation payments is a secondary issue in the context of arguments based on discrimination; and (b) the *status*-related discrimination rejected by the court, that is the granting of preferential rights to prisoners working in non-state institutions, is mandated expressly by the wording of the legislation, which applies exclusively to this category of prisoner.

On a related topic, the question arises whether and to what extent the *work safety laws* apply to prison labour. While some of the provisions of these laws refer to 'places of work', others refer to 'employers' and 'employees' which, as we have seen, are of doubtful applicability in this context. Even the term 'plant', employed in the context of the requirement of safety committees under the Work Supervision Organisation Law of 1954, raises some problems, in view of the somewhat enigmatic character of its definition.[46]

Underlying the 1996 Report of the State Comptroller was the assumption that the work safety laws were applicable to prison employment,[47] and public policy would surely dictate their observance, whatever the conclusions emerging from a formal legal analysis. The Work Supervision Organisation Regulations (Safety Plan) of 1984 require any plant which has more than 100 workers to have a safety plan and other safety-related programmes (safety training, for instance). The internal requirements of the Prison Service appear from the State Comptroller's report to have been more limited, and the records suggested that the instruction for committees of safety to be established, and to meet at least once in three months, seem to have been followed only partially. The State Comptroller also noted deficiencies in the collection of data on work accidents

    vacations, and not to make vacation-redemption payments: 'A vacation-redemption payment is given [only] after a minimal number of vacation days has been taken.'

46  Section 9 of that law refers to the Work Safety Ordinance [New Version], 1970, for a definition of this term. Section 2 of that Ordinance provides a detailed definition, culminating in the following conditions:
(1) The plant functions by way of occupation or for the sake of earning;
(2) If wage-earners are employed there, their employer has the right of approach or the right of control.'

47  Support for this principle is also found in the judgment of Judge Baizer in the *Hazan* case cited above.

and in the preparation of reports for consideration by the legal department.

## 2.6 Administration of the System: Structure and Information Flow

In practical terms, prison conditions may be less affected by legal issues than by the manner in which the system is administered. Historically, more attention has indeed been devoted to these aspects.

It will be recalled that, while the early nineteenth-century prisons placed great emphasis on the working habits of prisoners (Rothman, 1971; Foucault, 1977), the positivist school which developed subsequently set great store by the application of scientific methods in planning the prison regime – in particular, by means of the classification of offenders. In this context they adopted a 'medical model', involving diagnostic and treatment methods which, it was believed, would bring about positive change in the prisoner's conduct and personality (Grunhut, 1948).

The latter approach is reflected in the Prison Commissioner's standing orders for the organization of prison labour in Israel, but not in the reality of the system. Two standing orders are devoted to the organization of the system, the first laying emphasis on the processes involved (as well as the criteria), the second concerned exclusively with the constitution and functioning of one of the committees involved (the National Employment Committee).[48] An account of the process, as laid down in the standing orders, will follow, laying emphasis on the identities and functions of the agencies designated as having a role under these orders, and on the high level of organizational bureaucracy implicit therein.

The list of six objectives of prison labour in Standing Order 12.14.01 (section D) is followed by the 14 principles upon which it is based (section E), and a ninefold classification of prison labour (section F). Section G then elaborates the first stages in the classification process. This section provides for a 'Framework for Occupational Diagnosis' to be operated in conjunction with the Ministry of Labour and Welfare at three prison locations: for adult males, young prisoners and female prisoners, respectively. Adult males are to be processed at the Diagnosis and Classification Centre at the Ramle Detention Centre.

The same section of the standing orders provides that there will be a National Classification Committee which will receive up-to-

---

48  See Standing Orders 12.14.01 and 12.14.02.

date information from the Department of Employment (of the Prison Service) regarding the types of occupation required by the plants in the prisons, so that that their needs may be considered when prisoners are classified. The Diagnosis and Classification Centre will record employment-related information on each prisoner, which will be presented to the National Classification Committee.

Section H of the standing orders lists 12 factors which are to be taken into consideration in determining the employment placement of the individual prisoner. These relate mainly to the prisoner's personal profile, including the findings of his 'occupational diagnosis', as well as to prison needs. The decision, according to section I of the standing orders, will be taken by the Reception and Placement Committee of the prison. (This section mentions the recommendations of the National Classification Committee and the findings of the occupational diagnosis 'if one has been carried out' as the basis of the placement.) Provision is also made here for applications on the part of officials to change the placement, and for follow-up reviews at least once in six months. The Employment Officer of the prison is made responsible for the implementation of the decisions of the (Reception and Placement) Committee.

While the criteria referred to above apply to placements in general, special provisions apply to placement with private entrepreneurs (section I(6) of the standing orders) and to prisoners in certain wings of the prisons (section J). Section K lists the responsibilities of the Department of Employment (preparation of new projects, contact with prison governors, contact with employment officers, gathering data on the employment structure of the prisons, and contacts with Prisoner Administration regarding transfer of information, development of new types of employment, criteria for the placement of prisoners and so on). The section also specifies the responsibilities of the Prison Directorate: placement of prisoners in types of employment according to the standing orders, day-to-day management of the employment system, implementation of agreements with the entrepreneurs, and so on. Finally, section L purports to allocate responsibility for the implementation of different aspects of the order to different authorities within the prison system.

In addition to all the above, section K.2 provides that the allocation of responsibility between Financial Administration and Prisoner Administration on the topic of employment is the subject of another standing order.

Standing Order (12.14.02) specifies the structure and functions of the National Employment Committee. Its general purpose (section A) is the direction and development of projects, while its functions (section D) include providing guidelines to the employment department as to the types of plant and the work appropriate for the employment of prisoners. Other provisions relate to its procedures (that it must meet at least once a month), the factors it should take into account and its decision-making process. An Appendix of more than five pages lays down the procedures for preparing prisoner employment projects and their approval.

The 1996 Report of the State Comptroller, while it makes reference to the standing orders, also notes that, in the wake of the 1989 Master Plan, a Steering Committee was established, comprising representatives of the police and the prisons. This committee submitted its report in 1991 adopting the Master Plan, which emphasized the need for the provision of appropriate employment and training, and for the flow of information on prisoners' skills and preferences and on the numbers able to participate in manufacturing work or professional employment outside the prisons.

The system which the above provisions purport to establish seems to combine elements of a nineteenth century positivist belief in professionalization and centralization of the correctional system, a Foucauldian account of information control and a Kafkaesque bureaucracy. On the other hand, and perhaps not surprisingly in view of the complexity of the structure created, the reality bore scant similarity to the system that the standing orders were designed to create. This was revealed by the investigation conducted by the State Comptroller (1996), during the period March–July 1995 at the administrative offices of the Prison Commission and at a number of prisons.

The State Comptroller's report found that the joint frameworks for employment diagnosis were not functioning, that the information collected by the Diagnosis and Classification Centre was only partial, that the lack of data was an obstacle to the planning of appropriate employment and training, and that the National Classification Committee was lacking the relevant information when classifying prisoners. A Diagnosis and Classification Officer was appointed only in March 1995, and had not yet begun to classify prisoners at the time of the investigation. Further, there was a discrepancy between the number of prisoners referred to work and those actually working, but the data were not sufficient for the reasons for this to be analysed.

In four of the prisons investigated, the Reception and Placement Committees which, under the standing orders, were to determine the prisoner's employment track, did not do so; nor, in three of the prisons, did they conduct periodic reviews as required. The recommendation of the Steering Committee, to develop criteria for transferring prisoners from services to manufacturing, had not been carried out.

The State Comptroller found that the main responsibility for the functioning of the system was placed with the Employment Department, which was to be guided in policy matters by the National Employment Committee. This committee, which, as noted above, was obligated to meet at least once a month, did not meet throughout 1994 or up to the time the investigation ended (mid-1995); nor were any protocols located relating to earlier meetings.

Thus there appears to be a yawning gap between an almost pathologically detailed planning of the system of prison labour and a somewhat lackadaisical mode of implementation.

## 2.7 Administration of the System: the Exercise of Discretion

Whether the gap between the detailed formal norms governing the operation of the system and the somewhat haphazard character of their implementation serves to increase or decrease the discretionary powers of the decision makers, it is clear that considerable discretion is exercised under this system. This applies both to the wider policy decisions, for example to which employment facilities should be developed and, in particular, to the allocation of individual prisoners to particular facilities or to alternative options, such as training or study.

This topic is, of course, an inseparable part of a fundamental feature of the prison culture, the *classification* of prisoners. Classification is a routine part of the prison regime. In the present context it will be of great significance for the prisoner if he is classified as suitable for a better paid manufacturing job, on the one hand, or for a poorly paid service job, on the other. Frequently, classification assumes a more structural character, and is part of placement in a particular *category* (based on such variables as type of offence, term of sentence, recidivism and security risk) which will determine an array of outcomes, including selection of prison and type of employment (if any).

While the classification and even the categorization of prisoners appear to be universal characteristics of the prison system, these do not necessarily apply, or not to the same degree, in respect of the 'dynamic' (or 'vertical'), as opposed to the 'static' (or 'horizontal'), aspect. 'Horizontal' classification implies that prisoners are classified on entry into the system: for example, by age, previous record or type of offence. While this approach seems to be universal, how far should the system also be based upon the movement of individual prisoners from category to category ('vertical' classification)? Such was the ideology of the 'progressive stage system', which developed in the nineteenth century, pioneered by Crofton in Ireland (Grunhut, 1948). The assumption was that a prisoner would progress from the punitive stage of his sentence to the rehabilitative stage, thereby enhancing his motivation for positive conduct and contributing to the discipline of the prison in the process.

While much of this ideology is no longer fashionable, with the decline of the rehabilitative ideal and the support for a more structured or 'justice' model, elements of the old concepts or practices may remain. An implicit allusion to the 'progressive stage' model is found in the reference to the lack of criteria for transferring prisoners from service to manufacturing jobs.[49] The most notable illustration of the 'progressive stage' model in the contemporary Israeli prison system is the concept of 'Rehabilitation Work'. Here the law creates a category of prisoners who have the advantage of separate residential conditions (generally outside the main part of the prison), employment outside the prison attracting a real wage, and other privileges such as civilian dress.

While the minimum qualifications of eligibility for rehabilitation work are laid down in the prison regulations, there remains much scope for the exercise of discretion, particularly in the light of the limited availability of employment possibilities. Recognition of the importance of the topic and its complexities in terms of organization and responsibility for the prisoners' conduct when outside the prison is reflected in the detailed standing orders which have been issued; and, as noted earlier, most of the sections of the prison regulations dealing with prison labour are on this topic. Neverthe-

---

49   See also the account of incentives for 'prisoners who work with devotion' in a report of the State Comptroller (1989: 400). An early Supreme Court case was related to a practice of promotion from one employment level to the next, leading to an advancement in the pay scale from 10 to 40 Agorot per day: see *Atlani v. Prison Commissioner* (1962). In that case, the petitioner failed to convince the court that the grounds for his lack of promotion were unreasonable.

less, this remains one of the most important areas of discretionary decision making.

### 3  Special Categories

The legal provisions and the issues discussed thus far have focused on adult males who have been convicted and sentenced to prison for criminal offences. Space does not permit a general discussion here of other categories, on whom documented information is in any case sparse. Brief reference will be made only to specific provisions or salient characteristics of these populations.

*Female prisoners*  Section 26 of the Prisons Ordinance states that 'Women's work shall not be outside the prison except in accordance with a recommendation of the physician and in work that is appropriate for women.' This provision seems to combine the 'medical model' with a 'chivalrous' approach: for why should females be differentiated from males in these respects?

*Young prisoners*  The 1996 Report of the State Comptroller found that the training centre for young prisoners located at the youth prison had closed in 1991. At the time of the investigation, there were 58 minors (under 18) in the prison: 16 were receiving compulsory education and seven worked in maintenance. Thus most were not working, and no training courses were available. In the light of the report, the prison service sought to establish appropriate training courses and entrepreneurs who could provide work for minors.

*Civil prisoners*  Section 17 of the Prison Regulations permits the authorities to employ civil prisoners, with their consent.

*Pre-trial detainees*  The same section of the Prison Regulations applies also to pre-trial detainees if held in prison.[50] Recent legislation specifying the rights of detainees, whether held in prison or in police facilities, requires the detainee 'to maintain the cleanliness of his cell'.[51]

50  The Prisons Ordinance and Regulations are only applicable to the prison system. Pre-trial detainees who have had charges preferred against them are in principle transferred from police lock-ups to the prisons; but frequently this is not done for lack of space. There has, however, been a decision in principle to transfer the police lock-ups to the authority of the prison administration.

51  'A detainee will keep the peace and respect property in the place of his detention, he will maintain cleanliness in his cell and will

*Administrative detainees* For persons held without trial under emergency legislation (within the 'Green Line') regulations have been issued, consistent with international law. In respect of work, the regulations authorize the prison governor, at his discretion, 'to permit the detainee to perform at the location of the detention work which will be specified in the permit' for remuneration in accordance with the prison regulations. The governor may also permit such a detainee 'to do other work for himself'. However, as with the criminal detainees, the detainee is obliged to make his bed, and clean and tidy his cell, but 'beyond this duty, the detainee is exempt from working' (s.9 of the Emergency Powers Regulations (Arrests)(Conditions of Custody in Administrative Detention) 1981).

Other security prisoners, such as those convicted in military courts and held in military camps, are not normally employed. Indeed, even prisoners convicted of security offences under provisions of the Penal Law, who are formally subject to the regular norms applicable to prisoners, including the obligation to work, are as a matter of policy not generally *required* to do so.

## 4 Prison and the Community

Prison labour is, on many levels, a focal area for the forging of links between the prison, supposedly a closed total institution (Goffman, 1961), and the outside world. The link may be somewhat symbolic or indirect. Thus prison work is presumed to enable the offender to develop both the skills and the habits which will facilitate his rehabilitation on release into the community, as will any savings he may have accumulated as a result of such work. However, there are also more direct manifestations of the community connection, notably the system prevalent in Israel whereby industrialists establish plants inside the prison walls.

This is taken a stage further with the system of rehabilitation work, whereby prisoners, at an advanced stage of their sentence, are allowed to reside in the outer perimeter of the prison and travel daily to their place of work. In many respects such prisoners are at this stage more in the community than in the prison. They may, indeed, be able to continue in the same employment after final release. An intermediary position is held by prisoners who have not

> comply with the orders regarding order and the modes of conduct customary in his place of detention' (s.9(c) of the Criminal Procedure Law (Powers of Enforcement – Arrests), 1996).

yet qualified for rehabilitation work, but who are nevertheless permitted to travel daily to a place of work in the community. The prison standing orders require such prisoners to travel in groups, accompanied by a supervisory guard.

Such a linkage with the community may be perceived as being of significant value, for prisons have often been criticized as an inappropriate environment for any rehabilitative treatment by virtue of their isolation from the community in which the offender will have to function upon final release.

The prison–community linkage is taken to its extreme with the adoption in recent years of 'service work', whereby convicted offenders who have been sentenced to prison are directed to community employment without having to enter the prison gates. In this case it may be said, by contrast with the first example, that it is the idea of prison which is symbolic, the community placement being the reality. Whether or not this form of punishment is worthy of the title 'prison', its creation does suggest that traditional notions of prison as necessarily having the character of a total institution may have to be reconsidered. One element which in practice links this new form of sentence with the traditional prison is the emphasis on work; the arrangements for work in this case are a precondition for receiving the sentence.[52]

While some of the schemes described here have an element of *privatization* in them, this would apply to the use of private employers for prisoners on day release but more particularly to the entrepreneurs establishing plants within the prison walls; there have as yet been no plans for the privatization of prisons in toto. There has, however, been some involvement of private contractors in the transportation of prisoners to their work release destinations and

---

52    In the case of service work, however, the work allocated is designated 'public work', and is unpaid. It thus does not in principle provide the offender with appropriate employment on termination of the sentence. The legislative provisions on service work would also allow the courts to order the offender to undertake 'work for the economy', which would be paid (and could in principle continue after termination of the sentence); see ss. 51A and 51D of the Penal Law 1977. (Moreover, the latter provision specifies that an employer–employee relationship would be created.) However, the courts have proved unwilling to make use of this option, apparently because of a perceived absence of any punitive element, particularly during a period of unemployment.

even in their supervision. Proposals have also been made to employ a manpower company to assist in the placement of prisoners with employers, while other models of privatization, or for the organization of prison labour as a self-sufficient economic market, have also been proposed for consideration.

## 5 Conclusions

In terms of its own objectives, the development of prison labour in Israel still has a long way to go. Many prisoners remain idle, the majority earn paltry sums of money, and the fact that some are earning the minimum wage serves to emphasize the deprivation of the others, in particular insofar as the basis for selection of the 'real' wage earners is not clear-cut. Moreover, the provision of training programmes, especially for young prisoners, is inadequate. On the other hand, much attention has been devoted to the means of improving this situation, while a progressive programme of day release and alternative sanctions, whereby 'prisoners' remain (working or 'serving') in the community, appear to be enlightened innovations from a liberal, if not from a radical, perspective.

In terms of ideology, the developments described suggest a pragmatic combination of sometimes conflicting approaches. The formulation of the standing orders for the decision-making process with regard to prison labour and its implementation suggests a caricature of nineteenth-century principles of centralized planning and the application of 'scientific' methods of prisoner rehabilitation; but the involvement of private contractors for some of the administrative tasks involved suggests the recourse to contemporary market economy techniques.

Similarly, the development of programmes for work release on the part of prisoners still serving their sentences, while not entirely inconsistent with the nineteenth century model of the 'progressive stage system', appears to go far in the direction of diluting the 'pains of imprisonment' (Sykes, 1958). 'Service work', insofar as it is imposed upon 'genuine' prisoners, takes this process further still. Work, in this case in the form of community service, is all that remains of the prison sentence. This has practical as well as conceptual implications, not only for the meaning of prison labour, but also for the very notion of imprisonment. If, on the other hand, this sentence is merely an exercise in 'net widening' (that is, it is imposed on offenders who were not in fact candidates for prison terms),[53] the analysis would be totally different. Rather than revolutionizing the idea of prison labour and of imprisonment itself, it will be providing an additional community sanction to supplement the prison, enhancing the reality of the 'punitive city' (Cohen, 1979).

## References

Barak, Aharon. 1994. Human dignity as a Constitutional Right. *Hapraklit* 41: 270–90 (in Hebrew).
Cohen, B. 1992. The Practice of Israel in Matters Related to International Law. *Israel Law Review* 26: 559–73.
Cohen, Stanley. 1979. The Punitive City: Notes on the Dispersal of Social Control. *Contemporary Crises* 3: 339–63.
Eaton, Joseph. 1964. *Prisons in Israel*. Pittsburgh: University of Pittsburgh Press.
Feeley, Malcolm and Jonathan Simon. 1992. The New Penology: Notes on the Emerging Strategy of Corrections and its Implications. *Criminology* 30: 449–74.
Foucault, Michel. 1977. *Discipline and Punish: The Birth of the Prison*. Translated by A. Sheridan. Harmondsworth: Penguin.
Freeman, Michael. 1994. *Lloyd's Introduction to Jurisprudence*. 6th edn. London: Sweet & Maxwell.
Goffman, Erving. 1961. *Asylums*. New York: Doubleday.
Grunhut, Max. 1948. *Penal Reform*. Oxford: Clarendon Press.
Israel Prison Service. 1996. *Annual Report 1995*. Jerusalem.
Kretzmer, David. 1992. The New Basic Laws on Human Rights: A Mini-Revolution in Israeli Constitutional Law? *Israel Law Review* 26: 238–46.
Landau, Simha, Leslie Sebba, Bilha Sagiv, Ronit Nirel and Yoram Peles. 1994. *Punishment by 'Service Work' – An Evaluation Study*. Jerusalem: Hebrew University (in Hebrew).
Raday, Frances. 1996. Religion, Multiculturism and Equality: The Israeli Case. *Israel Yearbook on Human Rights* 25: 193–241.
Rodley, Nigel. 1987. *The Treatment of Prisoners under International Law*. Oxford: Clarendon Press and Paris: UNESCO.
Rothman, David. 1971. *The Discovery of the Asylum*. Boston: Little, Brown.

---

53  Recent research on this sanction (Landau *et al.*, 1994), while it suggested a degree of 'success' in terms of relative recidivism rates, indicated that a net-widening effect was partially operating, in that the profile of offenders sentenced to service work was 'better' than that of control groups of actual prisoners.

Sebba, Leslie. 1996a. Sanctioning Power in Israel – an Historical Overview. *Israel Law Review* 30: 234–75.
Sebba, Leslie. 1996b. Human Rights and the Penal System: Did the Nineties Produce Two Constitutional Revolutions? *Bar-Ilan Law Studies* 13:183–225 (in Hebrew).
Sellin, Thorsten. 1976. *Slavery and the Penal System*. New York: Elsevier.
Shavitt, Gavriel. 1976. Prison Labour and its Wages: A Review and Proposal. In *Israel Studies in Criminology 1975/6*, edited by S.G. Shoham. Jerusalem: Jerusalem Academic Press.
Shavitt, Gavriel. 1998. The Israeli Prison System. In *Crime and Criminal Justice in Israel*, edited by R. Friedman. Albany: Suny Press.
State Comptroller. 1989. *Annual Report 39*. Jerusalem (in Hebrew).
State Comptroller. 1990. *Annual Report 40*. Jerusalem (in Hebrew).
State Comptroller. 1996. *Annual Report 46*. Jerusalem (in Hebrew).
Sykes, Gresham. 1958. *The Society of Captives*. Princeton: Princeton University Press.

## Cases
*Ashkenazi v. Prison Service* 1992 92 (4) Takdin-Mechozi 187.
*Atlani v. Prison Commissioner* 1962 16 P.D. 2793, 2794.
*Golan v. Prison Service* 1996 96 (3) Takdin-Elion 704.
*Ketib v. Governor of the Central Prison Ramle* 1963 17 P.D. 2412–3.

## The Author
Leslie Sebba is professor in the Institute of Criminology and the Faculty of Law at the Hebrew University in Jerusalem, Israel.

# 7 Japan

## YUICHI KAIDO AND KATSUSHIKO IGUCHI

### 1 Imprisonment with Labour as Penalty

The Japanese Penal Code prescribes two types of imprisonment as penalties: mere imprisonment and imprisonment with labour. Article 12(2) of the Penal Code states that the sentence of imprisonment with labour shall be executed by detaining the prisoner in a prison and making him or her engage in assigned labour. Such prisoners perform most prison labour in Japan. Further prison labour is performed by prisoners who are obligated to work owing to non-payment of fines, as well as by those sentenced to 'mere imprisonment' and those awaiting trial, who are not legally compelled to do work but nevertheless apply to do so. Detailed legal provisions about prison labour are to be found in the Prison Act, the regulations and numerous standing orders.

Prison labour, as Table 7.1 reveals is performed by the vast majority of all Japanese prisoners.

Table 7.1: Overview of Prison Labour: November 1997

|  | Prisoners Detained | Prisoners in Work | Percentage |
|---|---|---|---|
| All prisoners | 50,755 | 39,405 | 77.6 |
| Imprisonment with labour | 41,595 | 39,080 | 94.0 |
| Imprisonment only | 121 | 117 | 96.7 |
| Pre-trial detainees | 8,842 | 31 | 0.4 |
| Others | 197 | 177 | 89.8 |

*Source*: Corrections Bureau, Ministry of Justice (1998: 66–70).

In 1997, the daily average figure of prisoners engaged in prison labour was 38,000. Revenue of about 12.6 billion yen (US$100 million) was generated by prison industry. The types of work performed at the end of December 1994 can be seen from Table 7.2.

Table 7.2: Types of Prison Work: December 1994

| | |
|---|---|
| Total number of prisoners engaged | 35,754 |
| Productive work (per cent) | 76.7 |
| Domestic work (institutional maintenance such as cooking, laundry, repair) (per cent) | 20.2 |
| Occupational training (per cent) | 3.1 |

Source: Ministry of Finance (1995: 85–91).

The 27,356 prisoners engaged in production in 1994 performed the various types of production work reflected in Table 7.3.

Table 7.3: Types of Productive Work

| | |
|---|---|
| Dressmaking | 20.6% |
| Assembling | 18.5% |
| Paper work | 17.3% |
| Miscellaneous work | 16.6% |
| Woodwork | 9.2% |
| Machine manufacture | 8.0% |
| Printing | 5.5% |
| Leather work | 4.3% |

Source: Ministry of Finance (1995, 85–91).

## 2 Prison Labour under Draconian Discipline

It is one of the strongest characteristics of Japanese prison labour that prisoners are forced to work under draconian discipline and inhuman conditions (Human Rights Watch, 1995). The daily prison regime follows a set pattern:

| | |
|---|---|
| 6h45 | Wake-up |
| 7h00 | Roll call |
| | Breakfast |
| 8h00 | Prison industry begins |
| 9h45–10h00 | Short break |
| 12h00–12h40 | Lunch |
| 14h30–14h45 | Short break |
| 16h40 | Prison industry ends |

| | |
|---|---|
| 17h00 | Roll call |
| | Supper |
| 18h00 | Free time |
| 21h00 | Sleep |

Prisoners work 8 hours daily, 40 hours weekly, except on Saturdays, Sundays and national holidays. The general approach to prison labour is illustrated by the *Handbook for Life in Prison* of the Fuchu Prison in Tokyo, which states:

> The most important part of your sentence is that you fulfil your duty of assigned labour. Prisoners who are sentenced to imprisonment with labour are obliged under the law to engage in the work to which they are assigned. If without good reason a prisoner refuses to work, skips work or demands to change the type of work, it will be considered as an action against that duty and severe measures may be taken. (Fuchu Prison, 1996: section 7)

In most prisons, prisoners are subjected to strip searches twice daily, when they move from cell to factory and from factory to cell, to check for illegal property. This examination requires the completely unclothed prisoner to raise his arms above his head and alternately raise each leg for the guard's inspection. (At some prisons, guards touch over underwear.) Many penitentiaries force the convicts to march in a military style to and from the work house or during transfers within the prison. They are made to chant 'one-two, one-two' as they march, swinging their arms to shoulder height and goose-stepping. In some facilities convicts are required to shout out the 'Five Principles' in unison every day before work begins (Japanese Federation of Bar Associations, 1992):

1. Always be honest.
2. Sincerely repent.
3. Always be polite.
4. Keep a helpful attitude.
5. Be thankful.

Prisoners work under constant and very stringent surveillance and monitoring by guards. They must concentrate on their work and are not allowed to look sideways or talk to fellow prisoners. They must work in complete silence. Making eye contact with prisoners or guards is strictly prohibited (ibid., 1992).

Violation of the rules results in punishment. There are short breaks of 15 minutes each in the morning and in the afternoon. The lunch break lasts only 40 minutes. Going to the toilet, acts such as wiping the sweat off one's face with a towel, or blowing one's nose are in principle authorized only during break times (ibid., 1992).

All the revenue of the prison industry goes to the national treasury. Prisoners receive no wages for their work, but receive a small gratuity that varies according to their work classification. In 1997, the average monthly gratuity amounted to about 3,905 yen (US $35) (Ministry of Justice, 1998). These payments are accumulated, and given to prisoners when they are released. A part may be spent to purchase goods in the facility.

Because prison labour is done as an execution of the sentence, the government is of the view that labour protection laws such as labour standard law, labour safety and hygiene law do not directly apply to prison labour. However, the government takes necessary measures so that prisoners in practice enjoy similar protection. Compensation is paid to prisoners for accidental death or injury. Compensation for death is approximately 1.4 million yen.

## 3 Compatibility of Japanese Prison Labour with International Norms

The practice of Japanese prisons forcing prisoners to make commercial goods for private companies has been strongly criticized in the USA and the UK on the grounds that it violates the International Labour Organisation (ILO) Forced Labour Convention. In June 1994, the Subcommittee on Asia and the Pacific of the Committee on Foreign Affairs, United States of America House of Representatives held a public hearing on Japanese prison labour practice (United States of America House of Representatives, 10 June 1994). An American who served time in the Fuchu Prison in Tokyo testified that he was forced to make commercial export goods for the Sega firm, under very harsh conditions including not being permitted to talk, look around or use the toilet without permission. He received the equivalent of only 3 US cents per hour for his work. Attorneys testified that in the USA use of prison labour for private companies is allowed only with the consent of the prisoner concerned. They added that wages were paid at a rate not lower than the minimum wage paid to the same labour in the normal labour market and that Japanese practice without such conditions constitutes a violation of the ILO Forced Labour Convention.

In May 1995, leading British newspapers reported the harsh experiences of a British former prisoner in a Japanese prison and that the practice of Japanese prisons forcing prisoners to make commercial goods for private companies, for a minimal wage, under draconian discipline and under threat of punishment, constitutes violation of the ILO Convention No. 29 (*The Independent*, 28 May 1995). The Director-General of the Corrections Bureau of the Japanese Ministry of Justice replied in *The Times* that a Japanese prisoner's work is mandatory because of the Penal Code and different from forced labour for private companies (*The Times*, 30 May 1995). These criticisms refer to three different things: unfair trade practice on the part of Japan, harsh treatment of prisoners and incompatibility with ILO Convention No. 29.

Article 1 of the Forced Labour Convention (No. 29) states that each member of the ILO which ratifies this Convention undertakes to suppress the use of forced or compulsory labour in all its forms within the shortest possible period. Article 2 defines the term 'forced or compulsory labour' as 'all work or service which is exacted from any person under the menace of any penalty and for which the said person has not offered himself voluntarily'. Article 2(2) lists forced labour exempted from the Convention:

> Any work or service exacted for any person as a consequence of a conviction in a court of law, provided that the said work or service is carried out under the supervision and control of a public authority and that the said person is not hired to or placed at the disposal of private individuals, companies or associations.

The production work in Japanese prisons mentioned above is divided into two types: firstly, operations for which a public corporation, The Correctional Association Prison Industry Corporation, provides the state with raw materials and sells the finished products, such as shoes and bags, that have been manufactured by prison labour; secondly, operations which the state contracts out to private companies and in which commercial goods are produced either in workshops in prisons or in workshops outside prisons and operated by private companies. In studying the problem of compatibility of the second type of production work with the ILO Convention No. 29, it would be useful to consider the arguments made at the ILO Expert Committee.

In 1974, this committee requested governments to supply information on the position of law and practice regarding the use of convict labour by private companies and other organizations. Since the general survey of 1968, a number of countries have repealed provisions under which prisoners could be placed at the disposal of a private enterprise. Other countries have indicated that measures have been taken to amend their legislation accordingly (ILO, 1979).

The use of the labour of convicted prisoners in workshops operated by private undertakings outside and inside prisons would be compatible with the Convention only if it were subject to the consent of the prisoners concerned and guarantees were given as to the payment of normal wages and social security. This became apparent in the Report on Austria (ILO, 1994) and the response of that country. The government of Austria argued that there was a vital distinction between the conditions of employment for prisoners in workshops operated by private undertakings and those of free workers: the prisoners have no contractual relationship with the private undertaking. The committee pointed out that compulsory prison labour was exempted from the Convention under a twofold condition: not only must the work be carried out under the supervision and control of a public authority, but also the persons concerned must not be hired to or placed at the disposal of private companies. It hoped that the Austrian government would soon report progress in raising remuneration and take steps with a view to seeking prisoners' explicit consent to working in workshops operated by private undertakings.

In Japanese prisons, prisoners are required, without their consent being sought and for a gratuity of only about 3,900 yen per month, to engage in making products for private companies such as Mitsukoshi. However, prison factories inside prisons are not actually run by private companies. They are operated by the prison and placed under the stringent supervision and control of prison guards. Whether in this case prison labour is placed at the disposal of private companies and, in the light of the discussions of the Expert Committee, should be considered as a violation of the Forced Labour Convention similar to the Austrian case, is an open question.

## References

Fuchu Prison. 1996. *Handbook for Life in Prison.* Tokyo: Government Printers. Reproduced in full in Human Rights Watch. 1995. *Prison Conditions in Japan.* New York: Human Rights Watch.

ILO. 1979. *CEACR General Survey.* Geneva: International Labour Organisation.

ILO. 1994. *CEACR Report on Austria 1990–1994 concerning Convention No. 29*. Geneva: International Labour Organisation.
Japan Federation of Bar Associations. 1992. *Prisons in Japan*. Tokyo: Japan Federation of Bar Associations.
Ministry of Finance. 1995. *White Paper on Crime*. Tokyo: Government Printers.
Ministry of Justice, Corrections Bureau. 1998. *Prison Administration in Japan*. Hosijiho: Government Printers.
*The Independent*. 28 May, 1995. British Prisoners used as Slave Labour.
*The Times*. 30 May, 1995. Prison in Japan.
United States of America House of Representatives. 10 June, 1994. Joint Open Meeting of the Committee on Foreign Affairs: Subcommittee on International Security, International Organisations and Human Rights and Subcommittee on Asia and the Pacific on Japanese Prison Labour Practice.

## The Authors

**Yuichi Kaido** is an attorney at the Tokyo Kyodo Law Office in Shinjuku-ku Tokyo in Japan.

**Katsushiko Iguchi** is an attorney at the Tokyo Kyodo Law Office in Shinjuku-ku Tokyo in Japan.

# 8 Namibia

GAIL SUPER

## 1 Introduction

### 1.1 Colonial Heritage

Namibia, known as South West Africa (SWA) until 1990, was formally colonized by Germany in 1884. In 1920, the League of Nations gave South Africa (SA) a Class C Mandate over Namibia and the policy of apartheid was systematically introduced into the country. On 29 September 1978, the UN Security Council adopted Resolution 435, which resolution was eventually implemented in 1989, and on 21 March 1990, Namibia received its independence from SA (see Department of Women Affairs, 1995). The apartheid system has had complex and far-ranging repercussions, the effects of which are still apparent today, not least of all in Namibia's prisons.

### 1.2 Establishment of the Prisons Service in Namibia

The first detention cells and lock-ups were built in 1898 and the Prisons Service was established in Windhoek between 1905 and 1907 – during the period of German rule. The Windhoek Central Prison was built in 1963 (Matongo 1995). The system of apartheid was entrenched in the Prisons Service of the former SWA administration and facilities and treatment were racially segregated and unequal.

With independence, a substantial complement of Prisons Service staff left Namibia and returned to SA. The Prisons Service headquarters were situated in SA and prison staff received training there, but this practice ceased after 1987 (Joutsen 1993). During the first five years of independence, the Prisons Service focused on restructuring in order to do away with past inequities, and affirmative action programmes were implemented within the Prisons Service. The name of the Prisons Service also changed from the SWA Prisons Service to the Namibian Prisons Service.

### 1.3 UNICEF Study

In January 1994, a study (Prisons Service, 1994) was undertaken as part of the Namibia/UNICEF country programme of cooperation. The study sought to assess the situation of youth in prison and was the first published study pertaining to the situation in Namibian prisons. The research team comprised representatives from the Prisons Service, Ministry of Youth and Sport, Legal Assistance Centre and UNICEF. The findings indicated that prisons, and particularly the Windhoek Central Prison, were overcrowded and understaffed. The physical layout of cells did not comply with United Nations standards, in that there was not enough provision of light, space, windows and sanitary installations. Prison staff were not only overworked but also lacked specialized training for dealing with prisoners, especially with regard to their rehabilitation. Prisoners tended to sit around in the courtyards during the day owing to a lack of trained staff. Moreover, there was a severe shortage of social workers with no more than one social worker attached to any particular prison; some prisons had no social workers at all and the Windhoek Central Prison had four social workers for over 1,000 prisoners. The Windhoek Central Prison was (and still is) the only prison in Namibia with workshops. Only a maximum of 100 prisoners can be accommodated, with the result that over 1,000 prisoners at this prison were found to be completely idle (Prisons Service, 1995). There was no central rehabilitation thrust, with directorates operating at a regional rather than national level. As such, vocational training and education were totally neglected and the sample indicated that prisoners actually lost literacy once admitted to prisons (Prisons Service, 1994).

### 1.4 The Ministry of Prisons and Correctional Services

A new prisons ministry, the Ministry of Prisons and Correctional Services, was established after the general elections of 1995. Its officials have been publicly outspoken in their emphasis on rehabilitation. A Prisons Bill which was produced in 1996 was passed by Parliament in 1998. As of 29 July 1998, the new Act had still not been brought into operation. However, when it becomes operational it will wholly repeal the South African Prisons Act of 1959. More prisons have also been established in Namibia, with the ostensible aim being differentiation of treatment: for example, the Elizabeth Nepemba Juvenile Centre in Rundu and the Divundu Open Farm Prison. There is no information yet on the impact that these institutions will have on the facilities available in the system as a whole.

## 2   Prison Labour in Namibia

### 2.1   Official Justification

The policy of prison labour in Namibia is rooted in the country's colonial history, in terms of which black prisoners served as a reservoir of cheap unskilled labour for white farmers. Section 40 of the Prisons Act 8 of 1959, which was repealed by the Prisons Amendment Act 13 of 1981, provided that 'any person declared to be an idle person' in terms of the Blacks (Urban Areas) Consolidation Act 25 of 1945, had to be detained in a 'farm colony'. A 'farm colony' was defined as being a prison where a black person would be sent to learn habits of industry and labour'.

It has been unofficially stated that the establishment of certain prisons in Namibia, such as the Hardap Prison at Mariental, was intended to provide a source of labour for the farmers in the surrounding area. Prisons in existence at independence were concentrated in the central, southern and western areas of the country, while the communal areas in the north and north-east had no prisons at all. The areas where the prisons were situated were, coincidentally or by design, heavily farmed areas.

In 1995, a ministerial task force committee made various recommendations concerning the hitherto largely ignored concept of rehabilitation, including that prisoners serving sentences of up to six months should be engaged in 'extra mural penal employment' as an alternative to imprisonment (Prisons Service, 1995); that prisoners sentenced for a period of six months to five years should work in 'open farm prisons'; and that prisoners sentenced for more than 10 years should concentrate on industrial training. It was further recommended that juveniles should receive vocational training and that prisoners who were elderly or ill could be employed to do work of a 'craft orientated nature'. Another recommendation was that training through 'gainful employment' should be provided, together with group work counselling, vocational training programmes and recreational activities supervised and conducted by social workers. Prison labour was perceived to be integral to the process of rehabilitation.

The task force committee also recommended that prison labour be used for the generation of income and that the prisons trade account be consolidated. This account would tender for the award of contracts on a competitive basis. Specific activities were envisaged for prisoners in gainful employment, including the supply of manufactured articles needed by government departments, the building of prison accommodation, the supply of labour to government departments engaged in 'development works', and the provision for prisoners' own needs such as food and clothing production. The task force committee proposed that 1,500 prisoners be employed on 'open farm' prisons, and that agricultural undertakings be initiated by the prisons trade account in the north of the country where 'farm colony' prisons were currently being established. Well-equipped workshops were also planned for these new prisons.

In 1997, an unpublished ministerial policy paper and mission statement, on the treatment of offenders, made reference to an alliance between prison officers and prisoners, through the slogan 'toil and sweat, service and sacrifice'. The idea expressed in this policy document is to instil in prisoners a 'working culture' so that they may 'understand that work, in itself, is a practical substitute for criminal activities'. At the same time, reference is made to the 'inhumanity' and 'unproductiveness' of allowing 'able-bodied men and women ... to remain idle all day'. The official justification for prison labour is that it should not be perceived to be a form of punishment, but rather, 'something to be proud of... work should not be equated with punishment'.

## 2.2  Legislative Framework

### 2.2.1  The Prisons Act 8 of 1959

The South African Prisons Act 8 of 1959, which was applicable prior to the enactment of the Prisons Act 17 of 1988, stipulates that one of the functions of the Prisons Service is, 'as far as practicable, [to] apply such treatment to convicted prisoners as may lead to their reformation and rehabilitation and to train them in habits of industry and labour' (s.2(*b*)).

The Act authorizes the Commissioner of Prisons to enter into agreements regarding the 'labour of prisoners' (s.75). The Commissioner and the employer are regarded as the parties to the contract, with the only proviso being that, as far as possible, prisoners should be employed in public works. The Act contains no limitations on the terms and conditions of the contract, and the payment of gratuities to prisoners for work rendered is discretionary (s.76). The option to work is limited to sentenced prisoners only. A prisoner is under a positive duty to perform labour, tasks or other duties as may be determined by the Commissioner (s.77).

Where articles are manufactured and can be supplied by the Prisons Service, government departments are under an obligation to purchase these at fair and reasonable prices that are determined by the Minister of Finance. The Act contains a proviso that the minister should ensure that competition with industries in the neighbourhood of the prison is prevented (s.75(3)). The minister may also order that certain work be rendered gratuitously if it is 'necessary or expedient in the public interest or in the interest of any deserving charity' (s.75(4)).

Women prisoners are prohibited from working outside the confines of the prison walls (s.45(5)). Section 77 of the Act makes it clear that a prisoner has no choice in the type of work, treatment or training assigned to him or her, and at the same time makes it obligatory for prisoners to be 'employed, trained and treated in such a manner as the Commissioner may determine and such prisoner shall at all times perform such labour, tasks and other duties as may be assigned to him for the purpose of such employment, training or treatment or for any other purpose connected with the prison, by any member of the Prisons Service'.

### 2.2.2 Regulations[1]

Regulation 141(a) states that 'intensive practical and theoretical training in suitable work which, as far as practicable, will equip and assist the prisoner on release in earning an honest living in free life', shall be given to a prisoner. Prisoners who are found to be idle, careless or negligent in their work, or who refuse to work, are guilty of contravening the regulations (Regulation 99(d)).

The regulations prohibit prisoners from being employed in a 'disciplinary capacity' in a prison, although they allow for specially selected prisoners to be granted a position of 'limited responsibility and leadership' (Regulation 98(4)). The Commissioner may order that a prisoner be segregated from other prisoners and work alone in his or her cell where 'such action appears to be in the interests of the treatment of such prisoner or the good order and discipline of the prison' (Regulation 98(5)).

The regulations provide for some basic conditions of service; for example: every sentenced prisoner is under an obligation to work

---

[1] Prison regulations promulgated in terms of s.94 of the Prisons Act 8 of 1959 by GN R2080 of 3 December 1965.

for a maximum of 10 hours per day unless the Commissioner, in terms of a classification scheme or course of treatment or otherwise, orders that a prisoner be exempted from work (Regulation 105(1)). Only work which is deemed to be 'absolutely essential for the hygiene and proper administration of the prison' (Regulation 105(5)) may be performed on Sundays and public holidays.

If a prisoner's earning ability is reduced as a result of an accident or injury sustained in prison, which was not due to his own negligence or fault, the Commissioner may, in consultation with the Treasury, grant to such prisoner an ex gratia compensation in money and may determine the manner in which such compensation will be controlled on behalf of such a prisoner (Regulation 107). A medical officer must certify that a prisoner is suitable for work (Regulation 105(2)(a)), and a prisoner may on the recommendation of the medical officer be certified wholly or partially exempt from work (Regulation 105(2)(b)).

A prisoner is prohibited from performing work for another prisoner, a member, a temporary warder or a private person or body without the explicit approval of the Commissioner (Regulation 105(4)).

## 2.3 Institutional Guidelines and Standing Orders

A prisoner serving a sentence of less than two years is classified as a 'non-board' prisoner and is placed in the B Group. Most first offenders who have committed crimes against property are placed in this group upon admission. Work within prison walls is limited to A Group prisoners, and a few selected B Group prisoners. There are severe limitations in respect of numbers. For example, at the Hardap Prison, where there was a total of 892 prisoners on 25 March 1996 (Prisons Service, 1996), five prisoners work in the kitchen, 11 work as cleaners and, depending on the season and the crops that are growing, 100 prisoners work in the fields (Gomelsky, 1996). A clean health report – which includes being HIV free – is a prerequisite for kitchen work. At the Windhoek Central Prison, where there are no agricultural activities, prisoners perform menial labour such as cleaning, serving tea and preparing food, as well as more skilled labour such as plumbing, mechanics, panelbeating and carpentry. The standing orders provide that where a prisoner has been allocated for vocational or other specialized training or work and is unable to be accommodated immediately, the prisoner should perform unskilled labour for the interim period (Standing Order No. 7: 12).

Working outside the prison is regarded as a privilege and only prisoners who have completed one-third of their sentence and are classified within the A Group category are eligible for this privilege. When a prisoner is paroled, he works outside the prison for a specific employer from the day that he is paroled until the expiry of his sentence. Juveniles and women prisoners are released on parole to their families only.

Prisoners at the Windhoek Central Prison work either in the workshops, the kitchen or the laundry. Women prisoners are restricted to laundry and limited kitchen work. Some women are employed as domestic workers for members of the Prisons Service. According to current gratuity scales, payment for work in the kitchen and laundry ranges from N$4.00 to N$7.00 (Namibian dollars) per month. Remuneration for work in the workshops is differentiated according to the degree of skill exhibited by the individual prisoner and the length of time for which they have been so employed. According to sources within the ministry, it takes six months to move from one gratuity notch to another. The scales range from N$7.00 to N$35.00 per month (Motinga, 1996). Neither cleaners nor agricultural workers at the Hardap Prison are remunerated.

No remuneration is made to individual prisoners who have been hired out on a daily basis, although a private employer is obliged to remunerate the Ministry of Prisons and Correctional Services by N$2.86 per day per prisoner for weekend work and N$4.13 for work performed during the week (Hübschle, 1996b).

During the week prisoners 'march out for labour' at 6h45 and return at 16h15 (Prisons Service, *Instructions to Temporary Warders*, n.d.). On Saturdays they return at 11h45. An hour's lunch is provided for, from 12h00 to 13h00. Fires in winter are prohibited and prisoners are enjoined to keep warm through labour. Prisoners are required to work continuously throughout the day, with no delays. They are prohibited from working with civilians, and temporary warders may only oversee; they are prohibited from working with the prisoners whom they supervise.

The instructions prohibit prisoners from doing 'schooled work' or from working with machines. Prison labour outside the prison is restricted to the performance of unskilled labour, with the only proviso being that prisoners are not allowed to work on mines and in diggings and are not allowed to carry heavy loads on their heads.

In a parole situation the prison is deemed to be the hirer of the prisoner's labour. The 'hirer' and 'parolee' sign an agreement in terms of which the parolee agrees to work for the employer. By signing the undertaking, the parolee acknowledges that the penalty for non-compliance with the stipulated conditions is a return to prison to serve the unexpired portion of the sentence and forfeiture of all remission of sentence previously granted. The parolee is informed of his right to file complaints against the employer, with specific reference being made to complaints about being assaulted or poorly treated.

The employer undertakes to keep the prisoner in his or her care or employment. The agreement prohibits the employer from paying the parolee in anything but cash. It is not stipulated whether this should be done on a daily, weekly or monthly basis, or only at the expiry of the parole period. Despite this prohibition, payment 'in kind' is a common practice. Sub-hiring of the parolee's labour is prohibited and the employer is required to provide the parolee with 'proper' accommodation, a balanced and nutritious diet, sufficient bedding and suitable working clothes. The prison regulations specify that, where prisoners do work that exposes their clothes to excessive wear or where the work is of such a nature that they may be injured, protective clothing should be provided by the hirer or, if the prisoners work for a government department, by the department (Regulation 155).

The Prisons Service reserves the right to inspect conditions. The employer is also under a duty to provide necessary attention to the parolee in the event of sickness or injury sustained by him and to pay for hospital and medical expenses. In the event of a parolee becoming ill, injured or dying while on parole, the employer is obliged to notify the head of the prison immediately and in the latter event to remit any outstanding wages and personal effects to the prison's administration. The employer is further obliged to register the parolee in terms of the Employees Compensation Act 30 of 1941.

The restriction of 10 working hours per day is reflected in the agreement, but it is silent as to overtime payment and registration with the Social Security Commission. Work on Sundays is limited to the performance of essential duties only, but the ambit of 'essential' is not explained and a farm labourer could conceivably have many essential duties to perform on a Sunday. The contract obliges the employer to return the parolee to the prison at his own cost in the event of a refusal to work, misconduct or the breach of parole conditions. If the parolee absconds, the employer is under a duty to notify the head of the prison immediately, to pay all money owing and to deliver all personal items belonging to the parolee to the prison.

There is no clause relating to liability for any damages suffered by a parolee during the parole period, although the employer is liable to the prison administration for 'any expenses incurred by the State' as a result of non-compliance with the agreement.

### 2.4 The Namibian Constitution

Articles 8 and 9 of the Namibian Constitution, which deal with respect for human dignity and slavery and forced labour, respectively, are to be found in the chapter on fundamental rights and freedoms. Article 131 entrenches the rights and freedoms contained in this chapter.

Article 8 provides that the dignity of all persons 'shall be inviolable' (art. 8(1)). In addition to this general provision, the article further provides that 'during the enforcement of a penalty, respect for human dignity shall be guaranteed' (art. 8(2)(a)) and that 'no persons shall be subject to torture or to cruel, inhuman or degrading treatment or punishment' (art. 8(2)(b)).

Article 9 prohibits slavery and 'forced labour', which is defined as excluding, inter alia, any labour required in consequence of a sentence or order of a court and any labour required of persons while lawfully detained which, though not required in consequence of a sentence or order of a court, is reasonably necessary in the interests of hygiene (art. 9(3)(a) and (b)). As yet, no cases have been brought to test prison legislation and practices against the Constitution.

### 2.5 The New 1998 Namibian Prisons Act

The new Prisons Act does not really change Act 8 of 1959 insofar as prison labour is concerned: for example, the function of the Prisons Service referred to in s.2(b) of the old Act is practically identical to that contained in s.3(b) of the new Act, namely 'as far as is practicable, to apply such treatment to convicted prisoners as may lead to their reformation and rehabilitation and to train them in habits of labour and industry'. Part 10, which is entitled 'Employment and Training of Prisoners', provides in general that 'as far as is practicable ... every prisoner shall be engaged in such work as will promote and nurture the training and industrial skills of such prisoner to equip him or her to manage his or her life in a productive manner after release' (s.81(1)(a)). In terms of ss.81(1)(b) and (c), a prisoner also has a duty to 'perform such labour, tasks on public works, and other duties as may be assigned to him or her by a prison member; and to keep his or her cell, the surroundings thereof and the furniture, clothing and utensils therein, clean'. A prisoner may be exempted from work or given lighter duties to perform on medical grounds. The Act also provides that a prisoner who is detained in prison 'pending the determination of criminal proceedings, pending the determination of appeal proceedings or pending arrangements for his or her removal from Namibia to another country shall be required to keep his or her cell clean, the surroundings thereof and the furniture, clothing and utensils therein clean, and to perform such other tasks in the prison as the Commissioner may determine' (s.82).

The Act makes provision for contracts to be entered into between the Commissioner and any 'institution, person or body of persons' for the employment of 'the labour or services of prisoners' (s.83(1)). The terms and conditions of such employment are as agreed upon between the Commissioner and the employer. Consequently, this section is almost identical to s.75(1) of Act 8 of 1959.

As is the case with the old Act, ministries and other government agencies are, in so far as is practicable, enjoined to purchase required articles and supplies from those which the prison service has produced or manufactured. (s. 83(2)). The minister has the authority to authorize specific services which are 'necessary or expedient in the public interest or for a charitable purpose' to be rendered free of charge (s. 83(3)).

Despite the ostensible policy of regarding prison labour as non-punitive in nature, the sections in the Act which refer to 'work' are phrased in the language of duties rather than rights to work. This is evidenced by the sanctions imposed for failure to work. A prisoner who 'is idle, careless or negligent at work or without reasonable cause refuses to work' is regarded as having committed a 'minor prison offence' (s.74(c)), the punishment for which could be 'confinement in a single cell for a period not exceeding fourteen days' (s.78(1)(a)(i)); 'forfeiture of remission of sentence ... not exceeding 30 days' (s.78(1)(a)(ii)); 'reduction in grouping ... or forfeiture of prison privileges' (s.78(1)(a)(iii)); 'removal from any earnings scheme for a period not exceeding three months, or forfeiture of gratuities ... but not exceeding one half of the amount earned' (s. 78(1)(a)(iv)).

Among the conditions for parole are that the prisoner must display 'meritorious conduct, self discipline, responsibility and industry' (s.95(1)(b)). Similar conditions apply in respect of remission of sentence, in that the prisoner should have displayed 'meritorious conduct and industry' (s.92(1)). The report on long-term prisoners must include a statement by the officer in charge of the prison on the 'work and conduct' of the prisoner (s.91(2)(a)), as well as by the Institutional Committee (s.91(2)(b)). As is the case with the old Act, the payment of gratuities to prisoners is discretionary.

Apart from these provisions, and certain general provisions in respect of probation, there is little else about labour. The Act merely provides that the minister may make regulations about the 'safe custody of prisoners when performing labour or otherwise' (s.124(1)(j)); the 'days and hours during which work or labour by prisoners may be suspended' (s.124(1)(q)); the 'provision and equipment of workshops for the training of prisoners and the supply of machinery, tools, or materials necessary for the purpose' (s.124(1)(s)) and the 'payment of monetary compensation to prisoners whose earning capacity is affected as a result of an accident or injury received in prison' (s.124(1)(ee)). The Act is silent about excluding female prisoners from working outside the prison.

## 3   Conclusion: International Human Rights Law and Prison Labour in Namibia

It is relevant to mention that Namibia has ratified the International Covenant on Economic, Social and Cultural Rights; the International Covenant on Civil and Political Rights; the Convention on the Elimination of All Forms of Racial Discrimination; the Convention on the Elimination of All Forms of Discrimination Against Women; the Convention Against Torture and Other Cruel, Inhuman or Degrading Treatment or Punishment; the Convention on the Rights of the Child; and the African Charter of Human and Peoples' Rights. Namibia is a member of the International Labour Organisation but has not ratified the ILO Convention No. 29 concerning forced or compulsory labour.

Current practices pertaining to prison labour in Namibia are not in keeping with the spirit of the provisions of the 1955 United Nations Standard Minimum Rules for the Treatment of Prisoners (SMR) despite official ministerial assurances to the contrary. It is questionable whether 'normal' working conditions prevail in the arena of prison labour. A court might well find that certain practices constitute a form of humiliating punishment for prisoners. The fact that prisoners are not allowed to communicate with members of the public while working outside is surely counterproductive with regard to the ultimate aim of reintegration into the community.

The present focus on manual labour does not encourage the development of skills; it provides little more than a reserve of cheap unskilled labour for callous entrepreneurs. Although the choice of labour is limited by logistics, the prisoners are not consulted about the choices, however limited, which do exist.

Prisoners are not afforded the same indemnification as free workers in the case of industrial injury (SMR rules 74(1) and 74(2)). Both the old and the new Prisons Acts merely provide for ex gratia compensation to be paid – at the Commissioner's discretion. Although the maximum daily working hours of prisoners are fixed in terms of the standing orders, it is questionable whether those prisoners engaged in work outside the prison have enough time for any other activities as recommended in SMR rule 75(2).

The proviso in the SMR that there be a system of 'equitable remuneration' (rule 76(1)) in respect of prison labour is disregarded and prisoners are only remunerated on a very basic level if they perform certain duties within the prison. This form of remuneration is not constant and it varies from prison to prison. Prisoners are not paid more for overtime work and have not been mentioned specifically in the Social Security Act 34 of 1994 which provides for pension, maternity and medical aid benefits. It is doubtful whether the prisons administration will register them as employees in terms of the Act. The prisons administration also does not provide for any form of release fund, apart from a train ticket, and there is only one halfway house operating in Namibia at present. Situated at Hardap and run by a non-governmental organization called The Bridge, it assists released prisoners in re-establishing contact with family members or with the necessary material support to enable the prisoner to purchase basic items such as clothing and shoes.

Women prisoners – a distinct minority grouping – are not protected by legislation, and as women they have fewer opportunities for work: women prisoners have no access to agricultural or vocational training and are trained in stereotypical and traditional 'female' activities which have little or no value in securing employment after release. Prior to 1992, women prisoners did not work at all and, in an attempt to alleviate this situation, UNICEF donated sewing machines to the women's section of the Windhoek Central Prison in 1992.

The practice of hiring prisoners out to private contractors is problematic in Namibia and is not carried out under the 'supervision or control' of a public authority as required by art. 2(2)(c) in the ILO Convention No. 29 (International Labour Organisation,

1982). It is disturbing that virtually any person, except an ex-prisoner, is eligible for appointment as a temporary warder, since this leaves outside prison labour subject to the control of persons who are not permanent employees of the prison system in anything but name. The appointment of temporary warders circumvents the stipulation in rule 73(2) that, where prisoners are employed in work outside the prison, they will always be under the supervision of prison personnel. Private individuals pay ridiculously low wages for the benefit of prison labour despite the enjoinder in rule 73(2) that normal wages be paid to the administration by the persons to whom the labour is supplied.

Regard being had to the above, prison labour in Namibia might well be said to be of an unduly 'afflictive nature' (rule 71(1)). Nor can it be held that the interests of prisoners and their vocational training are given higher priority than financial profits earned from their work, as is provided for in rule 72(1) and, contrary to rule 72(1), 'the organization and methods of work' do not 'resemble as closely as possible those of similar work outside institutions' (rule 72). The practice of hiring prisoners out to private persons with no de facto supervision leads to the exploitation and abuse of prisoners. Although there is a contract, its terms do not explicitly protect a prisoner's human rights.

In addition, there are no age restrictions on prison labour except for juveniles. Although prisoners can be exempted from work, or given lighter duties on medical grounds, there is a lack of medical practitioners attached to prisons: this could lead either to a delay in prisoners being declared medically unfit to work, or to a situation where this provision is not adhered to. The working day is also longer than that stipulated in the 1992 Labour Act (10 hours per day as opposed to eight hours). The mechanisms in place for the monitoring of conditions are inadequate. Once a prisoner goes on parole, the number of inspections or spot checks is entirely at the discretion of the head of the prison. Although the head of a prison is required to check on parolees, in practice, where parolees are paroled to farmers, this is highly unlikely.

The shortage of human resources within prisons makes it easier to occupy prisoners with unsupervised work than to provide education or vocational training. Although it is encouraging that the Ministry of Prisons and Correctional Services has publicly stated its intention to establish more prison workshops and to encourage more active non-governmental organization involvement (Hübschle, 1996a), consultation and transparency are needed for collaboration between the ministry and the non-governmental organization sector to succeed. Non-governmental organizations have not been consulted about the ministry's decision to establish new prisons and rehabilitation centres and, apart from the UNICEF study, non-governmental organizations are completely excluded from input on the administration and running of the Prisons Service. The new Prisons Act does not provide for non-governmental organization involvement and retains the characteristic secrecy of prisons.

In light of the escalating unemployment rate in Namibia (unemployment currently stands at 60 per cent of the total population) work is a scarce resource and the job market is extremely competitive. It is submitted that unemployment is a major cause of crime. There is, at most, an outside chance of acquiring a skill in prison. Moreover, criminal records will inevitably count against released prisoners and they will be at a substantial disadvantage when competing for jobs on the open market: the cycle of unemployment is likely to continue. It is therefore obvious that the environment inside the prison (where work is imposed) does not reflect life on the outside (where work is sought after). The afflictive and non-integrative nature of 'prison labour' is but one aspect of the contradiction. The question must thus be asked whether retaining the duty to perform unskilled work in prison is in fact penal policy which is conducive to rehabilitation. It is submitted that it would be far more 'rehabilitative' to expose prisoners, inasmuch as is possible, to life on the outside, inter alia, by encouraging non-custodial sentences. Collaboration with community organizations and non-governmental organizations, correctional supervision, furloughs, reintegrative programmes and the like are options that urgently need to be explored in the Namibian context.

In addition to the shortcomings in national policy, legislation and practice pertaining to prison labour, a specific international convention should be devised and adopted to deal with the conditions under which prison labour should occur. In this way international law can lay down certain fixed and readily ascertainable guidelines to give credence to the contention that work is an integral part of a prisoner's right to rehabilitation and not a sanctioned form of involuntary servitude. The 1955 United Nations Standard Minimum Rules for the Treatment of Prisoners are open to interpretation according to national conditions and as such are not always adhered to in a way that protects the prisoner's fundamental rights.

## References

Alexander, Neville. 1994. *Robben Island Dossier 1964-1974: Report to the International Community.* Cape Town: University of Cape Town Press.
Centre for Human Rights (Geneva). 1988. *Human Rights: A Compilation of International Instruments.* New York: United Nations.
Department of Women Affairs. 1995. *Namibia Country Report on the Convention on the Elimination of All Forms of Discrimination Against Women (CEDAW).* Windhoek: Office of the President, Government of the Republic of Namibia.
Gomelsky, Ulricke. 1996. Letter to the Legal Assistance Centre, Mariental. 7 March.
Hubbard, Diane and Andrew Corbett. 1993. *Namibian Labour Manual.* Volume 1. Windhoek: Legal Assistance Centre.
Hübschle, Michaela. 1996a. Speech to 'Workshop on Diversions for serious and Repeat Young Offenders' (facilitated by the Juvenile Justice Project of the Legal Assistance Centre). Windhoek.
Hübschle, Michaela. 1996b. Letter to the Legal Assistance Centre, March.
International Labour Organisation. 1982. *ILO Labour Conventions and Recommendations (1919-1981).* Geneva: ILO.
Joutsen, Matti. 1993. *Report on the Mission to Namibia.* Vienna: United Nations Crime Prevention and Criminal Justice Programme. 25-8 October, Windhoek.
Matongo, Crispin M. 1995. *A Special Message from the Commissioner of Prisons.* Windhoek: Ministry of Home Affairs, Government of the Republic of Namibia.
Motinga, Ben. 1996. Personal communication with the author. March.
Patel, E.M. and C. Watters. 1994. *Human Rights: Fundamental Instruments and Documents.* Durban: Butterworths.
Penal Reform International. 1995. *Making Standards Work: An International Handbook on Good Prison Practice.* The Hague: Penal Reform International & United Nations.
Prisons Service. 1995. *Rehabilitation of Prisoners: Policy as Envisaged by the Namibian Prisons Service.* Windhoek: Ministry of Prisons & Correctional Services.
Prisons Service. 1996. *Daily Incident Report.* Windhoek: Ministry of Prisons & Correctional Services, Government of the Republic of Namibia. 25 March.
Prisons Service. n.d. *Instructions to Temporary Warders.* Ministry of Prisons & Correctional Services, Government of the Republic of Namibia.
Prisons Service. n.d. *Standing Orders.* Windhoek: Ministry of Prisons & Correctional Services, Government of the Republic of Namibia.

Prisons Service, Legal Assistance Centre, Ministry of Youth & Sport, UNICEF. 1994. *A Study of Young Offenders in Namibia*. Windhoek: Ministry of Prisons & Correctional Services, Government of the Republic of Namibia.

van Zyl Smit, Dirk. 1992. *South African Prison Law and Practice*, Durban: Butterworths.

van Zyl Smit, Dirk and Frieder Dünkel, eds. 1991. *Imprisonment Today and Tomorrow: International Perspectives on Prisoners' Rights and Prison Conditions*. Deventer: Kluwer.

Ya Nangoloh, Phil. 1996. *Human Rights Report 1995*. Windhoek: National Society for Human Rights.

## The Author

Gail Super worked as an attorney at the Legal Assistance Centre at Windhoek, in Namibia.

# 9 The Netherlands*: Work in the Dutch Prison

CONSTANTIJN KELK

## 1 Introduction

It is no coincidence that throughout the ages work has always been an essential part of imprisonment. It has been recognized that regular work encourages a routine of order, rest and discipline, helps to resocialize prisoners, who are generally regarded as parasites on society, coincides with the age-old work ethic and contributes to the economic position of the prison. Think of the rasp and spin houses, which through the proceeds of the work (rasping wood for the paint industry and spinning) initially were able to support themselves completely. Discipline, resocialization, work ethos and commercial interest continue to reinforce one another.

After World War II, the ideal in the Netherlands was a new society with the worker as a new type of person who would distinguish himself by virtue, helpfulness and public spirit. 'Thereby human dignity, freedom and the person as a whole must be respected. Without freedom, virtue turns to compulsion, helpfulness to servility, public spirit to herd instinct' (Pompe, 1945: 39).

In a sense it is this same spirit which is reflected in the drastic reforms of the Dutch prison system that took place shortly after World War II. On the basis of the Fick Report of 1947,[1] the Prison Principles Act (*Beginselenwet Gevangeniswezen*) was enacted in 1953. This Act showed a high regard for the principle of

*Editorial note*: Penal labour in the Netherlands is portrayed in two chapters, one by Constantijn Kelk and the other by Miranda Boone, dealing respectively with penal work inside prison and work on the outside. This approach allows them to highlight an aspect of modern punishment which is often overlooked, namely the interconnections between what happens behind bars and what happens on the outside. These connections are as important in penal labour as in other spheres of prison life.

1  Report of the Commission for the further expansion of the prison system, under the chairmanship of W.A.J.M. Fick: The Hague, 1947.

resocialization, not only as one of the determinants of the prison regime as a whole, but also as a guide for other principles and starting points such as the differentiation of prisons, the social and psychological care of prisoners, education and the duty to work. Article 38 of the Act clearly states: 'Work shall also serve as much as possible to maintain, increase or acquire vocational skills.' For that matter, from 1937 onwards the courts were already able to send young offenders (18–23 years old), who were considered susceptible to improvement, to a special prison for juveniles where they could receive vocational training.[2] However, subsequent research revealed that, after release, the vocation learned during detention was relatively unattractive to these young offenders (Nijboer, 1971). Neither was there any greater work continuity than for a comparable group of young ex-prisoners who did not receive any vocational training during their detention.

The idealism of the post-World War II era did not remain unchallenged. In many areas, certainly not just that of work and vocational training, resocialization appeared to be too lofty an ideal. For this reason, from the beginning of the 1980's and onwards, this ideal was repeatedly redefined in more modest terms.[3] The age of neo-realism had dawned and was assuming more and more no-nonsense and businesslike airs. Nevertheless, the principle of resocialization has been retained unabridged in the new Penitentiary Principles Act (*Penitentiaire Beginselenwet*), which will soon replace the Prison Principles Act.[4]

In Dutch criminal law as a whole, however, the repressive and punitive aspects have become more prominent. There are more prosecutions, many more long prison terms and fewer short-term sentences (Moerings *et al.*, 1994). The concept of retribution, also sometimes called 'neo-retribution', has been rearing its head everywhere.

In addition, an entirely different development is also in progress: its objective is to arrive, by way of out-of-court settlements offered

[2] Since 1976, this prison has been closed, but there are now other types of prison for juveniles.

[3] In 1982, in the statement *Taak en Toekomst van het Nederlandse gevangeniswezen* (Task and Future of the Dutch Prison System) of the Minister of Justice; and afterwards much more fundamentally in the statement, *Werkzame Detentie* (Effective Detention) of 1994.

[4] The new Penitentiary Principles Act is scheduled to come into force on 1 January 1999.

by the Public Prosecutor, at pre-trial disposals for as many less serious criminal cases as possible and to impose alternative sanctions. All this points to the existence in practice of a two-track policy that the Ministry of Justice has been promoting for many years. For various reasons, including the continual shortage of cells (despite the repeated expansion of prison capacity), an increase in alternatives to the custodial sentence is very important to the ministry. Therefore the ministry has been supporting many projects providing for the implementation of work sentences or educational sentences. Such sentences may be imposed by the courts upon the recommendation of the probation service, which is charged with implementing the alternative sanctions.[5]

## 2 The Rights and Duties of Prisoners with Regard to Work

A fundamental difference in legal status between convicted offenders in prisons and untried detainees in houses of detention is that the former are obliged to perform the work assigned to them, while, owing to the presumption of innocence, the untried detainees do not have a duty to work. But if the latter do want to work, they are treated in the same manner as the convicted prisoners. In practice, an employment contract is concluded between the untried detainee and the governor of the house of detention. This is for a fixed time period that may be extended regularly. This prevents the detainees from being bound to a one-off choice of work during their entire period of detention. Convicted prisoners who refuse to work, as well as the untried detainees who breach the employment contract they signed, are subject to disciplinary punishment, for such behaviour is considered a disturbance of the proper order and discipline in the institution. But, in reality, what is at stake is mainly the organization of the work and the institution's obligation to deliver in good time the completed products ordered by its external clients. Furthermore, order at the institution is fostered when as many prisoners as possible have regular work.

The only exception to the duty to work is if a prisoner is ill. The institution's doctor must give the opinion that the prisoner is unable to work for that reason. In that case the sick prisoner will continue to receive sick pay. Those who feign sickness or sleep late may,

5  For a fuller exposition of these developments, see the section by Boone in chapter 10.

however, be subject to disciplinary punishment. The governor may exclude from the communal labour any prisoner who has reported sick or has not got up in time for some other reason. Essentially this means that a disciplinary punishment can be anticipated, despite the fact that it will not always be appropriate. The interests of the institution prompt this. Technically, if a detainee, having reported sick, is found by the doctor to be able to work, punishment is not allowed on that ground alone. Only if the governor in consequence of the doctor's findings gives the detainee an order to work and the detainee nevertheless refuses may punishment be justified. The possibility of a detainee refraining from consulting the doctor through fear of eventual punishment must be avoided.[6]

Many aspects of work, also the disciplinary ones, are regulated further in the case law on prisoners' rights of complaint and appeal. For example, the untried detainee is permitted to take along (limited) business records for the purpose of continuing his business (*PI*, 1986, no. 16). Remaining locked in one's own cell for not more than five days, during working hours, is generally considered a fair punishment for refusing to work (*PI*, 1981, no. 24).

An important question is to what extent the employment contract concluded by untried prisoners and governors is a contract governed by civil law. This question arose in the case of a prisoner who was punished after refusing to continue his work because a fellow prisoner had threatened him in the communal labour room (by throwing things at him). A warden watching them did not intervene at all, although the prisoner-victim requested him to do so. He lodged a complaint against the disciplinary punishment imposed on him because of his refusal to work and after that he appealed. The Committee of Appeal did not consider the employment contract to be a contract in the sense of civil law. Nevertheless, the action of this prisoner was judged to be correct on the grounds that he was not accountable for the circumstances under which he had stopped work and that he had prevented the situation from deteriorating: for these reasons, the disciplinary punishment was held to have been neither reasonable nor fair (*Sancties*, 1996, no. 26).

In practice, not participating in work in the communal labour room is not very appealing, since one must remain in one's cell during working hours and few or no staff are available to perform

---

6   See the judgment of the Committee of Appeal 22 March 1996, A 96/40, *Penitentiaire Informatie (PI)* 1996, no. 55.

services. On the other hand, particularly when the work is very simple, as is often the case in houses of detention, work is not very attractive either. Whether or not detainees apply for work thus often depends on their financial situation. Such considerations are only applicable to untried persons, for convicted prisoners must work. However, prison work for the convicted prisoners is not always of such a nature that vocational skills can be acquired or improved.

It is not always possible for the institutions to acquire qualitatively interesting work. Moreover, specialized work often requires sophisticated equipment. Nevertheless, some work of this kind is provided in a number of prisons, especially those meant for long-term prisoners. There are prisons that provide facilities for trades such as metalwork, woodwork, furniture making and electrical assembly that do indeed foster vocational skills, but for the rest the work is often simple, such as assembling plastic children's toys or electrical sockets. There may be waiting lists for communal work, so that simpler work that can be done in the cell has to be accepted first.

As long as enough possibilities exist, the prisoner may choose the type of work he wishes to do. The prisoner's background may play a role here. In one case the Committee of Appeal decided that, if no objections were raised, a detained hotel owner should be granted his request for a change of workplace, namely to be transferred from the sawmill to the plant nursery (*PI*, 1988, no. 45). In general, the prisoner's preference is taken into consideration and, of course, the right of complaint has a corrective function.[7]

Domestic tasks, such as cleaning the corridors, serving coffee, helping to serve food, assisting in the library, painting and working in the kitchen, are much sought-after forms of work. Apart from this, each prisoner is obliged to keep his own cell clean. The gradual disappearance of kitchen facilities from prisons, as they are replaced by outside caterers, has led to the disappearance of the traditional kitchen jobs, which is a great loss.

Those who apply for work or are obliged to work and cannot do so because no work is available are considered 'jobless' and are paid wages as if they were 'unemployed' people. In practice, a *right* to work already exists, although there has not been formal legal provision for it. In the new Penitentiary Principles Act such a right is expressly guaranteed.

7   On the key role played by the right of complaint in the Dutch Prison system generally, see Kelk (1991).

In the past the *working hours* in a number of closed institutions have been reduced to four hours a day (working block times) in order to provide for activities such as sport, visiting and contact with lawyers and probation officers. This has also meant that, during the blocks of hours earmarked for work, prison officers could refuse visits from lawyers, especially when there were sufficient other opportunities for this (circular of 7 September 1984, no. 811/384). In the future, the prisoners will work at least six hours a day, four days a week; that means 24 hours (or at most 26 hours) weekly. Commercial objectives will be pursued more rigorously than has hitherto been the case.

In penal institutions for *long-term prisoners* there is a regulation for work-free days, which makes it possible to take a day off (circular of 21 February 1980, no. 102/380, PI, 1980, no. 43). Staffing cutbacks, however, sometimes make this regulation difficult to implement in practice.

In *open prisons*, work is done for private employers for at least the minimum wage. Since 1980, it has even been possible for ex-prisoners, who had worked as prisoners in an open institution at the Post Office, to continue working at the Post Office after their detention (circular of 17 July 1980, no. 608/380, PI, 1981, no. 35). When a prisoner in an open prison is dismissed by his (external) employer because of problems at work, he may be transferred to a closed prison. This is laid down in the rules; also that the prisoner must be informed of this rule before beginning work in an open prison (PI, 1984, no. 55).

The question as to whether prisoners have the right to back up any protest on their part with a *strike* has arisen several times. In 1983, the Committee of Appeal decided that this was not the case, since there was no question of an employer–employee relationship, to which art. 6(2) of the European Social Charter has bound the right of collective action in the event of conflicts of interest (PI, 1984, no. 7). Disciplinary punishment may therefore justly be imposed on prisoners who strike (PI, 1984, no. 25). The prisoner also forfeits his wages for part of a working day which has been interrupted by a strike: the applicable wage regulation assumes payment for a whole day (PI, 1984, no. 77).

Where prison work is concerned, prisoners may have neither the status of employees nor that of public servants, but may not be viewed as 'slaves of the state', a viewpoint that, after all, was abandoned long ago by every civilized society. Since the point of departure, in the Dutch criminal justice system, is that the treatment of prisoners should be humane and society-oriented, legitimate actions for the preservation of one's human dignity deserve some consideration. This means that collective strikes by prisoners should certainly not be rejected under all circumstances, although it would be impracticable, in view of their exceptional nature, to draft rules for them. Apart from that, a weakness of the current system is that the prison governors act, not only as the employer–contracting party, but also as the criminal court. This is typical of the detention situation, in which the separation of the three powers of the state is largely absent. In the past, strikes by prisoners have not only led to disciplinary actions, but have also had a positive effect, such as in 1977, when a work stoppage led to the equalization of higher wages for long-term prisoners in different prisons.

On 1 September 1990, the Decree on Working Conditions in State Judicial Institutions (*Arbeidsomstandighedenbesluit Justitiële Rijksinrichtingen (AJR)*) took effect, while at the same time the Working Conditions Act became applicable in all penal institutions. The purpose of the latter Act is to promote safety, health and well-being at work generally. The *AJR* is tailored to the very specific situation in the institutions, so that a reasonable balance will have to be struck between the interests of the management of the institution in maintaining order and security, and the requirements set from the viewpoint of safety at work.[8] The question is to what extent the law on working conditions is applicable in penal institutions. This question arose in a case involving a prisoner who had doubts about the safety of a machine (for woodworking) with which he had to work: one button was held in place with gummed tape. In spite of the foreman's order to continue working because safety was supposed to be assured (the foreman had demonstrated several times how the machine could be used without any danger), the prisoner refused to do so because of his doubts. He received disciplinary punishment for this, although outside the institution the right to stop working does exist if, 'in the reasonable judgment' of the employee, there is a risk of personal injury (*PI*, 1995, no. 40).

---

8   See the circular of 9 November 1990, no. 34658 DJ 90, *Sancties*, 1990, no. 78 and the circular on the decree amending the *AJR* of 12 December 1990, no. 38100 DJ 90, *Sancties*, 1991, no. 14.

## 3   Remuneration for Work

The opinion has often been voiced that all working prisoners should receive the minimum wage instead of letting the family left behind depend on benefits. Among other things, this would mean a radical reform of the social security system (De Jonge, 1994). The Wage Regulation of 23 February 1948, which was considered provisional, is still the basis for remuneration. The prevailing remuneration system includes the granting of a basic wage with additional payments. At present one can earn an amount of about six guilders a day in this way. This has scornfully been called a 'tip' (De Jonge, in *Sancties*, 1995, no. 74). It is spent on purchases from the canteen (soft drinks, extra coffee, smoking materials, sweets and so on). The amounts involved are higher in institutions for long-term prisoners.[9] These amounts can be adjusted regularly by circular. A regulation has also been adopted to continue paying wages on recognized public holidays when no work is done (circular of 17 September 1981, *PI*, 1981, no. 57). This applies to the Christian holy days. In principle, Muslims are also exempted from work on the recognized Islamic holy days, but as yet no provision has been made for the continued payment of wages. Because prisoners who work in the kitchen in some institutions also work during the weekend, a special wage regulation applies to them.

The wages are deposited into a *pocket-money account*. (Except in open prisons and in prisons for those who turn themselves in, prisoners may not have money in their possession.) Money can also be transferred to the pocket-money account from the *personal account* into which money may also be deposited from outside. Purchases in the canteen can only be made via the pocket-money account; purchases that cannot be made from the canteen may be made, at the request of the prisoner, by the staff, using money from the prisoner's *personal account*. The amount that may be transferred weekly from the personal account to the pocket-money account is bound by a limit fixed by circular.[10]

In open prisons and the open sections of closed prisons, prisoners for whom no work is available from employers outside the institution can be obliged to perform household chores or work in other penal institutions for wages to be fixed by the Minister of Justice (circular of 1 March 1984, *PI*, 1984, no. 32). Prisoners in

---

9   This has been an experiment since 1977.
10  For the regulation of financial means, see arts 69 to 75 (III) of the internal regulations for houses of detention.

open institutions receive at least a week's wages of 40 per cent of the gross minimum wage.

## 4  New Policy and New Legislation: the Standard Regime

In 1994, the Minister of Justice made a statement to Parliament on a new policy for the prison service entailing cutbacks and a tightening of the reins. Although this was not expressed in so many words, it was clear that this statement was prompted by a strong wish to economize. The introduction to the statement, entitled *Werkzame Detentie* (Effective Detention), highlights the 'retributive purpose' of criminal law and the objective of promoting safety in society as the most important determinants of penal policy. The 'punitive nature' of the prison sentence will be safeguarded and safety furthered by a smooth course of detention, according to the statement. The 'essential precondition' for this is the humane and efficient execution of the prison sentence. This brief and concise credo appears to demand retribution as a goal in itself. Contrary to the opinion of many criminal law scholars, the statement implies that the demands of retribution are not satisfied with the argument that the deprivation of liberty is the essence of punishment, but that its implementation must serve individually and socially oriented goals. When the current prison legislation was drafted in 1953, clearly no room was deemed to exist for the infliction of *additional* suffering that went beyond the mere deprivation of liberty. It is evident that the retribution idea has been raked up in order to serve as a stepping-stone for an intensive programme of cutbacks.

Once cutbacks are deemed to be the result of retribution, the statement arrives with a hop, skip and a jump at the announcement of the introduction of a *standard regime* for all prisoners. The new Penitentiary Principles Act will provide the basis for such a standard regime. This standard regime includes a number of minimum requirements for the basic living conditions of the prisoners: 26 hours of work a week (this is an extension) and a shortened day programme spread over three days, which will best serve the optimal use of the scarce prison facilities and the effective control of the prisoners.

When the new Penitentiary Principles Act comes into effect this standard regime will apply uniformly to the vast majority of prisoners. Only a small segment of them (20 per cent has been mentioned) will, on the grounds that they have specific problems (for example of a psychological nature) or that they have sufficient motivation to break out of a drug-related criminal lifestyle or to follow education or vocational training, be given a different regime with less full-time work. Furthermore, the opportunity to perform more highly qualified labour must be earned by effort and diligence.

Work is central to the new regime: on a wider scale than has been the case up to now, work will have to be 'cost-effective' and remove the prisoners from the cell, so that there will be no more 'hanging about in the cell'. In short: there will be more emphasis on the commercial aspect, which is seen to bolster the no-nonsense approach.

The new approach will face considerable difficulties. One must realize that even today, with shorter working hours, it is very difficult to find enough work for the prisoners. Not every prisoner who wants to work can be given a job. The question is how one proposes to solve this problem when more work opportunities are required. In a number of prisons, experiments are already being conducted in this regard. Moreover, the prison service recently has taken part in the specialized exhibition of General Supply Companies (*Algemene Toeleveringsbedrijven*). This means that the Ministry of Justice had a stand at the exhibition to show what the prisoners were capable of producing: tiles, concrete feeding troughs, textiles, banners with the logos of popular football clubs, and so on. Another idea was the recycling of equipment (radios, computers). Orders were acquired at the exhibition, though not many (*NRC Handelsblad*, 3 February 1996). The business community will probably have to get accustomed to this modus operandi of the prison service. In general, the prison service is viewed as a competitor in the arena of sheltered employment with others who also have to rely on orders for relatively simple types of work. This makes the prison service an even greater factor in the labour market.

All in all, with the introduction of the standard regime there will be a new hierarchy of starting points for both the treatment of the prisoners and the organization of the prison service as a whole. Prisoners must prove themselves worthy of a more favourable regime by adjustment, diligence, motivation or psychological need. Only then can (expensive) resocialization in the complete sense of the word take place. The proposed new regime foresees that only a very limited segment of the prison population will be the 'lucky ones' in this respect (as mentioned above, about 20 per cent). In other words, the right to resocialization, because of the cost factor, must be acquired by way of a bonus–demerit system. The largest category of prisoners by far, if only because of their criminal past, will not succeed in achieving a convincing prognosis for a fruitful reintegration into society. Ironically, public safety would benefit most if something could be done for these unsuccessful candidates. Another consideration is the criteria for being admitted to a resocialization programme and who is in a position to apply them responsibly. One thing is certain: that writing off resocialization in advance for such a large group of prisoners (about 80 per cent) is more dangerous to society in the long run than at least risking a serious attempt at their reintegration, even if it does not seem very promising. One should not underestimate the extent to which hope and trust can strengthen a person mentally. Of course there are absolutely 'impossible' characters among prisoners, but their resocialization should be regarded as a challenge. It is clear that the 'front-line' workers among the staff will be involved in the decision making as to whether prisoners should be allowed to take part in resocialization programmes, and it is obvious that these staff members may easily be subject to great pressure, if not blackmail, by certain prisoners.

## 5  A New Concept: 'Work Preparation' for Certain Groups of Prisoners

The term 'Work preparation' (*Arbeidstoeleiding*) means that during detention prisoners are prepared for a job after their release, a job which as far as possible is reserved for them. This is what the probation service tried to achieve for each individual prisoner in the past. At present, however, this is the purpose of a number of specially organized projects aimed at special target groups among the prisoners. The same idea underlies the future development of the reservation of resocialization for only the most motivated prisoners. The ministers of justice and social affairs have successfully appealed to, amongst others, the European Social Fund, on behalf of several youth projects that have been operating for some years. The subsidy request concerns 20 projects. It is hoped that about 400 prisoners will find jobs via detention planning. This is 5 per cent of all male prisoners who are sentenced annually to non-suspended custodial sentences of at least several weeks.

In the new Penitentiary Principles Act the so-called *penitentiary programme* is introduced. This means that long-term prisoners who have entered the last year of their imprisonment (before their early release) are given the opportunity to participate in an educational or vocational training programme outside the prison walls. Such a programme takes at most 24 hours a week and lasts some months. For the remaining time the participant has to be in prison.

It will apparently not be possible to participate in a penitentiary programme and after that to stay in an open prison. The relationship between these two kinds of the execution of a prison sentence has not yet been clarified fully.

For young offenders, work preparation during detention is of utmost importance. First of all, there is the juvenile detention centre 'De Corridor', a semi-open prison for about 100 young men between the ages of 18 and 23, who (still) have to serve a maximum term of eight months' imprisonment. On working days there is a compulsory programme consisting of work, sport and educational activities. Once every four weeks they have weekend leave. In any case, sport and training as well as social activities are an important part of the regime. Most of the prisoners there have had no vocational training and hardly any work experience.

The adviser to the *'Binnenste Buiten'* ('Inside Out') project gives vocational aptitude tests to prisoners who want to participate in the project. Outside the institution, on several afternoons a week, a practical orientation programme is given in woodwork and metalwork. Companies in the vicinity of the institution (for a small amount of compensation) allow the young men to acquire work experience as employees there. A stable home situation is important for the period following detention, so the necessary precautions are taken by the project supervisors already during detention: a confidant from the prisoner's own environment is appointed 'Very Important Person' (VIP). This may be a parent, brother, sister or other family member, or someone with whom the prisoner has a good relationship. Since the beginning of 1994, many ex-prisoners have obtained jobs in this manner. Most of them work in technical vocations, crafts or industrial vocations. A number of ex-prisoners have begun a long-term training programme.

Another institution for young adults (from 18 to 23 years of age) is the youth work institution. It was hastily created in 1993 as an experiment, after police circles in the big cities had sounded the alarm about the constantly increasing number of young criminals who sometimes committed very dangerous crimes. The youth work institution was speedily completed and initially consisted of two stages: the lower level where very intensive work under strict discipline had to be done in the forest, and the higher level, which aimed at preparation for work. Such higher levels (in the form of open institutions) are to be found in different places in the Netherlands, so that those involved can be prepared for work as much as possible in the vicinity of their homes. Meanwhile, the first stage has ceased to exist because of a lack of youngsters for whom the regime was deemed to be appropriate. An attempt is being made to continue the second stage alone as it has important implications for the future of young prisoners.

Finally, there is the possibility that a stay in the open institution for adult prisoners (as the final stage of a long term of imprisonment) from which the prisoner goes to work for a private employer during the day may lead to obtaining permanent employment. This way of obtaining employment has existed for some time.

In addition, there are numerous projects, organized by the probation service, acting as intermediaries in obtaining *jobs for ex-prisoners* after their release. Part of the function of these projects is allowing them to gain practical experience, educational experience and social skills in a short time. In the future, such projects will probably be replaced by the activities belonging to the penitentiary programmes. Because of the generally low level of education and long-term unemployment (before their detention) of those involved, their chances of permanent employment are often remote. Moreover, their lifestyles, their patterns of drug use, their psychiatric history and their ethnic background often combine to make it difficult for them to find employment. In addition, because of its overall workload, the probation service is sometimes unable to give sufficient attention to this group of clients.

The probation service generally has to deal with a client population of which 90 per cent are men and 10 per cent women. Of the men, 80 per cent are under 40 years of age. The level of education is usually low: more than half have not completed lower general secondary or lower secondary vocational education. In more than half of the cases there is some form of addiction (drugs, alcohol, gambling), while difficult family situations are very common (Van Netburg, 1996). Almost half of the prisoners received benefits before detention. Of those who did not receive benefits, more than one-quarter supported themselves through paid employment. About 15 per cent have their own business, of which 63 per cent are in the hotel and catering sector (*Werkzame detentie*, 1994: 55–6).

A recent research report on the social perspectives of released prisoners confirms the poor work prospects that prisoners face on release (BONJO, 1998). Many released prisoners who did not have employment before detention wish to have lodgings and to work in the future, but often their attitude is too passive to realize their ambitions. For almost all released prisoners, even those with vocational training, it is very difficult to get a job honestly. Very often they have to keep silent about their past, otherwise the employers do not accept them. This is a problem worldwide.

## 6 Conclusion

The traditional rationale of regular work inside prison, namely that it is in the interest of order, rest and discipline, is again current since the introduction of a more restrictive standard regime for all prisoners. Furthermore, the extension of the number of working hours is meant to serve commercial purposes to a greater extent than was previously the case.

In general, the regular work in houses of detention is very simple, but also for prisons it is not easy to acquire interesting work that may improve the vocational skills of the prisoners. In some long-term prisons the work situation is more favourable.

A new development is the concept of 'work preparation' for certain groups of prisoners. This means that serious efforts are being made to bring about the type of resocialization that is most effective and fundamental for the prisoners: getting a job in society after release. It is clear that during detention a basis for this aim has to be laid by vocational training and other measures. In the future the so-called 'penitentiary programme' outside the prison will give the prisoner the opportunity to prepare himself effectively for acquiring such a job. It is understandable that in this respect the prison system is aimed in the first instance at the category of long-term prisoners who show themselves to be motivated. Nevertheless, one should strive for the gradual enlargement of this category, because generally not many people in prison are highly motivated to achieve social goals. As a result they often miss out on any significant training or the opportunity to build a labour record. Only time will tell whether the new policies will create prisoners who after release will carry on with the type of work they started inside the prison walls.

## References

BONJO. 1998. *Huisvestingsproblemen van (ex-) gedetineerden*. Amsterdam: de Woonbond.

De Jonge, Gerard. 1994. *Strafwerk*. Breda: Uitgeverij Papieren Tijger.

Kelk, Constantijn. 1991. The Netherlands. In *Imprisonment Today and Tomorrow: International Perspectives on Prison Rights*, edited by D. van Zyl Smit and F. Dünkel. Deventer: Kluwer.

Moerings, Martin, Johannes C.J. Boutellier, Frank Borenkerk, Marian Junger and Constantijn Kelk, eds. 1994. *Hoe punitief is Nederland?* Arnhem: Gouda Quint.

Nijboer, Jan. A. 1971. Opleiding tijdens detentie en recidive. *Tijdschrift voor Criminologie* 21.

*NRC Handelsblad*. 3 February 1996.

Pompe, Willem P.J. 1945. *Het nieuwe tijdperk en het recht*. Amsterdam: Uitgeverij Vrij Nederland.

Van Netburg, C.J. 1996. *Arbeidsmarkt-posisie van ex-gedetineerden*. The Hague: Ministry of Justice.

*Bibliographical note*: The judgments of the various tribunals that shape penal law in the Netherlands are recorded in two journals, *Penitentiaire Informatie (PI)* and *Sancties*. These journals also contain important official circulars. Reference is made in the text to both sources.

## The Author

**Constantijn Kelk** is professor of criminal law, penology and criminology at the Willem Pompe Institute for Penal Sciences (Willem Pompe Instituut voor Strafrechtswetenschapen) at the University of Utrecht, in the Netherlands.

# 10 The Netherlands: Labour Imposed as a Criminal Punishment outside the Dutch Prison

MIRANDA BOONE

**Foreword**

Labour for prisoners is designed to become a feature of growing importance in the Dutch prison system. The basis for this change is the new Penitentiary Principles Act (*Penitentiaire Beginselenwet, PBW*), also discussed in the previous chapter. In principle, every prisoner is to be placed on a (minimum) standard regime, in which a larger number of hours than before will have to be worked. But the interesting types of labour that really contribute to resocialization will be reserved for those among the long-term prisoners who show motivation in this regard; the estimates are that this will involve about 20 per cent of all prisoners. For the rest, prison labour will have to show more of a return and keep the prisoners 'calm' and 'busy'. After all, the proverb, 'an idle brain is the devil's workshop', is also true within penitentiary walls.

This development in the field of prison labour comes during a period when alternative sanctions are also burgeoning in the Netherlands. Many work projects in this area are rapidly getting off the ground. It is precisely there that resocialization plays an important role, to be achieved by means of useful activities without an intramural setting. This seems to have provided inspiration for the intramural situation: here and there projects have been initiated to prepare prisoners, while in prison, for work after release – so-called work instruction projects. In the future, during the last stage of the prison sentence, penitentiary programmes will be formulated to take prisoners outside the walls. The same programmes can also serve as alternative sanctions for non-detainees. In this way, some consistency will be created among the various types of punishment.

## 1 Introduction

Not only is work an important part of the prison sentence, but for the past 15 years work has also increasingly been imposed as a punishment outside the prison context. Work sentences, in addition to educational sentences, form the category of sanctions that are currently referred to as 'task sentences', although many are better known by the term 'alternative or community sanctions'.

In 1989, after years of experiments, community service (having to perform unpaid work for the benefit of society) was formally included in the Penal Code. The sentence can only be imposed by a court if it is considering a prison sentence of up to six months, or a prison sentence of which the non-suspended part is no more than six months. These prison sentences may be replaced by community service for not more than 240 hours. In order to avoid the prohibition of forced labour under international law, the accused himself must offer to do community service at an early stage of the trial and must confirm his consent again after the sentence has been imposed. In the near future, the regulation on community sanctions will be changed drastically. Community service will become a sentence which can be imposed independently of a prison sentence. Although the offender will still have to give his consent after sentence, the earlier offer to do community service will not be required.

Since the new juvenile act came into effect on 1 September 1995, community service has also had a statutory basis in juvenile law. A sentence of not more than 200 hours' community service can be imposed instead of a principal sentence. Under juvenile law, in addition to work sentences, educational sentences may also be imposed as independent penalties, that is penalties that consist of an obligation to follow a certain course, for example a course on social skills or sex education, or a course on the circumstances of victims. Unlike what happens in adult criminal law, the public prosecutor and police may also propose a task penalty to the accused in order to avoid criminal prosecution. The maximum number of hours for which an accused person may be subjected to such a penalty is 40.

The so-called HALT projects have a separate status. The police, under the supervision and with the authorization of the Public Prosecutions Department, may propose a HALT project to a young offender under the age of 18 years in order to avoid formally sending a report to the public prosecutor. The HALT settlement has two components: an arrangement to pay compensation and a work project. Both are laid down in consultation with the HALT bureau. The young offender (and his parents where a young offender under

16 years of age is concerned) must consent to the settlement and the project may not last longer than 20 hours. During the initial years only vandalism, including destruction of property, damage, overt violence against property, less serious forms of arson and hooliganism were eligible for referral to a HALT project. Recently, the category of HALT offences has been extended to include embezzlement and handling stolen goods to a maximum value of 250 Dutch Guilders (NLG).

There has been a great increase in the number of task sentences. In 1983, 1,668 work sentences were imposed on adults; in 1987, the number rose to 18,000. Similarly, in 1983, 298 work sentences and six educational sentences were imposed on young offenders. In 1977, the number of these two types of sentences rose to 3,000 and 2,000, repectively. It is estimated that 25,000 work sentences will be imposed in 1999 and the the number will increase annually (Interdepartementaal beleidsondonderzoek, 1997: 16–17; Rijksbegroting, 1998). The number of task sentences is increasing so quickly that, in addition to a shortage of cells, there is now also a shortage of project places. This is one of the reasons group projects have been started, in which large groups of community service offenders can complete their task sentences at the same time.

It certainly cannot be said that these task sentences are replacing non-suspended prison sentences or a principal penalty that can be imposed on young offenders, as was the original intention. Under adult criminal law, too, about half of the task sentences are used to replace non-suspended prison sentences (Junger Tas, 1993; Spaans, 1995). There are different ideas about the desirablity of this development because of its so-called 'net-widening' effect. What is clear is that the work sentence should no longer simply be considered as a favour, but as an independent penalty, which creates obligations for the authorities to clarify the legal status of such penalties and of the offenders who serve them.

## 2 Status with Regard to Labour Law

### 2.1 *The Status of the Community Service Offender under the Labour Laws*

Hardly any attention has been given to the legal status of persons who have been subjected to a work penalty. There has been more interest in the instrumental aspects of the penalty, such as its influence on recidivism and its cost-saving effects. It has also been suggested that the pedagogical nature of the work penalties is not compatible with the pursuit of stricter standards of legality (Van der Laan, 1992).

There have been recommendations made by various international panels for enforcing task sentences in so-called 'standard minimum rules'. For the Netherlands, the European Rules on Community Sanctions and Measures (Council of Europe, 1992) are the most important. They are complemented by the United Nations Standard Minimum Rules for Non-custodial Measures, the so-called 'Tokyo rules'. Although neither the rules of the Council of Europe nor the rules of the United Nations are laws with mandatory effect, they do have a moral value and form important guidelines for the contracting states for the further development of task sanctions. They are comparable to the very influential standards for the enforcement of prison sentences, that is the Standard Minimum Rules for the Treatment of Prisoners (United Nations, 1955) and the European Prison Rules (Council of Europe, 1987). The first-mentioned prison rules were prepared by the International Penal and Penitentiary Commission. The successor to this organization, the International Penal and Penitentiary Foundation (IPPF), working closely with the rules given by the United Nations, has enacted a third set of standards applicable to community sanctions: the Standard Minimum Rules for the Implementation of Non-custodial Sanctions, the so-called 'Groningen rules' (IPPF, 1989).

Rule 47 of the Council of Europe's minimum rules on community sanctions obligates enforcing authorities to facilitate participation in society by means of an agreement between the person doing community service and the probation service, in which the nature of the tasks and the manner in which they are to be performed are described. In practice, a contract is almost always drawn up. Up to now, this contract has been one of the most important sources of rights for the person sentenced to community service.

An important question is to what extent the labour laws apply to the person doing community service. If community service could be categorized as a contract for the performance of work, the position under labour law of the person doing community service would be considerably strengthened, since mandatory provisions which relate to the employment contract in particular offer the employee a high degree of protection. Strengthening the legal position of the person doing community service with respect to the project place (that is, the institution at which the community service is done) however, is not compatible with the general goal of keeping the requirements in respect of the project place to a minimum (see, for example, Voorbereidingsgroep Experimenten Dienstverlening, 1984: 29). Such a goal is linked with the dependence of the success of community service on the availability of sufficient project places.

One of the requirements set for a legally valid contract is the obligation of the other party to pay wages. It is immediately evident from the standard contract that this condition has not been fulfilled, for it provides: 'The person doing community service shall not receive compensation of any kind whatsoever.' The unsalaried nature of the community service is also apparent from the official term, 'unpaid work for the benefit of the community'. Since neither the coordinator nor the institution is obliged to pay wages, the conclusion must be drawn that no employment contract has been effected and the protective rules of the Civil Code do not apply.

This does not mean that the labour laws are wholly inapplicable. In addition to the concepts 'worker', 'employment contract' and 'gainful employment', labour law also uses the concepts 'employee' and 'employment relationship' (Koopmans, 1962). The concepts 'employee' and 'employment relationship' are broader than the concepts 'worker' and 'gainful employment'. The employment relationship usually includes gainful employment, although there are also legal relationships by virtue of which work is performed but which do not amount to employment contracts. The broader concept, 'employee', appears in various labour acts. The scope of these acts is therefore wider than it would be if they only applied to workers. We may assume from the legal history that community service in principle falls within the scope of labour law. The starting point is that community service is performed in society according to the rules which apply in society (Bill 20074, no. 11, p.3).

The consequences that the application of labour legislation can have for community service can be illustrated by two examples. First it could be argued that the Working Conditions Act (*Arbowet*) is applicable to the relationship between the project institution and the person doing community service. This Act also applies to employees and employers who, without being employers and employees within the meaning of art. 1637a of the Civil Code, have others perform work under their authority. Since the community service offender is obliged to follow the instructions of the project institution (art. 5 of the Standard Rules), this criterion of an employment relationship is fulfilled. The result is that the project agency is confronted with the need to provide for varying characteristics and abilities of the persons doing community work.[1] The employer must also avoid unvaried work as much as possible. If this is not possible, the work must be stopped at regular intervals or alternated with other work.

A second example concerns the obligations of the employer laid down in the Civil Code (*BW*) for the employer. In terms of art. 1638x, the employer must ensure that rooms, equipment and tools do not endanger the body, honour or property (*lijf, eerbaarheid en goed*) of the employee. Although this article only applies if there is an employment contract, the courts seem to give it a broader interpretation. In two judgments, the court applied the article analogously to the relationship between an agency providing temporary workers and its client (Ktr. *Bergen op zoom*, 13 Oktober 1982 en 30 Maart 1983, *Praktijkgids* 1984, nr. 2050; Rb's Gravenhage 23 November 1983, *Praktijkgids* 1984, nr. 2057). In both cases the business making use of temporary workers was held liable for the loss suffered by the temporary worker as a result of the injury incurred in the course of his work at the business. The relationship between a community service offender and the probation service project is comparable in many respects to that between a temporary worker and a temporary agency and its client. In both cases there is a three-way relationship and in both cases the authority of the temporary agency and probation service to give instructions is delegated to the client and the project, respectively. If art. 1638x of the Civil Code is declared applicable, this means that the 'employer' can be obliged to pay (supplementary) damages if the person doing community service is, as a result of an accident, no longer able to provide for himself independently. A more than marginal function may be ascribed to the applicability of art. 1638x of the Civil Code, since in many cases the offender doing community service cannot rely on disability insurance, and the insurance taken out by the probation service does not cover all forms of damage, particularly not emotional damage.

### 2.2 The Status of the HALT Client under the Labour Laws

There is even less clarity regarding the legal status of the HALT client in the implementation stage than there is regarding the legal status of the offender doing community service. The general instructions of the Public Prosecution Department concerning the

---

1 These include age, gender, physical and mental state, experience, skills and linguistic ability.

HALT settlement were published in 1995, but these mainly stipulate criteria which must be met by the offence and offender before a settlement may be instituted. The instructions are therefore meant primarily for the police and not for the bureaus responsible for the settlement (the so-called HALT bureaus). According to their preamble, the European Minimum Rules, strangely enough, are not applicable to the implementation of task sentences for young offenders. For the sake of completeness, the guidelines issued by the Council of Europe for social reactions to juvenile delinquency can be referred to here (European Committee on Crime Problems, 1989). In these guidelines the use of diversion or mediation programmes at the earliest possible stage is emphasized (guideline 2) and alternative settlements are chosen above custodial ones (guidelines 6 and 7). During the development and implementation of task sentences account must be taken of the rights of minors to education, their own personality and personal development (guideline 11). The criminal records of young offenders must remain confidential (guideline 10).

Because the HALT settlement concerns minors, special requirements are set by the labour laws on the nature of the work and the working hours. A 1983 circular from the Secretary of State for Social Affairs and Employment indicates that, when task sentences are being carried out (including HALT), the prohibitions of the Juvenile Employment Decree must be observed. This decree contains provisions on the types of work that under certain circumstances may not be performed by juveniles. These requirements take both the physical and mental well-being of the juveniles into account. For example, the decree forbids juveniles from using toxic substances for the removal of graffiti. During consultations between the Ministry of Social Affairs and Employment and the Ministry of Justice it was therefore decided that the removal of graffiti with toxic substances was under no circumstances whatsoever to be permitted as a HALT project or task sentence. The removal of graffiti with non-toxic substances is permitted.

On the basis of art. 92 of the 1919 Factories Act, the Minister of Social Affairs and Employment, in consultation with the Minister of Justice, has drawn up rules deviating from the Factories Act with regard to the work and the working hours of juveniles who are given task sentences (circular of 13 December 1995). The circular states that the project must provide non-industrial assistance of a light and educational nature or be an entirely educational project. The performance of any other work is prohibited during a week in which work is being done as part of a work sentence. Concerning working hours, the juvenile must have an uninterrupted rest period of 14 hours a day, which includes the hours between 8 pm and 7 am. The juvenile must have an uninterrupted rest period of at least 36 hours a week. During a school week, not more than 20 hours' work may be performed, of which not more than two hours a day may be worked on school days and not more than seven hours a day on other days. During holiday weeks a maximum of 35 hours a week and seven hours a day may be worked.

An important gap in the procedural protection of the rights of HALT clients is that, as yet, no complaints procedure has been developed. When disputes arise between the client and the HALT worker on the nature of the work, the number of hours of the settlement, or the amount of the compensation, the HALT client cannot do much more than refuse the settlement, thereby running the risk of criminal prosecution.

## 3 Punitive Nature versus Resocialization

Although the lack of cells is playing an increasingly larger role in the development of work sentences, work sentences arise primarily from the desire for sentences that are better suited to the individual offender than they were before. There was disillusionment with the possibilities for resocialization offered by (in particular short-term) prison sentences and the aim was to strengthen the deterrent function of criminal law by developing and applying work sentences. An attempt was made to find sanctions which reflect the seriousness of the offence committed. A large integrative capacity was attributed to labour in particular, and often project places were sought which could strengthen the individual abilities of the delinquents.

It was only early in the 1990s, after the introduction of community service as a principal penalty, that a rather heated debate was conducted on the retributive content of the work penalty. The basis of the debate was the fear that neither the public nor the courts would take the penalty seriously. During the debate, the Public Prosecutions Department argued that the retributive character of task sentences should be strengthened by making the work more onerous; those subject to community service orders should not do odd jobs in homes for the aged, but should pollard willows or cut peat. Aside from the nature of the work, other punitive aspects of the work sentence were mentioned, such as deprivation of liberty, the threat of alternative penalties, confrontation with the suffering of others, the supervision exercised, stigmatization and labelling in connection with the higher visibility of work sentences, and the shame attached to such sentences.

What is striking is the large measure of arbitrariness with which the punitive elements are ascribed to the task sentence. A consistent penal concept does not seem to underlie the different opinions. So, for example, no distinction was made between the intended retribution and suffering that must be considered to be an unintended side-effect of the penalty. It is interesting to draw a comparison with the prison sentence. For the prison sentence, the maxim still prevails that you go to gaol as a punishment and not for punishment. Kelk (1978) mentions the *generally accepted* point of departure that the penal element of the custodial sentence consists solely of the physical deprivation of liberty. On this basis, additional suffering during the enforcement stage is rejected. This starting point also underlies the resocialization principle laid down in art. 2 of the pending Penitentiary Principles Act (*Penitentiaire Beginselenwet, PBW*), which states that, while the nature of the penalty or measure must be preserved, its enforcement should also serve to prepare the prisoner's return to society, and the principle of minimal restrictions which holds that 'those who have not been convicted shall be subject to no other restrictions than those required for the purpose of their detention, or those absolutely necessary to preserve order'.

How do these principles relate to the objective of strengthening the retributive nature of work penalties either by having more strenuous work done, or by toughening supervision, or by adding elements of stigmatization and confrontation to the penalty? It is surely not proper suddenly to apply a totally different penal concept to work penalties. The introduction of task sentences may be viewed as a natural step in a process which had already begun in the nineteenth century in the Netherlands (Franke, 1990). This process is characterized by an increasingly open mode of enforcement of the prison sentence. Coercion, in the sense of the restriction of alternative behaviour, has remained unaffected as the essence of the punishment. Just like the deprivation of liberty, the enforcement of the work sentence should serve to resocialize the person concerned as much as possible. This means that, in searching for appropriate work, not the measure of retribution but the resocializing potential of the work should be the deciding factor.[2]

[2] For educational sentences, the same questions are even more difficult to answer, although in my opinion in the end the same conclusions can be drawn as for work sentences.

## 4 Conclusion

Kelk has commented in chapter 9 on the many job preparation projects that are meant to prepare prisoners during their detention for a job after their release. During the last stage of their detention, many are given the opportunity to work outside prison walls. In the Penitentiary Principles Act a new form of enforcement of the custodial sentence is introduced, namely the penitentiary programme. This means a 'series of activities to be participated in by persons for the further enforcement of the custodial sentence imposed on them or custodial measure in connection with their stay in an institution, and recognized as such by our Minister' (art. 4(1) of the Penitentiary Principles Act). Not much has been decided as yet regarding the exact form of the penitentiary programme. In the explanatory notes to the Act we read that the purpose is 'To provide for a multidimensional development of the enforcement of a custodial sentence or custodial measure *outside the walls of a penal institution*.... At this stage, the Act should serve as a solid basis for many experiments, while obstructing them as little as possible' (Tweede Kamer (Lower House), session 1994-1995, 24263, no. 3, p.16; emphasis added).

The penitentiary programme can be regarded as another step towards the development of a more open prison regime. Although this formally concerns the enforcement of a custodial sentence, essentially the same projects will probably be involved that are now used for the implementation of task sentences. The remarkable situation will then exist that the substance of the custodial sentence will be the same as that of sanctions for the purpose of avoiding the use of custodial sentences (Bleichrodt, 1994). This seems to reduce the distinction between the custodial sentence and the task sentence to a procedural difference. The substance of both the custodial and the task sentence may consist of performing work under the supervision of a monitoring body with the threat of total deprivation of liberty as an alternative penalty. This raises questions, for example, regarding the essence of the custodial sentence and the role of the courts. For can it still be maintained that the essence of the custodial sentence consists of physical deprivation of liberty? And what remains of the exclusive authority of the courts to determine the severity of the punishment, if the custodial sentence imposed by the court can be converted by the administration into a work sentence to be served outside the institution? Perhaps the concept of penal labour will be of further help in finding a coordinating penal philosophy.

## References

Bleichrodt, F.W. 1994. Het penitentiaire programma: invulling of uitholling van de vrijheidsstraf? *Sancties* 5: 268 ff.

Council of Europe. 1987. *Prison Rules*. Adopted by the Committee of Ministers of the Council of Europe on 12 February.

Council of Europe. 1992. *Rules on Community Sanctions and Measures*. Adopted by the Committee of Ministers of the Council of Europe on 16 November.

European Committee on Crime Problems. 1989. *Social reactions to juvenile delinquency*. Strasbourg: Council of Europe.

Franke, Herman. 1990. *Twee eeuwen gevangen, Misdaad en straf in Nederland*. Utrecht: Spectrum.

Interdepartementaal beleidsonderzoek substitutie vrijheidsstraffen door taakstraffen, mei 1997. *Substitutie van vrijheidsstraffen*, IBO-ronde 1996, rapport nr. 8.

International Penal and Penitentiary Foundation. 1989. *Standard Minimum Rules for the Implementation of Non-Custodial Sanctions* (Groningen Rules). Deventer: Kluwer.

Junger Tas J. 1993. *Alternatieven voor de vrijheidsstraf. Lessen uit het buitenland*. Arnhem: Gouda Quint.

Kelk, Constantijn. 1978. *Recht voor gedetineerden*. Alpen aan den Rijn: Samsom.

Koopmans, T. 1962. *De begrippen werkman, arbeider en werknemer*. Alpen aan den Rijn: Samsom.

Rijksbegroting. 1998. (National Budget). The Hague: Government Printing Office.

Spaans, E.C. 1995. *De toepassing van werkstraffen en korte vrijheidsstraffen in 1992*. Arnhem: Gouda Quint.

United Nations. 1955. *Standard Minimum Rules for the Treatment of Prisoners*. Adopted by the First United Nations Congress on the Prevention of Crime and the Treatment of Offenders, 30 August 1955; approved by United Nations Economic and Social Council resolution 663C (XXIV) of 31 July 1957; amended (new rule 95 added) by Economic and Social Council resolution 2076 (LXII) of 13 May 1977.

United Nations. 1990. *Standard Minimum Rules for Non-custodial Measures*. Adopted by the General Assembly resolution 45/110 of 14 December.

Van der Laan, Peter H. 1992. Een eeuwig dilemma: alternatieve sanctiesen rechtsbescherming. *Proces*: 280–87.

Voorbereidingsgroep Experimenten Dienstverlening. 1984. *Dienstverlening: van experiment naar wet, eindadvies van de Voorbereidingsgroep Experimenten Dienstverlening*. The Hague: Government Printing Office.

## The Author

**Miranda Boone** is lecturer at the Willem Pompe Institute for Penal Sciences at the University of Utrecht, in the Netherlands.

# 11 Poland

ZBIGNIEW HOLDA

## 1 Introduction

Poland has experienced fundamental changes in its criminal justice system since 1989, the year in which democracy and the rule of law, as well as the market economy, were restored (Bulenda *et al.*, 1994; Holda, 1995; Wasek and Frankowski, 1995). The protection of human rights has become one of the crucial components of the legal and political system.

Before 1989, prison labour played an important role in the prison system (Holda and Rzeplinski, 1991). The communist government demanded that all convicted prisoners be employed, either in prison enterprises such as factories, workshops or farms, or in factories and on farms outside the prisons. The economy was planned and the state administration managed industry which was largely state-owned. As a result, up to 90 per cent of convicted prisoners worked, approximately 40 per cent of them outside prisons, in state-owned industry.[1]

Notwithstanding provisions of the Criminal Code (CC) of 1969 and the Code on the Execution of Penalties (CEP) of 1969 referring to the ideology of resocialization, the exploitation of prison labour was the main purpose of the prison administration. In reality, prisoners were treated simply as a cheap labour force. The allocation of inmates, their education and even their medical care were to a large extent subordinated to the requirements of prison labour. Several prisons were built in areas where a labour force was lacking. Everyday prison life was determined by labour practices, and refusal to

---

1  For example, in December 1986, of the 76,112 convicted prisoners in Polish gaols, 62,983 (82.8 per cent) were employed and in December 1988, 83.9 per cent (47,232 out of 56,270) convicted prisoners. In addition, a small number of prisoners in pre-trial detention were also employed. However, at the same time thousands of employed inmates were engaged in the then totally unpaid domestic work and institutional maintenance labour or public works (11,628 and 116, respectively in December 1986 and 8,759 and 105, respectively, in December 1988).

work was the most frequent reason for the most severe disciplinary penalties, including solitary confinement for up to six months. Working conditions and legal norms pertaining to the prisoners' work were highly inadequate.

Since 1990, when the rules of a market economy were restored, most prisoners have been unemployed.[2] As a result of changes to the law in 1990, domestic work and institutional maintenance labour have ceased to be a legal category of unpaid labour. However, to some extent prisoners are obliged to do this kind of labour regardless of whether they are paid or not. Therefore some inmates are engaged without remuneration in domestic work and institutional maintenance labour, as well as in work for state institutions. (In May 1996, 3,154 convicted prisoners were engaged in the former and 302 in the latter.)

The prison administration cannot provide all inmates with work. Industry does not need prisoners any more and only between 12 per cent and 16 per cent of working inmates are employed by these outside employers. Employment in prison workshops, factories and farms has also been greatly reduced because of the poor economic performance of these undertakings, despite tax exemptions granted by the Minister of Finance. Approximately 20,000 prisoners were employed in these undertakings in the 1980s but this number dropped to approximately 3,500 in the 1990s. Only employment in domestic work and institutional maintenance, which are necessary for the smooth functioning of prisons, is still available and between 55 per cent and 60 per cent of inmates are employed in these functions, but unlike what happened in the past, most of them receive remuneration.

The prison population of approximately 60,000 inmates is still very high.[3] Although some prisoners cannot work for security reasons, especially those in pre-trial detention, or for health reasons, most can. Today approximately 20,000 convicted prisoners who are able to work have no work, although many really want to work and perceive the lack of labour opportunities as discrimination and

2   For example, 29.1 per cent in December 1992 and 26.7 per cent in December 1994 performed paid labour, plus a small group in pre-trial detention. In May 1996, still only 27.5 per cent (12,261 out of 44,570) of convicted prisoners and 6.5 per cent (1,020 of 15,769) of pre-trial detention prisoners were paid for their labour.

3   For example, in May 1996, the total number of prisoners was 60,339, of whom 15,769 were in pre-trial detention.

a violation of their rights. The whole prison system has been affected by this unemployment.

However, since 1990 the legal provisions concerning prison labour were changed in favour of prisoners. In 1990 and 1995, several provisions of the Code on the Execution of Penalties (CEP) were amended. New prison rules, which were issued by the Minister of Justice in 1989, were amended in 1995, to secure their conformity with the new version of the CEP.

The drafts of the new Criminal Code (CC), the CEP and also the Code of Criminal Procedure (CCP) were submitted to Parliament in mid-1995. The Central Directorate of Prisons of the Ministry of Justice prepared the draft of the Prison Labour Act in 1996. The Codes and the Prison Labour Act were adopted in May 1997. The Codes have been in force since 1 September 1998 and the Prison Labour Act since 1 January 1998.

It seems that the new legal provisions will better protect prisoners' rights and establish privileges and preferences required to enable the products of prison labour to compete on the open market. They provide for a wide range of exemptions from taxes for the prison enterprises, and also some exemptions for outside enterprises that employ prisoners. The Prison Labour Act states that prisoners should constitute at least 20 per cent of the workforce of prison enterprises; with a complement of at least 50 per cent of prisoners, the enterprise will enjoy the maximum range of exemptions. The same Act contains provisions for a special fund, devoted to the creation of new workplaces for prisoners and the modernization of prison enterprises which currently lack adequate infrastructure and equipment.

According to the estimates made by the prison administration, the Polish prison system needs approximately 30,000 to 40,000 workplaces for inmates; more than half of that number should be provided in prison enterprises. In 1995, the prison administration administered only 49, mostly small, workshops, factories and farms, which employed about 3,500 inmates. Tadeusz Zielinski, who was the national Ombudsman from 1992 to 1996, stressed in several papers and official reports submitted to Parliament that unemployment among prisoners had to be overcome and that it was the task of the state authorities to expedite this (see Zielinski, 1993: 11–12; Zielinski, 1995: 377).

The amendments to the legal provisions on prison labour in Poland, as well as the new CEP of 1997, have been influenced by academic writings on labour law theory and criminal law theory

(Holda and Wojcieszczuk, 1983; Bojarski et al., 1985; Liszcz, 1989; Kosut, 1992, 1993, 1995; Radzikowska, 1992).

## 2 Prisoners and Involuntary Servitude

Prisoners have a duty to work, but the scope of this obligation is determined by the law, and differs according to the category of prisoners involved. Involuntary work has been the essential element of the penalty of imprisonment for a long time. However, it seems that today prison labour should be subjected to a different legal regime and the prisoner's duty to work should be abolished.

According to the Codes of 1969, a convicted prisoner had the duty to perform that type of work which was decided by the prison administration (art. 80(2) of the CC, art. 47 of the CEP; see also para. 40 of the Prison Rules). It included simple domestic work, such as cleaning and maintaining order and more skilled, institutional maintenance labour such as cooking, running the central heating, water supply and library, and assisting in the office work of the prison administration. Of course, it also included normal paid labour in industry or services, inside or outside prison. The prisoner in pre-trial detention only had the obligation to perform domestic work 'within the house of detention'; any other type of work required his consent (art. 87 of the CEP). According to para. 6 of the Prison Rules of 1989 and para. 7 of the Prison Rules on Pre-Trial Detention of 1989, 'a prisoner is obliged to keep the rooms in which he stays clean and in order'.

The ability of a prisoner to work and, if required, the type of work and hours of work, were determined by a medical doctor (art. 50 of CEP of 1969). A prisoner could be engaged in work that was potentially injurious to his health, but only with his consent (para. 40 of the Prison Rules of 1989).

There was one special category of convicted prisoners who were exempt from the duty to work: prisoners of conscience, who fell under Convention 105 of the International Labour Organisation. According to the Regulations issued by the Minister of Justice in 1978, these prisoners had the right to decide whether they preferred to work or not. However, they were obliged to do some basic domestic work such as 'to keep rooms in which they stay clean and in order' (see para. 6 of the Prison Rules of 1989).

Legally, work cannot be imposed as a punishment for intra-prison rule violations or for certain special crimes (but one of the penalties adopted by the CC, the restriction of liberty, contains a duty to work as an essential element). In practice, however, it seems that the prison staff can compel prisoners to perform particularly hard or dirty tasks as informal punishment.

According to art. 49(4) of the CEP of 1969, a convicted prisoner was not entitled to remuneration for domestic work and institutional maintenance labour not exceeding 60 hours a month.[4] It was unpaid labour, but, if this unpaid work was exercised scrupulously, it could be rewarded financially by the prison director.

Since 1990, prisoners have not been obliged to work in state departments. According to art. 49(5) of the CEP of 1969, as amended in 1995, they could be engaged in unpaid work for the benefit of local government, but only with their written consent.

All prison labour, including domestic work and institutional maintenance labour, was regulated by legal norms of a general nature, for example occupational health and safety regulations (art. 50 of the CEP of 1969) or regulations on hours of work (art. 49(2) of the CEP of 1969). As a result, there were numerous restrictions with respect to matters such as type of work, hours of work and conditions of work.

The CEP of 1997 (art. 116), as well as the Prison Labour Act of 1998 (art. 1) state that the convicted prisoner has a duty to work. Provisions in the CEP of 1997 on the prisoner's duty to work are similar to the provisions mentioned above; art. 107, for instance, states that a prisoner of conscience is not obliged to work.

## 3 Prisoners' Right to Work

According to the CEP of 1969, a convicted prisoner not only had a duty to work, but he also had 'the right to employment and accident insurance' (art. 48). The Polish Constitution of 1952 (art. 68), as well as the Labour Code (art. 10), proclaimed the right to work as a human right. Labour law scholars (for example Liszcz, 1995: 22–4) viewed it as a social right of a promotional or programmatic nature since an individual cannot demand of the state the right to obtain employment. However, according to some legal provisions, certain groups of citizens (such as disabled soldiers) have an enforceable right to work. The majority of scholars, as well as courts and prison administration, have assumed (despite the

---

[4] In the period 1990–95, it was only 30 hours a month; before 1990, it was up to 42 and before 1981, up to 46 hours a week, as stated by general labour law regulations.

wording of art. 48 of the CEP of 1969) that prisoners did not belong to this privileged minority. But some scholars (Liszcz, 1989: 88–9; Kosut, 1992: 64–5; 1993: 36–8) have argued that prisoners enjoyed an enforceable, or at least a 'strengthened', right to work. In reality, unemployment among prisoners is very high.

Paragraph 40 of the Prison Rules of 1989 gave several guidelines for the employment of prisoners: their health, age, professional skills and interests, as well as security requirements, should be taken into account. Inmates who were obliged to give assistance to their families or to pay compensation to the victims of their crime should be preferred. However, even these preferred persons were often unemployed. In May 1996, out of 11,936 prisoners who were obliged to give assistance to their families, only 6,357 were working.

Prison administration could assign inmates to labour inside prison on tasks such as institutional maintenance or in an internal workshop or factory or outside prison. Prisoners serving their terms in closed prisons could work outside prison only under supervision of the prison service; prisoners in semi-open prisons could work under reduced supervision or without supervision; and those in open prisons could work outside prison without supervision, preferably in so-called 'individual labour positions' (paras 82–6 of the Prison Rules of 1989).

The new Polish Constitution adopted in 1997 does not proclaim the right to work. Nor do the CEP of 1997 or the Prison Labour Act provide that prisoners have the right to work. But the CEP of 1997 does state that a 'prisoner has the right to remuneration for labour and to social security benefits' (art. 102). The lack of work does not necessarily mean enforced idleness in prisons. Instead of working, prisoners may listen to the radio, watch TV, train at sport, take part in cultural or religious activities or attend the therapeutic programmes. Today prisoners have free access to media (through mostly private TV and radio sets and also newspaper subscriptions) and a wide range of organizations including religious associations, Alcoholics Anonymous groups and other social organizations. Some inmates attend schools.[5]

One can be of the opinion that enforced idleness in prison could constitute a form of cruel and degrading punishment, but unemployment alone does not offend human dignity and labour is not the sole measure of rehabilitation. Nevertheless, some prisoners demand work and say that the deprivation of work violates their

5    4,050 in 1993; 4,025 in 1994.

human dignity and human rights, including the right to rehabilitation. The Ombudsman himself (Zielinski, 1993: 12; 1995: 377), officers of the Office of the Ombudsman (for example Bramska, 1995: 287-8) as well as the Central Directorate of Prisons (Report, 1995: 55-6), have expressed the same opinion.

Prisoners' right to rehabilitation seemed to be entrenched in art. 80(1) of the CC of 1969 and art. 37 of the CEP of 1969. Art. 49(1) of the CEP of 1969 stated that employment of prisoners should aim at 'preparation for an honest life in freedom' and at 'the preservation and development of physical and mental abilities'. Provisions of the CEP of 1997 are founded on the idea that resocialization is an offer made to a prisoner, but not a duty imposed on a prisoner.

Very often unemployed prisoners have no money and are not able to give assistance to their families. For this reason, the prison administration can, 'in justified cases', grant a prisoner's family a subsidy for up to three months (para. 48 of the Prison Rules of 1989).

## 4 The Connection between Work and Release

Conditional release is regulated in the CC (arts 90 to 98 of CC of 1969; arts 77 to 82 of CC of 1997) and in the CEP (arts 78 to 81 of CEP of 1969; arts 159 to 163 of CEP of 1997).

Under the CC of 1969, a penitentiary court could order conditional release if it ascertained that the personality and behaviour of the inmate had given grounds for the prediction that he would observe legal order after his release and also that the aims of the punishment (general prevention and individual prevention) had been achieved. The equivalent art. 77 of the CEP of 1997 does not mention the aims of the punishment.

Refusal to work was always regarded by the courts as bad behaviour during imprisonment. In the past, the prisoners' attitude to labour was treated as the most important factor in decisions about release (Platek, 1985). But today, when work opportunities are scarce, refusals to work do not occur and mere unemployment does not disqualify a prisoner from parole.

## 5 Prisoners and the Labour Law

Prison-made goods are not prohibited from commerce by Polish legislation. Prisoners are only partly protected by basic labour law regulations. They have no right to collective bargaining.

Traditionally, working prisoners are not employees in the sense of labour law. A prisoner's work is an element of the public law relationship between him and the prison administration and does not constitute an individual employment relationship. The Supreme Court expressed this opinion in its decision of 11 February 1970 and in its decision of 30 March 1979. These decisions have met with widespread approval.

Until 1998, labour law was unfavourable to prisoners and did not provide for a special labour relationship between a prisoner and an employer whether the employer was the prison itself or another institution, for instance a factory outside prison. Prisoners who worked outside prison did not sign individual contracts with an employer. They were employed in terms of contracts drawn up between the prison administration and the employer.

Some scholars (Holda and Wojcieszczuk, 1983: 77; Liszcz, 1989: 90–92) proposed that working prisoners should be granted the full status of employees in terms of labour law. This point of view was partly adopted in 1990, when the CEP of 1969 was amended, extending some labour law rules to prisoners. However, even before 1990, prison labour was given some protection by labour law. According to art. 50 of the CEP of 1969, national occupational health and safety regulations applied to a prisoner's workplace. According to art. 49(2) of the CEP of 1969, labour law regulations of the hours of work were applicable to working prisoners. According to art. 49(3) of the CEP of 1969, the remuneration for a prisoner's labour should be equal to that of a free employee for the same kind of work.[6] According to art. 51 of the CEP of 1969, working prisoners were entitled to holidays every year.

Article 48 of the CEP of 1969 stated that a prisoner had the right to employment and accident insurance. Before 1990, insurance compensation and disability pension (or family pension) for prisoners' work accidents and occupational diseases were covered by the Civil Code, not by labour law. (Paradoxically, in some cases this worked in prisoners' favour, as labour law, before 1990, allowed for limited compensation only.)

According to art. 49(1) of the CEP as amended in 1990, the period of a prisoner's work was credited to the term of employment that determines employee and pension (social security) benefits. According to art. 49(2), the prisoner and his family had the same rights to social security benefits as a regular employee if, as a result

---

[6] However, there are compulsory deductions (art. 52 of the CEP).

of a work accident, he became sick, disabled or was killed, or if he fell ill with an occupational disease. The legal rules pertaining to employees' work accidents and occupational diseases were thus improved in 1990.

The 1990 amendments to the CEP of 1969 also reduced the extent of unpaid labour; the new version of art. 49(4) of the CEP of 1969 confined it to 30 hours a month. Compulsory deductions from remuneration for paid labour for the state budget and for the post-release assistance fund were reduced as well (the new version of art. 52(1) of the CEP of 1969 increased the minimum remuneration that an inmate had to get, after deductions, from 20 per cent to 25 per cent, following the Prison Rules of 1989). Article 53 of the CEP of 1969, specifying the deduction of a prisoner's legal debts (court costs, fines and so on) from his remuneration or from his award for unpaid labour, was changed in his favour. Article 51 of the CEP of 1969 was also reformulated: it stated that employed prisoners were entitled to 12 days' holiday annually.[7] The amendments of 1990 improved the status of the working prisoner and were welcomed in the academic literature (Kosut, 1993; 1995: 56).

Ex-prisoners are covered by unemployment law (the Unemployment Act of 1994, previously the Unemployment Act of 1989). They are entitled to assistance, including (if they have worked at least 180 days – since 1997, 365 days – during and before imprisonment) unemployment benefits (art. 23 of the Unemployment Act of 1994).

In 1995, the CEP of 1969 was amended again. Some of the amendments pertained to prison labour. The limit of unpaid labour was increased to 60 hours a month (new version of art. 49(4)) and the possibility of unpaid work for the benefit of local government was established (new art. 49(5)). Article 49(3) and art. 52, outlining the remuneration for prison labour, were also amended.

The CEP of 1997 contains detailed provisions on prison labour. Some are new; for example, art. 121 states that prisoners can be employed, with the consent of the prison director, as employees in terms of labour law.

## 6   Compensation for Work by Prisoners

According to the CEP of 1969, there were two types of prison labour: (1) paid labour in industry or services inside or

7   Before 1990, it was only seven days.

outside prison as well as domestic work and institutional maintenance labour, and (2) unpaid labour, that is, domestic work and institutional maintenance labour not exceeding 60 hours a month and work for state institutions.[8] Usually, domestic work and institutional maintenance labour were performed as paid labour, but the limit of 60 hours per month was not yet operational. Prison directors had to decide in advance whether the job would be treated as paid or unpaid labour.[9]

According to art. 49(3) of the CEP of 1969, the rate of remuneration for a prisoner's paid work should be determined in terms of the general rules applicable to a free employee's wage rate. Despite these provisions and for several reasons, such as lack of professional skills, low levels of efficiency and a disadvantaged social status, prisoners were actually paid very badly. In May 1996, the average remuneration for a prisoner's labour was 254 zloti (zl) per month, while the average wage in industry was 936 zl per month. What is more, since 1995, 'a prisoner can agree to lower remuneration' (art. 49(3) *in fine*), obviously in order to make it easier to find a job. However, according to the decision of the Constitutional Tribunal of 7 January 1997, 'lower remuneration' cannot be lower than the minimum wage established by the labour law.

Under national labour law and tax law regulations, the state deducts social security fees and taxes from the prisoner's remuneration. These deductions are transferred by the institution acting as employer. The Prison Labour Act provides for the deduction of the social security fees from a prisoner's remuneration (art. 6).

Other deductions were made from a prisoner's remuneration in terms of art. 52 of the CEP of 1969; 10 per cent of wages were deducted for the post-release assistance fund and up to 40 per cent for the state budget. A prisoner had to receive at least 50 per cent of his wage. Before 1995 this minimum was 25 per cent, and before 1989 (adoption of new Prison Rules) only 20 per cent. Before 1995, only 5 per cent was taken for the post-release assistance fund. Under para. 44 of the Prison Rules of 1989, no deductions in terms of art. 52 of the CEP of 1969 could be made from allowances paid for hard or dangerous labour, or labour which could be harmful to health, or from labour rewards and from money earned during overtime, or for special achievements.

8 Art. 49(3) to (5), see above.
9 Unpaid work in the prison, if performed well, can be rewarded by the prison director (art. 49, para. 4 of the CEP).

A prisoner could get more than 50 per cent of his wage, even up to 75 per cent, if he worked scrupulously and efficiently, if his family needed assistance or if he was obliged to pay compensation for injury caused by his crime. In the latter case the family or injured person got the full additional amount (paras 46 and 47 of the Prison Rules of 1989). In May 1996, 6,357 inmates who were obliged to give assistance to their families worked. In 1,563 cases, their remuneration had been increased, owing to the poverty of the family.

Before 1990, art. 53 was highly unfavourable to prisoners. Very often, the only money they ultimately received was pocket money (Holda and Rzeplinski, 1991: 456, 471-2). In 1990, art. 53 was amended, providing substantive protection to prisoners' remuneration.

The provisions of the new CEP of 1997 in respect of the compensation for work by prisoners are similar to the provisions of the CEP of 1969. The director of the prison decides on the employment of prisoners and determines the rate of remuneration for prisoners' labour. A prisoner has the right to file an appeal with the penitentiary court (art. 14(1) of the CEP of 1969, art. 7 of CEP of 1997). In practice, inmates rarely approach the court. They prefer other remedies: for example a petition to the Ombudsman.

## 7 International Human Rights Law and Prison Labour

There should be a convention against commerce in prison-made goods. However, it should not be applicable to countries where protective labour law rules have been extended to working prisoners and conditions of work are acceptable. Prisoners should receive special treatment under the international human rights law pertaining to employment. Today international law, especially the International Covenant on Civil and Political Rights and the European Convention on Human Rights, gives some protection to prison labour. Poland is party to these conventions.

## References

Bojarski, Tadeusz, Zbigniew Holda and Jacek Baranowski, eds. 1985. *Praca skazanych odbywajacych kare pozbawienia wolnosci.* Lublin: UMCS.

Bramska, Mieczyslawa. 1995. Zatrudnienie. *Biuletyn RPO Materialy* 28: 262–88.
Bulenda, Teodor, Zbigniew Holda and Andrzej Rzeplinski. 1994. Poland. In *Untersuchungshaft und Untersuchungshaftvollzug*, edited by F. Dünkel and J. Vagg. Freiburgi Br: Max-Planck-Institut für ausländisches und internationales Strafrecht.
Holda, Zbigniew. 1995. The Law of Corrections in Poland. In *Legal Reform in Post-Communist Europe*, edited by S. Frankowski and P.B. Stephan. Dordrecht: Kluwer.
Holda, Zbigniew and Andrzej Rzeplinski. 1991. The Polish Prison System in Mid-course: Prisoners' Rights and Prison Conditions in Poland on the Verge of Becoming Civilized. In *Imprisonment Today and Tomorrow*, edited by D. van Zyl Smit and F. Dünkel. Deventer: Kluwer.
Holda, Zbigniew and Jan Wojcieszczuk. 1983. Praca wiezniow – zagadnienia prawne. *Panstwo i Prawo* 3: 68–77.
International Labour Organisation. 1957. Forced Labour Convention (no.105).
Kosut, Anna. 1992. Prawo do pracy i obowiazek jej swiadczenia przez skazanych odbywajacych kare pozbawienia wolnosci. *Panstwo i Prawo* 2: 63–7.
Kosut, Anna. 1993. Prawne aspekty zatrudniania skazanych odbywajacych kare pozbawienia wolnosci. Unpublished PhD. thesis. Lublin: Maria Curie Sklodowska University Faculty of Law.
Kosut, Anna. 1995. Wplyw zatrudnienia w zakladzie karnym na uprawnienia pracownicze i prawo do zasilku dla bezrobotnych. *Praca i Zabezpieczenie Spoleczne* 10: 56–64.
Liszcz, Teresa. 1989. Zatrudnienie skazanych odbywajacych kare pozbawienia wolnosci. *Panstwo i Prawo* 2: 84–92.
Liszcz, Teresa. 1995. *Prawo pracy*. Gdansk: INFO-Trade.
Platek, Monika. 1985. Warunkowe zwolnienie a praca skazanych w swietle ustawy i praktyki. In *Praca skazanych odbywajacych kare pozbawienia wolnosci*, edited by T. Bojarski, Z. Holda and J. Baranowski. Lublin: UMCS.
Radzikowska, Barbara. 1992. Problemy zatrudnienia osob pozbawionych wolnosci. *Biuletyn RPO Materialy* 14: 49–62.
Raport o stanie wieziennictwa – perspektywy kontynuowania reform. 1995. *Przeglad Wieziennictwa Polskiego* 10: 51–70.
Wasek, Andrzej and Stanislaw Frankowski. 1995. Polish Criminal Law and Procedure. In *Legal Reform in Post-Communist Europe*, edited by S. Frankowski and P.B. Stephan. Dordrecht: Kluwer.
Zielinski, Tadeusz. 1993. Ochrona praw obywatelskich a reforma wieziennictwa. *Biuletyn RPO Materialy* 18: 5–20.

Zielinski, Tadeusz. 1995. Sprawozdanie Rzecznika Praw Obywatelskich za okres od 13 lutego 1994 r. do 12 lutego 1995 r. *Biuletyn RPO Materialy* 25.

## The Author
**Zbigniew Holda** is professor of criminology, penology and criminal law at the Universities of Lublin and of Kraków in Poland.

# 12 South Africa

DIRK VAN ZYL SMIT

## 1 Introduction

To a large extent the South African prison system has been shaped by the need for labour in the colonies out of which the Republic of South Africa developed. Yet the part played by prison labour in the modern South African economy is tiny. Even within the prison system, the current monetary value of prison labour is modest. The continuing importance of prison labour lies, it will be argued, in its symbolic embodiment of an ideal social order. Even this ideal is under severe strain. Moreover, the legal position in respect of prison labour is at odds with the reality on the ground, not to mention the demands of the new Constitution.

## 2 History

The beginning of the systematic exploitation of prison labour in southern Africa can be related quite specifically to a series of major social reforms introduced in the first half of the nineteenth century by the British authorities who had succeeded the Dutch as the colonial masters of the Cape Colony in the course of the Napoleonic wars.[1] The colony that the British inherited was one in which imprisonment was not a major form of punishment. Instead, punishments were harsh and physical and those serious offenders who were not put to death were generally banished from the colony. Forced labour was used, but it took the civil form of slave labour, rather than the systematic exploitation of sentenced offenders.[2]

---

1   The British first occupied the Cape from 1795 to 1802. It was returned to the Dutch for a brief period, 1803–6. Thereafter the formal British link was maintained until well into the twentieth century.

2   Not that the convicted were left entirely to their own devices: offenders banished to Robben Island off Cape Town in the seventeenth and eighteenth centuries were required to burn sea shells in kilns to make lime for the mainland, but this was a relatively isolated example of the use of convict labour.

The early nineteenth century saw major changes both in the penal system and in the demand for labour. Many of the harshest forms of physical punishment were abolished and fixed terms of imprisonment began to feature more prominently in sentences imposed on convicted offenders. At the same time, slave labour was phased out: the slave trade was outlawed in 1807 and slavery finally abolished in 1834 (Rayner, 1986).

These moves took place in the context of an increased demand for labour in a growing colony and a decline in the existing forms of social control. In 1823, a commission of inquiry was sent by the British authorities to investigate both labour problems and the administration of the Cape Colony generally. The Commission reported that the penal system needed to be overhauled to deal with labour matters on a racially neutral basis. It also reported that the existing gaols and lock-ups were not operating efficiently. In 1828, major new labour legislation was introduced which abolished formal racial discrimination in the control of workers, but nothing was done about the administration of prisons (Newton-King, 1980).

Against this background the prison population of the Colony was increasing. It grew from 861 in 1828 to 4,242 in 1842 (Van Wyk, 1964: 154). The virtual demise of the old system of harsh physical punishment of the criminal without its replacement by any coherent new approach was what confronted the newly appointed Colonial Secretary at the Cape, John Montagu, when, in 1843, he was charged with the control of the local penal system (Breitenbach, 1959; Van Zyl Smit, 1981). Before serving at the Cape, Montagu had been in Tasmania, where he had come into contact with Captain Maconochie, the superintendent of the well-known Norfolk Island prison. Maconochie had introduced major innovations in prison administration and Montagu had been party to drafting a detailed body of rules according to which the system should operate. These included provision for techniques designed to rehabilitate prisoners, not by solitary confinement (as was being attempted in European and North American countries at that time), but by rewards determined according to a system of points awarded for meritorious work and general conduct (Barry, 1958).

Soon after his arrival at the Cape, Montagu sought to introduce changes in accordance with the general approach adopted by Maconochie. The conditions for change were propitious: the agricultural sector of the economy was beginning to expand rapidly. For products to be marketed and state control of the hinterland to be maintained, a communications structure that would give easy access to the interior was required. At the same time, the rehabilitative ideal was gaining acceptance by the colonial authorities as a positive goal of punishment. That rehabilitation could be achieved by 'useful' labour made Montagu's ideas more attractive to them.

A new legislative framework was created by the enactment, in 1844, of an Ordinance 'For the Discipline and Safe Custody of the Convicts Employed on the Public Roads'. All convicts serving sentences of hard labour of longer than three months in the scattered lock-ups were consolidated into three major convict stations. Convicts housed in these convict stations (in fact, large, portable wooden prisons) were used to build a 'hard road'[3] across the flats surrounding Cape Town, and to build various mountain passes into the interior. At the same time, the existing convict station on Robben Island was reorganized and eventually disbanded as its inmates were transferred to road camps on the mainland (Van Wyk, 1964: 235).

Life in the convict stations was highly organized according to precise regulations drafted by Montagu himself. Regardless of race, prisoners were initially divided into two groups – the chain gang and the road party. A tripartite system of classification, based on Montagu's ideas, which consisted of a punishment class, a probationary class and a good conduct class, was introduced in 1854 (ibid.: 236). Prisoners could be promoted from one group to another for good behaviour. They could also earn small cash payments, privileges and even a limited reduction of sentence. The power of overseers to inflict physical punishment was carefully circumscribed in the regulations.

Important benefits followed from the improved system. Major roads and mountain passes built by convicts provided, at very little cost to the state, vital links with the interior. At the same time, the convicts were protected, to some extent, against ill-treatment by the bureaucratic regulations that limited powers of punishment. Diet and standards of hygiene improved and opportunities for secular and religious education increased (Newman, 1855: chs 6 and 7).

The benefits of the changes introduced by Montagu must be seen in the context of the changed conceptions of punishment which underpinned them. Conditions of detention remained harsh, although their purpose shifted. The state ceased to inflict pain as a

3    The term *hardepad* (Afrikaans for 'hard road') is still used colloquially to describe penal servitude.

direct form of social control and attempted instead to mould, through the reformative influence of the totally controlled environment of the prison, the attitudes and morals of convicts and, through them, of society as a whole. Indirectly, the sanction of physical punishment remained in the guise of penalties for disciplinary infringements in prison.

There was no attempt by the colonial authorities to disguise the fact that they were exercising penal power in a new way (cf. Foucault, 1977) and with specific objectives. Thus Lord Grey, the Secretary of State for the Colonies, wrote to the Governor at the Cape in 1850 about the advantages of the system in the new convict stations and noted that 'both the discipline upheld at the stations, and the testimony of men who have completed their sentences, bear evidence to the controlling influence exercised on the convicts' minds' (Newman, 1855: 152).

Nor was there any attempt to disguise the utilitarian benefits of the new system for the authorities. On the contrary, attention was drawn to the advantages of 'creating new men'. Thus Newman, Montagu's contemporary and biographer, emphasized:

> You may behold [at the convict station] indolence learning industry, and the idle and thieving Bosjesman, and the cattle-lifting Kafir, making a high-road for commerce and civilization, in which the spoor of theft shall give place to the rut of the farmer's wain. In those stations the savage nature is restrained by wholesome discipline, and yet the same savage by his penal toil turns the wild mountain-pass to a road of usefulness. (Ibid.: 109)

At one level of analysis, the comprehensive reform of the penal system introduced by John Montagu represents a signal achievement in penal policy in southern Africa. Indeed, its protagonists claimed that it was a system from which others could learn.[4] Its system of classifying prisoners was relatively sophisticated and is similar to that in use today in South African prisons, where it is considered to be an essential part of the rehabilitative process (Van Zyl Smit, 1992).

4   See, for example, the letter from W.E. Gladstone to Sir Peregrine Maitland (Governor of the Cape Colony) dated 26 April 1846, in which he describes Montagu's innovations as 'calculated to throw much useful light on the general question of convict management' (quoted in Newman, 1855: 486).

There is, however, another and perhaps more fundamental level at which the reforms of the 1840s and 1850s have significance. The use of prison labour opened the way, wrote Lord Grey in 1850, for closer control of colonial convicts (Newman, 1855: 152). This indicates the increasing importance of both the qualitative and quantitative aspects of surveillance by the state in the sense suggested by Foucault (1977). The fact that most of the labourers 'trained' by the system were indigenous inhabitants, and therefore outsiders drawn into the net for the first time, was to be a significant factor, in spite of the protestations of equality of treatment of the races.

In the period immediately after the introduction of Montagu's reform, there was little further development of the prison system. Montagu's innovations in the penal system were not abandoned after his departure from the colony in 1852, but much less attention was paid to penal questions. Nevertheless, prisoners sentenced to hard labour continued to be employed on public works and the emphasis in the following two decades shifted from mountain passes to harbours, with the construction of the breakwater[5] in Cape Town as the most prominent activity (Venter, 1959: 49–50). Nevertheless, during this period control of the prison system as a whole deteriorated and little effort was made to implement the positive, rehabilitative aspects of Montagu's penal policy.

At a structural level, however, major changes were taking place in southern African society. In particular, the successful mining of diamonds after 1871 drew a large number of additional colonists to the country. As diamond mining became more complex, a need arose for more labour than was freely available. In addition, the larger mines required stricter discipline than before (Turrell 1982a: 292; 1982b: 45–76). At the same time the demands of the mines disrupted the existing patterns on the colonial farms. Once again the prison system was to be put to use and public policy regarding incarceration was to be adapted.

Inevitably, the focus for change shifted to Kimberley, the centre of the diamond mining industry. In 1882, by government proclamation, the Kimberley prison became the first prison in the Cape to be

---

5  The term 'breakwater' eventually became synonymous with a long period of imprisonment. Cf. *R v. Heine* 1910 CPD 371 where the accused was identified by a mortally ill witness who said (at 373): 'I am going to die. Mrs Heine is the cause of it all. I want her to go to the Breakwater.'

legally segregated along racial lines (Van Wyk, 1964: 338–9). In 1885, the De Beers Diamond Mining Company became the first non-state corporate entity to employ convicts on a regular basis (Turrell, 1982a: 292). The mine owners were clearly pleased with this arrangement. As the official Commission of Inquiry of 1888 reported:

> Indeed, so satisfied are the De Beers Mining Company with the convicts, that they have agreed to take 300 completely off the hands of the Government, and pay in addition 2d. per man per day for them. Thus the country will make an actual profit of over 700 pounds per annum from the labour of these 300 convicts. (*Report*, 1888: 305)

The profit to the De Beers Diamond Mining Company was not mentioned.

In the two decades after 1885, the employment of convict labour on the diamond fields increased. Another mining company also used prisoners from the local Kimberley gaol (Turrell, 1982a: 292). The dominant De Beers Diamond Mining Company went a step further and built a branch prison which it staffed and where prisoners were housed, fed and controlled by the company. The number of convict labourers employed by De Beers increased from 300 per day in 1885 to 600 per day after 1888 (Venter, 1959: 50). By 1903, large numbers of prisoners convicted in the areas inhabited by black peasants were being transferred to the De Beers convict station. A parliamentary question in 1903 elicited the reply that, during the period from 1 June 1902 to 31 May 1903, 496 convicts had been transferred from the 'Native Territories' of Tembuland and Griqualand East to De Beers (*Hansard*, 1903). This was admitted to be part of a scheme by which 'government undertook to supply to De Beers native labour up to a daily average of 11 000 when practicable' (ibid.: 67). Although it was not stipulated that these labourers had to be convicts, 'it had been the practice to supply convict labour in this connection, the convict labour being considered suitable for the purpose' (ibid.). The role of the state as the provider of unskilled black labour for the mines through the penal system had become manifest.

The deployment of convict labour in this way had a profound impact on the whole mode of social control exercised by the state. As diamond mining developed in the 1880s, convict labour in the mines must be seen in conjunction with other means used to produce, primarily from the indigenous population, the large, docile, unskilled labour force required to work the deeper mines. One of these means was the system of 'pass laws' that required black men in the area (with the important exception of skilled, mixed-race Cape artisans) to carry passes showing that they had a fixed place of abode and employment. Failure to produce a pass resulted in a sentence of imprisonment and thus in forced labour. There is evidence that, by 1888, a significant proportion of the prison population had been created in this way (*Report*, 1888).

The second institution that paralleled the development of the company prison was the so-called 'closed compound', in which unskilled black workers who had entered into a contract with a mining company were housed for fixed periods during which they were not allowed free access to the outside world. It appears that the 'total institution' of the convict station provided the model for the compound system. The Inspector of Mines wrote in 1886: 'In these convict barracks, or branch gaols, the perfection of the compound system may be said to have been reached. The only important difference being that between compulsory and voluntary service' (*Report*, 1886: 12).

The use of convict labour in the mines disrupted labour patterns in other sectors as well. Prisoners had been hired out to individuals since early in the nineteenth century, but this had taken place on an ad hoc basis. In 1887, these procedures were reorganized and placed on a more systematic footing. Provision was made for convict labour to be made available, at standard rates of payment, to bodies such as municipalities and to private persons such as farmers. Such bodies or individuals were to provide implements and even guards, who were to be sworn in as special constables. Convicts who performed well received an allowance. An attempt was made to limit patronage and abuse by forbidding government officials to use convict labour in their private capacities (Van Wyk, 1964: 347–8).

Another aspect of penal policy that emerged in the 1880s was the first systematic attempt to segregate prisoners on racial lines. Here again the developments in the mining industry played a crucial part. Labour historians have noted that latent racial prejudice was used to shape the way in which labour was organized and controlled in the mines. Mine owners treated white workers differently from black workers. White workers were allowed some measure of freedom to organize and campaign for better conditions for themselves. Black workers were tightly controlled in the compounds and the prisons. To some extent the tolerance of white workers was conditional – on their not making common cause with their black co-workers. The distinction between 'civilized' (white) artisans and 'barbarous' (black) labourers was emphasized. This enabled mine owners to exploit unskilled black workers by encouraging what Johnstone (1976) has called a 'class colour bar', while buying off the more skilled white miners.

Changes in the penal system of the Cape Colony mirrored these developments. Montagu's ideals of formal equality of treatment were abandoned at precisely the time that a segregated labour force began to be deployed in Kimberley.

The model of convict mine labour proved to be influential outside the Cape Colony as well. Developments in the sphere of the application of prison labour were relatively slow in the Colony of Natal and in the republics of the Orange Free State and the Transvaal, that is in the other three southern African territories which would eventually make up the Union of South Africa. However, the British occupation of the two republics in the middle of 1900 led to a major reorganization of the penal systems of both territories. In the Transvaal in particular, the authorities were faced with an enormous increase in the prison population and with major disorganization of the supply of labour to the mines. Attempts to control the latter through a system of 'pass laws' further increased the prison population (Van Onselen, 1985: 68). As with the diamond mines in the Cape, the 'solution' adopted was to allow a mining company (in this case the ERPM gold mining company in Boksburg) to build a prison for approximately 800 black prisoners. The company then had to pay the government one shilling per day per prisoner to be allowed to use the prisoners as labourers on its mines (Venter, 1959: 122).

After the Union of South Africa was established in 1910, the administrations of the various territorial prison systems were centralized and their legislative bases were overhauled. Major changes in the internal use of labour took place with gradual development of prison workshops and the establishment of farm prisons, which were designed to produce food for the prisoners in the system. Allocation of prisoners to these work programmes was done on a specifically racial basis. Inside work, that is work in workshops, was reserved for 'Europeans' and work outside prisons for 'natives' (Department of Justice, 1917).

Prison labour policies, allowing only black prisoners to work outside the prisons, remained largely unchanged for the next 30 years. If anything, the demand for prison labour from private contractors expanded. Although the mines were not, proportionately, as large employers as in the past,[6] the demand from the agricultural sector increased. Farmers were severely hit by the depression of the 1930s. In 1934, a scheme was introduced whereby farmers could hire prisoners from the Prisons Department for 6d a day. These prisoners had to work for the farmers for the remainder of their sentences. The farmers in turn had to house them: that is, detain them in their private farm gaols (Lansdown Commission, 1947: paras 901 and 902; Corry, 1977: 129–30).

Prison labour policy in South Africa was reviewed comprehensively for the first and only time this century by a judicial commission in 1947. The Lansdown Commission on Prison and Penal Reform contrasted an ideal of reformative training for all prisoners with the bleak reality. It noted prominently that 'stone-breaking by hand, to provide necessary occupation, has been a feature in many prisons and gaols in the Union' (Lansdown Commission, 1947: para. 823). Constructive work in the sense of trade training was available only to a few 'European' men (ibid.: paras 835–6). The Commission's reform recommendations were far-reaching. Make-work routines were sharply criticized and it was suggested that there be a serious attempt to make training opportunities available to women and to prisoners of all races.

The Commission was also broadly critical of the provision of prison labour to outside institutions. In particular, it condemned the schemes such as the '6d-a-day' scheme where prisoners served part of their sentences under the direct control of 'outsiders', in this instance farmers (ibid.: para. 908).

In all, the Report of the Lansdown Commission may be viewed as presenting a vision of a prison labour system suitable to a liberal democratic society of the immediate post-World War II era. In 1947, South Africa was not such a society. The years after the publication of the Report of the Lansdown Commission saw prison labour increasingly becoming an issue of public debate and a focus for both practical and symbolic disputes. One dispute arose almost immediately, namely the proposed rejection of the '6d-a-day' scheme. On the basis of preliminary findings of the Commission, the government ordered the suspension of the '6d-a-day' scheme even before the Commission had presented its final report. However, as a result of 'urgent representations' made to the Minister of Justice, the

6   The use of prisoners in the mines seems to have declined gradually, until it was finally abandoned in 1955 (Corry, 1977: 154).

system of farm labour in lieu of imprisonment for short-term prisoners was reinstated almost immediately, with some minor additional safeguards, as the '9d-a-day' scheme. In its final Report, the Commission was highly critical of the new scheme. It reiterated its earlier findings on the importance of not hiring out prison labour, but to no avail (ibid.: para. 1105).

At the same time the fragile social consensus around prisons was breaking down in other aspects. Wide publicity was given to a series of articles on prison labour in the magazine *Drum*, which was aimed primarily at African readers. In an extraordinary series of investigations, the *Drum* journalist Henry Nxumalo managed to get himself employed on one of the farms where prisoners were sent in terms of the '9d-a-day' scheme (Nxumalo, 1952). Subsequently, he allowed himself to be arrested for a 'pass offence' and was admitted to the Johannesburg Central Gaol (Nxumalo, 1954). In both cases the reports, which were written under the pseudonym, 'Mr Drum', were vivid eye-witness accounts of abuses, accompanied by photographs of a mounted farmer with a whip, and in the case of the gaol, of prisoners forced to dance naked before others in the course of being searched. These allegations were widely reported in the daily press in South Africa as well as abroad (Sampson, 1956).

The immediate response was not to deal directly with these abuses or immediately to seek a new consensus. In fact the use of prison labour on private farms was increased during the 1950s by allowing 'bona fide Farmers' Associations' to build 'prison farm outstations' which were then handed over to the Department of Prisons to manage. Farmers who contributed were entitled to employ a number of convicts proportionate to their contribution to the construction of the prison (Corry, 1977: 155–6).

However, the government of the day was not unconcerned about the legitimacy of its prison system. In 1959, prison legislation in South Africa was modernized and, insofar as the, by then, explicit policy of apartheid allowed, formally brought in line with the United Nations Standard Minimum Rules for the Treatment of Prisoners (Prisons Act, 1959). In the course of these legislative changes, the sentence of imprisonment with hard labour was removed from the statute book (Criminal Law Amendment Act, 1959). In theory, all sentences of imprisonment were now subject to the same conditions. At the same time, the '9d-a-day' scheme was abolished.

The effect of the 1959 legal changes was not immediately apparent, since the allocation of work inside the prisons did not change for many years. Moreover, the '9d-a-day' scheme was replaced by a system of 'parole' in terms of which black prisoners were released on condition that they entered into contracts of employment with farmers who housed the parolees under closely supervised conditions for the remainder of their sentences. Failure to work meant immediate reimprisonment. This new system placed the farmers concerned in a position to take advantage of these parolees in the same way as they had done with prisoners under the earlier schemes, and in time similar allegations of abuse were made (Corry, 1977: 159–60).

Since 1959, changes in prison labour patterns have been piecemeal. Most dramatic has been the relatively steep decline in the significance of prisoners working in commercial agriculture. In the case of the so-called 'prison outstations', it is possible to point to a specific catalyst. South Africa was warned that the production of goods for export using forced labour was a contravention of the General Agreement on Tariffs and Trade and that the convict labour from the outstations was such labour (ibid.: 157). As a direct result, the outstations were closed down,[7] and the automatic provision of convict labour to the contributing farmers ceased. At about the same time, around the middle of 1988, the practice of hiring out short-term prisoners to farmers was discontinued (Van Zyl, 1996).

Patterns of labour use inside prison have been far more resistant to change. Accounts of conditions experienced by political prisoners in the 1960s and 1970s are full of descriptions of stone breaking and other hard and relatively pointless manual labour being performed by prisoners under harsh conditions (for example, Mandela, 1994: 390). But such conditions were not restricted to political prisoners. As late as October 1984, the Swiss criminologist, Dr Haesler, was shown prisoners who were breaking stones inside cages made of chicken wire at the maximum security Brandvlei prison in the Western Cape (Haesler, 1986). The cages were ostensibly to prevent prisoners from attacking one another with the heavy hammers they were using. Once the stones were small enough they were to be pushed through the gaps in the chicken wire. Only on 24 March 1992 was this practice formally abandoned (Van Zyl, 1996).

The biggest change to labour patterns inside prison has come with the abandonment of racial segregation inside prison. This has meant that access to workshops and other training is now available to all prisoners. The present author's own observations confirm a

---

7   The last outstation was closed on 30 June 1988 (Van Zyl, 1996).

high degree of racial mixing in prison workshops. Official and unofficial accounts from prison officers confirm that mixing in these facilities has been relatively problem-free.

## 3 The Current Situation

It is not possible to gain a clear quantitative impression of the deployment of prison labour from current published sources. The most recent Report of the Department of Correctional Services for the year 1 January to 31 December 1997 (Department of Correctional Services, 1998) does reveal that relatively few prisoners receive formal training. Thus training in the building trade, which could lead to the writing of a trade test, was given to 764 prisoners. In the workshops, 436 prisoners were trained. To these figures one may add a further 70 prisoners who received hairdressing training. If all these prisoners are added together (and it is assumed that no single prisoner was trained on more than one programme) a total of 1,270 prisoners received systematic training in a work situation (ibid.: 18).

The 1997 Annual Report also deals with less formal 'career-directed skills-training' which it reports as including welding, autobody repair work, fencing, bricklaying, basic woodwork, needlework, patchwork and leatherwork (ibid.: 19). Reference is also made to other agricultural training. In all these fields, 2,382 prisoners were involved in external courses in career skills training (ibid.). A further 4,726 prisoners received training in internal courses of the same kind and in 'entrepreneurial skills'. If one combines the number of prisoners involved in these two types of skills training and adds the 7,108 prisoners to the 1,270 prisoners involved in formal trade training, one reaches a total of 8,378 prisoners involved in any kind of systematic work-related training. These are the only figures that the Annual Report provides in this regard.

The conclusion to be drawn from this attempt to quantify available information is obviously that very few prisoners are being trained in a work situation. It is not entirely clear what percentage of the prison population was being trained. For comparative purposes, one may note that on 31 December 1997 there were 142,410 prisoners being detained within the national prison system. Of these, 41,435 were unsentenced prisoners (Department of Correctional Services, 1998). The result of comparing these figures, recorded on a particular day, with the number of prisoners trained throughout the year is inescapably that, even amongst prisoners serving long terms, very many are not receiving formal, work-related training of any kind.

Fortunately, at the time that the paper on which this chapter is based was originally written, the Department of Correctional Services was able to provide more detailed quantitative information than was available in the published sources (Van Zyl, 1996). Statistics of the average number of prisoners employed daily in each month of 1995 are contained in Figure 12.1, while Figure 12.2 contains statistics on the monthly prison population. From these figures it is clear that only a relatively small percentage of prisoners is employed at all. In the month of December 1995, for example, there were an average of 112,572 prisoners detained in South African prisons. Of these, 27,320 were unsentenced and therefore were not liable to work.[8] Of the remaining 85,252 prisoners, only 21,411 (25 per cent) were employed. Since 1995, the number of employed prisoners has declined even further. In 1997, an average of 10,750 'work opportunities' were provided for a prison population that reached 100,975 prisoners at the end of that year (Department of Correctional Services, 1998).

The employment patterns too are significant: 94 per cent of the prisoners (20,121) counted as employed worked inside the prison, 6 per cent (1,225) were hired out and a further 65 prisoners (less than 1 per cent) performed work outside prison on an ex gratia basis. These figures can be contrasted with those for earlier years. In the statistical year from 1 July 1972 to 30 June 1973, the average daily number of sentenced prisoners in the system was 76,034 (Corry, 1977: 195). Of these, 66,689 (88 per cent were recorded as being employed on the average working day. The number of prisoners recorded as working then included no fewer than 29,949 (39 per cent) working outside prisons, either as agricultural labourers provided by the prison farm outstations or otherwise. Unemployment amongst sentenced prisoners was only 12 per cent in 1972/73, as against 75 per cent in December 1995.

The conclusion to be drawn is that there has been a massive decline in the number of prisoners working outside prison. This can be attributed primarily to the prohibition on the hiring out of prison labour to farmers and also to other forms of commerce and industry. The prison authorities explain that, as a rule, prisoners who are hired out currently work mostly, although not exclusively,

---

[8] For details of the position of unsentenced prisoners, see below.

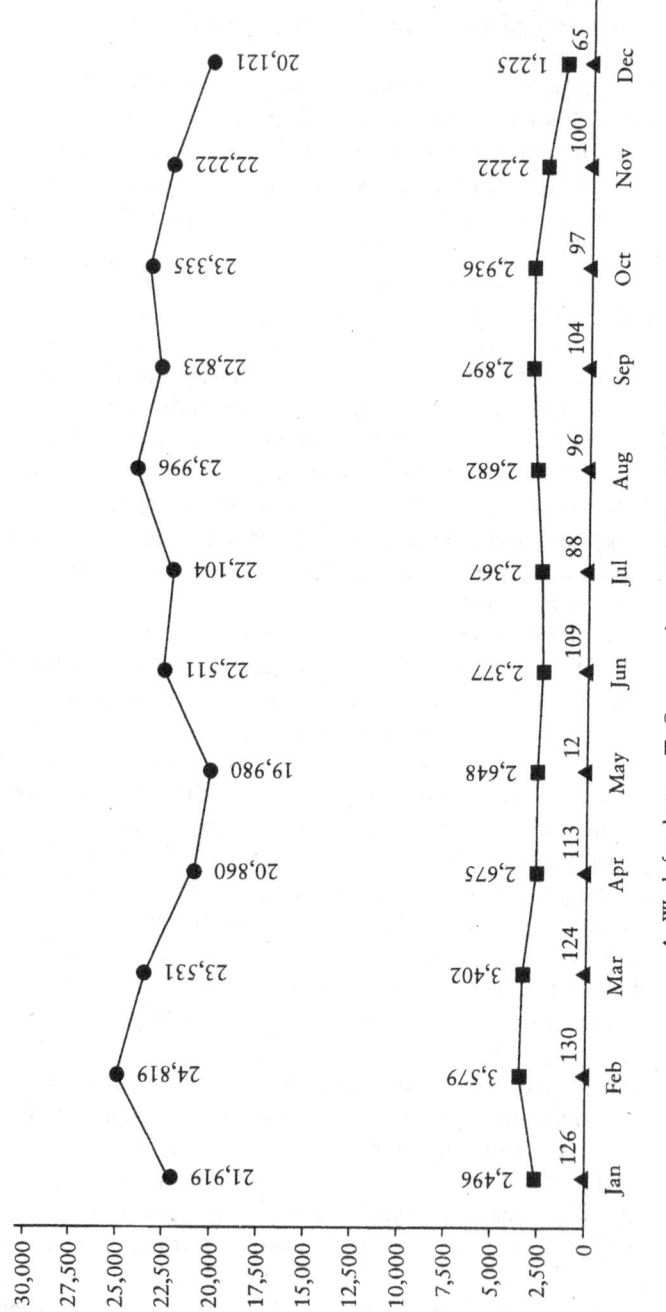

Figure 12.1: Monthly Labour Statistics for 1995

# SOUTH AFRICA

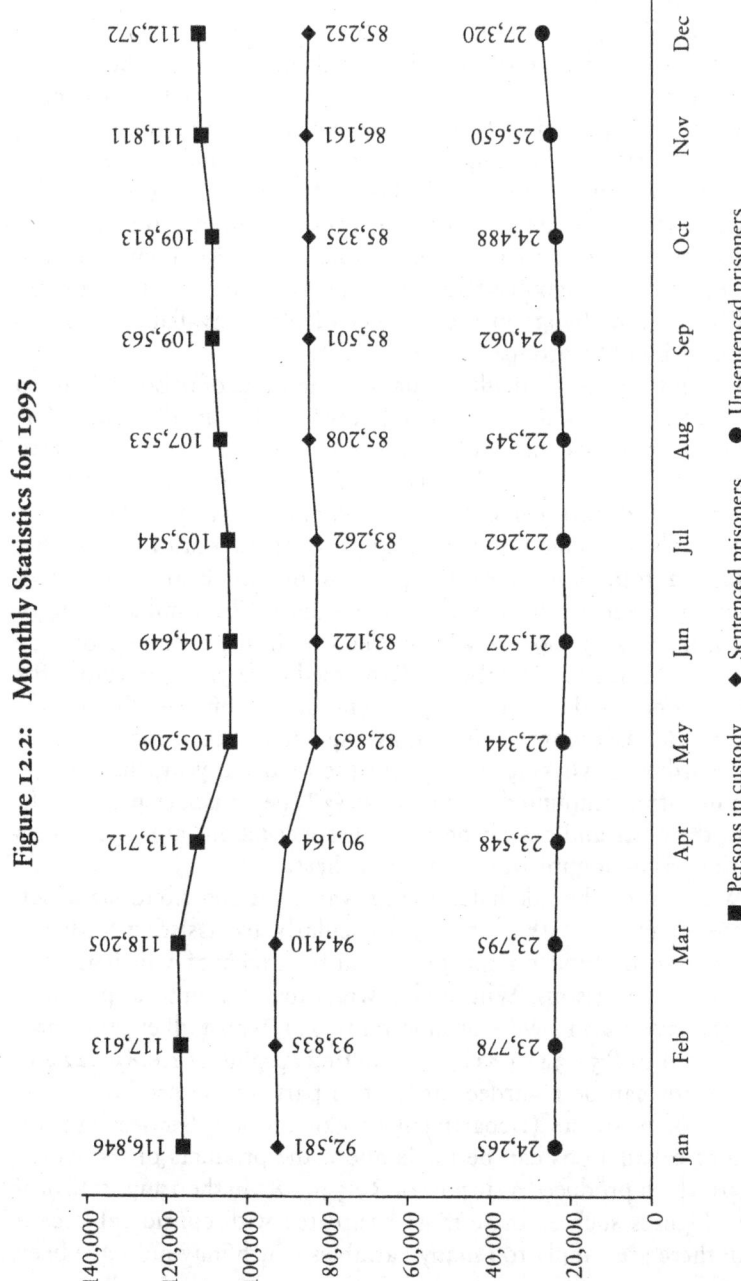

Figure 12.2: Monthly Statistics for 1995

for private individuals (in their gardens, for example) or for sports clubs and the like.

On available information, precise comparisons cannot be made in respect of the type of employment available inside the system. Corry (1977) recorded that in 1972/73 approximately 2,600 prisoners were employed daily in workshops, 3,000 in building groups, 6,000 on prison farms and a further 15,500 in maintenance. The total average of 27,100 is not very different from the figures for 1995 when, in some months, the average number of employed prisoners was just above 24,000 (Figure 12.1). 'Maintenance' is in any event a fairly flexible figure and the evidence suggests that there has been little change in the number of places available in workshops or building groups.

It is notoriously difficult to quantify the value of prison labour to the system as a whole. What is known is that in the fiscal year 1995/96 the Department of Correctional Services was reimbursed almost R4 million for the labour of prisoners who worked for other government departments. A further R2 million was paid by private individuals or companies who hired prisoners to work for them. Set against a total budget of R2,421 million, these are very small amounts. Even smaller is the total amount of R2.8 million paid in gratuities to all prisoners who worked both in prison and outside during the same statistical year. Expressed differently, gratuities for labour amounted to only 1 per cent of the budget. Or, if one assumes (conservatively) that an average of 20,000 prisoners could be regarded as working throughout the financial year, the average remuneration amounted to R140 (US$38) per prisoner per year. In sum, the costs and cash benefits of prisoner labour are small items on the prison administration balance sheet.

What cannot be calculated in this way is the contributions which prisoners make to the system, particularly by assisting with the production of food on the prison farms, much of which is consumed in the prisons. What is known is that agricultural products worth R57,178,212 were produced in 1997, whilst all expenditures amounted to R50,342,983. The resulting surplus of R6,835,229 in this sector can be regarded, at least in part, as the product of the labour of prisoners (Department of Correctional Services, 1998). Similar calculations can be made about the products of the workshops which produced a surplus of R9,330,485 in the 1997 statistical year. Figures such as these must be treated with considerable caution: there are simply too many variables which may not have been taken into account.

It is even harder to make generalizations about attitudes towards work. The 1994 Annual Report notes, however, that in that year there were various incidents of labour unrest both amongst prison staff and amongst prisoners and that this led to 'a decrease in the availability and productivity of members and prisoners' (Department of Correctional Services, 1995: 34). These careful words refer not only to the prison riots which took place in 1994, but also to the rise of trade unionism amongst prison officers. The impression, confirmed in discussion with prison officers and by the decline in prosecutions of prisoners who refuse to work (see below), is that the overall work ethic in the prisons has declined in recent years. This tendency is not universal. In some prisons, such as Pollsmoor prison near Cape Town, there are apparently more prisoners who wish to work than there are opportunities available. However, as far as can be ascertained, this is not true of the system as a whole.

## 4 Specific Issues

### 4.1 Involuntary Servitude

The formal legal position is that the duty of prisoners to work is expressly enacted by primary legislation. In the case of sentenced prisoners, s.77 of the Correctional Services Act (1959) obliges such prisoners to perform 'such labour, tasks and other duties as may be assigned to [them] by the Commissioner [of Correctional Services]'. What may be assigned to such a prisoner by the Commissioner is limited by the provisions of the Correctional Service Act. In theory, a special order of court may lay down how a prisoner shall be treated,[9] but since the abolition of the sentence of hard labour in 1959 the courts have had no power to order that a sentence of imprisonment include labour of a particular kind. In the light of the fact that the manner in which prisoners should be treated and trained is governed by legislation, it has been held that the courts have lost the authority to lay down binding instructions in this regard as part of their sentences (*S v. Nkosi* 1984). The powers of the Commissioner (that is, of the prison authorities) to order a prisoner to work are very extensive. They are restricted only by the somewhat vaguely stated purposes of imprisonment emerging from the Act as a whole.

9    Cf. s.31 of the Correctional Services Act, which provides that a sentenced prisoner is to undergo a sentence 'in the manner directed in the warrant by the court'.

The duty of unsentenced prisoners to work is far more limited. The general rule is that such prisoners are not compelled to work, except for such work as is required for purpose of hygiene. This is translated into a requirement that such prisoners clean the cells, adjoining courtyards, corridors, toilets, bedding and eating utensils they use (s.81 of the Correctional Services Act, 1959; Departmental Order B IV(2)(*d*)(ii)).

It is a disciplinary contravention for any prisoner to refuse to work when legally required to do so.[10] The prohibition is contained in Prison Regulation 99(1)(*d*) which provides that a prisoner who 'is idle, careless or negligent in his work or refuses to work' is guilty of a disciplinary contravention. The nature of the work required was considered in *S v. Pule* (1970) where the court emphasized that even a sentenced prisoner need only work when ordered to do so by a member of the department under whose control the prisoner is. Moreover, the work has to relate to the training of the prisoner as determined by the Commissioner. Both these elements have to be present before it can be found that Regulation 99(1)(*d*) has been contravened. Refusal of a prisoner to work when instructed by a member of the department to do so could also be prosecuted indirectly by, for example, charging a prisoner with the disciplinary offence of failing to obey a lawful order. Although the courts have on occasion been critical of the disciplinary charges brought on this ground, they have generally upheld convictions even where they have had doubts about the need for the instruction or order concerned (*S v. Saayman* 1987; *S v. November* 1988).

A new and as yet largely unexplored dimension has been added to South African prison law by the recognition of entrenched fundamental rights in the 1996 Constitution of the Republic of South Africa. Section 13 of the Constitution provides simply and without exception: 'No one may be subjected to slavery, servitude or forced labour.' Section 12 of the so-called 'interim Constitution' of 1993 (the Republic of South Africa Constitution Act 200 of 1993) contained an identical provision. Applied literally, this section could mean that a prisoner could mount a constitutional challenge to the lawfulness of legislation compelling prisoners to work or of instructions seeking to enforce such legislation in specific cases. The rule is that legislation which conflicts with a constitutionally entrenched fundamental right is unconstitutional unless it can be justified by

---

[10] Cf. *R v. Mtiyane* (1956) which deals with this point in the context of the previous 1911 Prisons and Reformatories Act.

the limitations clause of the Constitution. The limitations clause, s.36 of the Constitution, allows entrenched rights to be limited by law of general application. Such law must be reasonable and justifiable in an open and democratic society based on human dignity, freedom and equality. In addition, it must take into account all relevant factors including:

(a) the nature of the right;
(b) the importance of the purpose of the limitation;
(c) the nature and extent of the limitation;
(d) the relation between the limitation and its purpose; and
(e) less restrictive means to achieve the purpose. (Section 36 of the 1996 Constitution)

In practice, it would appear that, currently, disciplinary sanctions are rarely used against prisoners who refuse to work.[11]

Formally, additional work requirements cannot be imposed as punishments for infringements of prison discipline. Since the abolition of corporal punishment, dietary punishments and solitary confinement, the penalties which may be imposed for disciplinary contraventions are relatively mild. They are limited to the deprivation of 'one or more privileges and indulgences for a period not exceeding two months' (s.54(13) of the Correctional Services Act, 1959 as amended in 1993). The same legislation also provides specifically that prisoners should not be reclassified because they commit a disciplinary infringement. In practice, work allocation is determined by so-called 'institutional committees' at each prison. These committees are also responsible for discipline. There is a real possibility that disciplinary infringements will be met by prisoners being allocated different kinds of work or no work at all. Indeed, a

[11] In the six-month period from 1 July to 31 December 1995, a total of 346 prisoners were convicted of a contravention of discipline because they refused to work. A further breakdown of the figures reveals marked regional differences. During this period of six months, only one prisoner in the Northern Cape Command and six prisoners in the Eastern Cape Command were found guilty of refusing to work. During the same period, the number of convictions in the Western Cape Command was 146. These differences suggest significant variations in enforcement policies. *Source*: direct communication from the Department of Correctional Services, 10 May 1996.

prisoner who creates 'disciplinary difficulties' may not be dealt with through the disciplinary system. A reclassification of security or general privilege category will achieve the same result. Security classification is particularly important, for prisoners regarded as requiring maximum security detention generally do not work or, if they do, are involved only in the most repetitive forms of physical labour (Africa Watch Prison Project, 1994: 65).

### 4.2 Prisoners' Right to Work

Hitherto South African prison law has not recognized a positive right to work. The reality of the system is that there is not enough work of any description available for prisoners who wish to break the monotony of the prison routine.

In theory, there are arguments which could be advanced in favour of saying that South African prisoners have a legally enforceable right to work. In 1992, the position in South African law was analysed as follows:

> As a positive right to rehabilitation has not been fully recognized in South Africa, prisoners are not likely to be able to compel the prison authorities to provide them with work. The Department of Correctional Services does have a general duty to attempt to provide all prisoners with work, as one of its functions is 'as far as practicable ... to train [prisoners] in habits of industry and labour'. However, the qualification 'as far as practicable' makes this duty difficult to enforce. Absence of the opportunity to work for a long period may, of course, be a deprivation, which could damage the mental health of a prisoner. Prisoners may be able to enforce a right to work on this basis, but the problems of proving the causal nexus would be considerable. Where the opportunity to work is deliberately withheld as a subtle form of punishment, however, the prisoners will be able to ask a court to review the decision of the prison authorities to treat them in this way. (Van Zyl Smit, 1992: 217)

There have been no significant changes in the specific legislation dealing with prison labour since this analysis was undertaken.[12] However, the South African constitutional order changed drastically and specific constitutional recognition is now given to a number of the rights of prisoners. These include the provision that 'Every-

---

12  See, however, the draft Correctional Services Bill presented to Parliament in 1998 and discussed below.

one who is detained, including every sentenced prisoner, has the right ... to conditions of detention that are consistent with human dignity' (s.35(2)(e) of the Constitution, 1996). The Constitution also outlaws torture and treatment or punishment that is cruel, inhuman or degrading (s.12 of the Constitution, 1996). On the basis of these provisions it may now be easier than in the past to argue that long-term prisoners at least have to be given the opportunity to work in order to ensure that they do not deteriorate mentally and physically while in prison. Such deterioration would both impair their human dignity and be a cruel, inhuman or degrading form of punishment.

The constitutional commitment to legality and administrative justice (s.33 of the Constitution, 1996) could also be relevant to prisoners' right to work. Given that the opportunity to work is extremely valuable to prisoners, they may well have a legal interest in the fair allocation of work. What 'fair' might mean in this context has yet to be considered.

It is reasonable to assume that enforced idleness is inimical to rehabilitation. The legal question then becomes whether prisoners have a positive right to rehabilitation. The references in the Constitution to the right to human dignity may provide a basis for the development of a positive right to rehabilitation from which a right to work could be deduced.

Another and more direct avenue to the recognition of a positive right to rehabilitation may be an amendment specifying such a right in the primary legislation governing prisons. In 1998, an entirely new Correctional Services Bill was presented to Parliament. It specifies that the objective of the implementation of a sentence of imprisonment is to enable 'the sentenced prisoner to lead a socially responsible and crime-free life in the future'.[13] The new Bill does not, however, go as far as recognizing a positive right to work.

### 4.3 Work and Release

One of the most controversial aspects of the South African prison system is its release policy. The current policy, which came into operation in 1994, is that all prisoners are considered by a parole board for release on parole after serving half their sentences. (Since 1994, remission of sentence cannot be granted. All prisoners are supposed to serve their full sentences either in prison or in the community while on parole.) The requirement that prisoners must

---

[13] Clause 37.

serve half their sentences before being considered for parole sets only the outside limit before the matter is referred to the parole board. Prisoners may be *considered* for release before they have served half their sentences if they are awarded what are called credits.

The theory is that credits are awarded for good behaviour (s.22A of the Correctional Services Act, 1959, introduced by the Correctional Services Amendment Act 1993). An institutional committee considers the behaviour of a prisoner over a six-month period (s.62(a) of the Correctional Services Act, 1959). If the prisoner has performed in a way which meets maximum expectations, a credit of three months may be awarded. When reviewing behaviour, the institutional committee must take into account both positive and negative behaviour. Thus it is instructed to reward positive participation in a 'multidisciplinary programme'. Such a programme may include a requirement to work. Conversely, when reviewing behaviour over the past six months, institutional committees are also constrained to take disciplinary infringements into account. Infringements dealt with informally lose five days' credit and violations against which formal action was taken result in the forfeiture of 15 days (Departmental Order B VI(2)(d)). Deviation by institutional committees from these standards is strongly discouraged.

In practice, a large number of difficulties have arisen with the credit system, some of which are relevant to the question of the interrelatedness of work and release. One is that there is simply not enough work, particularly work which has a training component, to meet the requirements of 'multidisciplinary programmes' for all prisoners. The practice in the department is therefore to grant full credits to prisoners who are unable to take part in programmes which they would otherwise be expected to complete. At best this is a partial solution, for those prisoners who are placed in programmes but who do not perform as required may be in a relatively disadvantaged position.

Another danger is that, in practice, the failure to award a credit as a result of disciplinary infringement (related directly or indirectly to failure of a prisoner to work as required) is a form of double punishment. It is not unrealistic to assume that prisoners who keep out of trouble will be awarded maximum credits. Those who have disciplinary convictions will, as a rule, lose some credit. Even though credits are in theory only one factor to be considered in determining the date of release on parole, they are very often decisive. In this indirect way, disciplinary offences, including those related to work, can result in a delayed release for a prisoner. It is understandable that, because of the uncertainties inherent in the system of credits, prisoners have been overtly hostile to it.

The entire system of early release was changed by the 1997 Parole and Correctional Services Supervision Amendment Act.[14] The new Act, which was passed by Parliament but which has not yet been put into effect, will abolish the credit-based parole system and replace it with a new procedure in terms of which parole will be considered by independent parole boards on which there will be strong community representation. It is too early to say whether prison work records will influence the decisions of these boards.

### 4.4 Prisoners and Labour Law

There appears to be a loosening of the legal restrictions on the use of prison labour to produce goods which can be sold on the open market. Historically, with the major exceptions of the mining and the agricultural sectors, which used prison labour extensively, there was a strong bias against competition with private enterprise. However, amendments made to the Correctional Services Act in 1991 allow the Commissioner of Correctional Services to contract 'with any institution, person or body of persons' for the employment of sentenced prisoners.[15] Moreover, the old provision, which restricted the discretion of the Minister of Correctional Services to determine how the products of prison labour should be disposed of by requiring him 'as far as possible [to] prevent competition with industries carried on in the neighbourhood of [the prison concerned]', has been abolished.[16] The change in focus reflects the emphasis on conducting the affairs of the Department of Correctional Services according to 'business principles' which was added to the legislatively specified functions of the Department in 1991 (s.2(2)(d) of the Correctional Services Act, 1959).

The changes introduced in 1991 were somewhat tentative. A legislative requirement that government departments should, as far as practicable, purchase articles and supplies from the Department of Correctional Services has been retained (s.75(2)). Also retained is the power of the Minister of Correctional Services to 'authorize specific

14   Act 87 of 1997.
15   Section 75(1) of the Correctional Services Act as replaced by s.26(a) of the Correctional Services Amendment Act 122 of 1991.
16   Section 75(3) of the Correctional Services Act was replaced by s.26(b) of the Correctional Services Amendment Act 122 of 1991.

services necessary or expedient in the public interest or in the interest of any deserving charity to be rendered gratuitously' (s.75(4)).

The patterns of use of prison labour outlined above suggest that little or no systematic use has been made of increased opportunities to sell prison-made goods in a wider market. Discussions about such schemes are taking place, but have not reached fruition. Inside South Africa, the question of prisoners producing goods which might compete with commerce on the outside has not been a major issue of dispute. The danger that competition may not be welcomed is sometimes mentioned by prison officials as an excuse for inaction in the development of prison industries.

Prisoners are not regarded as employees in South African labour law. This means that they are not governed by basic national labour law. They do not have a legal right as workers to bargain collectively. It is a moot point whether this position is ideal. Certainly, attempts have been made in the last few years to organize prisoners. SAPOHR (the South African Prisoners' Organization for Human Rights) uses the rhetoric of unionism. However, its main focus has not been on the area of work. Instead, it has concentrated with some success on grievances relating to the release policy and more generally on complaints from prisoners of ill-treatment. SAPOHR has achieved a degree of recognition in that its leader, 'Golden Miles' Bhudu, an ex-prisoner, was a member of the Transformation Forum for Correctional Services. This was a non-statutory body on which the Department of Correctional Services and various non-governmental organizations were represented. As its name suggests, the Transformation Forum was involved in the process of change in corrections in South Africa. Although prison labour matters were not prominent in the Forum, its deliberations seemed to offer an important route for involving prisoners in policy issues. However, largely as a result of international politics, the Forum was disbanded at the end of 1996 without having had a major impact on correctional change in South Africa (Giffard, 1997).

From the general proposition that, legally speaking, prisoners are not regarded as having contracts of employment even when they work in prison, it follows that prisoners are excluded from the Wage Act (1957) and the Basic Conditions of Employment Act (1983). This means that they are not governed by wage provisions or by provisions relating to maximum hours. Both these issues are covered by prison legislation, albeit indirectly.

Working hours for prisoners are set by the regulations made in terms of the primary prison legislation, the Correctional Services

Act (1959). General conditions for the use of prison labour are laid down in the regulations. Regulation 105(1) specifies a standard period of work of no more than 10 hours a day. Further detail is contained in the Departmental Orders which provide that, on weekdays, prisoners should march out to work not later than 07h00 and return to prison before 17h00. Between 12h00 and 13h00 there must be a rest period for lunch (Departmental Order B V(5)(e)(1)(aa)). Except for such work 'as is absolutely essential for the hygiene and proper administration of the prison', no prisoner may work on a Sunday or certain public holidays (Regulation 105(5)). No prisoner may work unless the medical officer has certified that he or she is fit to work (Regulation 105(2)(a)). The medical officer has the power to exempt a prisoner wholly or partially from work (Regulation 105(2)(b)).

Prisoners in South Africa do not build up credits for purposes of unemployment insurance. The Unemployment Insurance Act (1966) does not apply to prisoners. They are not subject to contracts of employment from which compulsory deductions, which can serve to pay eventual unemployment benefits, may be made. Prisoners who may have contributed to the unemployment insurance fund before their incarceration cannot claim unemployment benefits while in prison, for such benefits are only available to persons who are actively seeking work, and prisoners are not in a position to do so while they are incarcerated.

State pensions in South Africa are means tested, that is, someone of pensionable age is entitled to a pension only if their income is below a certain level. They are not affected directly by employment in prison or elsewhere prior to reaching a pensionable age. Sentenced prisoners of pensionable age do not qualify for pensions while imprisoned, but may do so afterwards. Married women whose husbands have been sentenced to imprisonment for at least three months may be paid a parent's grant.[17]

The Occupational Health and Safety Act (1993) does apply to prisons because it applies to workshops rather than to individual workers. However, prisoners injured while working have no claim in terms of the Compensation for Occupational Injuries Act (1993), for once again they are not regarded as workers. The best they can hope for is ex gratia compensation. The Commissioner of

---

17  The amount of the grant was set at R410 per month with effect from 1 July 1995: Government Notice 1022 in *Government Gazette* 16537 of 7 July 1995.

Correctional Services is allowed to award such compensation in any instance where 'a prisoner's earning ability is reduced as the result of an accident or injury sustained in prison, which was not due to his own negligence or fault' (Regulation 107).

### 4.5 Compensation for Work by Prisoners

Legal provision for compensating prisoners for their labour is rudimentary. The primary legislative instrument, the Correctional Services Act, is merely facilitative. It provides only that 'gratuities or remuneration may be paid to prisoners according to the conditions and tariffs determined by the Commissioner, with the concurrence of the Department of Finance' (s.76 of the Correctional Services Act, 1959). The regulations made in terms of the Act take the matter only slightly further by stipulating that the Commissioner must determine 'the manner in which any earned gratuity shall be controlled and used or paid to or on behalf of the prisoner' (Regulation 106). These provisions allow the authorities a measure of freedom to develop their own policy towards the remuneration of prison labour.

In practice, the amounts involved are extremely modest. The maximum gratuity which a prisoner can currently be paid is R72.60 (about US$17) per month. The current scales vary from between 30 cents to R3 per day (Departmental Order B V(9)(c)). All prisoners who work are paid something, but this has only been the practice since the beginning of 1996 (Van Zyl, 1996). However, the financial incentives to work, even for those who are paid the maximum gratuity (less than one US dollar a day), are very small. Every sentenced prisoner is entitled to receive up to R300 per month spending money from sources outside prison.

The very small amounts involved, and the fact that prisoners do not have a statutory basis for claiming more, means that there is no provision in South African prison law for deductions from prison wages for taxes or maintenance of family members. Unemployment insurance payments are not required because, as has been seen, prisoners are not employees and therefore by definition are not liable to pay it.

### 4.6 International Human Rights Law and Prison Labour

The determination of what international human rights law has to say about prison labour is potentially very important in South Africa, for the country aspires to meet international standards.[18] In the past, the United Nations Standard Minimum Rules for the Treatment of Prisoners (SMR), have been particularly influential, as successive South African governments have referred to them as reflecting standards to which they aspire. Where these standards were not met, the courts and other critics of the prison system could use them as a point of reference (Van Zyl Smit, 1995). The formulation of what may be regarded as best international practice (Penal Reform International 1995) and the reinterpretation internationally of the standards set by the SMR, for example with regard to the requirement that all medically fit sentenced prisoners must work (SMR 71(2)), are likely therefore to be given considerable weight in South Africa.

## 5 Conclusion

Prison labour in South Africa is characterized by a declining number of prisoners who are employed. Those who do work are in theory compelled to do so. In fact, the compulsion has lost much of its efficacy: the nineteenth-century ideal of ordered ranks of labouring convicts has been lost. On the other hand, the incentives to work are limited as well: training opportunities are restricted and the remuneration is derisory.

The question facing those who wish to reform the prison system is whether it will be able to break with the past, not only in the negative sense of stopping the abuse of prison labour, but also in the more positive sense of making labour worthwhile for the prisoners concerned. This will undoubtedly require incentives to encourage prisoners to work; such incentives will have to include remuneration and training opportunities and be supported by changes to laws relating to insurance, compensation for injuries and pensions. Imaginative proposals have been made for schemes using small amounts of venture capital, which would involve prisoners in cooperative ventures (Appelbaum, 1996). In practice though, the inertia of a large and underfunded system is considerable. There is, as yet, little indication that these issues are being addressed systematically.

18    This is reflected by formal recognition granted to customary international law in the 1996 South African Constitution (s.232). Section 39(1) of the Constitution goes further and enjoins the courts to take cognizance of public international law and comparable foreign law when interpreting the fundamental rights which are entrenched in the Constitution.

## References

Africa Watch Prison Project. 1994. *Prison Conditions in South Africa.* New York: Human Rights Watch.

Appelbaum, H. 1996. Personal Interview. March.

Barry, J.V. 1958. *Alexander Maconochie of Norfolk Island. A Study of a Pioneer in Penal Reform.* Oxford: Clarendon Press.

Breitenbach, J.J. 1959. The Development of the Secretaryship to the Government at the Cape of Good Hope under John Montagu 1845–1852. *Archives Yearbook for Southern African History* 171–306.

Corry, T.M. 1977. *Prison Labour in South Africa.* Cape Town: NICRO.

Department of Correctional Services. 1995. *Annual Report for the period 1 January 1994 to 31 December 1994.* RP 146/1995.

Department of Correctional Services. 1998. *Annual Report for the period 1 January 1997 to 31 December 1997.* RP 82/1998.

Department of Justice. 1917. *Annual Report for the Year 1917.* UG 36 1918.

Department of Justice and Correctional Services. 1991. *Extension of the Mission of Correctional Services and the Implementation of Correctional Supervision as an Alternative Sentencing Option.* 6 May.

Foucault, Michel. 1977. *Discipline and Punish. The Birth of the Prison.* Translated by A. Sheridan. Hardmondsworth: Penguin.

Giffard, Christopher. 1997. Out of Step? The transformation process in the South African Department of Correctional Services. MSc in criminal Justice Studies thesis, University of Leicester.

Haesler, W.T. 1986. Südafrikanischer Strafvollzug. Eindrucke einer Studienreise im September/Oktober 1984. *Zeitschrift für Strafvollzug und Straffülligenhilfe* 35: 11–17.

Hansard. 1903. Debates of the Tenth Parliament of the Cape of Good Hope.

Johnstone, F.A. 1976. *Class, Race and Gold. A Study of Class Relations and Racial Discrimination in South Africa.* Lanham: University Press of America.

Lansdown Commission. 1947. *Report of the Penal and Prison Reform Commission.* UG47/1947.

Mandela Nelson. R. 1994. *Long Walk to Freedom.* Randburg: MacDonald Purnell.

Newman, W.A. 1855. *Biographical Sketch John Montagu.* London: Harrison.

Newton-King, S. 1980. The Labour Market of the Cape Colony, 1807–28. In *Economy and Society in Pre-Industrial South Africa,* edited by S. Marks and A. Atmore. London: Longman.

Nxumalo, H. 1952. Bethal Today. *Drum* March: 9–10.

Nxumalo, H. 1954. Mr. Drum Goes to Jail. *Drum* March: 3-4.
Rayner, M. 1986. Wine and Slaves. PhD dissertation, Durham, North Carolina: Duke University.
*Report of the Committee on Convicts and Gaols*. 1888. G2-88 (2nd Report). Cape Town: Government of the Cape Colony.
*Report of the Inspectors of the Diamond Mines in Griqualand West*. 1886. Parliamentary Papers 640. Cape Town.
Sampson, A. 1956. *Drum: A New Venture in Africa*. London: Collins.
Turrell, R.V. 1982a. *Capital, Class and Monopoly: The Kimberley Diamond Fields 1871-1888*. PhD dissertation, University of London.
Turrell, R.V. 1982b. Kimberley: Labour and Compounds 1871-1888. In *Industrialization and Social Change in South Africa: African Class Formation, Culture and Consciousness 1870-1930*, edited by S. Marks and R. Rathbone. Burnt Mill: Longman.
Van Onselen, C. 1985. Crime and Total Institutions in the Making of Modern South Africa: The life of 'Nongolozo' Mathebula 1867-1948. *History Workshop Journal* 62-81.
Van Wyk, M. 1964. Die Ontwikkeling van die Gevangeniswese in die Kaapkolonie vanaf 1806 tot en met Unifikasie 1910. PhD dissertation, Pretoria: University of South Africa.
Van Zyl, E. 1996. Letter with Appendices from the Deputy Commissioner of Correctional Services, E. Van Zyl. April.
Van Zyl Smit, Dirk. 1981. Convicts on the Hard Road: Reflections on the System of Convict Labour Introduced by John Montagu in the Cape Colony 1844-1853. *De Rebus*. 223-6.
Van Zyl Smit, Dirk. 1992. *South African Prison Law and Practice*. Durban: Butterworths.
Van Zyl Smit, Dirk. 1995. South African Prisons and the Standards of International Human Rights Law. In *The Protection of Human Rights in African Criminal Proceedings*, edited by M.C. Bassiouni and Z. Motala. Deventer: Kluwer.
Van Zyl Smit, Dirk. 1998. 'Change and Continuity in South African Prisons'. In *Comparing Prison Systems Towards an International Penology*, edited by R.P. Weiss and N. South. Amsterdam: Gordon and Breach.
Venter, H.S. 1959. *Die Geskiedenis van die Suid-Afrikaanse Gevangenisstelsel 1652-1958*. Pretoria: HAUM.

## Cases
R v. *Heine* 1910 CPD 371.
R v. *Mtiyane* 1956 (2) SA 597 (N).
S v. *Nkosi* 1984 (4) SA 94 (T).
S v. *Pule* 1970 (2) SA 330 (o).

S v. *Saayman* 1987 (2) SA 504 (C).
S v. *November* 1988 (1) SA 661 (C).

## The Author
Dirk van Zyl Smit is professor of criminology and director of the Institute of Criminology at the University of Cape Town in South Africa.

# 13 Spain

ESTHER GIMÉNEZ-SALINAS

## 1 Legal Background

Article 25(2) of the Spanish Constitution of 1978 states that it is the fundamental right of all Spaniards that sentences and security measures shall be oriented towards re-education and re-integration into society, that they shall not involve forced labour, and that those sentenced to terms of imprisonment shall be entitled to engage in paid work and receive the corresponding social security benefits.[1] Article 25(2) is of crucial importance in the prison sphere. It is the reason why the Prison Law, passed by acclamation in the Senate in September 1979, places special emphasis on guaranteeing fundamental rights against arbitrary government action. Furthermore, it prohibits forced labour and therefore regulates in great detail all aspects of prison work, so that at law it can never be confused with forced labour. Finally, it establishes prisoners' rights to paid work and the corresponding social security benefits. The provisions of art. 25(5) are further reinforced by art. 35(1), which stipulates that work is both a duty and a right of all citizens.[2] All these principles are included in the Prison Law and the regulations governing its implementation.

1. Article 25(2) reads as follows: 'Prison sentences and security measures shall be oriented towards re-education and social rehabilitation and may not consist of forced labour. The person sentenced to prison shall enjoy during his imprisonment the fundamental rights contained in this chapter, with the exception of those which are expressly restricted by the content of the prison sentence, the purpose of the sentence and the penitentiary law. In any case, he shall have the right to remunerated work and the pertinent benefits of Social Security, as well as access to culture and the integral development of his personality' (translated by Flanz: Blaustein and Flanz, 1991).
2. Article 35(1) states: 'All Spaniards have the duty to work and the right to work, free choice of profession or trade, advancement through work and sufficient remuneration to meet their own needs and those of their families, without discrimination on the grounds of sex under any circumstances.'

## 1.1 Regulations

Prison work is regulated in arts 26 to 35 of the Prison Law and arts 118 to 153 of the regulations governing its implementation, passed by Royal Decree 190 of 6 February 1996, known as the Prison Regulations. These are the result of a complete revision of the 1981 Regulations.

The first reason for this revision has to do with the need to broaden the activities and programmes available to enable treatment 'according to the principle of scientific individualization' which, in terms of art. 59 of the Prison Law, consists of the set of activities directly aimed at achieving the re-education and social rehabilitation of offenders. Thus the new provisions of the revised regulations include programmed outings, therapeutic community groups and, of particular significance in relation to the present topic, a special prison employment relationship.

The second reason for the amendments to the regulations is that it is now 16 years since the Prison Law was enacted and 14 years since the regulations were introduced, and during this time both prison reality and Spanish society have undergone substantial changes. In the last 10 years, the Spanish prison population has grown from 22,802 to 47,905, an increase of 110 per cent. Moreover, not only has the overall prison population doubled during this period, the female inmate population has increased by 286 per cent. In other words, it has more than tripled in size.

The third reason for an overhaul of the regulations is to be found in developments such as the disproportionate number of foreigners in prison, the appearance of AIDS and the link between AIDS and drug addiction.

Finally, major modifications are also required to bring the regulations into line with the two laws passed in 1995. On the one hand, in terms of Law 10/1995 of 23 November, the Penal Code will affect remission of sentences for work and parole. On the other hand, Law 13/1995 of 18 December, which amends art. 38 of the Prison Law, provides that children under three years of age may stay with their imprisoned mothers and imposes a statutory obligation to establish a specific visiting regime for children under 10 that are not living with their mothers.

## 1.2 Characteristics

Article 26 of the Prison Law is based on the provisions of the Spanish Constitution and states that work is to be considered 'a duty and a right and shall be a fundamental element in the treatment of prisoners'. Such work, art. 26 explains, should have the following characteristics:

- it must not cause distress;
- it must not undermine the inmate's dignity;
- it must be educational and prepare inmates for normal working conditions in the civilian community;
- the inmates' skills and qualifications shall be taken into account in organizing the work;
- it shall be arranged by the prison authorities;
- the person performing it shall be covered by social security provisions; and
- it shall not depend on the authorities' economic interests.

Thus the second part of the article, which defines the conditions governing prison work, simply expands on art. 25(2) of the Spanish Constitution, while the first part reproduces art. 35(1) and stipulates the inmate's right and obligation to work.

In regard to the obligation to work, the law restricts this to convicted offenders, in accordance with their physical and mental capabilities, and excludes the following types of inmates:

- those undergoing medical treatment as a result of an accident or disease, until such time as they are declared fit;
- those suffering from permanent absolute incapacity;
- those over 65 years of age;
- those in receipt of a retirement pension;
- pregnant women, for 16 consecutive weeks, or 18 consecutive weeks in the case of multiple births; and
- inmates prevented from working by *force majeure*.

In the case of prisoners remanded in custody, art. 29 of the Prison Law simply states that they may work in accordance with their capabilities and inclinations.

### 2   Different Kinds of Prison Work: what does Work Mean and what Work can be done?

Article 27 of the Prison Law lays down that the work done by inmates shall be of one of the following kinds:

- vocational training activities, where possible provided by the authorities;

- study and academic education activities;
- productive activities under an employment contract, cooperative schemes or similar arrangements in accordance with current legislation;
- occupational activities forming part of a treatment plan;
- personal participation in the provision of the establishment's communal auxiliary services; and
- craft, intellectual and artistic work.

The Prison Law devotes a specific chapter to the question of work[3] and the 1981 Regulations have a whole chapter fleshing out the framework outlined in the Prison Law.[4] The new prison regulations that came into force on 25 May 1996 approach the matter somewhat differently. The section on treatment includes several chapters which are of particular relevance to the present topic, such as Chapter III on training, culture and sport, Chapter IV on the special prison employment relationship, and Chapter V, on non-productive occupational work.

The new approach is not a matter of chance but rather the result of a definite policy that differs substantially from its predecessor. Earlier legislation, which has now been replaced completely, identified treatment with work, and all the activities listed above, ranging from vocational education, productive work and allocated tasks in prison domestic services, to craft, intellectual and artistic activities, were considered to be work. Some authors have noted that this model was chosen in view of the difficulties, at the time legislation was enacted, in carrying out productive activities within prisons. This was especially important given the direct relation between work and the possibility of obtaining penal benefits.

The recently passed regulations establish different categories. These prison regulations had no alternative but to respect art. 27 of the Prison Law and recognize occupations of all kinds as constituting work for the purposes of possible penal benefits. However, in regulating them, the aim was to differentiate very clearly between the various kinds of activity in order to dispel confusion over the issue.

It is one thing for a task assigned to a prisoner to confer on the person doing it a benefit or privilege, but quite another for it to be regulated as a form of work. The duty to work is once again set out

3   Under Section II, 'The Prison Regime', arts 26 to 35.
4   Under Section III, 'Services Provided by the Authorities', arts 182 to 219.

in art. 133, which states that all convicted offenders have the duty to work, although they are compelled to do only the types of activity described in art. 27. One can therefore distinguish between (a) educational, cultural and sports activities, (b) non-productive occupational activities and (c) the special prison employment relationship. The last of these is of primary concern here, as it is the only one which may strictly be considered prison work. However, all three categories require closer consideration.

## 2.1 *Educational, Cultural and Sports Activities*

These are dealt with in Chapter X of the Prison Law and Chapter III of the Regulations under the heading of 'Instruction and Education'. Educational, cultural and sports activities are arranged in every prison establishment on the basis of individualized programmes drawn up by the Treatment Boards. Inmates are encouraged to take part 'profitably' in these activities by being granted benefits and other rewards. The 1996 Prison Regulations divide these activities into the following four kinds.

*Basic education* This will be obligatory for inmates without the qualifications corresponding to the period of compulsory education and will be a priority for illiterates, foreigners and people with specific problems.

*Secondary education* This will be provided by the prison authorities and consist of educational programmes comprising both official and unofficial courses that can contribute to the inmate's personal development.

*Vocational and occupational training* Inmates will be able to engage in such training in accordance with the guidelines laid down by the Treatment Board and on the basis of the official curricula for vocational and occupational training and reintegration into the world of work.

*Social, cultural and sports activities* These are to be organized according to the Treatment Board's requirements and as many inmates as possible will be encouraged to participate all year round.

## 2.2 *Non-productive Occupational Activities*

Provision is made for prison establishments to set up occupational workshops where inmates can participate in activities organized in accordance with treatment programmes. Obviously, the inmates taking part in these activities will also be entitled to incentives, rewards or penal benefits. If there is any economic profit from the sale of the products made, this money will go towards replacing the materials needed to make the products and also towards paying for the inmates' incentives.

### 2.3 The Special Prison Employment Relationship

The special prison employment relationship is a legal employment relationship established between Prison Work and Services, an autonomous body, and the inmates carrying out productive activities for a third party. Productive activities undertaken on a cooperative basis and, of course, work done by inmates enjoying an open regime via an ordinary employment contract fall outside the scope of this special relationship.

Productive prison work is to be performed in the prison workshops, organized into sectors and subject to the relevant health and safety regulations. Organizing and monitoring productive work is the responsibility of Prison Work and Services, which also pays the wages earned into the inmate's account, depending on his or her occupational category.[5]

Wages are calculated on the basis of the current statutory minimum wage, the number of hours actually worked and the worker's performance. The final wage has to include an amount to cover weekends, paid holidays and bonus payments. The working week is five and a half days, with one and a half days' rest. Inmates are also entitled to all the public holidays of the locality where the prison is situated and annual leave of 30 calendar days or the proportion that is due to them, depending on the length of time for which they have been working.

This prison employment relationship will be suspended in the following cases:

(a) by mutual agreement of the parties concerned;
(b) temporary incapacity of the prison worker;
(c) pregnancy of women workers, for 16 consecutive weeks, or 18 weeks in the case of multiple births, as stipulated in art. 133(2) of the Prison Regulations;
(d) suspension from work, with attendant loss of pay, as a result of disciplinary sanctions imposing isolation on the prisoner;
(e) temporary *force majeure*;
(f) for reasons of treatment; and
(g) because of transfers, provided the prisoner's absence does not ex-

---

5 There are two such categories, basic operative and senior operative.

ceed two months, and while the prisoner enjoys leave from prison or authorized outings as defined elsewhere in the regulations.

The relationship will be rescinded:

(a) by mutual agreement of the parties concerned;
(b) upon expiry of the period established or upon completion of the work or service;
(c) by virtue of the prisoner's inability to perform the work having been discovered or having occurred after the job had already been assigned to him or her;
(d) as a result of the prisoner's death, major incapacity or total or absolute permanent incapacity;
(e) on the prisoner's 65th birthday;
(f) if *force majeure* definitively prevents the work from being carried out;
(g) by virtue of the prisoner's release from prison;
(h) by virtue of category 3 prisoners obtaining gainful employment outside the prison;
(i) if the prisoner is transferred to another penal establishment for a period of more than two months;
(j) by virtue of the prisoner resigning; and
(k) for reasons of prison discipline and security.

Prisoners are entitled to have the productive work they do factored into their prison regime and their treatment, as well as towards the granting of penal benefits. In addition, both the Prison Law and the prison regulations stipulate that paid work shall be covered by social security provisions, as specified in art. 26 of the Prison Law. Evidently, in 1979, the legislator did not want to spell out the social benefits to be received by prisoners, whereas the new regulations provide protective social security cover for prison work.[6]

6   The addition to the regulations stems from a claim filed by a group of prisoners with Social Court No. 1 in Barcelona requesting that:
    (a) inmates carrying out tasks to which they have been assigned in penal establishments (that is, personnel participation in the provision the establishment's communal services, as defined in art. 27(e) of the Prison Law), should be remunerated for the work performed and should enjoy the protection of the Social Security;
    (b) Social Security protection should cover so-called 'general contingencies' for prisoners and their beneficiaries.

In spite of this provision, all prisoners at present are entitled only to a reduced social security coverage that protects them in the event of industrial diseases and accidents. Other statutory benefits to which ordinary workers are entitled, such as invalidity, disability and retirement pensions, are not applied to prisoners despite the existence of Decree 573/1967 of 16 March on prison work and the inclusion of prisoners in the social security scheme, which appears to accord them such benefits. This has been possible because the authorities have classified productive prison work as pre-apprenticeship work,[7] arguing that it is a basic component of treatment that is educational and therapeutic, helps to create or maintain work habits and prepares prisoners for normal employment in society at large.

## 3  Penal Benefits

Penal benefits are legal mechanisms that allow prison terms to be reduced. They are based on prisoners' participation in the activities of the penal establishment. In other words, taking part in treatment activities and, in particular, work activities, is a necessary condition of obtaining these benefits.

Over the years, the different penal and prison regulations have provided for several schemes whereby prisoners who behaved appropriately could have their sentences shortened or their conditions improved. These included remission of sentence through work, parole, pardons or rewards.

### 3.1  *Remission of Sentence through Work*

Remission of sentence through work was provided for in art. 100 of the Revised Text of the Penal Code published by Decree 3096/1973 of 14 September in accordance with Law 44/1971 of 15 November and subsequent amendments. Offenders serving prison sentences of more than six months could have their term of imprisonment reduced.

The sentences stipulated in the Spanish Penal Code were in fact extremely long, and the possibility of remission of sentence through work was intended to affect this harshness. In 'prison circles',

---

[7]  Article 4(1) of Decree 573/1967 states: 'For the purposes set out in art. 1, prisoners who carry out pre-apprenticeship or vocational training work as students, for which they receive economic rewards that do not constitute payment or salary, shall also be regarded as employed workers.'

everyone was convinced that in most cases prisoners actually only served half their sentence.

Let us consider the history of this provision.[8] Precedents can be found in the Penal Codes of 1822 and 1928, and the General Regulations on Prisons of the Realm of 1834 provided for sentence remission through work and good conduct. The scheme as we know it today was introduced during the Spanish Civil War (1936-9) to alleviate the burden of the war effort by relieving pressure on the overcrowded prisons and prisoner-of-war camps. Thus Decree 281 of 28 May 1937 granted prisoners of war and political prisoners the right to work.

In view of the beneficial effects of this scheme, it was extended to common criminals by a Ministerial Order issued on 14 March 1939. It was later incorporated into the Penal Code of 1944 and applied to all sentenced prisoners, irrespective of the crime they had committed.

As we have already mentioned, remission of sentence through work was provided for in art. 100 of the Penal Code and arts 65 to 73 of the Prison Service Regulations, passed by the Decree of 2 February 1956, and remained in force as a result of the second transitional provision of the 1981 Prison Regulations. Article 100 of the Penal Code states that prisoners performing work shall be entitled to one day's remission for every two days worked, subject to authorization by the supervisory judge. This is known as ordinary remission and allows for sentences to be reduced by up to one-third. Naturally, this reduction is taken into account in granting release on parole.

Ordinary remission begins when the inmate starts work, or when he or she is due to start work but is unable to do so for one of the reasons listed in art. 29 of the Prison Law or because the prison authorities are unable to provide him or her with work. In the latter case, the prisoner must not have expressed a refusal to work.

Prisoners are rewarded for being particularly hardworking. They are assessed every three months on the basis of the number of hours spent on the activity in question, bearing in mind the laboriousness of the task and their degree of involvement. A proposal for a period of remission is then put before the supervisory judge who may approve or reject it.

The 1995 Penal Code reduced the length of many sentences and at the same time abolished this form of early release. Nevertheless,

---

[8] For a broader treatment of the subject, see Garrido Guzman (1983).

the transitional provisions envisaged that offenders, sentenced before the new Code came into effect, will still be entitled to benefit from any more favourable provisions previously in force. This means that in many cases the 1944 Penal Code will continue to be applied. Although sentences under the old Code tended to be considerably longer, with remission through work they actually turned out to be shorter than those under the new Code. It is therefore expected that remission of sentences through work will be in effect for approximately another 10 years.

At the moment, only one prisoner out of every four chooses to go by the new Code when their sentences are reviewed. Generally speaking, it can be said that the new Penal Code is more favourable for those sentenced to shorter terms of imprisonment (less than two years) and harder on those with longer sentences.

### 3.2   *Early Parole: Requirements and Conditions*

The concept of parole is defined in arts 90 to 93 of the 1995 Penal Code. It is granted automatically provided the stipulated criteria have been met.[9] In addition to the general conditions, art. 91 of the Penal Code[10] provides for the possibility of early parole being granted to prisoners who are in category 3 and have a favourable report, when they have completed two-thirds of their sentence, provided they have been of good conduct and have been continuously involved in work, cultural or occupational activities.

There is also another case of early release which, however, has nothing to do with work or participation in treatment activities.

9       Parole is granted to prisoners serving custodial sentences who:
        1   are in prison treatment category 3;
        2   have served three-quarters of their sentence;
        3   have been of good conduct and in respect of whom there exists a personal report, prepared by experts and approved by the supervisory judge, concluding that there is a favourable prognosis for social rehabilitation.

        In granting parole, the supervisory judge may require certain of the rules contained in art. 105 of the Penal Code to be fulfilled.

        The period of parole shall last until the sentence has been served in full. If the prisoner offends again during this period or fails to comply with the rules of conduct, the supervisory judge may cancel the parole and the convict must return to the establishment, without prejudice to the time spent on parole.

10      Together with arts 202 to 205 of the Prison Regulations of 1996.

The granting of parole may also be brought forward in the case of prisoners over 70 years of age and severely ill prisoners suffering from incurable diseases, provided they meet the requirements of being in category 3 and have a favourable report. This condition for early parole has been included in the 1995 Penal Code, but in fact it had already been envisaged in art. 60 of the 1981 Regulations. The extremely heavy incidence of AIDS among the prison population has made such arrangements necessary.

### 3.3 Individual Pardon

Individual pardon is defined in art. 206 of the 1995 Prison Regulations. It provides for the reduction of sentences, by an amount depending on the circumstances, of prisoners who have consistently and for a minimum period of two years met, in an exceptional manner, the following prerequisites: (a) good conduct; (b) performance of a normal work activity, either within the establishment or outside, that may be considered useful in preparing him or her for life in liberty; and (c) participation in re-education and social rehabilitation activities.

### 3.4 Rewards

These are set out in Chapter VI, section X of the 1996 Prison Regulations under the heading 'Disciplinary Regime Rewards'. Inmates showing good conduct, keenness to work and a sense of responsibility, and who take part in regulation and other activities, may be eligible for the following:

(a) additional special and extraordinary communications;
(b) study grants, books and other items used in cultural and recreational activities in the Centre;
(c) priority in going on programmed outings to take part in cultural activities;
(d) reductions in sanctions that have been imposed;
(e) cash premiums;
(f) special mentions; and
(g) any other reward of a kind similar to the above that is not incompatible with the Regulations' principles.

## 4 Selected Data on the Current Situation in Catalonia as an Illustration of Spanish Trends

After the enactment of the Spanish Constitution in 1978, Spain was organized into 17 autonomous communities each with its own political and administrative autonomy, although not all of them enjoy the same degree of self-government or have had the same powers devolved to them. Three of these autonomous communities, the so-called 'historical communities' of the Basque Country, Galicia and Catalonia, have their own language and culture.

The possibility of granting responsibility for the prison service was included in the autonomy statutes of only the Basque Country, Navarre, Andalusia and Catalonia. However, 20 years after the Constitution came into effect, only Catalonia has actually been granted powers in this respect, including the management, organization and inspection of the penal institutions in its territory. These powers were handed over to the Catalan government by Decree 3482/1983 of 28 December and came into force on 1 January 1984.

As in Spain as a whole, the prison population in Catalonia has increased greatly. It has almost doubled in the space of 10 years, leaping from 3,496 in 1985 to 6,429 in 1995. This represents a total increase of 84 per cent since 1985, at an annual average rate of 6 per cent. Even more dramatic has been the increase in the number of juvenile prisoners, from 217 in 1985 to 585 in 1994. In percentage terms, the increase was 170 per cent overall, at an annual average rate of growth of 12 per cent. In summary, then, the Catalan prison population is quite large and has experienced a major increase in the course of the last 10 years. Prison labour in Catalonia must be understood against this background.

In order to regulate work done by prisoners, the *Generalitat de Catalunya* introduced Law 5/1989 of 12 May to set up the Centre for Rehabilitation Initiatives (CIRE). This has the status of a company governed by public law and falls under the Department of Justice. Its functions are laid down in the above law and can be summarized as follows:

- organizing and managing the work;
- paying prisoners for their work;
- acquiring the necessary raw materials and machinery; and
- arranging the industrial and commercial activity relating to prison work.

The CIRE consists of three departments. There is a Commercial Department, which is responsible for finding potential customers, and a Production Department with a representative in each of the prisons. These representatives arrange and supervise the work in the workshops and feed back information so that the Administration Department can make up the payslips and make whatever payments and collect whatever moneys are due.

### 4.1 *Types of Work*

Prison work has the reputation of not being very good: there is little of it, it is badly paid and it is not very motivating. It does not have such a reputation for nothing, but over the past few years CIRE has tried to replace unskilled manual work (of which much is still done in prisons) with other types of work that allow inmates to acquire job skills which are more useful and in demand in the labour market.

In 1995, CIRE organized the job workshops listed in Table 13.1, with an average of 1,844 prisoners taking part at any one time.

Table 13.1: Job Workshops

| Type of Workshop | No. of Prisoners |
| --- | --- |
| General services | 41 |
| Graphic arts | 57 |
| Carpentry | 109 |
| Artificial flowers | 25 |
| Unskilled manual work | 692 |
| Sewing | 178 |
| Bakery | 47 |
| Assembly of electrical components | 500 |
| Silk screen printing | 2 |
| Cardboard boxes | 150 |
| Welding | 36 |
| Making up batches of hygienic products | 7 |
| Total | 1,844 |

*Source*: CIRE (1995).

### 4.2 *Number of Prisoners Involved*

It was noted above that there is generally little work available in prisons. The average number of prisoners working in Catalan prisons in 1995 was 1,844, which is only 29 per cent of the total inmate population. Table 13.2 shows that, between 1990 and 1995, the number of employed inmates, as a percentage of the total prison population in Catalonia, rose by 99 per cent.

Table 13.2: Numbers of Inmates Employed

| Year | Average Number of Prisoners Involved | Total Prison Population | Percentage |
|---|---|---|---|
| 1990 | 694 | 4,821 | 14.39 |
| 1991 | 924 | 5,444 | 16.97 |
| 1992 | 1,263 | 5,888 | 21.45 |
| 1993 | 1,316 | 6,411 | 20.52 |
| 1994 | 1,516 | 6,741 | 22.48 |
| 1995 | 1,844 | 6,429 | 28.68 |

*Source*: CIRE (1995).

A great deal of effort still has to be made to reach a situation of full employment. However, it is extremely hard to achieve full employment in prisons when, as in December 1995, unemployment in Catalonia as a whole stands at 11 per cent. There are also many additional difficulties created by restrictive prison regulations as well as by poor work records of prisoners.

### 4.3 *Earnings*

As already mentioned, the payment received by prisoners is directly dependent on the number of hours worked and the production achieved in relation to the statutory minimum wage, which for 1996 was set at 64,920 pesetas per month. In 1995, CIRE paid out a total of 310,302,398 pesetas, making an average wage of 14,023 pesetas a month. Naturally, such average figures encompass a wide span so that, according to CIRE, some prisoners earn as much as 60,000 pesetas a month. In other words, if they were to work eight hours a day they could earn 100,000 or even 120,000 pesetas a month. The differences in the amount of money earned are determined by the type of work. For example, those prisoners who make clothes earn more than those assembling electronic components, while the latter earn more than prisoners engaged in unskilled manual work.

Table 13.3 shows the evolution of total and average wages paid by CIRE over the period 1990-95.

Table 13.3: Wages Paid by CIRE, 1990-95 (pesetas)

| Year | Total Payments | Monthly Average | Average no. of Prisoners | Average Monthly Wage |
|---|---|---|---|---|
| 1990 | 99,578,576 | 8,298,215 | 694 | 11,957 |
| 1991 | 139,642,613 | 11,636,884 | 924 | 12,594 |
| 1992 | 192,553,094 | 16,046,091 | 1,269 | 12,704 |
| 1993 | 183,338,155 | 15,278,179 | 1,316 | 11,609 |
| 1994 | 240,817,455 | 20,068,121 | 1,516 | 13,237 |
| 1995 | 310,302,398 | 25,858,533 | 1,844 | 14,023 |

Source: CIRE (1995).

## 5 Conclusion

Spanish legislation on prison labour is generally progressive and reflects the broad prison principles established by the democratic prison law of the post-Franco period. Increasing numbers of prisoners and high unemployment make it difficult to implement the ideals of the legislation. However, developments in Catalonia represent a serious attempt to put the ideals into practice.

### References

Beltran Miralles, Sofia. 1995. *La relació de treball dels penats a les presons catalanes. Investigacions.* Barcelona: Centre d'Estudis Jurídics i Formació Especialitzada.

Blaustein, A.P. and G.H. Flanz, eds. 1991. *Constitutions of the Countries of the World (Spain).* Trans. G.H. Flanz. New York: Oceana Publications.

Bueno Arús, Francisco. 1988. De nuevo sobre el derecho de los reclusos a un trabajo remunerado. *Poder Judicial* 12: 111-20.

Campà i Ferrer, Xavier. 1992. El treball penitenciari i la redempció de penes pel treball: crisi i alternatives. *Papers d'estudis i formació* 10: 9-31.

Cuesta Arzamendi, José Luis de la. 1982. *El trabajo penitenciario resocializador: teoría y regulación.* Guipúzcoa: Caja de Ahorros Provincial de Guipúzcoa.

Cuesta Arzamendi, José Luis de la. 1986. Clases de trabajo penitenciario: régimen jurídico (VI/1). *Comentarios a la legislación penal* 439-54.

Cuesta Arzamendi, José Luis de la. 1986. Condiciones de trabajo. *Comentarios a la legislación penal* 499-508.

Cuesta Arzamendi, José Luis de la. 1986. El Trabajo: derecho y deber del interno y medio de tratamiento. *Comentarios a la legislación penal* 419-38.

Cuesta Arzamendi, José Luis de la. 1986. Obligatoriedad del trabajo de los penados: el trabajo de los preventivos. *Comentarios a la legislación penal* 463-76.

Cuesta Arzamendi, José Luis de la. 1986. Trabajo: enseñanza. *Comentarios a la legislación penal* 455-62.

Garrido Guzman, Luis. 1983. *Manual de Ciencia Penitenciaria.* Madrid: Edersa.

Giménez-Salinas i Colomer, Esther. 1995. Autonomía del Derecho Penitenciario. Principios informadores de la Ley Orgánica General Penitenciaria. *Cuadernos de Derecho Judicial* 33: 67-104.

Giménez-Salinas i Colomer, Esther and Anna Rifà i Ros. 1992. *Intoducció al Dret penitenciari. Teoria i pràctica.* Barcelona: Centre d'Estudis Jurídics i Formació Especialitzada. Generalitat de Catalunya.

Grijalba López, Juan Carlos. 1995. La redención de penas por el trabajo y el adelantamiento de la libertad condicional: la disposición transitoria 2ª a) del Reglamento penitenciario. *Revista de estudios penitenciarios* 246: 61—66.

Lledot Leira, Laura. 1996. La redención de penas por el trabajo y la firmeza de la resolución judicial de concesión. *Boletín de Información. Ministerio de Justicia* 1782-83: 3487-99.

Moral García, Antonio del. 1996: A vuelta con la redención de penas por el trabajo y el régimen transitorio del nuevo Código Penal. *Actualidad Jurídica Aranzadi* 258: 1-5.

Reunión de Jueces de Vigilancia penitenciaria (7:1993). 1994. *Vigilancia penitenciaria: VII reunión de jueces de vigilancia penitenciaria.* Madrid: Consejo General del Poder Judicial.

Ruiz Vadillo, Enrique. 1996. Algunas breves consideraciones sobre la redención de penas por el trabajo y el nuevo Código Penal. *La ley* 3: 1436-7.

Sánchez Jiménez, Basilio. 1990. *Relaciones laborales especiales: trabajos penitenciarios.* Barcelona: Centre d'Estudis Jurídics i Formació Especialitzada.

Tamarit Sumalla, Josep M, Francesc Sapena Grau and Ramón García Albero. 1996. *Curso de derecho penitenciario: adaptado al nuevo Reglamento penitenciario de 1996.* Barcelona: Cedecs.

Zurita García, Juan. 1989. La redención de penas por el trabajo: controvertido origen y dudosa justificación actual. *Revista de estudios penitenciarios* 241: 51–60.

## The Author

Esther Giménez-Salinas is professor of criminology and penal law at the University Ramon Llul in Barcelona in Spain.

# 14 Switzerland

ANDREA BAECHTOLD

## 1 Historical Development and the Current Legal Position

Only since the introduction of the Swiss Criminal Code in 1942 has there been a uniform system of prison labour in Switzerland. Until then prison labour, like other aspects of the implementation of prison sentences, was governed exclusively by the legislation of the individual cantons.[1]

As early as the first half of the seventeenth century, new prisons and *Schallenwerke*[2] were set up and compulsory labour was introduced as a general rule for the prisoners. It has always been difficult to implement this rule owing to a lack of suitable work for the prisoners.[3] In the nineteenth century, new prisons were introduced, which followed the Anglo-Saxon reforms in Auburn in the United States of America and in Pentonville in England as well as the grading system developed by Croften. In these institutions it was seen as particularly important to provide work for the inmates.[4] In the second half of the nineteenth century, pioneer

---

1   There was one exception during the time of the so-called 'Helvetia' (1798–1802). After the Swiss were defeated by the French under Napoleon, the Helvetian Criminal Code (introduced in 1799) applied in all of Switzerland.
2   *Schallenwerke* (a seventeenth-century Swiss term for prisons for the execution of sentences as opposed to remand prisons) were put into operation in the cities of Berne, Basle, Freiburg, Zurich and St. Gallen for the first time between 1614 and 1661.
3   See, for example, Anselmier (1992, 1993), Curti (1988), Fumasoli (1981), Hafner and Zürcher (1925), Roth (1981), Schaffroth (1898), Schweingruber (1981), Zwicky (1982).
4   The prisons of St. Gallen and Lenzburg were erected in 1839 and 1864, respectively. In the Criminal Code of Berne of 1866, the obligation to work was expressly set up for confinement and correction sentences (arts 10 and 11) but not for sentences which did not exceed 60 days (art. 13).

agricultural prisons were set up,[5] in which prisoners were used first to drain marshy land and later to undertake extended agricultural projects. At this stage, prison labour was approached from an ideological,[6] economic perspective, with a view towards special prevention.

In the draft prepared by Carl Stooss for a Swiss Criminal Code in 1893, the goal of special prevention was brought to the fore: 'The convict is detained in order that he works. He should if possible be given work which corresponds to his abilities and which enables him to earn a living after his release' (Stoos, 1893, art. 21(4)). The Statement published by the Federal Council of the Federal Government on the draft for the Swiss Criminal Code, admittedly much later, in 1918, emphasized this point:

> In prison, work is the main means of education to bring the prisoner back to the right path and put him in a position to follow it. This method of treatment has already been established and maintained in our bigger prisons ... . We hope that the correct implementation of a prison sentence can improve the prisoner through education to work and through the moral influence of the institution in all other respects. (Swiss Federal Council, 1918, 14)

Hafner and Zürcher (1925: 160–61) had a similar argument:

> Prison labour is no longer a punishment, even if individual prisoners might take it to be practically the same thing. Work and movement are the bases of physical and psychological vitality. Work helps to make discipline more pleasant, promote a sense of security and improve the prisoners' chances of coping after their release. Its highest goal, however, is to contribute to the improvement of the prisoners; to convey the conviction that it is only hard work which both provides the individual with a basis of personal satisfaction and a livelihood – in other words, his happiness – as well as providing the foundation for the well-being of the nation.
>
> Work also helps to maintain the health of the prisoner, which he needs as his own capital once he has left the institution. On release from prison, health makes prisoners aware of the necessity and advan-

---

5   In the late nineteenth century, the prison of Witzwil, in the canton of Berne, was admired worldwide.
6   The Calvinistic work ethic had a far-reaching influence in Switzerland.

tages of work and brings them to conduct their lives in a sober, sociable and improved way.

These quotations demonstrate the long-standing tradition in Switzerland of prison labour geared towards special prevention.

The Swiss Criminal Code, which came into force in 1942 for all of Switzerland, unified and harmonized the previous provisions of the cantons, using, almost verbatim, the draft of Carl Stooss: 'The prisoner is obliged to carry out the work which is assigned to him. He should, where possible, be given work which corresponds to his abilities and enables him to earn a livelihood after his release' (art. 37(1)(2) of the Swiss Criminal Code).

Detainees, unlike prisoners and convicts,[7] may organize appropriate work for themselves (art. 39(3) of the Swiss Criminal Code). The Federal Council is empowered to pass ordinances over and above this basic framework (art. 397bis(1)(*i*) Swiss Civil Code) but it has delegated this power back to the cantons (art. 6 of the First Regulation to the Swiss Criminal Code).

There was a partial revision of the Swiss Criminal Code in 1971. This, together with the first Regulation to the Swiss Criminal Code of 1973, allows prisoners to carry out their work outside their penal institutions. If they have behaved themselves well during their term of imprisonment and already served half of their sentences, they are allowed to work for an employer who is not connected to the penal institution. This is termed 'semi-freedom' ('*Halbfreiheit*') by art. 37(3)(2) and (3) of the Swiss Criminal Code. If they have a sentence of not more than 12 months, they may continue their previous work or education outside their penal institutions, a status of 'semi-imprisonment' ('*Halbgefangenschaf*') in terms of art. 397bis (1)(*f*) Swiss Criminal Code and art. 4 of the first Regulation to the Swiss Criminal Code.

All other issues which affect prison labour and the salaries received for it fall under the legislative competence of the cantons. Depending on the canton, these issues are provided for either in a separate, special canton prison act, in an introductory act to the Swiss Criminal Code passed by the canton or in the canton's

---

[7]  Swiss law distinguished between *Haft-*, *Gefängnis-* and *Zuchthaus-* sentences, here termed detention, prison sentence and confinement, respectively. The former is imposed for up to three months and may not be carried out with those undergoing prison sentences or confinement.

criminal procedure provisions. Further details are provided for in the ordinances and rules of the prisons themselves. In addition, the so-called 'Implementation Concordats', that is, the instruments by which the cantons established three regions for the implementation of prison sentences, laid down further guidelines for prison labour.

A draft of the Expert Commission for the revision of the Swiss Criminal Code does not suggest any essential changes to the regime of prison labour. The obligation to work is retained expressly. However, a specific provision is made that 'a prisoner may, if he/she agrees, be employed by a private employer', that a prisoner 'with the necessary aptitude shall be given appropriate opportunities for education and training where possible', and that 'prisoners shall be reimbursed appropriately for their participation in education and training programmes if they are engaged at the workplace as part of a prison programme' (Bundesamt für Justiz, 1993: 29).

## 2 The Obligation and the Right to Work

The obligation to work, provided for in the legislation, does not require that prisoners actually work for a specific number of hours per week. Prisons are permitted and sometimes even encouraged to provide work only for a limited number of hours per week. They are also allowed not to provide work at all if there are health or therapeutic reasons for this or if the prisoner is undergoing a programme of education or further education. The decision on the amount of work to be assigned is left to the penal institution itself, within certain parameters provided by the legislation. For internal reasons, the average working week within the prison is 10–15 per cent shorter than the usual 42-hour Swiss working week. The obligation to work can be enforced by disciplinary measures. However, short-term refusals to work are no longer dealt with in this way. This is possible because the rules allow for discretion in the enforcement of discipline.

The legislation does not provide the prisoner with any subjective right actually to be assigned work at any particular time. In practice, it happens occasionally that no work can be found for the prisoners (that is, for half a day or for a few days) because, for example, an instruction concerning the work arrives late. Prisoners could object if insufficient work is offered systematically, or over a long period. However, there is no case law on the subject.

The prisoner has no right to any specific job. The prisons administering the longer sentences do, however, offer a wide range of work: domestic tasks such as cleaning, maintenance and working in a library, and work in various businesses and industries. Some prisons also provide work in gardens and agricultural services. In these institutions prisoners can also obtain career training in conjunction with an external training institution. But the prisons also offer 'protected employment', in which those prisoners who cannot work in normal businesses and who are being prepared to change to another work environment are employed.

## 3   Prison Labour from the Perspective of Labour Law and Social Insurance

Prison labour is not regarded as 'labour' within the meaning of labour law. However, the labour law rules, protecting employees from threats to their health and accidents, are applicable to prison labour.

The prisoners are subject to obligatory medical insurance but not to obligatory accident insurance since they are insured by the prison authorities. Disability pensions continue during the prison sentence but may not be drawn. As far as the obligatory old-age insurance is concerned, prisoners are deemed to be unemployed; as such, they may secure their pensions by paying the so-called 'minimum contribution'. Finally, work carried out in prison is also taken into consideration for the purposes of unemployment benefits, as long as the sentence is longer than 12 months.

## 4   Salaries for Prison Labour

In this respect, the section of the Swiss Criminal Code on prison law contains unusually detailed provisions: 'People who are incarcerated in terms of this law shall receive a salary as determined by the canton' (art. 376). The provisions on access to and use of the salary during the prison sentence are as follows: 'The salary is credited to the prisoner for the duration of the prison sentence. The rules of the institution determine whether and to what extent payments may be made from this amount for the benefit of this prisoner or the prisoner's family' (art. 377). After the prisoner's release, 'the institution has the discretion to award the entire amount to the released prisoner or to the relevant probation or welfare authorities to be used as appropriate for the released prisoner' (art. 378).

The system of salaries for prison labour is unequivocally designed for special prevention. This option was already chosen in the draft for Swiss criminal law in 1918. In the relevant Statement of the Federal Council of that time, it was set out as follows: 'Provisions for the payment of salaries are justified in view of the meaning such an institution has for educating the prisoners to diligence and thrift, and also in easing their return to normal life, since the capital, which the prisoners themselves have earned, helps them through their early difficulties' (Swiss Federal Council, 1918: 91).

Because the level of the salaries is decided by the cantons, the rate differed greatly until a few years ago. In 1976, the average salary paid in the cantons of West Switzerland was 8.50 Swiss francs per day. In East Switzerland it was 9.00 Swiss francs per day and in the cantons of North-West and inner Switzerland it was 14.00 Swiss francs per day (Bundesamt für Justiz, 1983). Since then, the three regional prison Concordats have harmonized and raised these amounts: in 1995 and 1996, the average basic salary for all the cantons was set at 24.50 Swiss francs per day. In 1998, the salary was 26.00 Swiss francs. Prisoners are paid for days on which the assigned work is carried out, as well as for days on which they do not work through no fault of their own: this is when they are prevented by sickness or accidents or when they attend an education or training programme offered as an alternative to work.

## 5 Prison Labour and Execution of the Prison Sentence

Because the privileges granted to prisoners are dependent on good behaviour, prisoners who refuse to work cannot expect conjugal leave or a more beneficial grade of treatment such as semi-freedom.

Less clear are the consequences of adequate or inadequate work performances for the conditional release of prisoners after they have served at least two-thirds of their prison sentences. A conditional release is granted if the prognosis is favourable, and this in turn rests on an overall evaluation of the prisoner and his/her personality, life before imprisonment, conduct in prison and probable environment after release. While a satisfactory work record is therefore not sufficient basis for an early conditional release, it must, at least, be considered from the perspective of the prisoner's reintegration into the labour market. On the other hand, if the prisoner refused to work, or carried out inadequate work, a long time ago, this obviously is not taken into consideration for the evaluation. A current bad work record usually (exceptions are always possible) precludes a favourable prognosis.

## 6 Current Problems

First, a serious problem is that the number of prisoners who cannot be put to work in 'normal' industries and businesses is steadily increasing. People belonging to this group are those heavily addicted to drugs (who represent more than one-third of the population in some prisons) and prisoners from other cultures (such as female drug-smugglers from black Africa) who are not familiar with the work standards in Switzerland. The third group, which is admittedly less noticeable through being smaller, consists of prisoners with serious psychological handicaps. These prisoners require special jobs in therapeutically oriented 'protected workplaces'.[8] These workplaces are staff-intensive and therefore expensive and they are also relatively unproductive. In times of shrinking state resources, such workplaces can be made available only to a limited extent.

A second, equally serious problem results from the continually weak economy. The prisons are finding it increasingly difficult to provide full employment for the prisoners as provided for by legislation, and to find a market for the goods and services produced. As a result, the Prisons Department of Berne released a policy paper, in November 1995, which provides that the work projects of the prisons follow production, cost and management policies in line with other public and private employers and that they join the open market (Amt für Freihetsentzug und Betreuung, 1995: 5). In October 1996, a campaign was started with the help of the media and a prospectus on the prisons' products and services was issued to market prison labour.

The third and final point that must be made is that, increasingly, the duty to work as part of a prison sentence is a contradiction in the wider world of work. The ordinary worker, as a result of not only economic but also structurally-related unemployment, sees a job as a rare advantage, while the convicted prisoner receives work from the state. This conflicts with the widely accepted criminological viewpoint that the environment inside the prison should reflect

[8] For example, the pilot project of the '*Arbeitsprogression*' model in the prison centre of St. Johannsen, Berne or the programme for mentally handicapped inmates at the prison of Saxieriet in the canton of St. Gallen. See Brenzikofer and Baechtold (1992).

the environment outside the prison as much as possible. For this reason the question still remains, although it is still seen as pure heresy in Switzerland, whether retaining the duty to work in prisons is still an appropriate penal policy.

## References

Amt für Freiheitsentzug und Betreuung. 1995. *Grundzätze für die Arbeitsbetriebe im Straf- und Massnahmenvollzug un der Bewährungshilfe*. Berne: Government Publisher.

Anselmier, Henri. 1992. *Les prisons vaudoises (1795-1871)*. Lausanne: Bibliothèque historique vaudoise.

Anselmier, Henri. 1993. *Les prisons vaudoises, 1872-1942*. Lausanne: Editions Réalités Sociales.

Brenzikofer, Paul and Andrea Baechtold. 1992. Vollzug als Asyl. *Neue Kriminalpolitik* 3, no. 4: 36-7.

Bundesamt für Justiz. 1983. *Die finanzielle Entschädigung der Gefangenenarbeit. Eine Untersuchung des Bundesamtes für Justiz über die im Jahre 1976 den Strafgefangenen ausgerichteten Verdienstanteile*. Berne: Government Publisher.

Bundesamt für Justiz. 1993. *Vorentwürfe der Expertenkommission zum Allgemeinen Teil und zum Dritten Buch des Strafgesetzbuches und zu einem Bundesgesetz über die Jungendstrafrechtspflege*. Berne: Government Publisher.

Curti, Claudia. 1988. *Die Strafanstalt des Kantons Zürich im 19. Jahrhundert*. Zurich: Schulthess.

Fumasoli, Georg. 1981. *Ursprünge und Anfänge der Schallenwerke. Ein Beitrag zur Frühgeschichte des Gefängniswesens*. Zürich: Schulthess.

Hafner, Karl and Emil Zürcher. 1925. *Schweizerische Gefängniskunde*. Berne: Stämpfli.

Roth, Robert. 1981. *Pratiques pénitentiaires et théories sociales. L'exemple de la prison de Genève (1825-1862)*. Geneva: Droz.

Schaffroth, J.G. 1898. *Geschichte des bernischen Gefängniswesens*. Berne: K.J. Wyss.

Schweingruber, Max. 1981. *Thorberg in der ersten Hälfte des 19. Jahrhunderts*. Burgdorf: Haller und Jenzer.

Statements of the Swiss Federal Council. 1918. Berne: Government Publishers.

Stooss, Carl. 1893. *Motive zu dem Vorentwurf eines Schweizerischen Strafgesetzbuches. Allgemeiner Teil*. Basle and Geneva: Georg & Co.

Zwicky, Jürg Stefan. 1982. *Das Gefängniswesen zur Zeit der Helvetik*. Zurich: Schulthess.

## The Author

**Andrea Baechtold** is head of the prison department of the canton of Berne and professor of criminal law and penology at the University of Berne in Switzerland.

# 15 United States of America: Prison Labour: A Tale of Two Penologies

JAMES B. JACOBS

## 1 Introduction

Two spectres haunt American penology. The one that keeps liberals up at night is the picture of sadistic profit-obsessed managers driving prisoners in forced labour (enforced by brutal whipping) beyond the levels of human endurance.[1] The spectre that keeps conservatives awake at night is the image of idle prisoners spending their days watching television, listening to music, smoking marijuana, lifting weights and playing basketball.[2] The first vision anguishes about the risk that prison labour will deteriorate into a system of punishment, exploitation and even torture; the second is vexed about the anomaly that citizens pay taxes to support idle prisoners; it thus focuses on the relationship of prison labour to social equity.

1   It is interesting to note that the thirteenth Amendment which freed the slaves, abolished involuntary servitude except 'as punishment for crime whereof the party shall have been duly convicted'. Courts have consistently held that prisoners can be required to work and that their labour belongs to the state (Spitzer, 1987).
2   In 1995, US Rep. Dick Zimmer (R., NJ) introduced the 'No-Frills Prison Act'. This would make federal moneys for state and local prison and gaol construction available only to states that end inmate privileges such as smoking, weight-lifting and family visits. 'We shouldn't be using taxpayer dollars to turn prisons into vacation spas,' Representative Zimmer said in a written statement introducing the bill (Zimmer, 1995). Senator Richard Shelby (R., Ala.) has introduced a bill into the US Senate, the 'Prison Construction Block Grant Amendments Act' (s.930), that would withhold federal money from any prison that fails to establish a minimum 48-hour working week and a 16-hour a week study requirement for inmates before they can enjoy privileges.

There have certainly been periods in American history when the exploitation and abuse of prison labour justified the liberals' concerns. The greatest abuses occurred in the American south in the nineteenth century and, in some cases, into the twentieth century (Sellin, 1976). Prisoners were often leased out to private entrepreneurs who worked them unmercifully, sometimes to death, in mining, agriculture, road works and in other jobs (Cvornyek, 1993; Fierce, 1994; Lichtenstein, 1996). Even when the prison officials retained managerial control, there were outrageous abuses. That the prisoners oppressed by this penal slavery were almost all black reinforces liberals' anxiety about current calls to reintroduce hard labour.

Brutal labour more or less came to an end in the post-World War II period as a consequence of both ideology and the prisoners' rights movement (Garland, 1990). The southern plantation prisons, vilified in film, journalistic portrayals and lawsuits, were essentially dismantled. The southern prisons, epitomized by those of Texas, were forced to adopt the northern model of imprisonment that was characterized by greater bureaucracy and much less labour. However, in the last few years, legislatures in several southern states have voted to reinstate 'chain gangs' thereby rekindling liberals' fear that, under the guise of work programmes, prisoners will once again be abused (Curriden, 1995). The reinvested chain gangs are so recent that I am not aware of any scholarly assessments. My prediction, however, is that there is more symbolism here than reality. In large part, this is because prison officials no longer have the stomach or the disciplinary tools for implementing hard labour.[3] Furthermore, such programmes will be given tough scrutiny in the courts and in the mass media.[4]

3   Consider the following tepid definition of 'hard labour' that appears in a recent Iowa law (Ch.166(H.F.215); West's No. 166, Inmates – Hard Labour): '3. For purposes of this section, "hard labour" means physical or mental labour which is performed for useful and productive work, chain gangs, menial labour, substance abuse or sex offender treatment programs, any training necessary to provide any work required, and if possible, work providing an inmate with marketable vocational skills. "Hard labour" does not include labour which is dangerous to an inmate's life or health, is unduly painful, or is required to be performed under conditions that would violate occupational safety and health standards applicable to such labour performed by a person who is not an inmate.'

4   Legal attacks on the chain gangs are already under way. The plain-

We now come to the second spectre, the one of prisoners sitting around doing nothing, wallowing in indolence. As study after study and commission after commission have shown, American prisons suffer from pervasive idleness. Only a small percentage of prisoners are 'employed' in any serious sense of the word. For the most part, they serve their time in their cells watching television and listening to music on headphones or on the tiers talking and 'hanging out'. If they are fortunate, they may go to the gymnasium or the recreation yard an hour or two a day. They sleep much and do little. This idleness is not treated as a component of the intended prison regime but as an unintended, albeit unavoidable, consequence of too many prisoners and too few jobs.

The vast majority of prisoners who do have jobs work in institutional maintenance, carrying out chores that keep the prison functioning. In theory, such work is compulsory; there is no right to refuse. In practice, however, there are far more prisoners than jobs. They sweep, scrub, mop and wax. They work in the laundry, in the kitchen and on the prison grounds. Such jobs are neither challenging nor interesting, and they usually last only a few hours a day. But they get the prisoner out of the cell house and into a position, if he wants to, to wheel and deal in prison intrigues and rackets.

A very small minority, perhaps 5–10 per cent of prisoners, work in 'industries'. These industries are often laughably antiquated, using machinery dating back decades. The so-called 'industries' bear no resemblance to a modern factory. To the observer, the inmates work very slowly; there is much 'featherbedding'. There is no hustle and bustle, no sense of time pressure; the atmosphere certainly does not suggest productivity. There is an extraordinary amount of 'down time' because foremen are not available, supplies have not arrived, orders have not come in, machinery is broken, the prison is on lockdown and so forth.

The most work-intensive prisons in American history were the southern plantation-type prisons that sent hundreds of prisoners off to the fields every day to pick cotton, plant alfalfa and so on. Agricultural work was the ideal unskilled labour. By expanding acreage more prisoners could be accommodated and the produce could be consumed by the prisoners themselves and by inmates of other state institutions. Modest capital and practically no technical

> tiffs charge that this form of work constitutes cruel and unusual punishment forbidden by the Eighth Amendment (for example, *Wade v. Kirkland*, 1997).

skill were needed to implement or supervise these agricultural operations. The guards, drawn from the rural areas in which prisons were located, knew all about the way farms are supposed to operate. But these were the very labour programmes that resembled slavery and generated charges of ghastly abuse.

These plantation systems did not survive the prisoners' rights movement of the 1970s. The modern advocates of rehabilitation excoriated agricultural labour because it was completely divorced from what the mostly urban prisoners would do upon release. They denounced agricultural work as demeaning and irrelevant. Moreover, it was a kind of hard manual labour that looked to the critics a lot like punishment. In any event, the critics put their faith in treatment, therapy and education, not work. The courts proscribed the hard punishments, such as whipping, isolation and physical abuse, that had been used to compel inmates to work. Eventually, many of the prisons (like Stateville in Illinois where field research was carried out in the early 1970s) sold off their agricultural lands (Jacobs, 1997).

While liberals favour *meaningful* work and job training (as long as proper safeguards are established) for its rehabilitative effects and conservatives believe that work is a moral imperative, neither pundits nor penologists face up to the practical difficulties of providing acceptable work opportunities, especially in the face of the massive increase in the number of prisoners currently overwhelming prisons in the USA. Just as political discourse has not accepted the reality that significant unemployment is an endemic feature of modern capitalist economies, those who engage in prison policy debates do not recognize that a very high rate of unemployment is endemic to the organization and operation of American prisons.[5] Indeed, there is a certain naivety among legislators, reformers and penologists when it comes to making grandiose recommendations regarding the employment of prisoners.

It is not difficult for prison commentators of all political persuasions to pay homage to the ideal of a prison alive and humming with productively employed inmates. Like motherhood and apple pie, work, especially 'meaningful well-remunerated work', is a sym-

---

5  Jonathan Simon (1993) argues that the work system on which the whole concept of parole is based evaporated in the second half of the twentieth century. Yet the parole system closed its eyes to the reality, continuing to cling to the fiction that inmates were being released on parole to jobs.

bol that commands universal obeisance.[6] According to the ideal, prisoners should work away at tasks that are meaningful, interesting and remunerative. They develop good work habits, a powerful work ethic and improve their human capital, acquiring skills that will be utilized upon release. Prisoners who are absorbed in work will not become bored, alienated, frustrated, restless or rebellious. Therefore, the full-employment prison (like the full-employment society) is safe because busy inmates are contented (or at least preoccupied) inmates. This same belief in the social value of work undergirds all criminology and is the most common (at least liberal) recommendation for addressing the crime problem.

This picture becomes even more appealing when we add the claim that the value of the prisoners' labour will pay for or at least substantially defray the cost of running the prisons, a cost which has become a real drag on state and local government. The working prisoners will contribute to their room and board, make restitution to their victims, pay off their fines and pay their taxes. No matter how expensive (or perhaps *because of* how expensive) prisons become and how large a share of the government budget they consume, politicians continue to talk about the self-financing prison.[7]

[6] The prestigious National Conference of Commissioners on Uniform State Laws drafted a comprehensive Model Sentencing & Corrections Act that was released in 1979. It is an important document that, as well as anything else, expresses the modern-day consensus. The Model Act urges the director to 'provide confined persons with opportunities to engage in productive activity' (4801). It urges that prison officials 'assist confined persons to develop a sense of responsibility by developing a realistic employment environment in which wages are comparable to those paid in the free community'. The Act states that a prisoner can be required to work.

[7] The Oregon Constitution was recently amended by Initiative No. 17, The Prison Reform and Inmate Work Act of 1994 which declared 'that inmates should work as hard as the taxpayers who provide for their upkeep; therefore ... All inmates of state corrections institutions shall be actively engaged full-time in work or on the job training'. The intent of the people is that taxpayer-supported institutions and programmes will be free to benefit from inmate work. Thus prison work programmes will be designed and carried out so as to achieve net cost savings in maintaining government operations, or so as to achieve a net profit in private sector activities.

According to the ideal's advocates, once the costs and benefits are properly explained, no interest groups will oppose this vision of the productive, full-employment prison. The most likely opponents, free-world workers and free-world companies, will realize that prison industries will not displace private sector firms or will do this so marginally as not to be noticed. By judiciously choosing which industries to establish, the prison officials will manage not to compete with private sector businesses. Likewise, by paying the prisoners a minimum wage or even prevailing wage, union opposition will be allayed. Thus the legislature and the taxpayers will be happy.

## 2 The Bitter Reality

Unfortunately, the full-employment industrial prison, no matter how often it is conjured, has not even begun to materialize. Nevertheless, penologists, liberal reformers and moral conservatives continue to pass laws proclaiming that prisoners should work, that prisons should be self-supporting, and that free-world workers and businesses should not be displaced. Some academic commentators blame the seemingly intractable problem of prisoner idleness on lack of will. They argue that prisons could be transformed into 'factories within fences' simply by making a strong political and moral commitment. Some years ago the then Chief Justice Warren Burger was much applauded for urging the complete restructuring of American prisons around the concept of productive work. Likewise, in a leading review of scholarship on prison labour, the criminologist Gordon Hawkins wrote:

> The implementation on a national basis of the concept of the industrial prison would present economic problems. But the principal barrier over the years to the profitable employment of prisoners has been neither the conditions of the labour market, the prevailing mode of production nor any other aspect of the economy. The principal barrier to a rational solution to the problem of prisoners, work and prison has been the persistent influence on penal policy of the principle of less eligibility. (Hawkins, 1983: 120)

I disagree with Hawkins. I believe that the idea of a factory prison, at least in the US context, is utterly unrealistic. This is not, of course, good news. But unless we face the reality, we will not be able to experiment with different models of the day-to-day routine of imprisonment.

The obstacles to establishing viable work regimens in prison hardly need recounting. With respect to 'industrialization', the prison suffers the same problems as some underdeveloped countries. First, there is the problem of infrastructure. The typical prison is at least several decades old and was not designed to serve as a modern-day factory. Such essentials as water, electricity and basic physical plant are inadequate to support a serious factory operation. Modern factories in the USA today typically have enormous square footage, are frequently purpose-built, including reinforced foundations, appropriate lighting and electrical wiring and good access to transport. Even so, competition is fierce, markets are fickle and there is certainly no guarantee of success.

A second and related problem is location. Prisons are usually located in rural, sometimes remote, areas. Thus they are far from suppliers, repairmen, customers and auxiliary service providers. More important, prisons are usually located far from large labour markets. Consequently, prisons have a major problem recruiting and retaining competent staff to serve as foremen, teachers and executives. Competent industrial foremen are much in demand in the private sector. Prisons are a 'tough sell'. There are many obvious drawbacks to spending one's working life in prison. The working conditions are very unpleasant and even dangerous, and there is little chance of developing a social life around one's co-workers. Such a position does not carry high status or prestige and will not advance one's career.

A third problem is inadequate capital. It takes a lot of money to establish, nurture and operate a successful business. To produce high-quality products requires good and modern equipment which has to be upgraded, repaired and replaced. And over the past two decades American businesses and industries have become increasingly capital-intensive. Thus factories need continuous access to capital markets. They borrow money from banks, sometimes float bonds and sometimes offer stock. Prisons industries must depend upon unstable government financing which, among other things, can only be counted on one year at a time, if that. In recent years, many state governments lurch from fiscal crisis to fiscal crisis and even demand across-the-board mid-year cuts in operating and capital budgets.

A fourth major obstacle to establishing a viable industrial programme in prison is the unreliable and irresponsible workforce. Despite some romantic claims that our prisoners are diamonds in the rough and as qualified for work as free-world persons, that is hardly true. The prisoners are grossly undereducated, irresponsible, non-cooperative, prone to be drug abusers and, most importantly, unsocialized into the world of work. The majority have never held a real job; there is a great deal of hostility or, at best, indifference to work. In addition, they are constantly exposed to the frustrations and tensions of prison life, including sexual deprivation, gang conflict, physical insecurity, lack of privacy, and so forth. This is not a contented workforce.

Prisoners' motivation to apply themselves to their tasks is not likely to be high. Most prisoners do not see themselves as settling into a '9 to 5' working life upon release. Furthermore, prison officials can do little to motivate hard work with attention to accuracy and quality. Pay is poor, indeed so poor (for example, $0.50–$0.70 an hour) as to convey the message that the work is not valuable and not worthwhile. Opportunity for 'advancement' is quite limited. For reasons discussed above, and because of antiquated technology and machinery, it is almost inconceivable that the prison factory will equip a prisoner with skills necessary to compete in the outside job market. The inmates' main motivation is probably to avoid the boredom of sitting in the cell house or to qualify for remission time. The motivation to work may even be perverse: to enjoy opportunities for gang banging, socializing and so on. Some prisoners may even take malicious pleasure in sabotaging the industrial enterprise.

Even under the best of scenarios, jobs are not as important to prisoners as they are to free-world persons. The job rarely comes first. Sometimes prisoners leave the prison for days, weeks or months in order to appear in court. On particular workdays they may be absent because of visits from family, friends or lawyers. Prisoners who may be in key positions in the industrial enterprise may voluntarily and sometimes involuntarily transfer to other prisons. (Of course, they may also be paroled or otherwise reach the end of the prison sentence.)

A fifth problem is 'intervention of the state'. Even under the most optimistic assumptions, industry will never be more than a secondary or tertiary (at best) organizational goal. Prison officials will always consider industry a lower priority than safety and security. Thus the prison suffers from frequent lockdowns which may shut down all activity for an indefinite period. The prison workplace is subject to unannounced searches and periodic shutdowns in the name of security. Sometimes prisoners are 'incarcerated' (sent to the segregation unit) for rule violations on and off the job or reclassified as not qualified to serve in an industry. The industries almost by necessity will have potential weapons lying around, so security staff will not permit some inmates to work there. All this causes delays and unpredictability that would try the patience of even the saintly customer.

The sixth problem is a whole slough of legal and political impediments to prison industries. In the USA prison-made goods have been banned from inter-state commerce (The Hawes-Cooper Act (1929), 49 U.S.C. s.60; Ashurst-Sumners Act (1935) and the Sumners-Ashurst Act (1940), 18 U.S.C. 1761, 49 Stat. 1134).[8] Furthermore, the elaboration of free trade institutions at the international level has led to prohibitions on the export of prison-made goods (see Cowen, 1993). Most states limit the market for prison goods to state agencies and institutions, but this does not necessarily mean that government agencies have to make their purchases from prison industries. Some laws provide a caveat that government agencies must buy from the prisons only when the prison products are less expensive. It is also possible for government agencies to avoid purchasing from prison agencies by describing their desired purchase needs in a way that would exclude the prison products; or they can argue that the prison product is inadequate and/or does not meet their needs.[9] In other words, it is not easy to force shrewd government officials to become purchasers. Ultimately, to be dependable customers, they will have to be convinced of the superiority of the prison-made product.

Politically, with people already insecure about their jobs, it is not surprising that unions, politicians and people generally will be hostile to the displacement of free-world jobs by prison industry. A number of states have placed restrictions in their laws regarding work release and prison industries to the effect that inmates should

8   See also the Walsh-Healy Act (1936), 41 U.S.C. s.35. But see the Justice Systems Improvement Act of 1979, P.L. 96–157, 93 Stat. 1167, 1215.
9   The US Navy has been seeking a federal law that would make it easier to buy furniture and other products from private sector employers without having to obtain waivers. According to the Navy's spokesperson, 'the furniture produced by Federal Prison Industries is inferior, costs more and takes longer to procure' (Statement of John Hagan, US Navy Chief Petty Officer, before the Subcommittee on Military Construction of the House Appropriations Committee on Quality of Life, 29 February 1996).

not be employed in industries, crafts and skills that compete with free-world industry in the region.[10] This means that prison industry will have to succeed in businesses which no entrepreneur has seen as possibly profitable. It is utterly unrealistic to imagine the US federal and state prison systems, not to mention gaols, employing even a substantial fraction of their 1.4 million inmates in industrial-type production.

The seventh problem is that the massive increase of prisoners in the USA over the last two decades has seriously exacerbated the situation. The prison population has practically quadrupled. There were not enough jobs before and the situation has only worsened by orders of magnitude.

Thus it seems that prison industry is likely to be no more robust in the future than it is today. Indeed, the danger is that the modest amount of prison industry we have today will dwindle in absolute terms, as it already has in terms of the proportion of inmates involved. UNICOR[11] is even now under serious threat in Congress. In this environment it is difficult to tell whether demands that UNICOR pay inmates the minimum wage are sincere or simply a cynical way of dismantling federal prison industries. A minimum wage is completely unrealistic unless it is no more than an accounting gimmick that would register a transfer of funds into the inmate workers' accounts and then register a reverse transfer back to the prisons for room and board.

## 3 Conclusion

The obstacles to establishing a full-employment productive prison seem formidable. The prisons have not been located, constructed or configured with industrial production in mind. The prisons lack capital and access to capital. Prison officials lack expertise in and strong commitment to business. Security concerns

10   The following proviso in connection with a *work release* bill is typical: 'Such paid employment will not result in the displacement of employed workers, nor be applied in skills, crafts, or trades in which there is a surplus of available gainful labour in the locality or impair existing contracts for services' (11 South Carolina, Corrections–Paid Employment of Prisoners–Wages and Unemployment Compensation, Act 500, H.B. No. 4473, 1994).

11   For an extensive exposition of UNICOR, see the section by Fleisher and Rison in this chapter (Editors).

significantly affect the way prisoners can be assigned and how workshops can be run. The pool of prisoners from which workers must be recruited is uneducated, unskilled, unreliable, unmotivated and undisciplined.

The amazing thing is that there are any success stories (Federal Prison Industries (UNICOR), 1995). Indeed, so formidable are the obstacles that one might wonder whether claims of success by the Federal Prison Industries (FPI) or UNICOR could withstand rigorous evaluation. Moreover, to this author's eye, it is incredible that certain European countries seem to have succeeded in establishing viable prison industries. If true, it is important to determine whether this success can be explained by differences in these countries, national economies, size of prisoner population, absence of a large pool of unskilled low-wage labour, quality of prisoners or by other factors.

It is fascinating that penologists, beyond recommending in a general way productive work, have not focused on what prisoners should do all day. Is it a matter of indifference to penologists whether prisoners watch TV soap operas and game shows or meditate or play board games? The universal obeisance to work and full employment has completely diverted us from looking the hard questions in the eye.

## References

Cowen, Jonathan M. 1993. One Nation's 'Gulag' Is Another Nation's 'Factory Within a Fence', Prison-Labor in the People's Republic of China and the United States of America. *UCLA Pacific Basin Law Journal* 12: 190 ff.

Curriden, Mark. 1995. Hard Time. *ABA Journal* 81: 72 ff.

Cvornyek, Robert L. 1993. *Convict Labor in the Alabama Coal Mines, 1874–1928.* Unpublished PhD thesis, Columbia University.

Federal Prison Industries (UNICOR). 1995. *Annual Report.* Washington: Government Printing Office.

Fierce, Mifred C. 1994. *Slavery Revisited: Blacks and the Southern Convict Lease System, 1865–1933.* Brooklyn College, African Studies Research Center.

Garland, David. 1990. *Punishment and Modern Society.* Chicago: University of Chicago Press.

Hawkins, Gordon. 1983. Prison and Prison Industries. In *Crime and Justice: An Annual Review of Research*, edited by Michael Tonry and Norval Morris. Chicago: University of Chicago Press.

Jacobs, James. 1997. *Stateville: The Penitentiary in Mass Society.* Chicago: University of Chicago Press,
Lichtenstein, Alex. 1996. *Twice the Work of Free Labor.* London and New York: Verso.
National Conference of Commissioners on Uniform State Laws. 1979. *Model Sentencing and Corrections Act 1979.* Chicago: Uniform Law Commissioners.
Sellin, Jonathan T. 1976. *Slavery and the Penal System.* New York: Elsevier.
Simon, Jonathan. 1993. *Poor Discipline: Parole and the Social Control of the Underclass 1890-1990.* Chicago: University of Chicago Press.
Spitzer, John B. 1987. 60 *American Jurisprudence* 2d, Penal and Correctional Institutions: 1117, especially section VII, 1237-44.
Zimmer, Richard. 1995. Legislation to End Prison Perks Wins Endorsement. Press release from the office of Richard Zimmer. 31 January.

## Case
Wade v. *Kirkland*, #96-17119 (9th Circ. 1997).

## The Author
**James B. Jacobs** is professor of law and director of the Center for Research in Crime and Criminal Justice in the School of Law at New York University in the USA.

# 16 United States of America: Inmate Work and Consensual Management in the Federal Bureau of Prisons

MARK S. FLEISHER AND RICHARD H. RISON*

## 1 Introduction

Prisons do not have to be disruptive, dangerous places. The quality of life for prison staffers and inmates depends, in large measure, on the management philosophy of a correctional agency and how that philosophy is moulded into a model of administration and management (DiIulio, 1987: 95; Fleisher, 1989; Wright, 1994). This chapter discusses inmate employment as the core of the consensual model of correctional management used by the (US) Federal Bureau of Prisons. The Bureau of Prisons (BOP) organizational model advocates inmate employment as an essential element in daily prison life. Inmate work enables prison administrators and managers to achieve a high quality of life for staff and inmates in correctional institutions, ranging from low to high security level.[1]

---

\* We thank Warden David W. Helman and William G. Saylor, Deputy Chief, Office of Research and Evaluation, Federal Bureau of Prisons, for their contributions. An earlier version of this chapter, presented at the Workshop on Contemporary Prison Labour, Oñati International Institute for the Sociology of Law, in Oñati, Spain, benefited from the comments of workshop participants. The opinions expressed here are those of the authors and do not represent the official position and policies of the US Department of Justice, Federal Bureau of Prisons.

1 For a discussion of management issues in the BOP, see Boin (1998), DiIulio (1987, 1989, 1990), Fleisher (1989, 1995, 1996, 1998), Fleisher and Rison (1997), Fleisher et al. (1997), Keve (1991).

The BOP management philosophy stresses these goals: the humane treatment of inmates, the security of staff and inmates in institutions and the opportunity for inmates to work at jobs that will assist them in adjusting to a lawful, post-imprisonment life style. To accomplish these goals, the BOP management model focuses on inmate employment opportunities in two areas. These are Federal Prison Industries (UNICOR) and institution, or non-UNICOR, jobs (maintenance, food service, grounds crews). Institution jobs are vital and support UNICOR operations. UNICOR is the BOP's organizational centrepiece and, because of that, federal institutions have created an inmate-based consensual management model. This consensual model stresses mechanisms of formal and informal social control familiar to lawful citizens in the community.

UNICOR and the BOP's culture and management strategies have evolved together for more than 60 years. The outcome of this evolution is a form of institution life where inmate employment does much more than just occupy inmates' time (see Flanagan and Maguire, 1993; Funk et al., 1982; Johnson, 1994; Lightman, 1987; Nicholas, 1988; Robinson, 1931; Seligman, 1986). Inmate work has become so valuable to inmates that work opportunities have become a customary and an expected aspect of inmates' life, even in newly opened facilities (see Fleisher *et al.*, 1997 for a discussion of organizational development at a women's minimum security prison camp). As a management practice, both UNICOR and institution employment offer inmates practical work experiences in factories, landscape, food service and other real-life work environments, and a monthly income. Because most inmates have not had long-term on-the-job work experiences prior to imprisonment (Fleisher, 1995), the requirement of daily employment with inmate-worker performance evaluations, expectations of high-quality output, and inmate/inmate, inmate/staff teamwork train inmates for the real world of work.

This chapter discusses the BOP's organizational model and illustrates the importance of inmate work with an analysis of wage and discipline data from the United States Penitentiary (USP) at Lompoc, California, a high-security penitentiary for offenders with violent criminal histories, and a discussion of UNICOR with the management strategy at the medium-security Federal Correctional Institution at Pekin, Illinois.

## 2  Federal Prison Industries (UNICOR)

UNICOR, a financially self-supporting organization within the BOP, was created by an act of Congress on 23 June 1934, with an initial investment of $4 million. Since then UNICOR has operated without appropriated funds from Congress. UNICOR has a six-member board of directors appointed by the President of the United States. At the end of 1994, approximately 16,000 inmates from among the UNICOR-eligible inmates in BOP facilities were employed in product and service jobs in 51 prisons in 100 factories.

UNICOR factories manufacture goods sold only to federal agencies: over 60 per cent of sales are to the US Department of Defense. UNICOR sales in the fiscal year 1994 were $395 million (Federal Prison Industries, 1994) or approximately 15.1 per cent of the BOP's 1994–5 annual budget of $2.6 billion. The production of UNICOR goods requires the assistance of inmates employed by UNICOR and by inmates in institution jobs. The contribution of federal inmates to UNICOR can be measured as a function of revenue generated by UNICOR. Using UNICOR's 1994 revenue as a base, each federal inmate generated $4,177; UNICOR inmate-workers each generated $24,687. The revenue generated by UNICOR inmate-workers exceeded the fiscal year 1994 average cost of confinement ($21,352) by $3,335. Since its inception, UNICOR has returned to the US Treasury over $82 million.

UNICOR offers inmate-workers cost-free job training and reduces the cost of operating federal institutions. UNICOR has also had a dramatic financial impact on local communities. Of each dollar expended by UNICOR, 56 cents purchase materials from local communities, 22 cents are allocated to staff salaries, 13 cents to utilities, equipment, maintenance and supplies purchased from local communities, eight cents to inmate salaries, and one cent to new factories and equipment.

Approximately 90 per cent of all inmates in a federal prison are fit to work; others are medically idle, unassigned (have not yet been assigned a job) or confined in administrative detention and disciplinary segregation. Generally speaking, UNICOR employs about 30 per cent, and institution jobs about 70 per cent, of work-eligible inmates, but these percentages have varied. From 1984 to 1986, about 35 per cent of UNICOR eligible inmates were employed by UNICOR. In January 1992, the UNICOR employment rate was 32 per cent, by the end of the fiscal year 1993, it was 29.4 per cent. In the fiscal year 1994, the UNICOR employment rate was 25.8 per cent, and in December 1994 it was 22.2 per cent. The decline in the

UNICOR employment rate was, in large part, an effect of a rapidly increasing inmate population effected by the Comprehensive Crime Control Act of 1984. In the five-year period from 1980 to 1985, the federal inmate population increased by 15,860 inmates, from 24,363 to 40,223. But by 1990, the inmate population had increased to 65,526, adding another 25,303 inmates.

Staff and inmates have a vested interest in institution social control and UNICOR operations (see DiIulio, 1987: 240). This means that staff and inmates should behave in a communal fashion to resolve strife on and off the job, for the benefit of the prison as a factory community. Labour strikes and labour-related violence in a factory prison are anathema. On-the-job interpersonal problems, particularly in higher security facilities, that are serious enough to prompt inmate strikes are also likely to result in fights, assaults and killings off the job. With this in mind, the BOP has imposed upper and lower threshold benchmarks for UNICOR employment at low-, medium- and high-security institutions; benchmark thresholds are not in effect at minimum security and administrative institutions. Thresholds are 15–25 per cent at low-security, 20–30 per cent at medium-security and 30–40 per cent at high-security institutions.

Benchmark thresholds are related to UNICOR work distribution and to inmate social control. A UNICOR employment rate that is below the minimum threshold suggests that too few inmates are employed and factories may be working below capacity. But UNICOR employment that exceeds an upper threshold at one or more facility may threaten to lower rates of UNICOR employment at other facilities. Thus a balance of work is maintained among UNICOR factories. The link between UNICOR employment and inmate social control is expressed in benchmark thresholds. Generally speaking, the level of a benchmark threshold is inverse to the likelihood of institution violence. Medium- and high-security federal institutions have the highest UNICOR benchmark thresholds and also house the BOP's more violence-prone inmates.

Congress and the BOP are aware of union and corporate leaders' sensitivity towards goods produced by federal inmates. Congress limits the potential market share of UNICOR products by diversifying the UNICOR product line into dozens of items, and, in general, has tried to focus on products now manufactured offshore. But as prison growth has risen since 1990, the number of UNICOR factories has increased and output has expanded. UNICOR officials are therefore subject to criticism.

## 3 Consensual Management

Organizing a prison for factory activities effects administrative and managerial changes. In the free community, work stoppages and slow-downs are influenced by a number of issues, such as income, working conditions and strained relationships among workers and supervisors. To sustain an industrial operation in a prison, these issues exert equal if not more influence over the outcome of factory operations. In the free community, disgruntled workers are free to quit and find other jobs; however, unhappy inmate-workers do not have that option and staff and inmates must resolve on-the-job dilemmas. A peaceful resolution requires a management model that allows informal negotiation leading to an acceptable agreement between inmate-workers and supervisors. Such a management model is based on open and affable relations supported by efficient and accurate interdepartmental communication, passive security and efficient support services. For instance, food service should be able to serve factory workers and other inmates a noon meal within a prescribed lunch period, say, 60 to 75 minutes. A longer lunch period reduces the length of the working day, cuts into inmates' off-duty midday time and may facilitate off-the-job discord among inmates.

Efficient factory operations should operate within a carefully monitored environment. The rigour of programme review, institution character profiles (Fleisher, 1995), operational reviews, strategic management and the ability to compare the performance of one institution to all others at the same security level, on dozens of performance criteria using the Key Indicator/Strategic Support System (Saylor, 1990, 1994), has enabled UNICOR factories to operate, even at higher-security institutions.

In general, prisons that are converted into work communities normalize social and economic life for inmates and facilitate the integration of staff and inmates' activities (Fleisher, 1989). Inmates earn incomes which sustain both legal (commissary purchases) and illegal (gambling) activities. Staff rely on inmates to accomplish daily institution work (painting, plumbing, electrical) which is the basis for their performance evaluations. If inmates do a mediocre job, staff pay for it with lower evaluations. In short, a prison factory community that is successful creates stakeholders from the parties that might otherwise be antagonists.

## 4  United States Penitentiary (USP), Lompoc

Maguire et al. (1988: 16) observed that 'industry employment may promote better institutional adjustment among participants. On several grounds, improving the climate of the prison environment and the behavior of inmates while confined are worthy policy goals'. Fleisher (1989) is a detailed account of discipline and violence at USP Lompoc. A significant finding of this penitentiary research is that inmate employment guided the flow of daily operations within the institution and had a central role in the informal social control among inmates and between inmates and staff. One inmate at USP Lompoc noted how money and social control are integrally linked. Inmate Whitney: 'You can control us with guns or you can do it with money. I like the money better.'

Fleisher and McCarthy (1988) focused on the relationship between inmate work assignments and discipline, using inmate wage data for the period November 1987 to March 1988. During this period, 76.2 per cent of inmates were employed in UNICOR and institution work assignments (23.8 per cent were medically idle or unassigned). Table 16.1 shows inmate job assignments by custody levels.[2]

There were two wage categories for inmate-workers. The first was for institution work. These wages had four pay grades: $0.11, $0.16, $0.27, and $0.38. Work supervisors were permitted to issue

Table 16.1:  Type of Employment by Custody Level, 31 May 1988

| Type of Employment | In Custody | | Maximum Custody | | Total | |
| --- | --- | --- | --- | --- | --- | --- |
|  | Number | Per cent | Number | Per cent | Number | Per cent |
| UNICOR | 440 | 39.0 | 67 | 26.1 | 507 | 36.6 |
| Other work[1] | 428 | 38.0 | 120 | 46.7 | 548 | 39.6 |
| No work[2] | 259 | 23.0 | 70 | 27.2 | 329 | 23.8 |
| Total | 1,127 | 100.0 | 257 | 100.0 | 1,384 | 100.0 |

Notes:
1  Includes non-UNICOR jobs (food service, orderly and mechanical services).
2  Includes medical idle and non-assigned inmates.

2   See Fleisher (1989) for an explanation of BOP custody classification.

to inmate-workers a 50 per cent quality work bonus for each two-week pay period. These job assignments put inmates to work in Central Maintenance Services (CMS) in a number of jobs. For instance, 144 inmates worked in food service, 91 worked as orderlies and 63 worked in vocational training. In June 1988, 39.6 per cent of work-eligible inmates held institution jobs.

The second wage category was for UNICOR jobs. On 31 May 1988, 36.6 per cent of inmates worked in UNICOR assignments. These jobs had five pay grades: $0.22, $0.44, $0.66, $0.88 and $1.10. After 18 months, inmates received a longevity increase of $0.10 per hour. On the basis of the quality of their work, inmates' supervisors were allowed to issue an additional $0.5 per hour increase as premium (bonus) pay. UNICOR assignments included employment in a sign factory, a print plant and an electrical cable shop. The revenue generated by these UNICOR factories in the month of April 1988 was $1.4 million.

At USP Lompoc all inmates had full-time assignments at work, school, vocational training or a combination of these activities. Work days began at 7h40 in the morning, lunch was served around noon, with inmates returning to work by 1h10 in the afternoon. Quitting time was 3h50. UNICOR overtime workers returned to work after the 4h00 inmate count and remained in the factories until 9h00 in the evening. To reduce the costs of overtime work, grade 4 workers as well as inmates on UNICOR work waiting lists were assigned overtime work. Grade 1 workers, those who earn the highest incomes, were lead men and worked only from 7h00 to 9h00 in the evening. Maximum custody inmates never worked at night. Few inmates refused work assignments. For the two-year period 1985–6, there were 3,790 incident reports written, with 10 per cent for refusing to work.

Inmates working in UNICOR have a stake in keeping their jobs. There is a lot of cash on the line. At Grade 1 salary with a bonus and overtime, inmates say they can earn as much as $700 to $900 a month. Wage records verify inmates' claims. During the study period, the average monthly income for UNICOR inmates was $208.60, with a wage range from zero to $993. Assuming an average of 168 working hours per month, UNICOR inmates at Grade 1 income and full-time work should earn $184.80 per month.

Table 16.2 shows the median monthly earning to closely approximate this projection; however, the mean monthly income is much higher. In the five-month study period, the average amount of total income earned by UNICOR inmates was $963, with a range

Table 16.2: Average Monthly Income for UNICOR

| Inmate Pay | November | December | January | February | March | Combined Average |
|---|---|---|---|---|---|---|
| Average | 211 | 202 | 196 | 203 | 204 | 203* |
| Median | 184 | 182 | 169 | 186 | 183 | 181 |
| Min/Max | 0/636 | 0/620 | 0/685 | 1/593 | 5/993 | 0/993 |

Note: * This average is slightly lower than the one mentioned above, because of methods of calculating earnings of inmates working two part-time jobs.

from zero to $3,579 (in the study, an average of 510 inmates were employed by UNICOR). Projected over a 12-month period, the average annual UNICOR salary is $2,344, but the maximum range may be higher. A similar estimate for Grade 1 institution work projects an average annual salary of $766.08 (wage records of monthly earnings for institution employment were not available). A full-time institution worker earns an average of $63.84.

An underlying assumption in USP Lompoc's management model is that UNICOR inmate workers have both financial and social incentives for maintaining institution order. This proposition was supported by comparing wage earning with institution infractions. Infractions have four grades of severity, ranging from most severe (100 level) to least severe (400 level): 100-level infractions include, for instance, killing and serious assaults; 200-level violations include the use of intoxicants and similar offences; 300-level violations include gambling; and 400-level infractions include behaviour such as tattooing. During the study period, 590 inmates (42.6 per cent of the total inmate population as of 31 March 1988) received 1,080 incident reports (IRs; see Table 16.3).

Table 16.3: Severity Level of Most Serious Infraction Charged

| Severity Level | All Infractions | Per cent | Per Inmate | Per cent |
|---|---|---|---|---|
| 100 | 311 | 28.8 | 215 | 36.3 |
| 200 | 261 | 24.2 | 137 | 23.2 |
| 300 | 468 | 43.3 | 221 | 37.5 |
| 400 | 40 | 3.7 | 17 | 2.9 |
| Total | 1,080 | 100.0 | 590 | 100.0 |

INMATE WORK AND CONSENSUAL MANAGEMENT

Table 16.4 shows that UNICOR workers received significantly fewer IRs than both workers in institution jobs and inmates assigned to jobs. An independent study affirmed the findings at USP Lompoc: UNICOR inmate-workers were 'less likely to have a misconduct report ... and when they did, it was less likely to have been serious misconduct. [They] were also rated by their unit teams to have a higher level of responsibility than their ... counterparts' (Saylor and Gaes, 1992: 6).

Table 16.4: Infraction Rate by Work Status

| Work Status | Incident Report Status (frequency/expected) | |
|---|---|---|
| | No Incident Report | One or More Incident Reports |
| UNICOR | 366 (291) | 141 (216) |
| Other work | 319 (314) | 229 (234) |
| No work | 109 (189) | 220 (140) |
| Total | 794 | 590 |

Table 16.5 shows the incident report level for UNICOR employment, institution jobs and no work. These data illustrate two important findings about inmate work and conduct: (1) UNICOR inmates commit fewer infractions; and (2) UNICOR inmates commit a significantly lower number of 100- and 200-level offences.

Table 16.5: Infraction Rate and Severity by Work Status

| Work Status | Incident Report Status (frequency/expected) | | | | |
|---|---|---|---|---|---|
| | No Incident Report | 100 Level | 200 Level | 300 Level | 400 Level |
| UNICOR | 366 (291) | 47 (79) | 36 (50) | 54 (81) | 4 (6) |
| Other work | 319 (314) | 77 (85) | 56 (54) | 91 (88) | 5 (7) |
| No work | 109 (189) | 91 (51) | 45 (33) | 76 (52) | 8 (4) |
| Total | 794 | 215 | 137 | 221 | 17 |

## 5  UNICOR in the 1990s

UNICOR has a key role in management and rehabilitation in new federal institutions. At the Federal Correctional Institution (FCI) at Pekin, Illinois, a medium-security men's institution housing some 1,200 inmates, which was opened in October 1994, UNICOR has a central role in institution management. FCI Pekin inmates are required to work full-time. The majority of them work in institution jobs, such as CMS (125), food service (180), recreation (50), compound crew (100), education and law library (50) and chapel (15). Some 16 per cent of the institution's 1,160 inmates (17 April 1995) are employed by UNICOR doing jobs related to the welding of stainless steel, aluminium and carbon steel. FCI Pekin's UNICOR factory offers inmates 'the most advanced technological training in the Bureau of Prisons, including the use of computerized equipment,' according to FCI Pekin's warden, David Helman.

FCI Pekin's UNICOR factory produces metal storage racks for food service storage, food service containers, wire racks, storage shelving hefty enough to hold munitions and aluminium shipping containers for handling sensitive military equipment. Because of federal government 'downsizing', FCI Pekin's UNICOR factory has experienced a downturn in business. In response, the factory now manufactures prison security items, including bars and grills for cell doors and solid steel cell doors.

High wages are an incentive for FCI Pekin's inmates to seek UNICOR jobs. The UNICOR wage structure has increased since the mid-1980s. The lowest end of the wage scale for UNICOR employment exceeds the high end of the institution wage structure. UNICOR Grade 4 pay is $0.44, grade 3 is $0.75, grade 2 is $0.95 and grade 1 is $1.25. UNICOR's average monthly wage range is $60 to $80; institution jobs pay $20 to $40.

Despite UNICOR's advantages, a factory prison with good wages and a never-ending production schedule poses at least two dilemmas. First, there is disparity between the quality of work engaged in by UNICOR inmate-workers and that of inmates doing menial jobs (raking rocks and picking up cigarette butts). Limited opportunities for relatively high institution pay, as well as meaningful work, said Helman, sometimes lead to conflict. Inmates who perceive their jobs to be menial have a weaker bond to supervisors and are more likely to engage in on-the-job disputes with them. On the other hand, inmates know that disruptive behaviour will disqualify them for UNICOR employment. Thus inmates must learn to control their behaviour to achieve an objective.

UNICOR inmates must exhibit self-control. Infractions committed in the UNICOR factory itself and off-the-job violations serious enough to commit a UNICOR inmate to disciplinary segregation will lead to that worker's dismissal from UNICOR employment. UNICOR inmates behave well for the most part. Their compliant behaviour serves as an informal control on younger inmates who may be more likely to be less compliant but who are, at the same time, interested in UNICOR employment.

Secondly, a factory production schedule places demands on supporting departments. A profit motive may conflict with security expectations and with the requirements of case management. FCI Pekin inmates are required to meet counsellors and case managers to assess progress; however, UNICOR managers do not want to lose employees to case management sessions during the working day. Case management sessions have had to be rescheduled to evening hours, which meant that staff schedules had to be altered.

## 6 Organizational Implications of a Factory Prison

When a major factory operation is the focal point of prison activities, there are a number of management outcomes. First, a prison's organizational culture becomes highly bureaucratic and mirrors for-profit businesses. Thus organizational control is removed from the hands of correctional officers and inmates and is shared at each level of the organizational structure. This prevents a distortion of power in the hands of line-level correctional staff and the use of a few inmates to control the behaviour of inmates generally (see DiIulio, 1987: 238–9).

Second, the institution mission is shared by staff at all levels and by inmates. Staff have a strong stake in maintaining a smoothly functioning institution because their performance evaluations and incomes depend on it. Inmates rely on work for steady incomes and a high quality of life (Fleisher, 1989, 1995).

Third, a 'hands-on' management style is necessary to monitor the departments and relationships among them which keep UNICOR operating well. 'Hands-on' management leads to stronger rapport between staff and inmates and maintains institution quality of life at a constant high level (Fleisher, 1996).

Fourth, close scrutiny of institution life enables administrators to be proactive and to short-circuit management and personal dilemmas before disruptive incidents and serious personal injuries to staff and/or inmates stop factory production.

Fifth, policy makers and taxpayers want prisoners to work. Industry work is rehabilitation that cuts prison costs and focuses on staff teaching inmates to be proficient at jobs suitable for post-imprisonment work. Inmate-workers experience a real workplace and the demands of accomplishing work on time (Saylor and Gaes, 1985, 1986, 1987, 1992, 1995).

Sixth, controlling a prison requires, at least, securing the perimeter and controlling inmate movement, keys and dangerous tools. In all federal prisons, inmates know that staff control these things. FCIs and USPs are surrounded by secure perimeters, with concertina (razor) wire. Only staff have high-powered weapons. While custody is an ever-present feature of federal institutions, custody does not have to be flaunted. Correctional officers do not man catwalks in the cellhouses of high- and medium-security prisons carrying weapons. Instead, custody has become integrated into the prison community, as red lights and speed limits have become normal sights in the control of traffic in a community. The security of staff and inmates has been not jeopardized by moving correctional officers from centre to side stage. If an emergency occurs, federal correctional workers make a strong appearance.

By focusing on UNICOR rather than custody, inmate discipline is maintained with a system of financial and social incentives that accrue through productive employment. Productive employment means more than earning a relatively high salary in prison; it also means being able to choose a job that meets the personal needs of inmates (Fleisher and McCarthy, 1988). Some choose work in food service, others prefer more challenging employment in UNICOR. The important point is to offer a choice to inmates.

Finally, in a consensual organizational model, discipline may be understated, but inmates know they have a choice of behaviour. Their choice is the same one lawful citizens face: consent to community rules and freedom, within the limits set by community standards, is at one's disposal; break the rules and sanctions occur. When federal inmates have a choice between a high quality of life in a clean and safe institution, or a constrained life style locked up 24 hours a day in a segregation cell, the overwhelming majority of them choose good food, a regular income and the opportunities allowed by institution policy.

## 7 The Future of Prison Leadership

Under the most favourable conditions, prison leadership is difficult. Inmate rehabilitation faces progressively stiffer challenges as changes in the American economy offer low-skill former inmates fewer opportunities to earn wages high enough to support themselves and/or their families. High-security inmates, like those at USP Lompoc and FCI Pekin, whose incarceration costs are the highest, rarely leave prison to initiate college careers or move into well paid jobs. UNICOR and other types of in-prison work programmes have vocational counterparts in the community that offer employees wages that are relatively higher than low-skill and unskilled employment. Former inmates in their 20s, 30s, 40s and older who have been imprisoned, in some cases for decades, are, in a vocational sense, locked in economic adolescence and thus forced to compete against younger, more skilled and experienced employees who do not have criminal histories. UNICOR and other prison-based work programmes offer inmates real-life experiences that may prepare them for post-imprisonment life by offering both the practical training and socialization into the world of work.

The proliferation and success of education and work programmes for inmates are squarely in the hands of correctional officials. Today's political climate in the USA decries rehabilitation and limits funding for inmate programming; however, the integrity of correctional management depends to a large degree on the abundance and quality of well-managed inmate programmes. American correctional officials must respond to critics of correctional programmes and rehabilitation by designing and implementing realistic, cost-effective, meaningful inmate work opportunities that have a clear extension to the workplace in the free world. The key to institution social control, and to inmates' post-release success, has been placed in the hands of wardens. This may be a difficult challenge, particularly with moderate support from congressional leaders and cost-cutting measures, but it is a challenge that must be met directly by correctional leaders.

## References

Boin, Arjen. 1998. *Contrasts in Leadership: An Institutional Study of Two Prison Systems*. Delft: Eburon.

DiIulio, John J., Jr. 1987. *Governing Prisons: A Comparative Study of Correctional Management*. New York: Free Press.

DiIulio, John J., Jr. 1989. *Prisons That Work: An Overview of Management in the Federal Bureau of Prisons*. Washington, DC: National Institute of Corrections.

DiIulio, John J., Jr. 1990. Prisons that work – Management is the key. *Federal Prisons Journal* 1, no. 4: 1–14.

Federal Prison Industries. 1994. *The 1994 Federal Prison Industries Annual Report*. Washington, DC: Federal Bureau of Prisons, Federal Prison Industries.

Flanagan, Timothy J. and Katherine Maguire. 1993. A full employment policy for prisons in the United States. *Journal of Criminal Justice* 21, no. 2: 117–30.

Fleisher, Mark S. 1989. *Warehousing Violence*. Newbury Park, CA: Sage Publications.

Fleisher, Mark S. 1995. *Beggars and Thieves: Lives of Urban Street Criminals*. Madison: University of Wisconsin Press.

Fleisher, Mark S. 1996. Management Assessment and Policy Dissemination in Federal Prisons. *The Prison Journal* 76, no. 1: 81–91.

Fleisher, Mark S. 1998. Strategic Management in the Federal Bureau of Prisons. *Corrections Management Quarterly* 2, no. 4: 1–11.

Fleisher, Mark S. and Daniel K. McCarthy. 1988. The effects of wage earning on reducing serious violence among maximum-security federal inmates. Paper read at the American Society of Criminology Conference, Chicago, November.

Fleisher, Mark S. and Richard H. Rison. 1997. Health Care in the Federal Bureau of Prisons. In *Classical and Contemporary Issues in Corrections*, edited by J. Marquart and J. Sorensen. Los Angeles: Roxbury Publishing.

Fleisher, Mark S., Richard H. Rison and David W. Helman. 1997. Female Inmates: A Growing Constituency in the Federal Bureau of Prisons. *Corrections Management Quarterly* 1, no. 4: 28–35.

Funk, Gail S., Neal Miller and Billy L. Wayson. 1982. *Assets and Liabilities of Correctional Industries*. Lexington, MA: Lexington Books.

Johnson, Elmer H. 1994. Opposing outcomes of the industrial prison: Japan and the United States compared. *International Criminal Justice Review* 4: 52–71.

Keve, Paul. 1991. *Prisons and The American Conscience*. Carbondale, IL: Southern Illinois University Press.

Lightman, Ernie S. 1987. *Industrial Work by Inmates in Correctional Institutions*. Toronto: University of Toronto Press.

Maguire, Katherine E., Timothy J. Flanagan and Terence P. Thornberry. 1988. Prison labor and recidivism. *Journal of Quantitative Criminology* 4, no. 1: 3–18.

Nicholas, Stephen. 1988. *Convict Workers*. New York: Cambridge University Press.
Robinson, Louis N. 1931. *Should Prisoners Work?* Chicago: John C. Winston Company.
Saylor, William G. 1990. At your fingertips: Key indicator system provides federal managers with data. *Corrections Today*. February: 24, 28.
Saylor, William G. 1994. The design, development and maintenance of strategic support systems for correctional agencies. Paper for the 1994 International Symposium on Criminal Justice Information Systems and Technology: Building the Infrastructure. Washington, DC. August.
Saylor, William G. and Gerald G. Gaes. 1985. *PREP: Post-Release employment Project. Interim report (October 1)*. Washington, DC: Federal Bureau of Prisons, Office of Research and Evaluation.
Saylor, William G. and Gerald G. Gaes. 1986. *Post-release employment project. Update (September 17)*. Washington, DC: Federal Bureau of Prisons, Office of Research and Evaluation.
Saylor, William G. and Gerald G. Gaes. 1987. PREP: Post-Release employment project. The effects of work skills acquisition in prison on post-release employment (November 13). Paper prepared for the 39th annual meeting of the American Society of Criminology, Montreal, Ontario.
Saylor, William G. and Gerald G. Gaes. 1992. *PREP study links UNICOR work experience with successful post-release outcome (May 22, 1991 revised January 8, 1992)*. Washington, DC: Federal Bureau of Prisons, Office of Research and Evaluation.
Saylor, William G. and Gerald G. Gaes. 1995. *Interim report: The effect of prison work experiences, vocational and apprenticeship training on the long-term recidivism of U.S. federal prisoners*. Washington, DC: Federal Bureau of Prisons, Office of Research and Evaluation.
Seligman, Irving. 1986. *Prison Industries in New Jersey: A 200 Year Chronicle*. New York: Carlton Press.
Wright, Kevin. 1994. *Effective Prison Leadership*. Binghamton, NY: William Neil Publishers.

## The Authors

**Mark S. Fleisher** is professor in the Department of Criminal Justice Sciences at the Illinois State University in Normal in the USA.

**Richard H. Rison** is a retired warden in the United States Federal Bureau of Prisons.

# 17 International Perspectives

## HELENA HENRIKSSON AND RALPH KRECH[1]

### 1 Introduction

The origins of prison labour can be found in the ancient practice of slavery. In the nineteenth century, much prison work took the form of forced labour under inhuman conditions, such as chain gangs digging with picks in quarries under a burning sun with only bread and water for nourishment. Prison labour was at that time mainly regarded as a punitive and disciplinary measure, finding justification in the theory of deterrence (Johnson, 1977: 333, 337).

During the twentieth century, prison labour has been considered an important element in the rehabilitation of the prisoner during the period of incarceration. According to modern concepts, prison labour opportunities are provided to furnish prisoners with skills, knowledge and work experience, which is intended to improve their ability to find employment after release and thereby increase their prospects of re-integration into society (Penal Reform International, 1995: 132). Thus vocational training, education and remuneration have emerged as new, important features which play a crucial role in the concept of rehabilitation. Another often used argument for prison labour is that it prevents idleness as well as moral and physical degradation among the inmates, which can result in disruptive behaviour and endanger the order and security within the institution.

These more positive approaches to prison labour are enshrined in the United Nations Standard Minimum Rules for the Treatment of Prisoners, which were adopted in 1955 at the First United Nations Congress on the Prevention of Crime and the Treatment of Offenders. The rules cover a very wide area of different aspects related to prison management and the treatment of prisoners, such as registration, separation of categories and classification, accommodation, hygiene, bedding and food, recreation, medical services, religion and

[1] Although the authors are affiliated to the United Nations, and draw extensively on material produced by the United Nations Crime Prevention and Criminal Justice Division, the opinions and views expressed in this chapter do not necessarily reflect the position of the United Nations Secretariat.

communication with the outside world. Rules 71 to 77, which are introduced with the proclamation that prison labour must not be of an afflictive nature, contain a number of regulations concerning the right and duty to work, working hours, vocational training, working conditions and precautions, remuneration and education. Regarding prison labour, the following provisions are of particular interest.

(a) Rule 71(3), which states that the prisoners shall be provided with sufficient work of a useful nature to keep them actively employed for a normal working day;
(b) Rule 71(4), which stipulates that the work should be of such a nature that it will maintain or increase the prisoners' ability to earn an honest living after release;
(c) Rule 71(5), which provides for the prisoners' right to vocational training;
(d) Rule 72(1), which states that the organization and methods of work in the institution should resemble those outside with a view to preparing the prisoners for the conditions of a normal working life;
(e) Rule 72(2), which requires that the interests of the prisoners and of their vocational training must not be subordinated to the purpose of making a financial profit from an industry in the institution;
(f) Rule 76, which provides for a system of remuneration for prisoners' work; and
(g) Rule 77(1), which provides for the right of prisoners to further education.

Ever since the adoption of the Standard Minimum Rules for the Treatment of Prisoners, the United Nations Crime Prevention and Criminal Justice Programme has carried out regular surveys regarding the implementation of the rules, which have been submitted to the quinquennial United Nations Congresses on the Prevention of Crime and the Treatment of Offenders.[2] The next section will give an account of the results of the information-gathering process on the use and application of the Standard Minimum Rules for the Treatment of Prisoners as reflected in a report of the Secretary-

2 Previous surveys on the implementation of the United Nations Standard Minimum Rules for the Treatment of Prisoners have been carried out and submitted to the Fourth Congress in 1970 (A/CONF.43/3, annex), to the Fifth Congress in 1975 (A/CONF.56/6, annex), to the Sixth Congress in 1980 (A/CONF.87/11 and Add.1), to the Seventh Congress in 1985 (A/CONF.121/15, Add.1) and to the Eighth Congress in 1990 (A/CONF.144/11).

General to the 1995 session of the Commission on Crime Prevention and Criminal Justice.

## 2 Use and Application of the Rules

The Economic and Social Council, in its resolution 1993/34, section III, requested the Secretary-General to commence a process of information gathering to be undertaken by means of surveys initially focusing on, among other things, the Standard Minimum Rules for the Treatment of Prisoners.[3] In pursuance of the request, the Crime Prevention and Criminal Justice Division elaborated a draft questionnaire on the use and application of the Standard Minimum Rules for the Treatment of Prisoners, which was submitted for consideration to the Commission on Crime Prevention and Criminal Justice at its third session. The questionnaire was then sent out to all member states and interested intergovernmental and non-governmental organizations in 1994. Of these, 75 states replied,[4] together with the Holy See, and four non-governmental organizations.[5]

3  Also included, as a first step, were the Code of Conduct for Law Enforcement Officials, the Basic Principles of the Use of Force and Firearms by Law Enforcement Officials, the Basic Principles on the Independence of the Judiciary and the Declaration of Basic Principles of Justice for Victims of Crime and Abuse of Power.
   By ECOSOC resolutions 1995/13 of 24 July 1995 and 1996/19 of 23 July 1996, the Council decided to include further standards and norms in crime prevention and criminal justice in the information gathering process.

4  Armenia, Australia, Barbados, Belarus, Belgium, Cameroon, Canada, Chile, China, Colombia, Costa Rica, Ivory Coast, Croatia, Cyprus, Czech Republic, Denmark, Finland, France, Germany, Greece, Haiti, Hungary, Iceland, Iran (Islamic Republic of), Iraq, Ireland, Israel, Italy, Jamaica, Japan, Jordan, Latvia, Lebanon, Liechtenstein, Luxembourg, Malawi, Malaysia, Malta, Marshall Islands, Mauritius, Mexico, Mongolia, Morocco, Myanmar, Netherlands, Pakistan, Papua New Guinea, Peru, Philippines, Portugal, Qatar, Republic of Korea, Romania, Russian Federation, San Marino, Saudi Arabia, Singapore, Slovakia, South Africa, Sri Lanka, Spain, Sweden, Switzerland, Syrian Arabic Republic, Tajikistan, Thailand, Macedonia, Tonga, Turkey, Ukraine, United Kingdom (England and Wales), United States of America, Vanuatu and Venezuela.

5  Penal Reform International provided information on the use and

The task of gathering further information is continuing and efforts are being made to encourage more member states to return questionnaires. The difficult question of how best to validate official responses was considered at a workshop on the impact of United Nations standards and norms in crime prevention and criminal justice in national practice that was held at the International Institute for the Sociology of Law, Oñati, Spain, on 2 and 3 February 1998 (Report of the workshop on the impact of United Nations Standards and Norms in Crime Prevention and Criminal Justice in National Practice, submitted to the seventh session of the Commission on Crime Prevention and Criminal Justice, E/CN.15/1998/NGO.4). However, it is apparent that, for the United Nations, data from official governmental sources will remain the primary source of information. It is hoped that increased publicity given to the information submitted from these sources will enable the scientific community to comment, where appropriate, on the accuracy of the information.

From the information received on prison work in response to the 1996 questionnaire, the following picture emerged. Less than a third of responding countries[6] indicated that they provided *all* prisoners with sufficient work of a useful nature to keep them actively involved for a normal working day (Rule 71(3)), while 13 countries reported that *almost all* prisoners (that is to say more than 80 per cent of the total prison population) were offered sufficient work in prison,[7] and 11 states reported that *most* prisoners received sufficient work opportunities.[8] In 17 countries, *half* the prison population was provided

application of the Standard Minimum Rules in Uganda; the Andean Commission reported on the implementation of the Rules in Bolivia, Chile, Colombia, Ecuador, Peru and Venezuela; Friendship Foundation International gave an account of the use and application of the Rules in Cameroon; and the Centre for the Study of Violence and Reconciliation reported on the implementation of the Rules in South Africa.

6     Armenia, Australia, Cyprus, Finland, Germany, Hungary, Ivory Coast, Japan, Jordan, Korea, Liechtenstein, Mauritius, Mexico, Myanmar, Peru, Russia, Saudi Arabia, Switzerland, Tajikistan, Thailand, Tonga and Vanuatu.

7     Canada, China, Denmark, Macedonia, Malawi, Malaysia, Netherlands, Philippines, San Marino, Singapore, Sweden, United Kingdom and Ukraine.

8     Iceland, Iraq, Ireland, Israel, Pakistan, Papua New Guinea, Portugal, Sri Lanka, Syria, Uganda and the United States (Missouri).

with sufficient work in prison,[9] and in Italy, Jamaica and Latvia a *quarter* of the prisoners received sufficient work. Barbados, Chile, the Marshall Islands, Qatar, Turkey and Venezuela replied that only *some* prisoners (less than 20 per cent of the total prison population) received work and, in Haiti, no work was offered to prisoners at all.

Almost every country in which prisoners were required to work indicated that a normal working day usually lasted between five and eight hours, except in those situations where work was temporarily unavailable.[10] Greece, Ireland, Netherlands, Peru, Qatar and Thailand reported that prisoners were normally required to work less than five hours a day, while in Tonga the working day of the prisoners was nine hours long. In Malta and Saudi Arabia, prisoners were not required to work at all. Over half of responding countries required prisoners to work for five days a week,[11] and in nearly a third of the countries,[12] the prisoners worked six days a week. A few countries reported that the number of working days varied from week to week.[13]

Nearly half of the responding countries reported that they provided *all* or *almost all* prisoners with opportunities for skills and trade training (Rule 71(5)),[14] but, when asked how many trade

[9] Belarus, Belgium, Cameroon, Colombia, Costa Rica, Croatia, Czech Republic, France, Greece, Iran, Lebanon, Luxembourg, Malta, Mongolia, Morocco, Romania and South Africa.

[10] That is, 63 countries.

[11] Cameroon, Chile, Costa Rica, Croatia, Cyprus, Czech Republic, Denmark, Finland, France, Germany, Iran, Ireland, Israel, Jamaica, Japan, Lebanon, Liechtenstein, Luxembourg, Marshall Islands, Mexico, Morocco, Netherlands, Pakistan, Papua New Guinea, Philippines, Portugal, Qatar, San Marino, Slovakia, South Africa, Sweden, Switzerland, Thailand, Turkey, United Kingdom, the United States (Missouri), Vanuatu and Venezuela.

[12] Armenia, Belarus, Colombia, Italy, Ivory Coast, Jordan, Korea, Latvia, Macedonia, Malawi, Malaysia, Mauritius, Mongolia, Myanmar, Peru, Russia, Singapore, Tajikistan, Tonga, Uganda.

[13] China, Romania, Belgium, Greece and Sri Lanka.

[14] *All*: Armenia, Australia, Belarus, China, Cyprus, Denmark, Finland, Germany, Hungary, Iceland, Iran, Japan, Korea, Liechtenstein, Macedonia, Mauritius, Myanmar, Netherlands, Peru, Portugal, Romania, Russia, San Marino, Slovakia, Tajikistan, Thailand, Ukraine and Vanuatu. *Almost all*: Canada, Croatia, Malawi, Malaysia, Mexico, Sweden, Switzerland and United Kingdom.

instructors were employed in prison service, it appeared that 12 of these 36 countries employed no trade instructor at all or less than one trade instructor per 100 prisoners.[15] In nine countries,[16] seven of which are Members of the Council of Europe, trade instructors would have fewer than 35 prisoners to supervise, which would allow meaningful trade instruction. Five countries replied that trade training was available to *most* prisoners,[17] and in another five countries, *half* the prison population received trade training opportunities.[18] In 23 of the responding countries the trade training opportunities were available for only a quarter of the prisoners or fewer.[19] Haiti reported that prisoners were not provided with trade training at all, and Latvia and Venezuela mentioned that reforms were expected in 1995 or 1996.

Twenty-three of the responding countries reported that *all* prisoners received education in prison (Rule 77).[20] In a further 19 countries, at least half of the prisoners were provided with education,[21] and in the remaining 33 countries, no more than a quarter or some of the prisoners received such facilities.[22] In Haiti, Uganda

15 Armenia, Belarus, Hungary, Korea, Malawi, Malaysia, Myanmar, Portugal, Romania, Slovakia, Tajikistan and Ukraine.
16 Australia, Cyprus, Denmark, Finland, Germany, Iceland, Ireland, Mauritius and Sweden.
17 Czech Republic, Jordan, Luxembourg, Singapore and Sri Lanka.
18 Ireland, Lebanon, Saudi Arabia, South Africa and the United States (Missouri).
19 *Quarter*: Costa Rica, France, Latvia, Malta, Mongolia and Uganda. *Some*: Barbados, Belgium, Cameroon, Colombia, Chile, Greece, Israel, Italy, Jamaica, Marshall Islands, Morocco, Pakistan, Papua New Guinea, Qatar, Tonga, Turkey and Venezuela.
20 Belarus, China, Cyprus, Denmark, Germany, Iran, Italy, Japan, Korea, Liechtenstein, Macedonia, Malawi, Mexico, Netherlands, Peru, Qatar, Romania, Russia, Saudi Arabia, Syria, Thailand, Turkey and Ukraine.
21 *Almost all*: Australia, Canada, Costa Rica, Croatia, Finland, Portugal, Sweden and Switzerland. *Most*: Barbados, France, Ireland, Jordan, Malaysia and Tajikistan. *Half*: Colombia, Iceland, Lebanon, Mongolia and the United States (Missouri).
22 *Quarter*: Armenia, Chile and Israel. *Some*: Belgium, Cameroon, Czech Republic, Greece, Jamaica, Latvia, Luxembourg, Malta, Marshall Islands, Mauritius, Morocco, Myanmar, Pakistan, Papua

and Vanuatu, education in prison was not available at all. In only one country[23] did a full-time teacher have fewer than 35 prisoners to supervise, and in only another four countries[24] was the number fewer than 100 prisoners per full-time teacher.

As an explanation of the difficulty of providing all prisoners with a sufficient volume of work, 13 of the responding countries[25] reported that a shortage of resources prevented them from applying the relevant provisions. For instance, Belarus and Latvia stated that prisoners could not all be provided with sufficient work and education because of the weak national economy, and Jordan remarked that the increase and improvement of trade training programmes always faced the problem of funding. The difficulty of financing prison work and vocational training became even more evident in view of the fact that it was mainly Western countries (that is, developed countries) which were able to employ a sufficient number of trade instructors.

Some states also referred to the shortage of work opportunities due to overcrowding and the fluctuating nature of the prison population, as well as the lack of qualified, specialized personnel who could act as technical instructors, work leaders and vocational trainers. Apart from a lack of sufficient resources, the problem of overcrowding in prison is probably one of the major reasons why developed as well as developing countries struggle to comply with the prison labour standards. During the last 15 years, the number of prisoners has, for several reasons, increased dramatically in relation to the facilities available, and the problem is aggravated by the fact that the prison administration has to spend more funds on security to keep up with the growing prison population. In addition, the governments give a lower and lower priority to criminal justice as a whole in the allocation of the national budget, which worsens the situation even more.[26]

|    | |
|----|---|
|    | New Guinea, Slovakia, South Africa, Sri Lanka, Tonga, United Kingdom and Venezuela. |
| 23 | Ireland. |
| 24 | Denmark, Israel, Macedonia and Tajikistan. |
| 25 | Belarus, Belgium, Cameroon, Canada, Chile, Colombia, Costa Rica, Germany, Jordan, Latvia, Luxembourg, Malawi and Morocco. |
| 26 | 'Criminal Justice Processes and Perspectives in a Changing World', Working paper prepared by the Secretariat, Seventh United Nations Congress on the Prevention of Crime and the Treatment of Offenders, A/CONF.121/5, 1985: 13–14, 22; 'Criminal Justice |

## 3 From Prison Labour to Vocational Training and Education

In general, not all member states ensure the full implementation of the rules stipulating that all prisoners should be provided with sufficient and useful work to keep them actively employed for a normal working day. Less than half of the countries replied that they provided all or almost all prisoners with sufficient work, and only in a few countries[27] was a sufficient number of trade instructors employed. This suggests that the work performed is of a simple and monotonous nature, for which specific skills are not required. In some cases, hard labour still seems to be used as a disciplinary sanction. The kind of work provided is all too often guided by considerations of cost and, in general, work assignments are not aimed at giving the prisoners skills and work experience. When comparing the results of the last survey with earlier reports submitted by the Secretary-General in 1980, 1985 and 1990, it becomes clear that the situation has remained largely the same. For instance, in the 1990 report on the implementation of the Standard Minimum Rules for the Treatment of Prisoners, as in 1995, less than half of the responding countries reported that sufficient work was available for all prisoners (*Implementation of the Standard Minimum Rules for the Treatment of Prisoners*, 1990: 9).

As to vocational training, the situation seems to have improved during the five years from 1990. In the 1990 report, only three countries out of 27 replied that more than 80 per cent of the prison population participated in vocational training courses, while in the 1995 report as many as 36 countries stated that all or almost all were involved in such activities. However, considering the very limited number of trade instructors employed, one may ask whether the real function of the trade instructors is to maintain order in the workplace instead of assisting, advising and instructing the prisoners during their work.

From the 1995 report, it is obvious that prison education still plays a marginal role in many countries, despite the fact that it

---

Policies in Relation to the Problem of Imprisonment, Other Penal Sanctions and Alternative Measures', working paper prepared by the Secretariat, Eighth United Nations Congress on the Prevention of Crime and the Treatment of Offenders, A/CONF.144/10, 1990: 3.

27  Australia, Cyprus, Denmark, Finland, Germany, Iceland, Ireland, Liechenstein, Mauritius and Sweden.

constitutes a preferable alternative when sufficient work is unavailable. In fact, both work and education are considered human rights according to the Universal Declaration on Human Rights (arts 23(1) and 26(1)) and the International Covenant on Economic, Social and Cultural Rights (arts 6(1) and 13(1)). However, in practice, prison education is often regarded as less of a priority than prison labour. This is probably due to the fact that prison education is not financially profitable, in contrast to prison labour.

The opportunities for receiving appropriate education in prisons differ considerably from country to country. Some countries offer the prisoners a wide choice of programmes of primary, secondary and higher education, to suit every individual prisoner's level of knowledge and capacity. Others, however, view education as a simple recreation activity which the prisoner has to undertake on his own initiative after working hours, without any teaching or assistance. Nevertheless, some new, positive trends have been observed during the last decades. For instance, one can observe a change of attitude towards prison education, which previously was regarded as a 'privilege' provided for a few, selected prisoners. Today, education in prisons has gained wider recognition as an important component of rehabilitation, and a greater number of prisoners are given the possibility to participate in educational programmes, on a part-time as well as a full-time basis (*Basic Education in Prisons*, 1995: 13). In many cases, they receive wages equal to those of inmates who work in prison industries, which is extremely important when trying to motivate prisoners to follow education programmes instead of working (ibid., 45, 166). Furthermore, the use of computers and audiovisual material, as well as other specialized techniques, has been on the increase. Computer training, in particular, is an important element in the preparation of the prisoner for a post-release occupation, in light of the demand for computer skills on the free labour market.[28] In addition, when inmates have a wide choice of self-improvement activities or constructive leisure-time programmes, tensions may be reduced and thus, also, internal infractions. For instance, a training course on anger control involving 18 participants in a UK prison resulted in a clear reduction in the number of reported disciplinary offences. Three months before the course there were 21 reports of offences; three months after, there were only 11 (McDougall, 1989).

28 See Council of Europe, 1990: 32–3 and *Basic Education in Prisons*, 1995: 33.

In addition, education in prison can perhaps contribute to socialization or resocialization, and at the same time it helps the inmate to develop a positive self-image as well as self-respect. A survey of 220 inmates of Sing Sing prison in New York State revealed, for instance, that of those who attended education courses (175 out of the 220), 91 per cent agreed that they felt prison school had helped them during their post-release social integration.[29]

A new feature in correctional treatment, which so far is limited to a small number of countries (predominantly Scandinavian), is the integration of education with prison labour and vocational training: so-called 'project work'. Project work involves task- or problem-oriented assignments, where the task itself is similar to those undertaken during vocational training, but where a greater emphasis is placed upon learning than on production. This is expected to increase the prisoner's motivation and interest in learning and work, and to see how the two elements relate to each other. Project work has so far been applied with allegedly positive results in Denmark and Sweden to unemployed juvenile delinquents who lack a complete education, vocational training or work experience. Given that many adults, too, have the same lack of education, project work could perhaps be successfully applied to them as well (Council of Europe, 1990: 33–4). A similar programme, which combines vocational training and education, is carried out in Nantes, France, where the inmates are trained in job-seeking skills as well as literacy with the goal of helping them to find employment on release (*Basic Education in Prisons*, 1995: 34).

Recently, a growing trend has emerged towards community-based non-custodial measures which, in practice, oblige the offender to perform paid or unpaid work in the community for a certain number of hours. The work assignment is organized by the probation service, and is arranged in the offender's local area. Apart from contributing to national development, community service is also considered by an increasing number of member states as an effective way to safeguard existing employment and allows the offender to continue to work with a minimum of disruption to remaining social structures, which will facilitate his/her reintegration into society after the sentence is served.[30] The USA tried to enhance resocialization through the use of

29 See *Basic Education in Prisons*, 1995: 2, 46, 52–3; Penal Reform International, 1995: 138; Bell 1989, 547; American Correctional Association 1981: 19; Council of Europe, 1990: 15–16, 19, 21–2.
30 See *Deinstitutionalization of Corrections and its Implications for*

'halfway houses', where qualifying inmates are offered an opportunity, prior to the end of their imprisonment, to work in the community without supervision (Saylor and Gaes, 1989: 537). An alternative to community-service and 'halfway houses', which also focuses on the resocialization of the offender, is to offer the prisoner, instead of money, a reduction of his or her sentence as compensation for work in prison. This model is used, for instance, in Romania, where five days of prison work can be compensated by the reduction of one day from the prisoner's sentence (Association pour la Prévention de la Torture, 1996: 22). However, the risk is that the courts may impose longer sentences, assuming that some fifth of the time will be reduced by prison work.

During the last two decades there has been a marked increase in the establishment of workshops within prisons with varying levels of private sector involvement. These workshops use modern industrial skills and equipment, and employ prisoners on the same conditions as workers outside, sometimes paying the same wages. In the USA, the Federal Prison Industries (UNICOR) constitute a historical example of this type of arrangement. Other examples are the PRIDE Corporation in Florida, the Best Western programme at the Arizona Women's facility, and Zephyr Industries in Kansas (*Correction Counseling and Treatment*, 1989: 174–8). In the UK, Prison Enterprise Services and Prison Enterprise Partnerships produce goods for the public service as well as for the 'external market', that is, on contract for private companies. Similar schemes have been carried out in Germany. Also, in Iraq and Pakistan, workshops, productive units and small-scale industries have been established in prisons, and in Luxembourg and Malta, the development of new workshops is expected before the turn of the century.

The workshops resemble, to a much greater extent, the outside work environment, and the assignments and equipment are more realistic and better adapted to present-day outside working conditions. The inmates are provided with an appropriate vocational training which could benefit them when seeking employment after release. While the chances of finding a job after release also obviously depend on such factors as unemployment rates, the skills and

> *the Residual Prisoner*, 1989: 28–9. The Standard Minimum Rules for Non-custodial Measures, adopted by the Eighth United Nations Congress in 1990, and approved by the General Assembly in its resolution 45/110, provide policy guidance for the strengthening of such tendencies.

experience the prisoners gain are nevertheless important for their personal development (Penal Reform International, 1995: 133). The models could perhaps also contribute to increased security at the institutions, in the sense that they keep the prisoners actively involved with interesting and meaningful tasks, which function as an outlet for tension and aggression. Idleness is considered by many scholars a major reason for physical and mental degradation, disruptive behaviour and riots.[31]

While many states claim that training and educational systems cannot take priority over matters of security, it is likely that meaningful activities, such as those just mentioned, can contribute to a safer and better-controlled prison environment. Finally, models managed cost-effectively can help the administration to balance the prison budget. However, the risk with these types of projects is that they can lead to abuses of prison workers, negating the original purpose of rehabilitation in the pursuit of financial profits. The lessons of history must always be kept in mind when considering reforms in this particular field. Thus whether the new models are to be considered as a positive approach depends on the type of assignments the prisoners are given, and under what kind of conditions they have to work. Also the question of supervision, and security within the institution, must be taken into account in this context.

## 4  Remuneration

As for remuneration (Rule 76), a clear majority of the responding countries reported that most of the prisoners (at least two-thirds) received wages for the work performed in prison. However, the scale of payment varied considerably. For instance, in Korea, the Marshall Islands, Peru, Syria and Ukraine, the prisoners were reported to receive between 91 per cent and 100 per cent of the average wage paid to the lowest category of prison officer, while in 18 of the responding countries the pay received was no more than 10 per cent of the level of pay of the lowest prison officer category.[32] In a

[31]  See Johnson (1977: 334), Saylor and Gaes (1989: 535), *Corrections Today* (December 1986: 126); American Correctional Association (1981: 3, 19), *Basic Education in Prisons* (1995: 33).

[32]  Under 3 per cent: Ireland, Jamaica, Malaysia, Malta, Mauritius and South Africa; 3–7 per cent: Australia, Cyprus, Luxembourg, Morocco, Singapore, Sri Lanka and the United Kingdom; 8–10 per cent: Finland, Germany, Greece, Netherlands and Turkey.

similar number of countries the pay exceeded 10 per cent, but was no more than 50 per cent of the average pay of the lowest category of prison officers.[33] In four countries,[34] the wages varied between 51 per cent and 90 per cent of the average pay of the lowest category of prison officers, and in Myanmar, Papua New Guinea, Tonga and Vanuatu, the prisoners received no wage at all. In the USA, prisoners received less than 3 per cent of the average salary for the lowest category of officers, and other inmates who worked in a special project received between 3 per cent and 7 per cent of the average wage paid to the lowest category of prison officers, after reduction of mandatory contributions to pay off court-ordered financial obligations, such as fines. Twenty countries did not provide any information on remuneration to prisoners.[35]

Financial difficulties were mentioned as the major obstacle to paying wages to prisoners. For example, Malawi reported that it did not have adequate resources to meet the conditions in Rule 76. Some countries reported that the scale of remuneration depended upon the type and quality of the work performed by the prisoner. As the prison wages in general were very low, this would seem to indicate that the work provided usually requires only simple skills.[36]

The significant differences in the levels of remuneration between countries are not new phenomena. In the 1990 report, for instance, the earnings of prisoners ranged from 0.2 per cent to 100 per cent of the national average wage according to those 25 countries that provided such information. Five states reported that prisoners were

33   11–20 per cent: Belgium, Canada, Chile, Colombia, Costa Rica, Macedonia, Romania, Saudi Arabia and Sweden; 21–30 per cent: Croatia, Iceland, Jordan and Thailand; 31–50 per cent: Armenia, Denmark, France, Ivory Coast, Liechtenstein, Mongolia and Tajikistan.

34   51–70 per cent: Czech Republic, Iran and Slovakia; 71–90 per cent: Philippines.

35   Barbados, Belarus, Cameroon, China, Haiti, Hungary, Iraq, Israel, Italy, Japan, Lebanon, Malawi, Mexico, Pakistan, Portugal, Qatar, Russia, San Marino, Switzerland and Venezuela.

36   On the other hand, it should be kept in mind that the type of work provided depends on the skills of the workforce, and since many prisoners have inadequate skills training, and lack previous work experience, it is not always possible to give them highly qualified and specialized assignments (Bell, 1989: 543–4; *Basic Education in Prisons*, 1995: 19, 22).

paid the full average weekly wage, and 15 of the other countries paid wages no higher than 30 per cent of the national average. Nevertheless, one can observe a growing trend by some states to apply market-level wages in the remuneration of prisoners, in particular to those who work in prison industries. The reasons for this are fourfold. First, the rise in prison salaries is in accordance with the principle of victim compensation, where prisoners work to earn money, which is then used to indemnify their victims. Secondly, it has become more common for the prison administration to set aside a part of the wage for the maintenance of the prisoner's family, which prevents the family from becoming dependent upon social allowances during the period of incarceration (Johnson, 1977: 340). Thirdly, within the framework of the principle of normalization, there is a growing opinion that prisoners should be required to support themselves as they would have to do outside (*The Standard Minimum Rules for the Treatment of Prisoners in the Light of Recent Developments in the Correctional Field*, 1970: 7-8, 47). Fourthly, there is a belief that adequate remuneration can function as an incentive for prisoners to participate in work and educational programmes (Johnson, 1977: 334, 340). In fact, low motivation among inmates has sometimes been used as an explanation for states not providing prisoners with work possibilities. Additionally, it has been claimed that adequate salaries might result in a more peaceful atmosphere within the institutions if the inmates were satisfied with the remuneration. This, however, is highly uncertain, when one considers that higher salaries can also provoke a more stressful atmosphere at work. On the other hand, wage reductions can also be used as a threat and sanction for misconduct in order to achieve security and order within the institution: a practice which, however, must be applied carefully in order not to lead to abuse.

Apart from the reasons stated above, there is another argument for paying prisoners market-level wages. There have been objections, for instance by trade unions, to the selling of prison-manufactured goods, the argument being that the low cost of inmate labour gives the prison industries and workshops an unfair advantage in the market (Penal Reform International, 1995: 136). However, if the prisoners receive the same wages as free workers, the costs of production will be the same as in an ordinary factory, and the goods manufactured will comply with the pricing of the outside market. There would consequently be no real arguments against the prison industry extending the sale of its products to the private market as well.

## 5 Concluding Remarks

It is obvious that major challenges still exist for governments in the implementation of the relevant provisions of the Standard Minimum Rules for the Treatment of Prisoners. These include the provision of meaningful work, vocational training and education for prisoners. However, new projects and experiments are being carried out in the field, such as the establishment of workshops and 'work projects', as well as remuneration reforms. The situation is therefore far from static. Whether such schemes will be regarded as beneficial will depend on the final results of the treatment process. Treatment should therefore include adequate after-care and post-release counselling, which should be guided by the gains of a law-abiding life, rather than purely economic considerations. All these programmes should be carefully evaluated.

Even the best projects may not guarantee that resocialization will be effective. The lack of vacancies on the job market and the increased difficulty of entering higher education constitute obstacles which are hard to overcome. In times of high unemployment in the outside world, providing prisoners with strategies to deal with unemployment may also be important. Awareness-raising campaigns on the situation of prisoners, particularly as regards prison labour, may be necessary to improve prison conditions in the long run.

## References

American Correctional Association. 1981. *Riots and Disturbances in Correctional Institutions.* Washington, DC: Government Printing Office.

Association pour la Prévention de la Torture. 1996. *Rapport sur les mauvais traitements et les conditions de détention en Roumanie.* Geneva.

*Basic Education in Prisons.* 1995. ST/CSDHA/25, United Nations Publication, Sales No.: 95-IV-3.

Bell, Raymond. 1989. We Must Educate Prisoners. In *Correctional Counseling and Treatment.* 3rd edn, edited by P.C. Kratcoski. New York: Waveland Press.

*Corrections Today.* December 1986. The Case for Prison Industries.

Council of Europe. 1990. *Education in prison* (Recommendation No. R(89)12). Strasbourg: Council of Europe.

*Criminal Justice Policies in Relation to the Problem of Imprisonment, Other Penal Sanctions and Alternative Measures.* 1990. Working paper prepared by the Secretariat, Eighth United Nations Congress on the Prevention of Crime and the Treatment of Offenders, A/CONF.144/10, 29 June.

*Criminal Justice Processes and Perspectives in a Changing World.* 1985. Working paper prepared by the Secretariat, Seventh United Nations Congress on the Prevention of Crime and the Treatment of Offenders, A/CONF.121/5, 31 May.

*Deinstitutionalization of Corrections and its Implications for the Residual Prisoner.* 1989. United Nations. A/CONF.87/7.

*Implementation of the Standard Minimum Rules for the Treatment of Prisoners.* 1990. Report of the Secretary-General, Eighth United Nations Congress on the Prevention of Crime and the Treatment of Offenders, A/CONF.144/11.

Johnson, Elmer H. 1977. Prison Industry. In *Correctional Institutions.* 2nd edn, edited by M. Carter, D. Glaser and L.T. Wilkins. Philadelphia: J.B. Lippincott Company.

Kratcoski, P.C., ed. 1989. *Correctional Counseling and Treatment.* 3rd edn. New York: Waveland Press. In particular, see the chapter, Model Approaches – Examining Prison Industry That Works.

McDougall, C. 1989. *Anger control training with young offenders (United Kingdom).* Paper presented at the Second International Conference on Prison Education, Oxford.

Penal Reform International. 1995. *Making standards work – an international handbook on good prison practice.* The Hague: Penal Reform International.

Saylor, W.G and G.G. Gaes. 1989. The Post-Release Employment Project. In *Correctional Counseling and Treatment.* 3rd edn. New York: Waveland Press.

Seiter, Richard P. 1989. *Federal Prison Industries – Meeting the Challenge of Growth.* In *Correctional Counseling and Treatment.* 3rd edn. New York: Waveland Press.

*The Standard Minimum Rules for the Treatment of Prisoners in the Light of Recent Developments in the Correctional Field.* 1970. United Nations A/CONF.43/3.

## The Authors

Helena Henriksson is a Swedish lawyer.

Ralph Krech is a crime prevention and criminal justice expert working at the Centre for International Crime Prevention, Office for Drug Control and Crime Prevention, United Nations in Vienna, Austria.

# 18 Still 'Slaves of the State': Prison Labour and International Law

GERARD DE JONGE

### 1 Some Remarks on Origins, Explanations and Actual Meaning of Prison Labour

The practice of incarcerating delinquents in prison workhouses can be traced back to the Amsterdam *Rasphuis*, which, presumably under the influence of Coornhert's book *Boeventucht*, published in 1587, opened its doors in 1596. This signalled the birth of a new sanction, imprisonment, which, in north-western Europe, replaced the death penalty and corporal punishment. At that time, there was no general agreement about the purposes of the new sanction. In the minds of some, compassion with the fate of the poor wretches who were arrested was dominant; others saw it as a means of strict control over criminals. Although the new institutions were supposed to be economically self-sufficient, this aim was never realized. Some scholars, like Sellin (1976), view the first prisons as state-run factories, integrated into a mercantilist economy. Others, especially Spierenburg (1991), attribute the same symbolic value to imprisonment as to the former practice of public executions.

During the seventeenth and eighteenth centuries, the prisons/workhouses were managed according to the particular insights of the various local administrators. The regimes were characterized by simple, poorly paid manual labour (Howard, 1777). Only in the twentieth century did scholars start questioning the axiomatic character of obligatory prison labour. Rusche (1933) put forward the idea that the way prisoners are treated, especially with regard to the use of their labour, is determined by the dynamics of the labour market. Formulated in 1933, his *labour market theory* is still being investigated. However, this has not led to general conclusions about relations between economic systems, variations in the economic cycle, the size of prison populations and the way the labour force of these populations is used.

The economic approach of Rusche (1933) (also in his joint work with Kirchheimer (1939)) has been criticized as being too one-sided. Others (Steinert and Treiber 1978) have emphasized concepts such as 'discipline' and 'work ethic' as having a more explanatory value. It was Foucault (1975) who attributed to prison labour primarily a disciplinary function. The main effect of imprisonment, if any, was to produce individuals adjusted to the norms of an industrial society. Melossi considered 'discipline' to be a bourgeois concept of great use in organizing the labour process along capitalist lines. With Pavarini (1981) he described prison as a factory for the production of proletarians.

Without denying the relative importance of the Marxist and Foucauldian approaches, Garland (1985) saw the sanction of imprisonment, including prison labour, as part of a strategy aimed at the management of social problems in the modern welfare state.

In a world where slavery has been abolished, at least officially, state administrations are free to confiscate the labour force of prisoners. With few exceptions, governments put detainees to work and, again with few exceptions,[1] leave this compulsory labour unpaid or 'reward' it with a token salary.

This worldwide penitentiary practice is viewed as quite normal and rarely attracts the attention of the general public or human rights organizations. Only the most excessive forms of forced prison labour lead to international protest. Such was the case with three American states where chain gangs have been reintroduced, and with the 'reform through labour' practice in the People's Republic of China (Wu, 1992, 1994). Because of their symbolic and economic impact, these two systems of forced labour, which have drawn worldwide attention, will now be outlined.

[1] In a (non-comprehensive) survey, conducted by Penal Reform International, Chile reports that working prisoners are paid the basic minimum wage. Danish prisoners are said to receive payments equal to supplementary benefits (Penal Reform International, 1993).

Since the end of 1991, in two open prisons in the German city of Hamburg, prison labour has been based on realistic market conditions. The 'Hamburg Model' operates with two private businesses whose products are sold on the free market. The prisoners receive market-oriented (standard) wages and are included in the social insurance schemes. (See Hagemann, 1995; Justizbehörde Hamburg, 1995.) See also Chapter 4 in the present volume.

## 1.1 The Reintroduction of Chain Gangs in the USA

It was Amnesty International (AI) that blew the whistle in its report, *United States of America: Reintroduction of Chain Gangs*, published in November 1995. AI notes that chain gangs – forcing prisoners to do hard manual labour while shackled together – have been reintroduced into the prison systems of Alabama and Arizona. Florida and Utah, AI writes, have passed legislation reintroducing chain gangs in those states, and it fears that other states may soon follow suit.

In May 1995, inmates (reportedly most of them African–American) were assigned to chain gangs at the Limestone Correctional Facility in Northern Alabama, a state prison for convicted adult prisoners. Since then, chain gangs have been introduced into three more Alabama prisons. Chain gang members are drawn from Alabama's medium-risk offenders and spend between one and three months on the chain gang. While working on the gangs, the 400 prisoners live in one large dormitory built to house 200 prisoners. According to AI, they are woken up in the early hours of the morning and are taken to the work site in buses, dressed in white work suits, wearing caps with the word 'Alabama chain gang' emblazoned on the front. They are then made to kneel down and are chained together at the ankle in groups of five with a large 'handcuff' and a 2.5 metre steel chain weighing 1.5 kilos. Work on the site lasts for 10 to 12 hours, often in the hot sun, with very brief breaks for water and an hour for lunch. The only toilet facility available to chain gang inmates is a portable chamber pot behind a makeshift screen. Inmates remain chained together when using it. When the chamber pot is inaccessible, inmates are forced to squat on the ground in public.

Prisoners' tasks include cleaning draining ditches and tidying road verges. In August 1995, rock-breaking chain gangs were introduced. Prisoners engaged in rock-breaking (crushing chunks of limestone with sledgehammers to make gravel for roads) are chained together with leg irons and a 2.4 metre chain. They work for 10 hours a day with a break every 20 minutes, for five days a week. It appears that the rock-breaking programme is used mainly as a means of punishment; state highway officials are reported to have said that they have no use for the crushed rock produced by the prisoners. AI reports that prisoners who refuse to work are handcuffed to a 'hitching rail', which is a metal post used for tying up horses, and spend hours standing in the hot sun.

Arizona reintroduced chain gangs in May 1995. Inmates are not chained together, but each inmate has his legs chained together with a 20-inch chain. Some gangs are assigned to work projects, such as breaking rocks or digging and filling holes. AI has received unconfirmed reports alleging that prisoners who refuse to work on a chain gang are chained to a pole and forced to stand all day without food or water.

On 21 November 1995, Florida became the third state to use chain gangs. In Florida, the official term for chain gangs is 'restricted labour gangs'. According to the Amnesty Internal report, press reports indicate that chain gangs were last used in Florida in the 1940s. Florida prisoners are reportedly not shackled to each other, but their own legs are chained together. The prisoners are made to work eight hours a day, five days a week, tidying and cleaning land surrounding the prison. They are supervised by guards armed with shotguns, who are under orders to shoot, after one warning shot, anyone trying to escape. According to reports, inmates in Columbia County, North Central Florida, were put to work on a chain gang in black-and-white-striped trousers, caps and shirts with 'SHERIFF'S CHAIN GANG' written on the back.

It will not surprise anyone that AI believes that the practice of using chain gangs constitutes cruel, inhuman or degrading punishment, prohibited under art. 7 of the International Covenant on Civil and Political Rights, which was ratified by the US government on 8 June 1992. It is remarkable, however, that AI does not voice any protest against the use of forced labour, by mostly black prisoners, as a means of racial and social discrimination, which is forbidden by art. 1 of the Abolition of Forced Labour Convention (No. 105), adopted on 25 June 1957 by the General Conference of the International Labour Organisation and which was ratified by the USA in 1991.

The relatively small number of prisoners involved in chain gang labour (the Amnesty International reports mention about 1,000 prisoners in Alabama, an unknown number in Arizona and 210 in Florida) does not alter the *considerable symbolic meaning* of the reintroduction of chain gangs. It represents the reactionary mentality of the responsible criminal justice officials in those southern states and makes it clear that slavery may have been abolished, but still lingers as a concept in the minds of the local enforcers of law and order.

AI is aware of only two other countries in which prisoners are put in chain gangs. One of these is Burma, the other China, where

PRISON LABOUR AND INTERNATIONAL LAW                     317

chain gangs are used for transferring prisoners. But it is not for that
reason that the focus here is on the People's Republic of China.

### 1.2  Laogaidui: *Labour Reform Camps in China*

However cruel and inhuman the reintroduction of the chain
gangs in the USA may seem to many of us, these are mere incidents
compared to the systematic use of forced labour in the People's
Republic of China. It is dissident Harry Wu, survivor of 19 years of
imprisonment in a labour reform camp, who, in two books (Wu,
1992, 1994), reported in detail on the Chinese 'Reform Through
Labour' policy and practice. The communist Chinese labour reform
camps (*laogaidui*) have been in existence for over 40 years and – in
Wu's view – rival the Nazi and Soviet camps in terms of scope,
cruelty and the number of people imprisoned. The labour reform
system in the People's Republic of China (PRC) consists of three
distinct categories: convicted labour reform (CLR, *laogai*), re-
education through labour (RTL, *laojiao*) and forced job placement
(FJP, *jiuye*).

Generally referred to as 'labour reform camps' (LRCs, *laogaidui*),
the labour reform system functions as the prison system of the
Chinese Communist Party (CCP). This system is intended to eliminate all 'class enemies' and 'anti-socialist elements'. Wu cites Mao,
who states: 'Towards enemies, the people's democratic dictatorship
uses the method of dictatorship ... [that] compels them to engage in
labour, and, through such labour, be transformed into new men'
(Wu, 1992: 2) *Laogai* is the mainstay of the LRC system. Re-
education through labour (*laojiao*) is often seen as a supplementary
or auxiliary part of *laogai*. Forced job placement (*jiuye*) is a deriva-
tive of the two.

The *laogaidui* system consists of six parts: detention centres,
prisons, labour reform disciplinary production camps; juvenile offenders' camps, re-education through labour (RTL) camps and forced
job placement camps (FJP). In the PRC, labour reform camps are an
economic enterprise. The products of the prisoners' labour are sold
on domestic as well as foreign markets and have become an indis-
pensable component of the national economy. Wu estimates that
the present population of the forced labour camps is between 16
and 20 million.[2]

2   In his afterword to his book, *Laogai; the Chinese Gulag*, Wu says:
    'After my recent trip to mainland China, it is my impression that
    the numbers given in the book regarding [the] number of LCRs

Detention centres house accused persons who have not yet been sentenced as well as people sentenced to terms of imprisonment of less than two years. All of them, sentenced or not, are required by law to engage in forced labour. The average number of prisoners in a typical detention centre is about 200. The total number of such prisoners in mainland China is estimated by Wu to be as high as 500,000 or 600,000.

Offenders that have received severe sentences are confined in prisons. Except in name, there is no basic difference between prisons and labour disciplinary production camps. All prisons incorporate factories or workshops in which all prisoners are forced to work. The total prison population is estimated by Wu to be between 500,000 and 700,000.

Some 87 per cent of 'criminal' prisoners are confined in labour reform disciplinary camps. For this reason, the term 'labour reform' camp is often used when discussing the whole Chinese labour reform system. These camps are organized along military lines. Nationwide, there could be a total of about 600 labour reform camps with a total population of 3 to 4 million. Juvenile offender camps house approximately 200,000 to 300,000 prisoners, who are all forced to work. The camps are organized along the same military lines as the labour reform camps. Re-education through labour camps, entirely under the control of the Public Security Bureau, have an estimated population of 3 to 5 million. The forced job placement camps house those who have completed their labour reform or re-education through labour camps. These camps are arranged along the exact military lines as CLR and RTL camps. The number of FJP 'personnel', on the basis of Harry Wu's analysis, must be somewhere between 8 and 10 million.

The purpose of the compulsory thought reform, practised in the LRCs, is to radically change a person's consciousness, political views, religious beliefs and moral values. The communist government uses a sort of production 'theory' to justify forcing convicts into slave labour: people commit crimes only because their thoughts are dominated by the ideology of the exploiting class; in order to eradicate the problem, it is necessary to reform the criminal's ideology; and only by undergoing hard labour can a criminal be reformed into a 'new socialist person'. This serves both purposes of produc-

and the size of LRC populations are possibly a bit higher than is actually the case today' (Wu, 1992: 143).

tion and political education. The CCP sees forced 'criminal' labour as a dependable source of wealth.

All within the LRC system are forced into slave labour. Those awaiting sentences and short-term prisoners in detention centres are no exception. Most convicts labour at least 12 hours a day. The average income of the prisoners of the labour camps is 40 per cent of that of regular workers.

Labour reform enterprises have developed into an essential component of the economy of the People's Republic, though it has been impossible to establish with any certainty what portion of the economy and production of the PRC is made up of labour reform enterprises. Labour reform production is included in overall national production planning and constitutes a large proportion of the national economy of the PRC. The communist government refers to labour reform enterprises as 'special state-run enterprises', encompassing agriculture, industry, transport and construction. LRCs are not only encouraged to improve their products, but they are also encouraged to enter the competitive international market and export their products like other enterprises. An enterprise that can earn foreign exchange is considered a reform success.

Harry Wu's politically motivated whistle blowing has resulted in academic follow-up research by Seymour and Anderson (1997), who put Wu's allegations into a somewhat different perspective. They estimate the total prison population at about two million. Though they describe the conditions of imprisonment in the *laogai* as brutish, cruel and far from being ideal, they do not think the conditions can be called inhuman. As to the importance of the work camps for the Chinese economy, Seymour and Anderson disagree with Wu's assertions regarding the importance of forced labour for the Chinese national product. They found that the contribution of prison labour to the growth of the national economy was only marginal, productivity of the badly motivated prisoners being too low, and if Wu's assertions in respect of the importance of forced labour were accurate, outright sabotage of prison labour would be common practice.

The international community has begun to take notice of the LRCs and their labour reform products (forced labour products). The USA, Great Britain and other countries have laws prohibiting the import of forced labour products, but implementation of these laws is often hindered by considerations of political and economic expediency.

### 1.3 Tolerance for Compulsory Prison Labour in International Law

Wherever international law prohibits compulsory labour, it simultaneously makes reservations in respect of prison labour. The rationale for this must be sought in the *travaux préparatoires* of the first convention ever to oppose forced labour, Labour Convention no. 29 of the International Labour Organisation. The second article of this Convention excludes sentenced prisoners from the ban on forced labour. Remarkably enough, none of the parties involved in the preparation of this convention ever questioned the legal basis for requiring obligatory work from sentenced prisoners. All parties seem to have tacitly agreed that labour is *inherent* in imprisonment. In this respect, nothing much seems to have changed since the Richmond Court, in 1871, defined the position of a convict in the following way: 'For the time being, during his term of service in the penitentiary, he is in a state of penal servitude to the State. He has, as a consequence of his crime, not only forfeited his liberty, but all his personal rights except those which the law in its humanity accords to him. He is for the time being the slave of the State' (*Ruffin v. Commonwealth* 1871, 796).

## 2 Protection against Forced Labour as a Human Right

Forced labour, which until the end of the nineteenth century was a rather unproblematic issue, especially in the colonies of the various western European nations, made its appearance on the international agenda only in the twentieth century. In the 1930s and 1950s, the International Labour Organisation enacted two conventions directed against forced labour. From then on, protection against compulsory labour was a human right, which has been confirmed in corresponding articles of more recent conventions, such as the International Covenant on Civil and Political Rights and the European Convention of Human Rights and Fundamental Freedoms.

Strangely enough, all these international documents make an exception for forced labour where prisoners are involved. They belong to the few categories of workers whose labour force – within certain limits – is at the disposal of their governments. The question that is raised here is whether this exception should be removed from these international conventions.

## 2.1 Forced Labour Conventions No. 29 and No. 105

The International Labour Organisation (ILO), which originated in 1919, was linked in 1946 with the United Nations as a specialized agency. It brought about two international treaties against forced or compulsory labour, better known as the Forced Labour Conventions. The first one, No. 29, dates from 1930 and the second one, No. 105, dates from 1957. Although these conventions cover different phenomena, they are both relevant to prison labour.

### 2.1.1 Forced Labour Convention No. 29

The 1930 Convention was created mainly to fight slavery and other involuntary labour in colonial settings. Article 2 of this Convention points out that, under certain conditions, prison labour is not to be seen as forced or compulsory labour as defined in this Convention. This can be inferred from the text of the same article:

> (1) For the purposes of this Convention the term 'forced or compulsory labour' shall mean all work or service which is exacted from any person under the menace of any penalty and for which the said person has not offered himself voluntarily.
> (2) Nevertheless, for the purposes of this Convention, the term 'forced or compulsory labour' shall not include: ... (c) Any work or service exacted from any person *as a consequence of a conviction* in a court of law, provided that the said work or service is carried out under the supervision and control of a public authority and that the said person is not hired out to or placed at the disposal of private individuals, companies or associations. (Emphasis added)

It is striking that, during the drafting of this Convention, none of the parties involved questioned the legal grounds on which convicted persons could be compelled to work. Such an obligation was seen as a normal part of the prison sentence. Mr Vernon, acting as the Government Adviser of the British Empire, is recorded as saying:

> We *felt* that prisoners under sentence and labouring under the terms of their sentence did not represent the kind of forced labour contemplated, and that therefore such labour should be excepted. (International Labour Conference, 1930: 269; emphasis added)

Representatives of some countries felt that, contrary to the meaning of the draft text, prisoners should be allowed to work for private enterprises. The delegate of the government of South Africa proposed – in vain – to remove from the draft the provision that convicted prisoners could not be hired out to or placed at the disposal of private individuals (ibid.: VII). The representatives of Belgium proposed, also without success, to waive the ban on prisoners' labour for private interests in favour of contractors of public works that were supervised by the government.

Mr Latifi, acting as Adviser of the Government of British India, tried to amend the draft text in a drastic way: he proposed to remove the ban on all prisoners' labour for private interests and thus make it possible to allocate paroled prisoners to 'philanthropic individuals and associations', which would help their rehabilitation. Mr Shiva Rao, acting as the Workers' Adviser of British India opposed this amendment. He feared that Latifi did not have the rehabilitation of ex-prisoners at heart: 'What the Government of India wants, under the cover of this amendment, is to utilise prisons as potential sources for the supply of black-leg labour.' Shiva Rao cited a recent instance in India, where the government had used the labour of sentenced prisoners to break a big railway strike. For this reason, he asked the International Labour Conference whether it would allow, under the cover of a Draft Convention of the ILO, 'the forging of a new weapon to be used against the free workers of India, who are struggling against great force in asserting their elementary rights'. To Rao's relief, Latifi's amendment, though seconded by the government delegate of South Africa, was rejected by a large majority of the Conference.

But Latifi had more than one string to his bow. He introduced a new amendment proposing to except 'criminal' classes or groups from the ban on forced labour. Again it was Shiva Rao who successfully opposed this proposition, asking the Conference the rhetorical question whether it would permit these so-called 'criminal tribes' to be used in a way which was even worse than the treatment proposed for convict labour (ibid.: 302–5).

The drafters of the Forced Labour Convention No. 29 were only concerned with the question as to whether, and if so, to what extent, the free market should be permitted to make use of the labour force of prisoners. In the *travaux préparatoires*, the legitimacy of compulsory prison labour itself was never questioned. The position of prisoners was only a minor issue in the debates preceding the adoption of the Forced Labour Convention No. 29, which first of all intended to end the exploitation of native labour in the colonies of those days.

Shortly after the adoption of the Forced Labour Convention and before it came into force on 1 May 1932, the position of the prisoner, in his role as a worker, was the central issue in two publications by the International Labour Office (ILO, 1932a, 1932b). These publications were not – contrary to what one might expect – a spin-off from the effort to draft the Forced Labour Convention No. 29, but were instigated at the request of the League of Nations to comment on the draft text of the Standard Minimum Rules for the Treatment of Prisoners, as drafted by the International Prison Commission (the Berne Commission). The International Labour Office did not question the compulsory nature of prison labour: on the contrary, the requirement that prisoners should work was viewed as the essential element of the punishment of deprivation of liberty. The Office added,

> But wherever human labour is performed in conditions of subordination, dangers arise; and with prisons these conditions and the resulting dangers are pushed to the extreme. As a rule the work of prisoners is performed under compulsion. Thus a penalty involving the obligation to work may easily become the cause of social evils; *it is therefore important to bring it within the field of social policy*. (Emphasis added)

Free workers could also be compelled to offer their labour on terms similar to those imposed on prisoners, and international trade could suffer from the competition between free and prison labour. These risks did not prompt the Office to reject prison labour. It limited itself to an analysis of the known forms of prison labour: contract labour, the piece-price system and the state management system. In the view of the ILO, only an in-depth study of every individual case could determine whether any of these systems fell foul of the ban on prison labour for private interests. The Office limited itself to the recommendation that the Standard Minimum Rules be brought into line with the Forced Labour Convention No. 29 (ILO, 1932a: 312–13, 318–24).

After World War II, the matter of prison labour was first recommended for inclusion in the United Nations programme of work in a meeting by the first Group of Experts in the field of crime prevention and the treatment of offenders, which was convened in August 1949. The focus of the debate shifted from the dangers of exploitation by private interests to the role of prison labour in the training of prisoners and in the economy of the institution, as well as in its relationship to the national economy and the maintenance of the prisoner's dependants. The work of the first Group of Experts formed the basis of the report 'Prison Labour' which, in 1955, served as a principal working document for the First UN Congress on the Prevention of Crime and the Treatment of Offenders (UN Prison Labour, 1955: vi). One of the conclusions in this UN research document was that in almost all countries people sentenced to imprisonment were obliged to perform labour. The legitimacy of this obligation was – again – not questioned at all. But the UN added a new element to the discussion: it introduced prison labour both as a *right* and as an obligation, a right that at that time had only been expressly formulated in the laws of Denmark, Norway and Sweden (ibid.: 2). This 1955 UN report regarded pre-release work programmes for the benefit of private employers, intended primarily as preparation for freedom, as an important new direction in prison labour.

The UN report denounced lease and contract systems of prison labour as a violation of the Forced Labour Convention No. 29, but was lenient with regard to forms of extramural labour by prisoners for private employers. The report pointed out that even state-managed systems did not always prove to be a guarantee against exploitation or bad working conditions. The authors of the report hoped that the ILO would change art. 2 of the Forced Labour Convention No. 29 in such a way as to make it also possible to compel non-sentenced prisoners to work and to hire out convicted prisoners to private employers, albeit with strict guarantees against exploitation (ibid.: 22–9).

### 2.1.2 *Abolition of Forced Labour Convention No. 105*

The ILO Convention No. 29 was not able to cope with a special form of forced labour: the large-scale deportation of people to labour camps for political reasons. After receiving complaints from various member states of the Economic and Social Council, in 1953 a UN Ad Hoc Committee reported on the nature and extent of this phenomenon (UN Ad Hoc Committee on Forced Labour, 1953). Of the approximately one hundred imputations against 24 states, almost one-third related to working conditions in the USA and the UK and a little over two-thirds concerned the USSR and its then 'satellites'. The Committee had not been able to gather data on the People's Republic of China. Debating the draft of the Forced Labour Convention No. 105, the Soviet government delegate, Mr Arutiunian, claimed that the Ad Hoc Committee had been set up with the sole intention of creating animosity towards the Soviet Union (ILO, 1957: 351).

The USSR was accused of maintaining a system of forced labour to suppress opposition against the *regime*. The USSR in turn accused the USA of exploiting (uninsured) workers in such a way and on such a large scale that it amounted to forced labour: black people would be detained in order to make them work and Mexicans and other foreigners were allegedly performing de facto compulsory labour. Thus 'Cold War' rhetoric dominated the debate on this Convention.

The enquiry of the Ad Hoc Committee had revealed the existence of facts, relating to systems of forced labour, of so grave a nature that they seriously threatened fundamental human rights and jeopardized the freedom and status of workers in contravention of the obligations and provisions of the Charter of the United Nations. The Commission suggested international action be taken, either by framing new conventions or by amending existing conventions, so that these would be applicable to forced labour conditions (UN Ad Hoc Committee on Forced Labour, 1953: 127, 561). On 25 June 1957, the General Conference of the International Labour Organisation adopted the Convention concerning the abolition of forced labour: the Forced Labour Convention No. 105, which came into force in 1959. The aims of this Convention are expressed in article 1:

> Each member of the International Labour Organisation which ratifies this Convention undertakes to suppress and not to make use of any form of compulsory labour
> (a) as a means of political coercion or education or as a punishment for holding or expressing political views or views ideologically opposed to the established political, social or economic system;
> (b) as a method of mobilising and using labour for purposes of economic development;
> (c) as a means of labour discipline;
> (d) as a punishment for having participated in strikes;
> (e) as a means of racial, social, national or religious discrimination.

## 2.2 *The Implementation of the Forced Labour Conventions*

From time to time, the ILO used regular surveys to check the extent to which the Forced Labour Conventions were implemented and in the process gave special attention to the status of the prisoner-labourers. In a first account of the situation in 1962, it is stated that art. 2(2)(c) of the 1930 Convention No. 29, which stipulates that persons forced to perform work should have been convicted 'in a court of law', implicitly demands that all the guarantees prescribed by the general principles of law recognized by civilized nations should be granted to such persons. These include the presumption of innocence, equality before the law, regularity and impartiality of proceedings, independence and impartiality of courts, guarantees for the defence and non-retroactivity and precise definition of the criminal law.

Nevertheless, at that time the Committee felt that it could not be sure, from the information available, that this situation prevailed in every country in which the Conventions were in force. Furthermore, the Committee was aware of the fact that, in some countries, people under detention who had not been convicted by a court of law were required to perform work, which the Committee considered not to be in conformity with the Convention. On the other hand, it did not object to detainees having a right to work *at their own request*, provided this was in accordance with the Standard Minimum Rules for the Treatment of Prisoners. On the application of the 1957 Convention, which was to supplement the 1930 Convention, the Committee remarked that the Convention did not prohibit forced or compulsory labour, and *a fortiori* prison labour, except when it is used in one of the five instances referred to in art. 2 (International Labour Conference, 1962: paras 47–57).

In 1968 and 1979, a second and third International Labour Conference survey reported on the observance of the Forced Labour Conventions. It proved that in most countries the Conventions were being observed, though in several countries *unconvicted* prisoners were still compelled to work, which ran counter to Convention No. 29. The reporting Committee pointed expressly at Indonesia, where large numbers of detainees awaiting trial were obliged to perform (agricultural) work (International Labour Conferences, 1968, 1979).

## 2.3  Forced Labour in the International Covenant on Civil and Political Rights (ICCPR) and the European Convention for the Protection of Human Rights and Fundamental Freedoms (ECHR)

The ban on forced labour, first laid down in the Forced Labour Convention No. 29, can also be found in art. 8 of the ICCPR and art. 4 of the ECHR. The latter international treaties, like their ILO predecessor, allow compulsory prison labour. What all three documents have in common is that they are silent on the remuneration of (compulsory) prison labour. Complaints about the lack or low level of remuneration have been declared inadmissible by the European Commission of Human Rights on the simple ground that the ECHR does not contain any provision regarding the remuneration of prison labour (Council of Europe, 1988b).

An analysis by Smaers (1994) of the case law of the European Court of Human Rights in Strasbourg on art. 4 of the ECHR shows that this court holds that work is *not* a prisoner's right; detainees have no say in the organization of prison labour, nor are they entitled to remuneration or social security. Furthermore, the court holds that compulsory prison labour is lawful, provided the detention itself is lawful, the work required is done in the ordinary course of detention, it contributes to the rehabilitation of the offender and is founded on national law.

In the ICCPR and the ECHR, the exception, prison labour as a lawful form of forced labour, is formulated more broadly than in the ILO Convention No. 29. The relevant texts are the following:

> the term 'forced or compulsory labour' shall not include: (i) Any work or service ... normally required of a person who is under detention in consequence of a lawful order of a court, or of a person during conditional release from such detention; ... . (ICCPR, art. 8(3)(*c*)):

> For the purpose of this Article the term 'forced or compulsory labour' shall not include:
> *a.* any work required to be done in the ordinary course of detention imposed according to the provisions of Article 5 of this Convention or during conditional release from such detention; ... (ECHR, art. 4(3))

Whereas the ILO Convention No. 29 only allows forced labour by prisoners serving a sentence and does not expressly mention the possibility of exacting labour during conditional release, the ICCPR and ECHR do not distinguish between untried or convicted prisoners, provided they are detained lawfully, and allow for involuntary labour to be performed during conditional release. This poses a problem of priority: which text is binding on national jurisdictions? Where texts of treaties that are applicable to the same case are incompatible or even conflicting, it is up to the national courts to decide which one is valid (Heringa and Zwart, 1991: 210). The UN

Standard Minimum Rules and/or European Prison Rules discussed below may be decisive for the interpretation of the texts mentioned.

Another difference between ICCPR/ ECHR and the ILO Convention No. 29 is that the latter, in art. 2(2), contains a proviso prohibiting the use of prison labour by private enterprises, whereas this is not prohibited under ICCPR and ECHR. The European Commission for Human Rights declared inadmissible a complaint of violation of art. 4(3)(a) ECHR, lodged by German prisoners, who were hired out to private enterprises. The Commission held that this paragraph did not contain anything that could restrain a member state from contracting with private enterprises or that could restrict prison labour to state use only. The Commission noted expressly that the restrictions in this field, incorporated in the ILO Convention No. 29, were intentionally left out of the ICCPR and ECHR, because of the general practice of having prisoners work for the private sector. It follows that the ILO Convention does not provide complete protection against exploitation of prison labour by private enterprises and that there is still work for national legislatures.

## 2.4 The UN Standard Minimum Rules and the European Prison Rules

The UN Standard Minimum Rules for the Treatment of Prisoners (UN-SMR, drafted in 1955, approved in 1957 and most recently amended in 1977) dedicates arts 71 to 76 to the labour issue. As to the nature of the work, art. 71(1) reads: 'Prison labour must not be of an afflictive nature.' Article 71(2) provides rather imperatively: 'All prisoners under sentence shall be required to work.' And art. 89 states: 'An untried prisoner shall always be offered opportunity to work but shall not be required to work. If he chooses to work, he shall be paid for it.'

Preferably, institutional industries and farms should be operated directly by the prison administration and not by private contractors (art. 73(1)). Where prisoners are employed in work not controlled by the administration, they shall always be under the supervision of the institution's personnel (art. 73(2)).

In this respect, the prison administrations of the member states of the Council of Europe (including Russia since 1996!) are morally bound by the 1987 European Prison Rules (EPR). The rules enjoy the status of recommendations only and do not form an enforceable body of law. The EPR define the objective of prison work in a more positive way than do the UN-SMR: art. 72(1) formulates this as follows: 'Prison work should be seen as a positive element in treatment, training and institutional management.' The compulsory character is found in para. 2 mentioned earlier: 'Prisoners under sentence may be required to work', thus leaving it to the national penitentiary law and practice to determine whether or not this will be the case. In any case, art. 96 EPR states: 'Untried prisoners shall, whenever possible, be offered the opportunity to work.'

The EPR (in art. 73(1)(*b*)) leaves room for contract work from private employers to be performed in and outside the penal institutions. Both the UN-SMR and the EPR require that private firms using prison labour pay to the prison administration the same wages as they would pay for free labour. The various rules have no provisions as to how much of this money should be passed on to the prisoners themselves and limit themselves to stipulating that there should be a system of 'equitable' remuneration of the work of prisoners.[3]

## 3 Some Conclusions

As my excursion into the origins of Labour Convention No. 29 has shown, the compulsory character of prison labour has never been a matter of serious international debate. That convicted prisoners (and sometimes untried prisoners also) must work is pure conventional wisdom which has never been challenged seriously. It is a punishment within a punishment that needs reconsideration. Even if one does not consider compulsory labour as an additional punishment, it is often used as a means to manipulate prison populations: the good guys, that is to say, the ones willing to adapt to the system, get the jobs and with them a relatively privileged

[3] There are still other international texts on prison conditions, such as the 'Body of Principles for the Protection of all Persons under any form of Detention or Imprisonment', adopted by the UN General Assembly in December 1988. This Body of Principles does not contain a single reference to the problem of compulsory labour. The 'Basic Principles for the Treatment of Prisoners', adopted by the UN General Assembly in 1990, do include a provision on prison labour. Article 8 of these Principles reads: 'Conditions shall be created enabling prisoners to undertake meaningful remunerated employment which will facilitate their reintegration into the country's labour market and permit them to contribute to their own financial support and that of their families.'

position. The unmotivated ones have to put up with minimal prison conditions.

An analysis of the various international texts covering prison labour shows such differences in wording and meaning of the forced labour item that reconsideration of this issue seems no more than logical. It is time to turn the tables in favour of the prisoners and to normalize their status as workers. A prison sentence means no more and no less than deprivation of liberty, than restriction of free movement. It does not implicitly license prison administrations to rob the prisoner of his only remaining asset: the value of his labour. In this respect, the prisoner should not be treated more or less favourably than his free colleagues: if there is work to do in a prison and he accepts this, he should receive normal pay for it and if work is lacking he should receive compensation. There is no rational ground to look at it in another way. Forcing people to work must be considered a cruel and unusual form of punishment.

### 3.1 *How to Get Rid of Forced Prison Labour*

Some scepticism about the role and the rule of international law is justified. Nonetheless, if one notes that, for instance, neither the USA nor the PRC has ratified Forced Labour Convention No. 29 and, of those two countries, only the USA has ratified Convention No. 105,[4] the right approach would be to amend Forced Labour Convention No. 29 and remove from its Second Article the exception made for convicted prisoners. A simple thing to say, but who is going to take such an initiative to the ILO in Geneva?

The 'natural' institutions to act in this respect seem to be the trade unions. But, alas, on the national level, trade unions hardly show any positive interest in the position of prisoners as (potential) workers and even block initiatives to improve their fate.

In the USA, Charlie Sullivan, prisoners rights' activist and the director of National Citizens United for Rehabilitation of Errants (CURE), a Washington-based advocacy and policy group, recently criticized the mighty AFL-CIO trade union. This trade union successfully blocked an amendment to the Crime Bill of 1990 which was meant to expand the Prison Industries Enhancement Act (the PIE Act) to all 50 states. Sullivan could not help but conclude that

---

4 As confirmed by the International Labour Bureau in Geneva in May 1996.

this indirect if not direct prisoner-bashing by the unions is caused by its frustration in the loss of important and essential union clout over the last 30 years. ... Prisoners have always been society's scapegoats, but I am frankly surprised at the vehement opposition of the unions, whose early, legendary leaders were not only murdered and clubbed for organizing but also spent years in prison. (Sullivan, 1995: 15)

It is sad, but hardly surprising, that, at the national level, trade unions show little positive interest in the treatment of offenders and reserve their positive action for the prison service personnel as civil servants. If the unions were to defend the labour rights of both personnel and prisoners they would be putting themselves in a double bind, as it were; their position would be almost unjustfiable to their members, the free workers, with whom they seem to share a stereotyped view of crime, criminals and how they should be treated (Leder, 1978: 41, 49).

Let us note the three reasons Schumann (1975) gives why trade unions *should* be actively interested in the way prison sentences are being executed. First of all, he states that most (ex-) prisoners belong to the working class; secondly, prison systems maintain extremely low labour conditions; and thirdly, the interests of the prison personnel are served best by normalizing the living conditions of the people they keep detained. Schumann regrets seeing German trade unions react towards convicts just like the rest of the population. He would rather see the German unions recruiting prisoners as new members and trying to change the system from within.

As I know from my own experiences as a prisoners' rights lawyer and from talks with high-ranking trade union officials, this road is a dead end. No national trade union will risk the scorn of their members by advocating a better position for prisoners as workers. Perhaps a better result could be expected if this controversial item were transferred to a more abstract level, that of the International Confederation of Free Trade Unions (ICFTU), which does not fear a direct confrontation with individual union members on this issue. If it were possible to put the problem of forced or compulsory prison labour on the agenda of ICFTU and ICFTU were willing to introduce it onto the agenda of the International Labour Organisation, an important step could be taken towards the abolition of this last trace of slavery.

## References

Amnesty International. 1995. *United States of America. Reintroduction of Chain Gangs – Cruel and Degrading.* London: Amnesty International.

Amnesty International. 1996. *United States of America: Florida reintroduces chain gangs.* London: Amnesty International.

Coornhert, Dirk V. 1985. *Boeventucht.* Muiderberg: Dick Coutinho. Original edn 1587.

Council of Europe. 1988a. Decision 9449/81 of 3 May 1982.

Council of Europe. 1988b. *Digest of Strasbourg Case-Law relating to the European Convention on Human Rights.* Cologne.

Foucault, Michel. 1975. *Surveiller et Punir.* Paris: Gallimard.

Garland, David. 1985. *Punishment and Welfare: A History of Penal Strategies.* Aldershot: Gower.

Hagemann, Otmar. 1995. *Leistungsgerechte Entlohnung der Arbeit von Strafgefangenen im Justizvollzugsanstalten.* Hamburg: Strafvollzugsamt der Justizbehörde der Freien und Hansastadt Hamburg.

Heringa, Aalt-Willem W. and Tom Zwart. 1991. *De Nederlandse Grondwet.* Zwolle: Tjeenk Willink.

Hermann, Michele G. and Marilyn G. Haft. n.d. *Prisoners' Rights Sourcebook: Theory – Litigation – Practice.* New York: Clark Boardman.

Howard, John. 1929. *The State of the Prisons.* London: Dent. Original edn 1777.

International Labour Conference, League of Nations. 1930. Fourteenth Session. Geneva.

International Labour Conference. 1957. *Record of Proceedings XL, twenty-second sitting, Friday, June 21 1957.*

International Labour Conference. 1962. *Forty-Sixth Session, Report III (Part 4).* Geneva.

International Labour Conference. 1968. *Fifty-Second Session, Report III (Part 4).* Geneva.

International Labour Conference. 1979. *Sixty-Fifth Session; Abolition of Forced Labour, General Survey by the Committee of Experts on the Application of Conventions and Recommendation.* Geneva.

International Labour Office. 1932a. Prison Labour: I. *International Labour Review* XXV, no. 3: 311–31.

International Labour Office. 1932b. Prison Labour: II. *International Labour Review* XXV, no. 4: 499–524.

Justizbehörde Hamburg. 1995. *Gleicher Lohn für gleiche Arbeit; das Hamburger Modell.* Hamburg: Strafvollzugsamt der Justizbehörde der Freien und Hansastadt Hamburg.

Krantz, Sheldon. 1986. *The Law of Corrections and Prisoners' Rights.* St. Paul: Minn. West Publishing Co.

Leder, Carl. 1978. *Arbeitsentgeld im Strafvollzug der Bundesrepublik Deutschland. Paradigma für fehlende soziologische Problemsicht.* Rheinstetten-Neu: Schindele.
Melossi, Dario and Massimo Pavarini. 1981. *The Prison and the Factory: Origins of the Penitentiary System.* London and Basingstoke: Macmillan. Original edn 1977. *Carcere e fabrica.* Bologna: Mulino.
Penal Reform International. 1993. *Penal Reform International, Newsletter No. 14,* September.
Rusche, Georg. 1933. Arbeitsmarkt und Strafvollzug. Gedanken zur Soziologie der Strafjustiz. *Zeitschrift für Sozialforschung:* 63–78.
Rusche, Georg and Otto Kirchheimer. 1968. *Punishment and Social Structure.* New York: Columbia University Press. Original edn 1939.
Schumann, K. 1975. Was geht die Gewerkschaften ein Strafvollzug an? Ein Tagungsbericht. *Kriminologisches Journal* 3: 237 ff.
Sellin, Jonathan Th. 1976. *Slavery and the Penal System.* New York, Oxford and Amsterdam: Elsevier.
Seymour J.D. and R. Anderson. 1997, *New Ghosts Old Ghosts – Prison and Labour Reform Camps in China,* New York: M.E. Sharpe.
Smaers, Greet. 1994. *Gedetineerden en mensenrechten.* Antwerp: Maklu.
Spierenburg, Pieter. 1991. *The Prison Experience: disciplinary institutions and their inmates in early modern Europe.* New Brunswick and London: Rutgers University Press.
Steinert, T. and H. Treiber 1978. Versuch, die These von der strafrechtlichen Ausrottungspolitik im Spätmittelalter 'auszurotten'. Eine Kritik am Rusche/Kirchheimer und dem Ökonomismus in der Theorie der Strafrechtsentwicklung. *Kriminologisches Journal* 10: 81–106.
Sullivan, Charles. 1995. Private Prisoner, Prison Industries & Rehabilitation. *Texas Observer,* 30 June, p.15.
United Nations, Department of economic and social affairs. 1955. *Prison Labour.* New York: United Nations.
United Nations–International Labour Office, Ad Hoc Committee on Forced Labour. 1953. *Report of the Ad Hoc Committee on Forced Labour.* Geneva: United Nations.
Wu, Hongda Harry. 1992. *Laogai; The Chinese Gulag.* Boulder: Westview Press.
Wu, Hongda Harry. 1994. *Bitter Winds: a memoir of my years in China's Gulag.* New York: Wiley.

## Case

*Ruffin v. Commonwealth.* 62 Va. (21 Gratt.) 790 (1871).

## The Author
**Gerard de Jonge** is associate professor of penal law and penology at the University of Limburg in Maastricht in the Netherlands.

# 19 Conclusion: Prison Labour – Salvation or Slavery?

DIRK VAN ZYL SMIT AND FRIEDER DÜNKEL

There can be little doubt that controversy continues to be a feature of debates about prison labour, as it has been at least since American prison reformers clashed on its value in the early nineteenth century.[1] The studies of prison labour nationally and internationally that are included in this volume, as well as the debate at the meeting at Oñati at which most of them were first presented, reveal the extent to which the image of the working prisoner continues to reflect both the hopes of the prison reformers for a system that will be of value to both the prisoner and to society as a whole, and the fears of critics who see prison labour as a tool for exploitation and abuse.

The social and economic context within which prison labour is being performed, however, has changed greatly since the nineteenth century. With only limited exceptions, described in the reports on various countries in this volume and quantified in the survey material collected by the United Nations and presented in Chapter 17 of the present volume, the position is that there is a shortage of work with educational value for prisoners, and often no work at all. This does not mean that prison labour cannot continue to be highly exploitative or deliberately afflictive. Chapter 7, on Japan, gives a graphic account of a system with such predominant characteristics. In his overview chapter, De Jonge presents further examples with particular reference to practices in China and the reintroduction of chain gangs in some states in the USA. However, the overall implication of the empirical material in this volume is that in both

---

[1] See Rothman (1995) for a useful summary of this controversy and its wider impact on international penal policy. As Morris and Rothman, the editors of the *Oxford History of the Prison* in which Rothman's article appears, comment, prison labour is an issue that resonates throughout prison history (1995: ix).

developing and developed countries the discussion about issues of principle in respect of prison labour must take place against a background in which the commitment of the authorities to providing sentenced prisoners with useful and meaningful work (or indeed, with any work at all) is uncertain and their ability to do so, even if they want to, is limited.

The discussion at Oñati took place against the background of knowledge of this changed context. Shortly after the seminar, the discussion was distilled by two of the participants (Boone and De Jonge, 1996) as focusing on three major themes: the duty as opposed to the right of prisoners to work; the legal status of the prisoner as a worker and the related question of payment for prison labour; and the normalization of prison labour.[2] A fresh exposition of these themes, drawing also on material not presented at Oñati, is a useful way of reviewing the extensive comparative information to indicate tendencies in prison labour other than the merely economic.

## 1  The Duty versus the Right to Work

In most countries there is at least theoretically a duty on all sentenced prisoners to work. This is true of countries as diverse as the Netherlands, Hungary and Botswana. The duty to work does not usually apply to all prisoners. Unsentenced prisoners normally have only very limited obligations to perform minimal tasks related to health and hygiene. Some categories of sentenced prisoners, too, may be excluded from the duty to work. An obvious exclusion is of those who are medically unfit. A potentially more controversial exclusion was reported from Poland, where even sentenced prisoners of conscience are not required to work. This, however, assumes that the state is prepared to recognize that certain categories of convicted offenders stand in a different relationship to its authority because of the motive for their formally criminal conduct: this is not an approach which many states would appear to be prepared to adopt.

The question of whether there ought to be a general duty on sentenced prisoners to work is raised in a numbers of ways. Legal prohibitions on compelling prisoners to work are rare. In Chapter

2   With the permission of Boone and De Jonge, the present chapter relies heavily on the distinctions made by these authors and uses many of the same examples.

12, Dirk van Zyl Smit points out that the new South African Constitution outlaws all forms of forced labour. It does not, like most other national and international instruments, make an exception for labour by sentenced prisoners. However, van Zyl Smit believes that the principle that sentenced prisoners have a formal duty to work is so well established in South Africa that this particular provision of the Constitution is likely to be regarded as subject to an implicit limitation.

The duty to work is also criticized by Andrea Baechtold in his contribution on Switzerland – a chapter subsequently written for this volume and not available at the time to the participants at Oñati. Baechtold argues that the reality of structural unemployment in society as a whole means that, if life in prisons is to resemble life on the outside, a life of work for prisoners cannot be taken for granted. Under these circumstances, the duty to work should be reconsidered as well – a position which Baechtold recognizes is still 'pure heresy' in Switzerland. Indications are that this is happening. In countries not included in this volume, such as Denmark and France, the duty to work is formally being abandoned, at least to the extent that the disciplinary offence of failing to work has been abolished (Dünkel and van Zyl Smit, 1998; Hammerschick, 1997).

Gerard de Jonge forcefully expounds principled arguments in support of this 'heresy' in Chapter 18 of this volume. He argues that a close analysis of the various conventions against forced labour of the International Labour Organisation shows that the exceptions they contain for prison labour were not well motivated. In De Jonge's view, compulsory labour is an additional pain of imprisonment which cannot be justified.

Both in his chapter and in the discussion at Oñati, De Jonge was concerned to find practical means of ensuring that prisoners cannot be compelled to work. He noted that national trade union organizations, which often included unions representing prison warders, were not the ideal instruments for achieving the change he supported. He therefore proposed attempting to get the International Confederation of Free Trade Unions to take up the matter with the International Labour Organisation and sought the active support of the participants at the Oñati seminar for such an approach. The support was not forthcoming. Some participants were clearly opposed to the principle and felt that a duty to work was an appropriate part of the punishment of imprisonment, as long as the work itself was not specifically punitive. Even if they recognized that it might not be possible to enforce the duty in respect of all sentenced prisoners, it was, they argued, politically unrealistic to attempt to change the status quo.

Other participants argued that the most important problem raised by structural unemployment in many societies was not whether the duty to work should be abolished but whether a *right* to work should or could be recognized under the current circumstances. In recent years, the availability of work in prison has declined in most countries. In western European countries this decline has been relatively gentle and has followed the gradual loss of employment opportunities in the wider society. In the societies of eastern Europe and in South Africa the change has been far more dramatic. In Poland, for example, more than 90 per cent of prisoners were employed prior to 1989 as their labour was a central element in a planned economy which depended on prison labour to meet crucial aspects of its production targets. Currently, only 30 per cent of Polish prisoners are still employed, and employment inside prison, as on the outside, has become a scarce and relatively desirable resource. A similarly dramatic reduction in available employment has taken place in South Africa, and can be attributed almost solely to the abolition, under international pressure, of the practice of hiring out prison labour to commercial farmers.

In practice, it would seem that only limited recognition is given to the right to employment. In the Netherlands and Germany, there is no legal recognition of such a right, but where prisoners cannot be offered employment they are remunerated nevertheless. Also, in Switzerland, prisoners have a right to work, although there is no jurisprudence on its enforcement.

A difficulty with acknowledging a right to work specifically for prisoners is that most constitutions and social charters recognize a right to work only in general terms, if at all, for the population as a whole. The jurisprudence of the courts on this subject tends to be somewhat vague as well. Thus the Constitution of Spain, for example, provides that sentenced prisoners are not only protected against forced labour but also have a right to paid work. However, the latter part of this right has been described as a developing right, which is limited by the means available to the prison system. Even this limited recognition of the right to work could raise problems for prison administrators, for it would require them to determine which prisoners had the greatest entitlement to the scarce commodity, work. The problem is not, however, insurmountable and there is clearly a duty on prison administrators at least to distribute the available work according to rational and procedurally fair criteria.

It was suggested that depriving prisoners of the right to work may be inherently inhumane and a form of punishment that denies the goal of resocialization to which many penal systems explicitly subscribe. However, there was some scepticism about whether, legally speaking, a right to work for an individual prisoner could be deduced from a statutory goal of resocialization set for a prison system.

A more radical approach to the whole question of the duty and the right to work was suggested by James B. Jacobs in his overview of prison labour in American prisons. Jacobs pointed out that one has to recognize that most prisoners (and this applies to many, if not most, modern prison systems) are unemployed or underemployed in prison and that they are unlikely ever to spend their time doing serious, meaningful work on the outside. In attempting to create prison industries, prison managements have to deal with many of the same problems that many third-world countries face in attempting to develop industrial capacity. Prison industries are located in out-of-the-way places and tend not to attract capital investment. In many instances, there are restrictions on their ability to market their products. In addition, the prisoners who make up the workforce have a poor work record, are poorly educated and are often addicted to drugs and generally unmotivated to work. Under these circumstances, Jacobs argued that debates about a duty to work were largely irrelevant. Instead, penologists should ask why policy makers remain so obsessed by the ideal of work for all prisoners and why they do not pay more attention to the problem of how prisoners can use their time more meaningfully than by simply watching television or idling, as is currently the case.

## 2 Legal Status and Remuneration

The practical uncertainties about prisoners' duties and rights to work are reflected also in the ambiguity about their status as workers in terms of national law. To some extent, the variations in status in different countries can be described as a spectrum at one end of which prisoners are almost in the same position as workers in the open labour market, whilst at the other they have none of the rights and protections available to such workers, but are subject to additional restrictions, including a duty to work. On this spectrum, prisoners in Austria are probably closest to the ideal of equality with outside workers, for since 1993 their income as prison workers has formally been determined by wages bargained nationally between employers and employees. However, 75 per cent of the wages are deducted for accommodation and food: the prisoners keep only 25 per cent of the wages for their personal use. With this change has come access of prisoners to unemployment insurance, but also a duty to contribute to the maintenance of themselves and their families and even to pay compensation to the victims of their crimes. However, as Pilgram points out in Chapter 1, the 1993 reforms were not as far-reaching as outside observers have suggested. Prisoners are still not included in all aspects of national social security arrangements and even their wages are only roughly aligned to national agreements. Practical studies show that, in many respects, patterns of prison labour are unlike those on the outside. Transfers and 'dismissals' from employment in prison industries, for example, are dealt with very differently, while the requirements of maintaining prison discipline and, most important of all, releasing prisoners at the end of their sentences disrupt work patterns.

Other western European countries follow the Austrian model, but are generally not as close to it on formally equating prisoners to workers on the open market. In the Netherlands, for example, prisoners are paid while they are ill or unemployed, but the actual wage is relatively low, and not linked to wages on the outside. In Germany, too, the actual wage has hitherto been very low: DM250 per month on average. The German example is of particular interest since the 1976 German Prison Act specifically provides both that prison conditions should be normalized to resemble conditions on the outside as much as possible and that the state should systematically increase the remuneration of prison labour generally to reflect the outside market. That has not happened in the 20 years since the Act came into force. In July 1998, however, the German Federal Constitutional Court declared the existing practice unconstitutional and ordered the state to introduce a more equitable system of rewards for working prisoners before the end of the year 2000.

The judgment of the German court is an important precedent, not only for Germany but also for other countries in which it is accepted that the state has a (constitutional) duty to provide sentenced prisoners with the means of leading a crime-free and socially responsible life on release (Rotman, 1986). According to the German court, compulsory prison labour is a justifiable exception to a general prohibition on forced labour only when it is used for this purpose. Moreover, the court is clear that only appropriately rewarded labour can serve to 'resocialize', for the prison labourer has to experience, like the worker in a free society, the nexus between work and reward. The court is careful not to prescribe what appropriate labour is. It does not have to be financial: indeed, the court raises the possibility that the legislature may decide to reward prisoners for their work by bringing forward their release dates: that is, by a system of 'good time', something that hitherto has been foreign to German law but which is a feature of some other countries discussed in this volume including some states in the USA and, recently, Spain. This relative flexibility shown by the German court is a good example of the way in which the principle of reward may be accommodated in conditions where full monetary compensation may be difficult. However, the danger that 'good time' rewards may be manipulated by the authorities should not be ignored (see Jacobs, 1982).

Outside western Europe, prisoners tend to be excluded not only from minimum wage legislation but also from other forms of protection that workers generally enjoy. This does not necessarily mean, however, that they have no protection at all. Typically, some arrangement is made to pay them, although the payment may be so small that it is referred to as a gratuity rather than a wage or salary. The nomenclature is of more than mere symbolic importance as it indicates that the society does not regard prisoners who work as closely akin to labourers in free society. And in many societies there is an important difference, for prisoners may be rewarded for their labour in a way which is unique to them, that is by giving them credits towards early release for work well performed. In its simplest form, prisoners are released a specific number of days earlier for each day they work. (Conversely, their release may be delayed if they commit a disciplinary offence of failing to work when required to do so.) Where labour is not universally available and where a duty is not clearly placed on prisoners to work, the link between work and release may not be so obvious. However, it may continue to exist, for in any system which allows for discretionary release the commitment of the prisoner to work is a factor which may be considered in making an overall evaluation. Whether it is fair to consider work performance in making decisions on release is a different question.

Conditions of work in prison tend to be regulated by a mixture of general rules that apply to all labour and specific conditions applicable to prisoner labour only. For example, most systems have some rules to protect prisoners against physically dangerous forms of work. As in South Africa, these may be derived from national legislation relating to factories and machinery which for this limited purpose is applied to prisoners. On the other hand, legislation relating to minimum hours of work is applied to prisoners more rarely. In this area there is often a paradox: legislation which appears to be punitive may allow for prisoners to work for longer hours than workers in freedom, whilst the practical exigencies of feeding large numbers of prisoners and generally administering prisons have the effect of producing shorter working days for prisoners than for other workers.

Finally, with regard to the status of working prisoners, one may note that, while one end of the spectrum may be a closely regulated system in which the status of the working prisoner is carefully defined in law as closely akin to that of the free worker, the forms found at the other end of the spectrum are more diffuse. They could be closely regulated, as in Japan, where the (low) status of the prisoner is closely defined and labour discipline rigorously enforced. Equally, though, the absence of regulation could result in the denial of the status of the prisoner. This further paradox emerged clearly in the discussion at Oñati. One of the participants, Luis Gonzalez Placencia, graphically described Mexican prisons, in which an absence of internal control allowed conditions to develop in which patterns of entrepreneurship and labour resembled those on the outside. Businesses ranging from pizza parlours to drug running are conducted freely by prisoners who employ other prisoners. Such a system allows some prisoners to live in relative luxury and comfort. However, it is open to corruption and offers little or no protection to the employed prisoners who may be exploited both by the guards and by their fellow prisoners for whom they work.

### 3   The Normalization of Prison Labour

The idea that prison labour should be treated as 'normal' labour is deceptively simple. Its primary meaning is that prison labour should be deployed in a similar way to labour in a free society in work that is profitable. The implications of normalization applied in this sense are far-reaching and vary from society to society.

One trend that was noticeable was a movement towards the creation of specialized industries and industrial management structures within prison systems. In Catalonia in Spain, for example, the

CIRE serves as a separate management structure for prison industries. In the federal prison system in the USA an independent organization called UNICOR manages all industries in the prisons. It is financially autonomous and makes a profit out of the enterprises it manages.

In the American federal prison system, UNICOR is responsible for all prisoners who work, but this is not typical. In many systems there is a trend towards developing specialized prison industries which are run on business lines but which employ only a relatively small percentage of prisoners. This is the case in England, where Prison Enterprise Services employs 17 per cent of prisoners. Recent developments in that country are moves towards creating smaller, specialist enterprises in prison that would compete for niche markets.

Similarly, in Germany, attention is being paid to the creation of relatively small-scale undertakings in which skilled prison labour could be deployed. Prisoner workers are being employed in this way in Hamburg. In this model, which it is proposed to follow in England, the situation of this small group of prisoners is 'normalized' by getting prisoners to sign contracts of employment and paying them full salaries. In this way, 'normalization' can have a real impact on the status of these particular prisoners as workers, as well as giving them much larger incomes than other prisoners: a development which raises difficult issues of equity.

The link between normalizing prison labour in the sense of making it productive and paying market-related wages is not made everywhere. UNICOR, in the federal prison system in the USA, does not depend primarily on financial incentives to encourage prisoners to be productive. According to Fleisher and Rison, paying prisoners full wages would be politically unacceptable in the USA, and other means of encouraging productivity can be found. Similarly, in Japan, full productivity is expected apparently without the encouragement of significant wages.

Providing work which is both productive and resembles work that is done generally often drives prison authorities to seek employment for prisoners outside prison. In this case, they run into the restriction contained in Convention 29 of the International Labour Organisation which specifies that prisoners have to consent to working for outside employers. In practice, such consent is not difficult to obtain and such work is generally welcomed by prisoners as it brings them into contact with the outside world and provides other advantages. Increased pay is not necessarily one of the advantages. Accounts from African countries, in particular Ghana, Namibia and South Africa, all record that the payment for such prison labour by outsiders is small, that it goes mostly to the authorities and, particularly in Ghana, that the system offers scope for corruption by the prison authorities. Moreover, the labour may not resemble what the individual prisoner would normally do. In Namibia, prison labourers who are hired out are prohibited from doing 'schooled work'. Also, in South Africa, one may question how 'normal' agricultural work is for prisoners who mostly come from, and are likely to return to, urban areas.

In some instances, work on the outside may be provided precisely because it is similar to that which the prisoner will do after release. This is particularly common towards the end of a prison sentence, when prisoners are being prepared for release. In many systems, the next step is to allow them out of prison for shorter periods on what is sometimes called 'day parole' to work as ordinary employees doing 'normal' work during the day. One could argue that, when a prison sentence is being implemented in this way the work component has ceased to be prison labour, although the person allowed day parole is still, at least in part, a prisoner. The matter cannot be dealt with so simply. Boone, in her contribution on labour imposed in the Netherlands as punishment outside the prison system, points out that there are important ways in which a sentence to do compulsory work outside prison resembles a prison sentence. In extreme cases, work without custody may even be a harsher punishment than a (short) prison term where no work is required. Various hybrid forms are possible. In Israel, prison sentences of less than six months are executed in the form of extramural work. Such work is supervised by the prison authorities and runs for the full period of what would otherwise be a prison sentence. It differs from the community service orders, which are supervised by other authorities and which entail a different kind of work, and apparently is attractive to the courts who feel that the offender is still serving a 'real' punishment.

## 4 Conclusion

Sooner or later, any discussion of prison labour must consider the wider debate about sentencing and punishment. Inevitably, age-old questions arise both about the purposes of punishment and about its acceptable limits. In the meeting at Oñati, the discussion recognized and underlined the fact that the approaches adopted towards prison labour often reflect the wishful thinking applied also to other aspects of punishment which are deemed able simultaneously to fulfil diverse purposes. Thus labour is easily seen as serving both rehabilitative and retributive objectives, without any thought being given to the possible tension between them. In addition, untested claims are made that the further sentencing objectives of special and general prevention are also met by appropriate forms of compulsory labour in prison. The reality, as reflected in the contributions to this book, is that prison labour is not implemented in a way which allows it to meet these diverse objectives.

Finally, the material collected here provides a basis for further sociological reflection on the place of prison labour in modern societies. Most macrosociological theorization on this subject takes a long-term historical view (Rusche and Kirchheimer, 1939), but relatively little attention has been paid to complex recent trends. In studying such trends, one must be careful to recognize the impact both of wider economic forces and of modern ideological developments. Some of these forces can already be observed: the growing recognition, not only by scholars but by policy makers in some western Europe countries at least, that many offenders are likely to remain unemployed for considerable periods is clearly having an impact on the willingness to reconsider the duty of prisoners to work and also on any (residual?) idea that the state has a duty to provide work for all prisoners. At the same time, the experiments with entrepreneurial solutions reflect an ideological shift and also an aspect of a more pragmatic reassessment of the role of the state in the implementation of punishment. What appears to be happening is that the role of prison labour is becoming more differentiated. The focus is not so much on disciplining the mass of prisoners through work, in the manner described by Foucault (1977), as on developing an elite of prison workers who can contribute to the economy of the prison system and, after their release, to the wider society. The rest of the prisoners need only to be 'managed' so that they do not create major disturbances. The actual contribution of their labour in prison or subsequently is of relatively minor significance. What is required is theory that takes into account that not all prisoners are 'disciplined' in the same way, that the role of prison labour in this process may be much more differentiated than in the past.[3]

Recognition of the complex new realities may also assist reformers in understanding the interplay between their ideas and the practice

[3] For an attempt at reinterpreting grand theory about prison labour to take account of some of these developments, see Melossi (1997).

of penal labour; the debates about the right to work and the duty to work, the legal status and remuneration of prisoners and the normalization of prison labour matter. Although the wide range of empirical evidence collected suggests very strongly that prison labour cannot resolve the dilemmas of penal philosophy, what emerges clearly is that the manner in which prison labour is approached and managed by the authorities can make an enormous difference to the pains of imprisonment experienced by individual prisoners. Both by making work of certain kinds and under certain conditions compulsory and by denying work to prisoners, prison life can be made intolerable. As the research summarized in Chapter 4 suggests, however, a careful evaluation of a person's whole work record and assistance in employment both inside prison and thereafter can make a significant positive contribution to reintegration of the offender in the community.

Yet some controls over the work that is required are necessary: a laissez-faire approach to prison labour in the artificial environment of the prison can result in conditions as harsh as any imposed by the most draconian authorities. There is also the lurking danger that harsh community sentences may be new and uncontrolled forms of forced labour.

These findings indicate strongly that, even if there is no philosophical unanimity on penal objectives, it is still possible to identify standards that national practices regarding prison labour should meet if imprisonment is to be implemented with at least minimum levels of humanity. In this respect, instruments such as the United Nations Standard Minimum Rules of the Treatment of Prisoners and the conventions of the International Labour Organisation have a vital role to play. What is required is the further development of both the instruments and the means of ensuring their implementation nationally, regionally and internationally. The controversy about the duty to work notwithstanding, a consensus about practical minima should not be impossible. Moreover, the material presented in this collection should give ample support to those who wish to argue comparatively for practices that are more humane than the minimum standards.

## References

Boone, Miranda and Gerard de Jonge. 1996. Gevangenisarbeid wereldwijd. *Sociaal Maandblad Arbeid* 51: 638–44.

Dünkel, Frieder and Dirk van Zyl Smit. 1998. Arbeit im Strafvollzug – ein internationaler Vergleich. In *Internationale Perspektiven in Kriminologie und Strafrecht. Festschrift für Günther Kaiser zum 70. Geburtstag*, edited by Hans-Jörg Albrecht, Frieder Dünkel, Hans-Jürgen Kerner, Josef Kürzinger, Heinz Schöch, Klaus Sessar and Bernhard Villmow. Berlin: Dunker und Humblot.

Foucault, Michel. 1977. *Discipline and Punish: The Birth of the Prison*. Translated by A. Sheridan. Harmondsworth: Penguin.

Hammerschick, Walter. 1997. Arbeit im Strafvollzug – Rechtslage und Realität im europäischen Vergleich. In *Jahrbuch für Rechts- und Kriminalsoziologie '97. Arbeitsmarkt, Strafvollzug und Gefangenenarbeit*, edited by W. Hammerschick and A. Pilgram. Baden-Baden: Nomos.

Jacobs, James B. 1982. Sentencing by Prison Personnel: Good Time. *University of California Los Angeles Law Review* 30: 217–70.

Melossi, Dario. 1997. Economy, Labour and Penalty. In *Jahrbuch für Rechts- und Kriminalsoziologie '97. Arbeitsmarkt, Strafvollzug und Gefangenenarbeit*, edited by W. Hammerschick and A. Pilgram. Baden-Baden: Nomos.

Rothman, David. 1995. Perfecting the Prison: United States 1789–1865. In *The Oxford History of the Prison: The Practice of Punishment in Western Society*, edited by D. Rothman and N. Morris. Oxford and New York: Oxford University Press.

Rotman, Edgardo. 1986. Do Criminal Offenders Have a Constitutional Right to Rehabilitation? *Journal of Criminal Law and Criminology* 77: 1023–68.

Rusche, Georg and Otto Kirchheimer. 1939. *Punishment and Social Structure*. New York: Columbia University Press.

## The Authors

**Dirk van Zyl Smit** is professor of criminology and director of the Institute of Criminology at the University of Cape Town in South Africa.

**Frieder Dünkel** is professor of criminology, penology and juvenile justice at the Ernst-Moritz-Arndt-University of Greifswald in Germany.

# Index

'9d-a-day' scheme 220-1
Abolition of Forced Labour
  Convention (No.105), International Labour Organisation
  316, 321, 324-6
absolutism 2
abuse of prisoners
  South Africa 220, 221
  United States 270, 272
accidents *see* injury at work
accounting practices, England &
  Wales 69
administration, Israel 134-9
administrative detainees, Israel
  140
Advisory Council on the Employment of Prisoners, England &
  Wales 52-3
Africa
  *see also* Botswana; Ghana;
    Namibia; South Africa
  alternatives to prison 36
  outside labour 343-4
African Charter of Human and
  Peoples' Rights 163
agriculture
  England & Wales 60-1
  Ghana 30-1
  Namibia 155, 156
  South Africa 218-19, 220, 221,
    226
  Switzerland 260
  US plantation prisons 270, 271-2
AIDS 242, 251
AJR *see*
  *Arbeidsomstandighedenbesluit
  Justitiële Rijksinrichtingen*
Albany prison 64
alternatives to prison 306-7, 344
  *see also* community service
  Africa 36
  Germany 96
  Israel 118, 141, 142
  Netherlands 171, 185-96

Amnesty International, American
  chain gangs 315, 316
Andean Commission 300n5
Anderson, R. 319
Annual Report of the Israel Prison
  Service 126
Annual Vacation Law 1951, Israel
  131, 132n45
apartheid
  *see also* racial discrimination
  Namibia 153
appeal, rights of, Netherlands 172,
  173
*Arbeidsomstandighedenbesluit
  Justitiële Rijksinrichtingen
  (AJR)* 175
*Ashkenazi v. Prison Service* (1992)
  132
Austria 1-24
  early release 19
  forced labour 2, 3, 15-17
  history and tradition of prison
    labour 2-5
  integration 94
  international human rights law
    22
  Penal Amendment 1993 5-15
  prisoners' rights 7, 17-18, 19-21
  private sector employment 150
  wages 6, 7, 10-14, 20, 21-2, 82-3, 339-40

Baechtold, Andrea 259-67, 337
Barak, Aharon 131
Barbados 301
basic education, Spain 245
Basic Laws, Israel 117, 119-20,
  127, 128-9, 131
Belarus 303
Belgium 322
benchmark thresholds, UNICOR
  284
Berne Commission 323
Best Western programme, Arizona
  307

Bhudu, 'Golden Miles' 234
Blath, Richard 92
Blauner, Robert 53
'Body of Principles for the Protection of all Persons under any form of Detention or Imprisonment' 329n3
Boone, Miranda 185–96, 344
BOP *see* Bureau of Prisons, United States
borstal training, England & Wales 45
Botswana 25–30, 33–5
  overcrowding 34
  prisoners' right to work 33–4, 35
  resources 34
Brandvlei prison 221
Britain
  *see also* England & Wales
  colonial South Africa 211–12
Bureau of Prisons (BOP), United States 281–95
bureaucracy, Israel 134–7
Burger, Warren 274
Burma 316
Busch, Max 97
business orientation
  Coldingley industrial prison 53–6
  South Africa 233–4

case management, United States 291
Catalonia 252–5, 342–3
Catholicism, Austria 4
Central Maintenance Services (CMS), United States 287, 290
centralisation, England & Wales 43–4
Centre for Rehabilitation Initiatives (CIRE), Spain 252–3, 254–5, 343
Centre for the Study of Violence and Reconciliation 300n5
CEP *see* Code on the Execution of Penalties
chain gangs
  People's Republic of China 316–17
  South Africa 213
  United States 270, 314, 315–16, 335
Channings Wood prison 54
Chile 301, 314n1
China *see* People's Republic of China
CIRE *see* Centre for Rehabilitation Initiatives, Spain
Civil Code, Netherlands 189, 190
civil prisoners, Israel 139
classification of prisoners
  Israel 121–4, 134–5, 136, 137–8
  Namibia 158–9
  South Africa 213, 230
'closed compounds' 217
CMS *see* Central Maintenance Services
Code on the Execution of Penalties (CEP) 1969, Poland 197, 199, 200–7
Coldingley industrial prison 51n12, 53–6, 58, 64–5, 66
colonialism
  Africa 25–6
  Namibia 153
  South Africa 211–18
communism 197, 317, 318, 319
community, Israeli prison relationship 140–2
community service 306–7, 346
  Israel 124, 141, 142, 344
  Netherlands 186, 187–90, 192
compensation of victims 310
  Austria 6
  England & Wales 71, 73
  Germany 81
  Israel 129
  Poland 202, 207
competition
  Austria 5, 8, 10
  Netherlands 178
  South Africa 233–4
  United States 274, 277–8
  wage regulation 310
Comprehensive Crime Control Act 1984, United States 283
computer training 305
conditional release, Poland 203
conditions of work *see* working conditions

INDEX

conduct
    see also discipline issues
    Namibia 162–3
    South Africa 232
    Spain 249, 250, 251
    Switzerland 264
    UNICOR work relationship 286, 288–9, 290–1
consensual management, United States 281–2, 285, 292
conservatism, United States 269, 272
constitutional issues
    Germany 77, 81–4
    Hungary 111
    Namibia 161
    Poland 201, 202
    South Africa 228–9, 230–1, 237n18
    Spain 241, 252, 338
Controller of Accounts and Stores on Prison Industries, England & Wales 44–5
Convention Against Torture and Other Cruel, Inhuman or Degrading Treatment or Punishment 163
Convention on the Elimination of All Forms of Discrimination Against Women 163
Convention on the Rights of the Child 163
'convict prisons' 43
convict stations, South Africa 213, 214
Correctional Services Act 1959, South Africa 227–8, 229, 232, 233, 234–5, 236
Correctional Services Bill 1998, South Africa 231
corruption 2, 342
Corry, T.M. 226
costs
    Austrian reforms 7–8
    England & Wales 57–8, 70
    full-employment ideal 273
    Germany 77, 78, 85–7, 97
    industrialization of US prisons 275
    South African prison labour 226

UNICOR 283
Council of Europe
    European Prison Rules 188, 328
    European Rules on Community Sanctions and Measures 188
    juvenile delinquency 191
    prisoners' education 111
credit system, South Africa 232
Criminal Code (CC) 1969, Poland 197, 199, 200–1, 203
Criminal Justice Act 1991, England & Wales 38, 47, 65
Criminal Law Amendment Act 1959, South Africa 220
criminal law theory 199
cultural activities, Spain 245
CURE see National Citizens United for Rehabilitation of Errants
cutbacks, Netherlands 177

data collection, international research 300–3
Davis v. The Prison Commissioners (1963) 50–1
day-release 123, 344
De Beers Diamond Mining Company 216
de Jonge, Gerard ix, 313–34, 335, 337
de-institutionalization, Austria 4
debts, prisoners' 93, 96–7
Denmark 306, 314n1, 324, 337
Diagnosis and Classification Centre, Ramle Detention Centre, Israel 134–5, 136
dignity
    International Covenant on Civil and Political Rights 120
    Israeli law 131
    law viii
    Namibian Constitution 161
    South African Constitution 231
discipline issues 314
    Austria 16
    England and Wales 47, 48–9, 56
    Japanese draconianism 144–8
    Netherlands 171–2
    Poland 198
    South Africa 214, 228, 229–30, 232–3

training availability relationship 305
UNICOR work relationship 286, 288–9, 291
discretion, Israeli prison system administration 137–9
discrimination
  private v. state employment, Israel 132–3
  racial
    England & Wales 71–3
    Namibia 153, 155
    South Africa 212, 215–18, 221–2
    US chain gangs 316
Divundu Open farm prison 154
draconian discipline, Japan 146–8
drug addiction
  Israel 117
  Mandatory Drug Testing 39
  Spain 242
  Switzerland 265
du Cane, Edmund 44
Dünkel, Frieder vii–x, 77–103, 335–47
duty to work *see* obligation to work

early release 341
  Austria 19
  Spain 248–50
  Switzerland 264–5
'earned privileges' scheme, England & Wales 39
East Germany 89
East Sutton prison 64
eastern Europe, economic development 9, 10
ECHR *see* European Convention of Human Rights and Fundamental Freedoms
economic approaches 313–14
economic development, Austria 2–3, 9–10
ECPT *see* European Committee for the Prevention of Torture and Inhuman or Degrading Treatment or Punishment
education
  Austria 17–18

Council of Europe recommendations 111
Germany 80, 94
international comparisons 302–3, 304–8
Israel 124, 127
Spain 245
Switzerland 260, 262
United Nations Standard Minimum Rules 298
Young Offender Institutions 50
educational sentences, Netherlands 171, 186, 187
elderly prisoners 251
Elizabeth Nepemba Juvenile Centre 154
Elmley prison 55
employer-prisoner agreement, Namibia 159–60
employers, community service obligations 189–90
employment *see* private sector employment; work ouside prison
England & Wales 37–76
  Advisory Council on the Employment of Prisoners 52–3
  characteristics of prison labour 40–1
  chronology of events 1986–97 38–9
  current situation 58–73
    enhanced wages 64–5, 66, 67–8
    ideology 70–1
    private prisons 65–6
    racial discrimination 71–3
    Workshop Expansion Scheme 63–4, 68, 69
  historical development 37, 42–7
    borstal training 45
    Enquiry Committee report 1922 45–6
    late 1950s 46–7
    late nineteenth-century 43–5
    pre-1840 37, 42–3
  industrial prisons 53–8
  legislative/administrative frameworks 47–52

# INDEX

Prison Enterprise Services (PES) 58n15, 59, 60, 64, 69, 307, 343
enhanced wages, England & Wales 64–5, 66, 67–8
EPR *see* European Prison Rules
ethnic minorities, discrimination 71–3
European Commission for Human Rights 68–9, 327, 328
European Committee for the Prevention of Torture and Inhuman or Degrading Treatment or Punishment (ECPT) 38
European Convention of Human Rights and Fundamental Freedoms (ECHR) 68, 207, 320, 326–8
European Court of Human Rights 327
European Prison Rules (EPR) 188, 328–9
European Rules on Community Sanctions and Measures 188
exemption from work 336
  Austria 16
  Botswana 33
  England & Wales 40, 48
  Hungary 105
  Israel 118, 126, 127
  Namibia 158, 165
  Netherlands 171–2
  prisoners of conscience 200
  South Africa 235
  Spain 243
Exeter prison 54
exploitation vii, 325

factories, Austria 4
Factories Act 1919, Netherlands 191
'false work release' 83–4
'farm colonies', Namibia 155, 156
Featherstone prison 69
Federal Bureau of Prisons (BOP), United States 281–95
Federal Constitutional Court, Germany 77, 79n3, 81–4, 98, 340–1

Federal Correctional Institution (FCI), Pekin 282, 290–1
Federal Prisons Industries (UNICOR), United States 278, 279, 282–9, 290–1, 292, 293, 307, 343
female prisoners
  Germany 96–7
  Israel 139
  Namibia 157, 159, 164
Fenner Brockway, A. 45–6
Fick Report 169
Fleisher, Mark S. 281–95, 343
forced labour 314, 319, 330–1, 337
  *see also* involuntary servitude
  Austria 2, 3, 15–17
  England & Wales 68
  German prohibition of 83
  international instruments 320, 321–30
  Japan 148–50
  Namibian Constitution 161
  South Africa 211, 221
  Switzerland 259
Forced Labour Convention (No.29), International Labour Organisation 148–50, 163, 164–5, 320–8, 330, 343
Forsythe, William J. 42
Foucault, Michel vii, 215, 314, 345
Fox, Lionel W. 42n2, 45
France 306, 337
Frankland prison 57
free enterprises, Germany 84, 87
free trade, United States 277
freedom of occupation, Israel 128–9
'Fresh Start' programme, England & Wales 38, 58
Friendship Foundation International 300n5
Frimpong, Kwame 25–36
Fuchu prison 147, 148

Gaes, Gerald G. 289
Garland, David 314
Genders, Elaine 71–2
Germany 77–103
  *see also* East Germany

constitutional principles 81–4
empirical research 92–7
normalization 343
practice of prison labour 84–7
Prison Act 1976 77, 79–81, 88, 89
prisoners' right to work 338
private sector employment 307
trade unions 331
wages 314n1, 340–1
work release programmes 84, 85, 88–92
Ghana 25–6, 30–5
  outside labour 343–4
  overcrowding 34
  prisoners' right to work 33–4, 35
  resources 34
  training 32–3
gifts 32
Giménez-Salinas, Esther 241–57
Gladstone Report 1895 26
*Golan v. Prison Service* (1996) 128
'good time' system 83, 341
gratuity payments, Japan 148, 150
Greece 301
Grey, Lord 214, 215
Groningen rules 188

Haesler, W.T. 221
Hafner, Karl 260–1
Hagemann, Otmar 98
Haiti 301, 302
'halfway houses' 307
Halmos, Paul 53
HALT projects, Netherlands 186–7, 190–2
Hammerschick, Walter 94
'hands-on' management 291
'hard labour' definition 270n3
Hardap Prison 155, 158, 164
Hawkins, Gordon 274
health and safety
  see also safety issues
  England & Wales 41, 51–2
  Germany 81
Helman, David 290
Henriksson, Helena ix, 297–312
Hindley prison 55

HM Chief Inspector of Prisons 38, 51, 54–5, 56, 69
hobbies 128, 129n33
'hobbies and handicrafts incentives' 30
Hobhouse, Stephen 45–6
Holda, Zbigniew 197–209
Holme House prison 55
'horizontal' classification of prisoners 138
hours of work *see* working hours
Hours of Work and Rest Law 1951, Israel 131
Howard, John 42
Hull community prison 61, 62–3
human rights law
  international ix
  international
    Austria 22
    Hungary 111
    Israel 117, 120
    Namibia 163–6
    Poland 207
    South Africa 236–7
Hungary 105–14
  compensation of prisoners 106, 109, 110–11
  international human rights law 111
  involuntary servitude 105–6
  labour law 109–10
  main features of work 111–12
  prisoners' right to work 108
  release of prisoners 108–9

ICCPR *see* International Covenant on Civil and Political Rights
ICFTU *see* International Confederation of Free Trade Unions
ideology, England & Wales 70–1
idleness 304, 308
  *see also* involuntary passivity
  Hungary 108
  Israel 125
  Poland 202
  South Africa 231
  United States 269, 271
Iguchi, Katsushiko 145–51
ILO *see* International Labour Organisation

INDEX 355

incentives for prisoners
    see also motivation of prisoners; privileges; rewards
    hobbies and handicrafts 30
    South Africa 236, 237
India 322
individual pardon, Spain 251
Indonesia 326
industrial prisons
    England & Wales 53–8
    United States 274
'industrialization'
    international trends 342–3
    United States 274–9
infractions
    see also discipline issues
    training availability relationship 305
    UNICOR work relationship 286, 288–9, 291
infrastructure, US prisons 275
injury at work
    Austria 20
    England & Wales 51
    Hungary 110
    Japan 148
    Namibia 158, 163, 164
    Netherlands 190
    Poland 204–5
    South Africa 235–6
inmates see prisoners
institutionalization, Austria 3
insurance
    Austria 6, 7, 8, 14, 20–1
    Germany 79
    Poland 204
    South Africa 235, 236
    Switzerland 263
integration see reintegration
International Confederation of Free Trade Unions (ICFTU) 331, 337
International Covenant on Civil and Political Rights (ICCPR) 120, 124n28, 163, 207, 316, 320, 326–8
International Covenant on Economic, Social and Cultural Rights 163, 305
international human rights law ix

international human rights law
    see also legal instruments
    Austria 22
    Hungary 111
    Israel 117, 120
    Namibia 163–6
    Poland 207
    South Africa 236–7
International Labour Organisation (ILO) ix, 337, 346
International Labour Organisation (ILO)
    Abolition of Forced Labour Convention (No.105) 316, 321, 324–6
    Forced Labour Convention (No.29) 148–50, 163, 164–5, 320–8, 330, 343
    prisoners of conscience 200
international law
    see also legal instruments
    forced labour 320, 321–30
International Penal and Penitentiary Foundation (IPPF) 188
international perspectives 297–312
    education and training 304–8
    remuneration 308–10
    United Nations Standard Minimum Rules 297–303
involuntary passivity, Austria 18
involuntary servitude
    see also forced labour
    Hungary 105–6
    Poland 200–1
    South Africa 227–30
IPPF see International Penal and Penitentiary Foundation
Iraq 307
Ireland 301
Israel 115–44
    community issues 140–2
    extramural work 344
    legal status of prisoners 120–1, 131–4
    objectives of prison labour 125–6
    obligation to work 126–7
    policy orientation 116–24
        legislation 118–21
        prisoner categories 121–4

prisoners' right to work 127–9
remuneration of prisoners 122–3, 127, 129–31, 142
special categories 139–40
system administration 134–9
Italy 301

Jacobs, James B. 269–80, 339
Jamaica 301
Japan 145–51, 335
    compatibility with international norms 148–50
    prisoner status 342
    productivity 343
    working conditions 146–8
Jehle, Jörg-Martin 93n22
Johnstone, F.A. 218
Jordan 303
juvenile offenders *see* young offenders

Kaido, Yuichi 145–51
Kelk, Constantijn 169–83, 193, 194
*Ketib v. Governor of the Central Prison Ramle* (1963) 131n42
Key Performance Indicators (KPI) 50
Kimberley prison 215–16
King, Roy D. 58
Kingston prison 54
Kirchheimer, Otto vii, 314
Korea 308
KPIs *see* Key Performance Indicators
Krech, Ralph ix, 297–312

labour law 339–42
    Hungary 109–10
    Japan 148
    Netherlands
        community service offender status 187–90
        HALT client status 190–2
    Poland 199, 201, 203–5
    South Africa 233–6
    Switzerland 263
labour market theory 313
labour reform camps (LRC), China 314, 317–19, 335
labour rights 19–21

Lancaster Farms prison 55
Lansdown Commission on Prison and Penal Reform 219–20
Latchmere House 64
Latifi, Mr 322
Latvia 301, 302, 303
law
    *see also* international human rights law; legal instruments; legislation
    Israel
        freedom of occupation 128–9
        work safety 133–4
    labour 339–42
        Hungary 109–10
        Japan 148
        Netherlands 187–92
        Poland 199, 201, 203–5
        South Africa 233–6
        Switzerland 263
    sociology of viii
leadership, United States 293
League of Nations 323
Learmont Report 1995 39, 67
leave of absence 89
*Lebach* judgment 84n11
legal claims by prisoners, Israel 127–8
legal instruments
    African Charter of Human and Peoples' Rights 163
    'Body of Principles for the Protection of all Persons under any form of Detention or Imprisonment' 329n3
    Convention Against Torture and Other Cruel, Inhuman or Degrading Treatment or Punishment 163
    Convention on the Elimination of All Forms of Discrimination Against Women 163
    Convention on the Rights of the Child 163
    European Convention of Human Rights and Fundamental Freedoms (ECHR) 68, 207, 320, 326–8
    European Prison Rules (EPR) 188, 328–9

# INDEX

ILO Abolition of Forced Labour Convention (No.105) 316, 321, 324–6
ILO Forced Labour Convention (No.29) 148–50, 163, 164–5, 320–8, 330, 343
International Covenant on Civil and Political Rights (ICCPR) 120, 124n28, 163, 207, 316, 320, 326–8
International Covenant on Economic, Social and Cultural Rights 163, 305
United Nations Standard Minimum Rules for the Treatment of Prisoners (SMR) 297–303, 311, 323, 326, 328–9, 346
implementation 304
Namibia 163, 164, 166
Netherlands 188
South Africa 220, 237
legal status
community service offender, Netherlands 187–90
HALT client, Netherlands 190–2
regulation 342
legislation
see also law; legal instruments
Austria
Penal Amendment 1993 5–15
*Strafvollzugsgesetz* (StVG) 15–17, 19–20, 21
Unemployment Insurance Act 20–1
Botswana, Prisons Act 27–8, 33
England & Wales
Criminal Justice Act 1991 38, 47, 65
Prison Act 1865 26, 43
Prison Act 1877 43–4
Prison Act 1898 44, 45
Prison Act 1952 47–8
Prison Rules 1964 44, 47, 48–9
Prisoners Earnings Bill 1996 68
Race Relations Act 1976 72
Young Offender Institution Rules 49–50

Germany, Prison Act 1976 77, 79–81, 88, 89, 340
Ghana, Prisons Service Decree 30, 33
Hungary
labour law 109–10
Prison Act 105, 108–9, 111
Israel 117, 118–21
Annual Vacation Law 1951 131, 132n45
Basic Laws 117, 119–20, 127, 128–9, 131
Hours of Work and Rest Law 1951 131
Penal Law 1977 118–19, 125, 126, 129–30, 132, 140
Prisons Ordinance 118–19, 121, 125
Work Supervision Organisation Law 1954 133
Japan
Penal Code 145, 149
Prison Act 145
Namibia
Prisons Act 1998 154, 161–3, 166
Regulations 157–8
Social Security Act 1994 164
South African Prisons Act 8 (1959) 154, 155, 156–7
Netherlands
Civil Code 189, 190
Factories Act 1919 191
Penitentiary Principles Act 1999 170, 173, 177–8, 179, 185, 193, 194
Prison Principles Act 1953 169–70
Working Conditions Act 1990 175, 189–90
Poland
Code on the Execution of Penalties (CEP) 1969 197, 199, 200–7
Criminal Code (CC) 1969 197, 199, 200–1, 203
Prison Labour Act 1997 199, 201, 202, 206
Unemployment Act 1994 205
South Africa

1996 Constitution 228–9, 230–1, 237n18
Correctional Services Act 1959 227–8, 229, 232, 233, 234–5, 236
Correctional Services Bill 1998 231
Criminal Law Amendment Act 1959 220
Occupational Health and Safety Act 1993 235–6
Ordinance 'For the Discipline and Safe Custody of the Convicts Employed on the Public Roads' 1844 213
Parole and Correctional Services Supervision Amendment Act 1997 233
Prisons Act 8 (1959) 154, 155, 156–7
Spain
  Penal Codes 242, 248–50
  Prison Law 1979 241–5, 247
Switzerland, Criminal Code 1942 259, 260, 261–2, 263
United States
  Comprehensive Crime Control Act 1984 283
  Prison Reform and Inmate Work Act 1994 273n7
working hours 342
leisure activities
  Poland 202
  Spain 245
Leyhill prison 64
liberalism
  Austria 4, 5
  United States 269, 270, 272
light industry, Hungary 112
Limestone Correctional Facility, Alabama 315
Lompoc Penitentiary, California 282, 286–9
long-term prisoners
  Netherlands 173, 174, 179–80, 185
  South Africa 231
Lösel, Friederich 95
LRC *see* labour reform camps, China

Luxembourg 307

McCarthy, Daniel K. 286
McDermott, Kathleen 58
Maconochie, Captain 212
Maguire, Katherine E. 286
maintenance work
  Austria 10, 16, 21
  Botswana 27
  Hungary 105, 106
  Israel 122
  Japan 146
  Poland 198, 200, 201, 206
  South Africa 226, 228
  Switzerland 263
  United States 271, 286–7
Malawi 309
Malta 301, 307
management
  consensual 281–2, 285, 292
  'hands-on' 291
Mandatory Drug Testing (MDT), England & Wales 39
Marshall Islands 301, 308
Marxism 314
Max Planck Institute 92
May Committee, England & Wales 56–7
MDT *see* Mandatory Drug Testing
medical care, Austria 21
medical insurance, Switzerland 263
'medical model' 117, 134
Melossi, Dario vii, 314
Mexico 342
minimum wage 341
  Austria 20
  Hungary 109
  Israel 123, 129, 130, 142
  Netherlands 174, 176
  Poland 206
  United States 278
mining industry, South Africa 215–18
Ministry of Prisons and Correctional Services, Namibia 154–5, 159, 165–6
mission statements, England & Wales 57
monasteries, Austria 4
Montagu, John 212–15

INDEX 359

Morris, Pauline 46–7
Morris, Terence 46–7
motivation of prisoners
 see also incentives for prisoners
 Dutch training programmes
  178–9, 182, 185
 'progressive stage' model 138
 United States 276
 wages 310
The Mount prison 54
'multidisciplinary programme',
 South Africa 232
Myanmar 309

Nagy, Ferenc 105–14
Namibia 153–68
 colonial heritage 153
 Constitution 161
 institutional guidelines 158–61
 international human rights law
  163–6
 justification of prison labour
  155–6
 legislation 156–8
 outside labour 343–4
 UNICEF study 154
National Citizens United for
 Rehabilitation of Errants
 (CURE) 330
National Conference of Commissioners on Uniform State
 Laws, United States 273n6
National Employment Committee,
 Israel 135–6, 137
national insurance, England &
 Wales 41
Neild, John 42n2
neo-retribution 170
Netherlands 169–96, 301
 prisoners' right to work 338
 wages 176, 176–7, 340
 work outside prison 171, 185–
  96
 community service offender
  status 187–90
 HALT client status 190–2
 work in prison 169–83
  standard regime 177–9, 185
  'work preparation' 179–82
Newman, W.A. 214

non-custodial measures 306–7, 344
 see also community service
 Africa 36
 Germany 96
 Israel 118, 141, 142
 Netherlands 171, 185–96
non-governmental organizations,
 Namibia 165–6
non-productive occupational
 activities 245–6
Norfolk Island prison 212
normalization 70, 74, 310, 342–4
Northallerton prison 54
Norway 324
Nxumalo, Henry 220

obligation to work 324, 336–9
 Botswana 33
 Hungary 105
 Israel 126–7
 Namibia 157
 Netherlands 171–5
 Poland 200–1
 South Africa 227–9
 Spain 241, 242–3, 244–5
 Switzerland 262–3, 265–6
Occupational Health and Safety
 Act 1993, South Africa 235–6
Oñati International Institute for
 the Sociology of Law viii–x
'open farm' prisons, Namibia 155,
 156
open prisons
 Germany 88
 Netherlands 174, 176–7, 180,
  181
 Poland 202
Ordinance 'For the Discipline and
 Safe Custody of the Convicts
 Employed on the Public
 Roads' 1844, South Africa 213
organizational factors, United
 States factory prisons 291–2
overcrowding
 Botswana/Ghana 34
 international population increases 303
 Israel 116
 Pakistan 307

Papua New Guinea 309
pardon, Spain 251
Parkhurst prison 39
parole
  *see also* release
  Austria 19
  England & Wales 41
  Namibia 159–61, 162, 165
  South Africa 221, 231–3
  Spain 250–1
Parole and Correctional Services Supervision Amendment Act 1997, South Africa 233
'pass laws' 217, 218
'Pathfinder' scheme, England & Wales 64, 69
Pavarini, Massimo vii, 314
Pekin Federal Correctional Institution 282, 290–1
Penal Amendment 1993, Austria 5–15, 7
penal benefits, Spain 248–51
Penal Code, Japan 145, 149
Penal Codes, Spain 242, 248–50
Penal Law 1977, Israel 118–19, 125, 126, 129–30, 132, 140
Penal Reform International 299n5, 314n1
Penitentiary Principles Act 1999, Netherlands 170, 173, 177–8, 179, 185, 193, 194
'penitentiary programme', Netherlands 179–80, 181, 182, 185, 194
pensions
  Austria 20, 21
  Germany 79, 98
  Hungary 110
  Poland 204
  South Africa 235
  Switzerland 263
Pentonville Prison 46–7
People's Republic of China
  chain gangs 316–17
  'Reform Through Labour' policy 314, 317–19, 335
personal accounts 176
Peru 301, 308
PES *see* Prison Enterprise Services
physical punishment 2, 272

Pilgram, Arno 1–24, 340
Placencia, Luis Gonzalez 342
plantation prisons 270, 271–2
Player, Elaine 71–2
POA *see* Prison Officers' Association
pocket money 81, 176
Poland 197–209
  conditional release 203
  exclusion from work 336
  international human rights law 207
  involuntary servitude 200–1
  labour law 203–5
  prisoners' right to work 201–3
  remuneration of prisoners 205–7
  unemployment 338
positivism 134, 136
poverty, Austria 3
pre-trial detention
  Austria 10, 18, 21
  forced labour 326
  Germany 85
  Hungary 107
  Israel 121, 139
  Netherlands 171
  Poland 200
prevention, Switzerland 260–1, 263–4
PRIDE Corporation, Florida 307
Prison Act 1865, England & Wales 26, 43
Prison Act 1877, England & Wales 43–4
Prison Act 1898, England & Wales 44, 45
Prison Act 1952, England & Wales 47–8
Prison Act 1976, Germany 77, 79–81, 88, 89, 340
Prison Act, Austria (*Strafvollzugsgesetz*) 15–17, 19–20, 21
Prison Act, Hungary 105, 108–9, 111
Prison Act, Japan 145
'Prison Enterprise Partnerships' scheme, England & Wales 63
Prison Enterprise Services (PES), England & Wales 58n15, 59, 60, 64, 69, 307, 343

INDEX

Prison Labour Act 1997, Poland 199, 201, 202, 206
Prison Law 1979, Spain 241–5, 247
Prison Officers' Association (POA), England & Wales 38
Prison Principles Act 1953, Netherlands 169–70
Prison Reform and Inmate Work Act 1994, United States 273n7
Prison Rules 1964, England and Wales 44, 47, 48–9
Prison Service Industries and Farms (PSIF), England & Wales 57–8
Prison System Enquiry Committee, England & Wales 45–6
prisoners
　Austria
　　forced labour 15–17
　　labour rights 7, 19–21
　　penal reform 14–15
　　population figures 9, 10, 11, 12
　　release of 8, 19
　　right to work 17
　　secret arrangements with staff 1–2
　　wages 6, 7, 10–14, 20, 21–2, 82–3
　Botswana
　　overcrowding 34
　　right to work 33–4, 35
　　wages 28, 29–30
　of conscience 200
　early release 341
　England & Wales
　　Advisory Council on the Employment of Prisoners 52–3
　　population figures 60, 61
　　racial discrimination 71–3
　　rights 39, 40, 51
　　wages 40, 41, 56, 62, 64–8, 70–1, 73
　Germany
　　proportion employed 86
　　release 92–7
　　resocialization 81, 82, 84, 93, 96
　　wages 77, 80–1, 82–3, 84, 87, 98
　　work release programmes 84, 85, 88–92
　Ghana
　　overcrowding 34
　　right to work 33–4, 35
　　wages 31–2
　Hungary
　　population figures 106–7
　　professional skills 111–12
　　release 108–9
　　right to work 108
　　wages 106, 109, 110–11
　international population increases 303
　Israel
　　classification of 121–4, 134–5, 136, 137–8
　　legal status 120–1, 131–4
　　obligation to work 126–7
　　population figures 116
　　right to work 127–9
　　special categories 139–40
　　wages 122–3, 127, 129–31, 142
　Japan
　　forced labour for private enterprise 148–50
　　harsh conditions 146–8
　　proportions in work 145–6
　legal status 342
　Namibia
　　classification of 158, 159
　　conduct 162–3
　　parole agreement 159–61
　　poor treatment of 163–6
　　wages 159, 164
　　work regulations 157–8
　Netherlands
　　community service offender status 187–90
　　HALT client status 190–2
　　resocialization 169–70, 178–9, 182, 185, 192–3
　　rights and duties 171–5
　　wages 176–7
　　work preparation 179–82, 194
　new ideologies 345
　normalization 70, 74, 310, 342–4

Poland
  involuntary servitude 200–1
  labour law 203–5
  obligation to work 200–1
  population figures 198
  release 203
  right to work 201–3
  wages 205–7
'project work' 306
right versus duty to work 336–9
South Africa
  abuse of 220, 221
  attitudes 227
  classification of 213, 230
  employment figures 223–6
  labour law 233–6
  obligation to work 227–9
  racial discrimination 212, 215–18, 221–2
  release 231–3
  right to work 230–1
  training 219, 222–3
  wages 226, 234, 236
Spain
  Catalonia employment figures 253, 254
  early parole 250–1
  individual pardon 251
  obligation to work 241, 242–3, 244–5
  remission of sentence through work 248–50
  rewards 251
  right to work 241
  special prison employment relationship 245, 246–8
  wages 246, 254–5
Switzerland
  conditional release 264–5
  labour law 263
  obligation to work 262, 265–6
  right to work 262
  'semi-freedom' 261
  wages 263–4
United States
  full-employment ideal 273–4
  idleness 269, 271
  integration with staff 285
  population increase 278
  self-control 290–1
  UNICOR employment 282, 283–4, 293
  unreliability of 275–6, 279
  wages 278, 286–8, 290
  wages 308–10, 339–42, 343
Prisoners Earnings Bill 1996 68
Prisons Act 1998, Namibia 154, 161–3, 166
Prisons Act, Botswana 27–8, 33
Prisons Ordinance, Israel 118–19, 121, 125
Prisons Service Decree, Ghana 30, 33
private sector employment
  see also competition
  Austria 6, 10, 19, 150
  Botswana 28
  ECHR 328
  England & Wales 69
  EPR 329
  Ghana 31, 32
  Hungary 112
  ILO Conventions 321–2, 324
  international trends 307
  Israel 130–1, 141
  Japan 148–50
  Namibia 159–61, 164–5
  South Africa 216, 217, 218–19, 226
  Switzerland 262
  United States 270
  vacation payments 132–3
privatization of prisons
  England & Wales 51n12, 65–6
  Germany 83, 98
  Israel 141–2
privileges
  England & Wales 39
  United States 269n2
probation service, Netherlands 171, 179, 181, 188, 190
productivity
  Austrian reforms 8, 14
  enhanced work 64
  Germany 87, 98
  wages relationship 343
profitability vii, 87, 97
'progressive stage' system 138, 142
'project work' 306
promotion 138n49

# INDEX

'protected employment', Switzerland 263, 265
*Pullen v. The Prison Commissioners* (1957) 50
punishment
    colonial South Africa 211–12
    disciplinary issues
        England & Wales 49
        Netherlands 172
        South Africa 214, 229, 233
    failure to work, Namibia 162
    forced labour as 329–30
        Botswana/Ghana 25–6
        England & Wales 40, 43, 44, 73
        Hungary 106
        Israel 126n30
        Poland 200–1
    objectives 344–5
    physical 2, 272
    rock-breaking 221, 315
    work outside prison, Netherlands 171, 185–96

Qatar 301

*R v. Heine* (1910) 215n5
*R v. Mtiyane* (1956) 228n10
Race Relations Act 1976 72
racial discrimination
    England & Wales 71–3
    Namibia 153, 155
    South Africa 212, 215–18, 221–2
    US chain gangs 316
Ramokhua, Lucas 25
Ramsbotham, David 56
rationality 1
recidivism, Germany 92, 94, 96
reconviction rate, Germany 95
Red or Dead 63
reform
    Austria 5–15
    Germany 77, 79–81, 97–8
    Netherlands 169–70
    South Africa 212–15, 219
    Spain 242
    'Reform Through Labour' policy, China 314, 317–19, 335
    'reformative labour', Hungary 105–6

reformers vii, 42, 335, 345–6
rehabilitation
    Austria 4, 8–9, 18
    education 305
    German prison labour 80
    international perspectives 304
    Israel 116–17, 119, 123, 125, 138, 140, 142
    Namibia 155, 166
    Poland 202–3
    South Africa 212, 213, 230, 231
    Spain 242
    United States 272, 293
'Rehabilitation Work', Israel 123, 128, 138
reintegration
    Austria 8, 14–15, 18
    education relationship 306
    Germany 81, 92–7
    Hungary 108
    Netherlands 179
    prisoner's work record 346
    Spain 241
    Switzerland 264
relaxation of restrictions 91–2
release
    *see also* day release; parole; work release programmes
    Austria 8–9, 19
    Germany 80, 92–7, 341
    'good time' system 341
    Hungary 108–9
    Namibia 164
    Netherlands 181–2
    Poland 203
    South Africa 231–3
    Spain 248–50
    Switzerland 264–5
religious study 124, 127
remission
    *see also* release
    England & Wales 41
    Spain 248–50
remuneration *see* wages
'repressive de-institutionalization', Austria 4
research
    Austria 1
    Germany 92–7
    international 300–3

Israel 121–4
  Pentonville Prison study 46–7
  UNICEF Namibia study 154
resocialization 306, 311, 339
  Austria 9
  Germany 81, 82, 84, 93, 96, 341
  Netherlands 169–70, 178–9, 182, 185, 192–3
  Poland 203
  United States 306–7
resources, Botswana/Ghana 34
'restrictive reformative and educational labour', Hungary 105–6
retribution, Netherlands 170, 177, 192–3
rewards
  *see also* incentives for prisoners; privileges
  Germany 341
  sentence reduction 307
  Spain 251
Riesenfelder, Andreas 94
rights
  of appeal, Netherlands 172, 173
  Austria 7, 17–18, 19–21
  England & Wales 39, 40, 51
  International Covenant on Civil and Political Rights 120
  international law 320
  labour law 234, 331
  protection of 166
  to work 324, 336–9
    Austria 17
    Botswana/Ghana 33–4, 35
    Hungary 108
    Israel 127–9
    Netherlands 173
    Poland 201–3
    South Africa 230–1
    Spain 241
    Switzerland 262
riots, South Africa 227
risk, relaxation of restrictions 91–2
Rison, Richard H. 281–95, 343
road parties 213
rock-breaking 221, 315
Romania 307
Rosenthal, Michael 79n3
Rothman, David 335n1

*Ruffin v. Commonwealth* (1871) 320
Rusche, Georg vii, 313–14

*S v. Nkosi* (1984) 227
*S v. November* (1988) 228
*S v. Pule* (1970) 228
*S v. Saayman* (1987) 228
safety issues
  England & Wales 41, 51–2
  Israel 133
  Netherlands 175
  Poland 201, 204
  South Africa 235–6
SAPOHR *see* South African Prisoners' Organization for Human Rights
Saudi Arabia 301
Saylor, William G. 289
Scandinavia
  'project work' 306
  right to work 324
Schumann, K. 331
Sebba, Leslie 115–44
secondary education, Spain 245
security issues
  industrial prison 53
  Israel 116–17
  training/education effect on 308
  United States 276–7, 292
security offenders, Israel 117, 120–1, 140
self-control, UNICOR employment 290–1
self-esteem 306
self-sufficiency, Austria 9
Sellin, Jonathan 313
'semi-freedom', Switzerland 261
sentence reduction 307
service work, Israel 124, 141, 142
Settlement Farms, Ghana 30
Seymour, J.D. 319
Sharon prison 117
Shelby, Senator Richard 269n2
Shepton Mallet prison 57
Shiva Rao, Mr 322
Simon, Jonathan 272n5
slavery 211, 212, 297, 304
  *see also* chain gangs
Smaers, Greet 327

# INDEX

Smartt, Ursula 37–76
SMR *see* United Nations Standard Minimum Rules for the Treatment of Prisoners
social control
  consensual management model 282
  money relationship 286, 288
  South Africa 212, 214, 215, 216
  UNICOR benchmark thresholds 284
social order, Austria 3
Social Security Act 1994, Namibia 164
social security provisions
  *see also* insurance; pensions
  Poland 204–5
  Spain 241, 243, 247–8
  Switzerland 263
social theorists vii
social training 95–6
social workers, Namibia 154
sociology of law viii
South Africa 153, 211–40
  current situation 222–7
  history 211–22
  international human rights law 236–7
  involuntary servitude 227–30
  labour law 233–6
  obligation to work 337
  outside labour 343–4
  prisoners' right to work 230–1
  private sector employment 322
  release of prisoners 231–3
  safety legislation 342
  unemployment 338
South African Prisoners' Organization for Human Rights (SAPOHR) 234
South African Prisons Act 8 (1959), Namibia 154, 155, 156–7
Soviet Union 324–5
Spain 241–57
  Catalonia 252–5
  legal background 241–3
  management structure 342–3
  penal benefits 248–51
  prisoners' right to work 338

types of prison work 243–8, 253
special prevention, Switzerland 260–1, 263–4
special prison employment relationship, Spain 245, 246–8
Spierenburg, Pieter 313
sports activities, Spain 245
staff
  Austrian penal reform 13–14
  confiscation of gifts 32
  Dutch resocialization programmes 179
  'Fresh Start' programme 38, 58
  Namibian temporary warders 165
  secret arrangements with prisoners 1–2
  trade unionism 227
  United States
    inmate integration with 285
    organizational factors 291–2
    recruitment problems 275
    security issues 292
  wages 308–9
Standard Minimum Rules for the Implementation of Non-custodial Sanctions (Groningen rules) 188
standard regime, Netherlands 177–9, 185
state
  role of 345
  subsidies 112
  surveillance 215
State Comptroller, Israel 120, 121, 127, 133, 136–7
Stern, Vivien 57–8
Stoke Heath prison 54
Stooss, Carl 260, 261
*Strafvollzugsgetsetz* (StVG) 15–17, 19–20, 21
Strangeways prison 38, 65
strike action 174–5, 284
*Stufenvollzug* 7
Styal women's prison 65
subcultures 1–2
Sullivan, Charlie 330–1
Super, Gail 153–68
surveillance, social control 215
Sweden 306, 324

Swiss Criminal Code 1942 259, 260, 261–2, 263
Switzerland 259–67
  conditional release 264–5
  current problems 265–6
  historical development 259–62
  labour law 263
  obligation to work 262, 265–6, 337
  prisoners' right to work 262, 338
Syria 308

'task sentences', Netherlands 186–7, 191, 192, 193, 194
Thailand 301
Tokyo rules 188
Tonga 301, 309
trade instructors 301–2, 303, 304
trade unions 67, 227, 310, 330–1, 337
training
  Austria 4–5, 6, 8, 17–18
  Botswana 27
  England & Wales 43, 46, 52, 54, 55, 63, 73
  Germany 80, 92, 93–4, 95, 97–8
  Ghana 32–3
  Hungary 108
  international comparisons 301–2, 303, 304–8
  Israel 122, 124, 127, 139
  Namibia 155, 158, 161
  Netherlands 170, 180, 182
  South Africa 219, 222–3
  Spain 243, 245
  Switzerland 262, 263
  United Nations Standard Minimum Rules 298
  Young Offender Institutions 50
Transformation Forum for Correctional Services, South Africa 234
transportation 37
Tumim, Judge Stephen 39, 65, 67, 70
Turkey 301

Uganda 302
Ukraine 308
unemployment 311, 337, 338
  Botswana/Ghana 35
  Germany 85, 95, 97
  Hungary 108–9
  Namibia 166
  Poland 198–9, 202, 203, 205
  United States 272
Unemployment Act 1994, Poland 205
unemployment insurance
  Austria 6, 7, 8, 14, 20–1, 340
  South Africa 235, 236
Unemployment Insurance Act, Austria 20–1
UNICEF
  donations to Namibian women 164
  Namibia research study 154
UNICOR see Federal Prisons Industries, United States
United Kingdom see England & Wales
United Nations ix
United Nations
  see also Conventions
  Ad Hoc Committee on Forced Labour 324–5
  Commission on Crime Prevention and Criminal Justice 299, 300
  Congress on the Prevention of Crime and the Treatment of Offenders 297, 298, 303n26, 324
  Group of Experts 323–4
  Standard Minimum Rules for Non-custodial Measures (Tokyo rules) 188
  Standard Minimum Rules for the Treatment of Prisoners (SMR) 297–303, 311, 323, 326, 328–9, 346
    implementation 304
    Namibia 163, 164, 166
    Netherlands 188
    South Africa 220, 237
United States of America 269–95
  chain gangs 314, 315–16, 335
  exploitation 325
  Federal Bureau of Prisons (BOP) 281–95

consensual management 281–2, 285, 292
Lompoc Penitentiary 286–9
organizational culture 291–2
UNICOR 278, 279, 282–9, 290–1, 292, 293, 307, 343
non-ratification of international treaties 330
obstacles to industrialization 274–9
penologies 269–74
prison leadership 293
resocialization 306–7
wages 309
United States Navy 277n9
United States Penitentiary (USP), Lompoc 282, 286–9
Universal Declaration of Human Rights 305
unpaid labour
community service 189
Japan 145–9
Poland 197–8, 201, 205, 206

vacation entitlement, Israel 131–3
Vagg, John 37–76
Van Zyl Smit, Dirk vii–x, 211–40, 335–47
Vanuata 303, 309
Venezuala 301, 302
victims *see* compensation of victims
violence, UNICOR benchmark thresholds 284
vocational training *see* training
'voluntary' labour houses, Austria 3–4

*Wade v. Kirkland* (1997) 271n4
wages 314n1, 339–42
Austria 6, 7, 10–14, 20, 21–2, 82–3
Botswana 28, 29–30
England & Wales 40, 41, 56, 62, 64–8, 70–1, 73
Germany 77, 80–1, 82–3, 84, 87, 98
Ghana 31–2
Hungary 106, 109, 110–11
international comparisons 308–10

international law 327
Israel 122–3, 127, 129–31, 142
Namibia 159, 164
Netherlands 176–7, 189
Poland 205–7
productivity relationship 343
South Africa 226, 234, 236
Spain 246, 254–5
Switzerland 263–4
United States 278, 286–8, 290
Wakefield prison 37, 42, 65
Wales *see* England & Wales
Whitemoor prison 39
Widdecombe, Ann 39, 66
Windhoek Central Prison 153, 154, 158, 159, 164
Wirth, Wolfgang 94, 95n25
The Wolds prison 39, 65
women prisoners
Germany 96–7
Israel 139
Namibia 157, 159, 164
Woodcock Report 1994 39
Woolf Report 1991 38
work outside prison 343–4
*see also* day release; private sector employment
Botswana 28
England & Wales 64
Germany 84, 85, 88–92
Ghana 30, 31, 32
Hungary 112
Israel 123, 127, 128, 140–1
Namibia 159
Netherlands 171, 185–96
Poland 202, 204
South Africa 213–21, 223
Switzerland 261
'work preparation', Netherlands 179–82, 194
work release programmes, Germany 84, 85, 88–92
Work Supervision Organisation Law 1954, Israel 133
workhouses, Austria 2–3, 16
working conditions 340, 341–2
Austria 16–17
England & Wales 41, 51–2
Germany 81
Japan 146–8

Namibia 154, 163, 166
Netherlands 175
Poland 201, 204
Working Conditions Act 1990,
    Netherlands 175, 189–90
'working culture', Namibia 156
working hours
    Austria 16–17
    Botswana 29
    England & Wales 40–1, 50, 59, 60, 62
    Hungary 110
    international comparisons 301
    Israel 131
    Japan 147
    legislation 342
    Namibia 157–8, 160, 164, 165
    Netherlands 174, 176, 182, 191–2
    Poland 201, 204
    South Africa 234–5
    Spain 246, 254
    Switzerland 262

United States 287
Workshop Expansion Scheme, England & Wales 63–4, 68, 69
Wu, Harry 317–18, 319

Young Offender Institutions (YOIs), England and Wales 49–50
young offenders
    England & Wales 45, 49–50
    Israel 139
    Namibia 154, 155
    Netherlands 170, 180–1, 186–7, 190–2
    social integration 93
youth work institutions, Netherlands 180–1

Zephyr Industries, Kansas 307
Zielinski, Tadeusz 199
Zimmer, Dick 269n2
Zürcher, Emil 260–1